SOCIAL POLICY REVIEW 23

Analysis and debate in social policy, 2011

Edited by Chris Holden, Majella Kilkey and Gaby Ramia

First published in Great Britain in 2011 by

The Policy Press
University of Bristol
Fourth Floor
Beacon House
Queen's Road
Bristol BS8 1QU, UK

Tel +44 (0)117 331 4054
Fax +44 (0)117 331 4093
e-mail tpp-info@bristol.ac.uk
www.policypress.co.uk

North American office:
The Policy Press
c/o International Specialized Books Services (ISBS)
920 NE 58th Avenue, Suite 300 • Portland, OR 97213-3786, USA
Tel +1 503 287 3093 • Fax +1 503 280 8832
e-mail info@isbs.com

British Library Cataloguing in Publication Data
A catalogue record for this book is available from the British Library.

Library of Congress Cataloging-in-Publication Data
A catalog record for this book has been requested.

ISBN 978 1 84742 830 1 hardback
ISBN 978 1 84742 831 8 paperback SPA members edition (not on general release)

The right of Chris Holden, Majella Kilkey and Gaby Ramia to be identified as editors
of this work has been asserted by them in accordance with the 1988 Copyright,
Designs and Patents Act.

The statements and opinions contained within this publication are solely those of the
editors and contributors and not of The University of Bristol or The Policy Press. The
University of Bristol and The Policy Press disclaim responsibility for any injury to
persons or property resulting from any material published in this publication.

The Policy Press works to counter discrimination on grounds of gender, race, disability,
age and sexuality.

Cover design by The Policy Press
Front cover: photograph kindly supplied by www.istock.com
Printed and bound in Great Britain by TJ International, Padstow
The Policy Press uses environmentally responsible print partners.

Contents

Notes on contributors

Stephen J. Ball is Karl Mannheim Professor of Sociology of Education in the Department of Educational Foundations and Policy Studies, Institute of Education, University of London. Stephen's main areas of interest are in education policy analysis and the relationships between education and education policy and social class.

Hugh Bochel is Professor of Public Policy in the School of Social Sciences, University of Lincoln. Hugh has wide-ranging research interests in both politics and social policy. His current research includes a study of parliamentary scrutiny of the intelligence and security services and work on participation, including its relationship with representative democracy.

Edward Brunsdon is Honorary Research Fellow in the School of Social Policy and the Centre for Household Assets and Savings Management (CHASM) at the University of Birmingham. His research and publication interests include: pension policy and asset management, occupational welfare and human resource management.

Andrew Butcher is Director, Policy and Research at the Asia New Zealand Foundation (Asia:NZ). Andrew holds a PhD in Sociology from Massey University and is author of over 40 reports, articles and book chapters. Andrew is a member of the International Institute of Strategic Studies and a Professional Member of the Royal Society of New Zealand. In 2011 he will be a Visiting Fellow at the Institute of Southeast Asian Studies in Singapore.

Nick Ellison is Professor of Sociology and Social Policy and Head of the School of Sociology and Social Policy, University of Leeds. Nick's main research interests are contemporary UK social policy, 'globalisation' and the changing politics of welfare.

Dan Finn is Professor of Social Inclusion in the School of Social, Historical and Literary Studies, University of Portsmouth. Dan has a particular research interest in the role that third and private sector organisations are now playing in delivering welfare to work programmes; he has completed comparative studies of such developments in Australia, the USA and the Netherlands.

Neville Harris is Professor and Director of Research in the School of Law, University of Manchester. Neville's research interests lie in the field of social (welfare) law, especially: education law and policy, social security law and policy, administrative justice, human rights and the rights of the child.

Tina Haux is a Senior Research Officer at the Institute for Social and Economic Research. Tina is interested in social justice, family policy, welfare reform and evidence-based policy-making. Her current work focuses on lone parents and work activation.

Chris Holden is Senior Lecturer in International Social Policy at the University of York and Honorary Lecturer in Global Health at the London School of Hygiene and Tropical Medicine. He has published widely on the relationships between the global economy, transnational corporations and health and social policy.

Majella Kilkey is Lecturer in Social Policy in the Department of Social Sciences, University of Hull. Majella researches in the field of family social policy, making strong disciplinary links to sociology. Her current research interrogates family policies and practices through the lens of migration.

Ben Kisby is Research Fellow in Policy Studies at the School of Social Sciences, University of Lincoln. Ben's research interests include British politics, comparative public policy, social capital, political participation, citizenship theory and comparative citizenship education.

Ruth Lister is Emeritus Professor of Social Policy in the Department of Social Sciences, Loughborough University and a member of the House of Lords. Ruth's research interests include citizenship, gender, poverty, social security, welfare reform, children and young people.

Terry McGrath is National Director, International Student Ministries of New Zealand.

Simon Marginson is Professor of Higher Education in the Centre for the Study of Higher Education, The University of Melbourne. Simon works in two domains: higher education studies with an emphasis on policy and history, and comparative and international education.

Margaret May is Honorary Research Fellow in the School of Social Policy and CHASM at the University if Birmingham. Her research and publication interests include: employment policy, occupational welfare, human resource and welfare service management, and comparative social policy.

Nicholas Mays is Professor of Health Policy in the Department of Health Services Research and Policy, London School of Hygiene and Tropical Medicine, University of London. Nicholas is scientific coordinator of the Department of Health-funded Health Reform Evaluation Programme, 2006–12, and has experience of the evaluation of system-level reforms of healthcare in the UK and New Zealand.

Rajiv Prabhakar is a Lecturer at The Open University and also teaches public policy at UCL (University College London). Rajiv's interests cover assets and wealth, public services and welfare policy.

Gaby Ramia is Associate Professor in the Graduate School of Government at the University of Sydney. His research is in comparative and international social policy.

Erlenawati Sawir is a Research Fellow in the International Education Research Centre, Central Queensland University. Erlenawati is particularly interested in international education in the context of globalisation, that is, any research on the academic and social issues of international students.

James Sloam is a Senior Lecturer in Politics and International Relations in the Department of Politics and International Relations, Royal Holloway, University of London. James's research interests include German politics, political parties/European social democracy and youth participation in democracy/civic education.

Kitty Stewart is a Lecturer in Social Policy at the London School of Economics and Political Science (LSE) and Research Associate at LSE's Centre for Analysis of Social Exclusion. Kitty's current research interests include child poverty and disadvantage, international comparisons of policy and outcomes relating to poverty and inequality, and employment trajectories for the low-skilled.

Jay Wiggan is Lecturer in Social Policy in the School of Sociology, Social Policy and Social Work, Queen's University Belfast. Jay's research interests include comparative analysis of public employment services and social security administration and the political economy of welfare states.

Part One
Symposium on the Coalition government

Chris Holden and Majella Kilkey

Introduction

Never let a good crisis go to waste. That would seem to be the logic of the Conservative-led Coalition which, having come to office in May 2010, has embarked on a profound restructuring of the welfare state and the public sector more broadly. While there is much continuity with previous New Labour policy, there are important differences and the scale of change envisaged is substantial. Public expenditure across the board is being drastically reduced and the welfare system reshaped. Citizens are being left to rely more on themselves and an ambiguously defined 'Big Society', while being required to demonstrate that they are sufficiently 'responsible'. The context that is being used to justify all this is the need to reduce the huge public sector debt resulting from the bailout of the financial industry and New Labour's Keynesian response to the economic crisis which began in 2007. Yet these changes entail something far more than what is necessary simply for deficit reduction; they will leave a structural legacy for the welfare state that will endure well beyond this Parliament, and involve a very particular view of where the balance of sacrifice and responsibility should lie.

This issue of *Social Policy Review* casts a critical eye over many of the reforms being advanced by the Coalition government. In doing so, and given the profound long-term importance of these reforms, we have breached tradition by merging the first two sections of the *Review* into one extended symposium. We are acutely aware that the delay between the writing and publishing of a volume like this leaves a time lag during which events will inevitably have progressed; if a week is a long time in politics, a few months is an eternity during a crisis. Yet we are satisfied that we have gathered here a range of incisive contributions which provide analyses of the ideas, evidence, continuities and breaks relating to the government's evolving reforms that will continue to be essential reading for some time.

We start with an overview of Conservative social policy by Hugh Bochel in Chapter One, which sets the context by examining the development of Conservative Party social policy while in opposition and the challenges posed to the Conservatives by New Labour governments. As Bochel shows, the degree to which David Cameron's Conservative Party has left behind its 'nasty party' image and broken from its Thatcherite past is a matter of contention. Regardless, its performance in the 2010 General Election was modest given the extent of the economic crisis and the unpopularity of Gordon Brown's Labour government. The lack of an outright majority has brought the Party into coalition with a Liberal Democratic Party which itself contains a variety of political positions, from enthusiastic support for economic liberalism favoured by the *Orange Book* wing of the Party to those with a slightly more social democratic bent. As Bochel notes, the longevity and policies of the Coalition will be affected by these ideological issues, by electoral calculations on both sides and by the success or otherwise of its economic policies.

Chapters Two and Three, by Jay Wiggan and Nick Ellison respectively, interrogate more closely the ideological underpinnings of Cameron's Conservative Party. Both authors argue that at an ideological level, while there is evidence of a serious attempt to construct a 'progressive conservatism' – something that in broad terms combines a concern for social justice with a reduced role for the state and an emphasis on civil society – understanding of what precisely this entails differs considerably within the Party. Jay Wiggan focuses on the dividing lines between, on the one hand, the civic conservative ideas articulated by Conservative politicians such as David Willetts and Oliver Letwin, and on the other hand, what he sees as 'one of the most striking ideas within contemporary Conservative thinking', Phillip Blond's 'Red Tory' critique of neoliberalism. Wiggan argues that the distinctiveness of Red Toryism lies in its attempt to 'break conservatism from neoliberalism by establishing that the latter is not the champion of free markets, but of monopolistic big business'. While Wiggan notes that the Conservative Party leadership may on occasion have flirted with the Red Tory critique of monopoly capitalism, this remains at a rhetorical level, for as he demonstrates through an analysis of the Coalition government's welfare to work reforms, current policies will both extend the reach of private monopolistic practice and strengthen the power of capital. Such policy outcomes, Wiggan suggests, are consistent with the economic and class interests of leading members of the Conservative Party. As Wiggan concludes, it is civic conservative thought which is the more useful to the Conservative leadership as its attempts to construct a 'progressive conservatism', precisely because 'it does not necessitate a break with neoliberalism'.

The 'Big Society' is a dominant theme within Cameron's 'progressive conservative' agenda. Nonetheless, during and following the 2010 General Election campaign, it was an idea frequently criticised for its vagueness. Appropriately, therefore, in Chapter Three Nick Ellison sets out to examine the origins and nature of the Big Society 'project', to consider how the idea fits with the Coalition government's social policies and to reflect on what its implications might be, especially for the relationship between the state and the individual. Ellison argues that the idea of the Big Society has been informed by three broad perspectives within the Conservative Party: 'Burkean', 'pragmatic' and 'compassionate'. He notes that while the perspectives have much in common in advocating decentralisation and the promotion of civil society, there are critical differences in 'tone, emphasis and task', which not only result in the Big Society remaining a 'fairly unfocused and heterogeneous "vision"', but which also might result in it taking different forms in the different policies of government ministries. Ellison warns in particular that the 'vision' of the Big Society being played out in the Coalition government's welfare to work reforms, under the ministerial leadership of Iain Duncan Smith, risks imposing new forms of discipline and social control on the most vulnerable in society. To such a warning, Ellison adds concerns about the feasibility of the Big Society, in terms of both the adequacy of the level of government funding committed to supporting Big Society initiatives, and the capacity of the third sector to fill the gaps created by the withdrawal of central government, in a way that is 'socially and spatially coherent'.

The Big Society 'project' can be understood as part of a longer-running agenda in UK politics to shift responsibility away from the state towards the individual, an agenda that Ruth Lister captures in the title to her chapter – 'The age of responsibility' (Chapter Four) – and which she analyses through the lens of citizenship. Lister begins by outlining the dominant discourses of citizenship responsibility, discussing in particular how they have been articulated previously by New Labour governments, and currently by the Coalition government. She examines the ways in which social policy has been used to encourage or enforce responsibilities and obligations. A key critique developed by Lister is that the responsibilisation agenda has been directed overwhelmingly at the poorest and least powerful in society through increasing conditionality, exclusivity and selectivity of social citizenship. While Lister concludes that the Coalition government is continuing with this broad approach towards citizenship, she also notes that some critical differences are already apparent. These include a greater hostility towards the state on the part of the Coalition, a position reflected in the absence of a discussion of the rights that might accompany the obligations of citizenship.

With Rajiv Prabhakar's chapter, Chapter Five, we move on to examine more discreet policy areas. His focus on wealth and its taxation is particularly pertinent given the discourse on responsibilities discussed by Ruth Lister earlier and the current debate over who should shoulder the burden of reducing the public deficit following the financial crisis. The tactical advantage gained by the Conservative Party over the issue of inheritance tax shortly after Gordon Brown's assumption of the Premiership, when the then shadow Chancellor George Osborne promised to raise the threshold at which inheritance tax is paid to £1 million, is widely credited as having persuaded Brown to back away from calling a snap general election which he might have won. This debate has also become linked to that concerning how social care should be paid for, following Labour's proposals when in office for a capital levy to pay for such care. Prabhakar discusses how the debate on the issue of inheritance tax, and wealth taxes more widely, has changed in the aftermath of the financial crisis and the formation of the Coalition government. He notes the importance of considering wealth taxes within the context of the wider tax system and, despite their apparent unpopularity, argues that supporters of such taxes are in a position to shape, rather than simply follow, public opinion.

In Chapter Six Edward Brunsdon and Margaret May examine the arguments for and against the reform of public service occupational pension schemes. As they note, various journalists, politicians and employers' organisations have been highly vocal in designating these as 'unaffordable' and 'unfair', contrasting them with apparently less generous schemes in the private sector. Brunsdon and May do an expert job in explaining and analysing such arguments, presenting complex debates in a clear and concise way. Whatever the merits of the various arguments, however, they note that when considered in the broader political and economic context, what will count is the wider political agenda and the government's commitment to spending cuts and reform of the state. Yet they conclude that what is really required is a holistic approach to pensions, including occupational pensions, state pensions and personal savings, rather than the fragmented and piecemeal changes that have characterised previous policy.

Dan Finn, in Chapter Seven, examines the welfare to work policies of the Coalition government, noting both continuities and changes with those of New Labour. While the principles of activation pursued by New Labour governments have been retained by the Coalition, the latter's distinctive policies have involved the proposed transformation of all working age benefits into a 'Universal Credit' and the introduction of a single 'Work Programme', under which the scale and pace of the outsourcing of job placement services to private contractors will be increased. While these policies have been widely seen as principally those of the Conservatives, Finn notes that they also reflect the position set out by the Liberal Democrats prior to the election. Finn argues that New Labour's activation policies achieved relative success, during a period of economic growth, in reducing unemployment and poverty, and that together with economic stimulus and other measures introduced during the recession they were able to mitigate the rise in unemployment when compared to previous recessions. However, the Coalition will face difficulties in implementing its reforms against a background of wider public sector cuts and unemployment that will persist at high levels for some time; while assistance and work incentives may be improved for some, out-of-work incomes will be reduced for many.

In Chapter Eight Tina Haux focuses on lone parents, a group that, she argues, has represented a challenge for policy makers in the UK for three decades or so. Under New Labour, the 'lone parent problem' was constructed primarily as one of benefit dependency and poverty, and the policy response was to get more lone parents into paid work through a mix of encouragement and compulsion. The latter, Haux demonstrates, has intensified over time, with the point at which lone parents' receipt of out-of-work benefits becomes conditional on seeking work shifting from when their youngest child turns 16 (the situation prior to 2008), to when their youngest child turns seven (the situation at October 2010). In line with the continuation of New Labour's principles of activation discussed by Finn earlier, the Coalition government will extend compulsion to lone parents with a youngest child aged five from 2011–12. Haux cautions against a potential point of discontinuity between New Labour and the Coalition government when it comes to lone parents, however, and that is the moralisation of lone parenthood. The construction of lone parents as a social threat was a dominant perspective under the Thatcher and Major Conservative administrations, and Haux suggests that under the influence of The Centre for Social

Justice and its problematisation of family breakdown in particular, this perspective is at risk of re-emerging.

With Kitty Stewart's chapter, Chapter Nine, we turn to an examination of child poverty. Stewart begins by evaluating the evidence on child poverty under New Labour and during the recession of 2008–09. She illustrates the modest progress made by Labour governments in reducing child poverty during its time in office and points to the protective effect during the recession of Labour's macroeconomic and benefits policies. However, the impact on children in low-income households in the forthcoming period will depend on the nature of the economic recovery and on the Coalition government's deficit reduction and welfare reform policies. The latter involve a range of ambitious cuts and reforms that are likely to be regressive. As Stewart notes, the government's anti-poverty strategy relies heavily on substantial job growth in the private sector. She concludes that children in low-income households have suffered a 'treble blow': 'the continuing impact of the recession, the need to reduce the structural deficit and the arrival of a new government committed to particularly steep cuts to public spending and placing a lower priority both on income poverty and on children'.

The symposium ends with Chapter Ten by Nick Mays that assesses the implications of the Coalition's plans to restructure the National Health Service (NHS) in England. The plans involve taking another big step towards an NHS based on a publicly funded regulated market, by abolishing strategic health authorities and replacing primary care trusts with GP-led commissioning consortia. Given the continuities with New Labour policy, Mays begins by evaluating the evidence on the market changes introduced by New Labour governments, arguing that these have had some success, although this was relatively modest compared to the impact of additional resources and the setting and enforcement of targets. However, the absence of any regional intermediary organisations in the Coalition's plans may lead to 'inefficient duplication, fragmentation and destabilisation', given the tendency towards market failure in healthcare. Undertaking the scope and pace of reform envisaged in a context of restricted financial resources is a risky process, and a more complete, more competitive, NHS market could have negative effects on equity.

ONE

Conservative social policy: from conviction to coalition

Hugh Bochel

Although implied by the opinion polls during the course of the campaign, the result of the May 2010 General Election, and the first 'hung' Parliament for the United Kingdom for more than 35 years, came as a surprise to many. So too did the subsequent creation of the Coalition government by the Conservatives and the Liberal Democrats. For the Conservative Party the return to government after 13 years in opposition came after a succession of leadership changes and attempts to make the Party more acceptable to the electorate. For the Liberal Democrats it was perhaps even more of a surprise, but provided their first real opportunity to directly influence policy from within government since 1912.

This chapter focuses primarily on the Conservatives, considering the Party's journey since the Premiership of Margaret Thatcher, well known as a conviction politician, and the impact of a series of leaders prior to David Cameron taking on that role in late 2005. It examines changes in the Conservatives' approach under Cameron and their implications for social policy, before providing an early assessment of the Coalition with the Liberal Democrats and the work of the new government.

Margaret Thatcher and her legacy

Any analysis of the development of Conservative policy from the late 1970s has to take account of the impact of Margaret Thatcher and the influence of the New Right. Although the Thatcher period and the policies of the time have been widely analysed, especially in relation to social policy, it is worth reflecting on them briefly here because of their long-lasting implications for the Conservative Party.

Under Thatcher's leadership the Conservative Party was significantly influenced by New Right critiques of the welfare state, including by writers such as Hayek (see, for example, 1944, 1976), Friedman (1962) and Harris and Seldon (1979). The welfare state was seen as leading to excessive public expenditure and an unfair tax burden on citizens and entrepreneurs, negating choice, weakening the family and creating dependency. With its emphasis on the supremacy of the market and the reduction of the role of the state, the New Right was viewed by many (see, for example, Bosanquet, 1983) as representing a break from the paternalistic 'One Nation' Conservatism that had been seen as dominating the Party for much of the post-war period (however, see Seawright, 2009; Bochel, 2010). The Thatcher governments pursued policies designed to cut taxation, in particular direct taxation, and expenditure on public services, to reduce government involvement in and regulation of the economy and society, and to encourage private enterprise and markets, including the privatisation of state enterprises. While the Conservatives' success in reducing public expenditure was limited, in part because of high levels of unemployment, and consequently benefits payments, for much of their period in office, they did make a number of significant policy changes. In the first term these included the 'right to buy' council houses and curbs on trades union powers; in the second term, privatisation, including utilities such as British Gas and British Telecom, and greater targeting of social security benefits; and in the third, the creation of quasi-markets in health and social care, the introduction of the National Curriculum and grant-maintained schools, and transfers of council housing stock, generally to registered social landlords. Thatcher's three successive general election victories in 1979, 1983 and 1987 meant that many of the Conservatives' policies and ideas became embedded, while at the time cementing her popularity among Conservative Party members.

Following Thatcher's resignation in 1990, further changes under John Major's Premiership included the introduction of the Jobseeker's Allowance, a new Incapacity Benefit, the creation of Ofsted (Office for Standards in Education, Children's Services and Skills) and attempts to enhance the 'rights' of users of public services through the Citizens' Charter. However, while prolonging the period of Conservative rule and maintaining a broadly similar pattern of policy development to that of Thatcher, Major faced almost continual internal divisions and attacks on his leadership, which arguably foreshadowed many of the problems that the Conservatives would face over much of the next two decades. From having been a Party which was widely described as pragmatic and flexible in its pursuit of government up to the 1970s, from 1979 the Conservatives had become strongly attached to Thatcherite ideas, and this, together with the dominance of the right of the Party, were soon to be reflected in their struggle to respond to Tony Blair and New Labour, and their own position in opposition.

The Conservatives' problems, including their attachment to Thatcherism and the Party's loss of its claim to economic competence following Black Wednesday, 16 September 1992, when sterling was forced out of the European Exchange Rate Mechanism, were made worse by ongoing internal divisions, particularly over Europe, and, set against the context of a Conservative emphasis on family values, the improper personal conduct of a number of the Party's Members of Parliament (MPs) and ministers. However, the difficulties facing the Conservative Party were increased further by the creation of New Labour.

New Labour: a new challenge for the Conservatives

Under the leadership of Neil Kinnock (1983–92) and John Smith (1992-94), the Labour Party made a series of organisational and policy changes designed to show that the Party was again 'fit' for government, and was performing increasingly well in the opinion polls and to some extent in other tests of electoral popularity. However, following Smith's sudden death in 1994 Tony Blair became leader and, together with other 'modernisers', sought to rebrand the Party as 'New Labour', in an attempt to appeal beyond the core vote that had proved insufficient in four successive elections. This involved changes in economic policy (accepting the strengths of the market, deregulation of financial markets and a more tentative approach to state intervention) and social policy (including the acceptance of the centrality of paid work, a more 'active' welfare state, changing family structures, a focus on social exclusion rather than poverty and more consumerist approaches to service provision) (see, for example, Driver and Martell, 2006). Whether as a result of the creation of New Labour, the problems and weaknesses of the Conservatives, or indeed a combination of the two, Labour returned to government in May 1997 with 43.2 per cent of the vote and a majority of 179 seats in the House of Commons.

While some were able to argue that elements of Labour's policies, particularly towards the National Health Service (NHS) and some parts of the education system, reflected longstanding Labour concerns and were social democratic in nature, others suggested that there were greater similarities with the New Right-influenced approaches of the Thatcher and Major years (Powell, 1999; Driver and Martell, 2006). However, regardless of such views, Labour's policies, together with its commitment to increased public expenditure, especially on mass services (education and the NHS), and its apparent success in maintaining economic growth over a long period, found public favour and meant that it was able to dominate the political agenda. At the same time, many of the issues which appealed to Conservative members and core voters were now seen as of less salience by the bulk of the electorate. There was therefore a tension for the Conservatives between securing their core vote and attempting to reach out to potential new supporters. These factors were reflected in further general election defeats for the Conservatives in 2001 and 2005. As with the Conservatives' victories under Margaret Thatcher, by historical standards Labour's share of the vote in these elections was not high, but the Conservatives' failure to poll more than 32 per cent in any of these contests consigned them to substantial defeats.

During Labour's third term in power, however, the government began to encounter more difficulties. In addition to policy challenges, including a series of crises around the work of the Home Office, and difficulties over public service reforms, including persuading the electorate that the reforms were effective, the government was damaged by the decision to go to war in Iraq, and further weakened by Blair's statement prior to the 2005 General Election that he would stand down before the end of the third term, and rivalry and disagreement between allies of Blair and Brown. All of this too, came before the financial crisis of 2007 onwards.

Changing Conservative leadership – William Hague, Iain Duncan Smith, Michael Howard and the 'nasty party'

As noted above, the Thatcher era left the Conservative Party more ideologically driven than previously and dominated by the right, while Major's period as Prime Minister was overshadowed by divisions over Europe, and issues of sleaze and morality among the parliamentary Party. Following Major's resignation after the 1997 General Election, and given these challenges, William Hague clearly sought to draw on some of the lessons of New Labour in attempting to modernise his Party. In particular he sought to increase the role and power of Party members by embracing the principle of one member, one vote, and by giving them a ballot on the final two candidates to emerge from the parliamentary Party in a leadership contest. He also created a new policy forum to discuss and debate Party policy.

In relation to policy, Hague initially sought to take a rather different line from his predecessors. He apologised for the Party's failure to listen to voters and adopted a softer approach on many social issues, particularly gender, 'race' and sexuality. However, at a time when public opinion appeared to be strongly supportive of many public services, the Conservatives' continued commitment to privatisation and tax cuts lacked broad appeal, and over time the Party turned to its core vote, with Hague's most distinctive policy shift being to further harden the approach to Europe, promising that under the Conservatives the UK would not join the Euro for at least two Parliaments. At the 2001 General Election the Conservatives were therefore calling for a smaller state, including less welfare provision, and for tax cuts, but at the same time for increased expenditure on the NHS, greater freedom for schools from local authorities, increases in police numbers and tougher sentences.

Following the 2001 General Election, with the Conservatives having increased their share of the vote by just over one per cent and with a net gain of only one seat, Hague resigned, and after the ballot of MPs left a choice between the pro-European Kenneth Clarke and the Eurosceptic Iain Duncan Smith, it was no surprise that Duncan Smith won the ballot of Party members with 61 per cent of the vote. Like Hague, Duncan Smith initially sought to take the Conservatives on a different path, with more positive statements about public services, a new emphasis on social inclusion and recognition of the Party's continuing poor reputation with much of the public, memorably summed up by the then Party chair, Theresa May, when she described the public's perception of the Conservatives as the 'nasty party'. While Duncan Smith's vision of 'compassionate conservatism' and helping the vulnerable (Seldon and Snowden, 2005) may not have received much support from within the Party, and in particular the shadow Cabinet (although he did receive support from David Willetts, who held the Conservatives' social security portfolio; see Willetts, 2005a, 2005b), his ideas did receive attention from some younger Conservative MPs, who would come to prominence in the future. Despite an improvement in the Conservatives' performance in European and local elections, Duncan Smith faced continued opposition within the Party, and concerns about payments to his wife for work done for his office weakened his position further. In autumn 2003 the backbench MP, Derek Conway, supported by at least 25 Conservative MPs, requested a no-confidence vote which Duncan Smith subsequently lost.

In many respects the next Conservative leader, Michael Howard, represented a step back to the Thatcher-Major era. He had a degree of status and experience as a former Home Secretary, and made the Conservative Party more of a force in Parliament, but introduced only relatively minor changes to policy. Indeed, having backed the Iraq War he was unable to exploit the Labour government's biggest weakness, and ultimately fought the 2005 General Election on what was seen by many as a tax (cuts) and (anti-)immigration campaign. While the Conservatives did gain 33 seats, the improvement appeared to be largely as a result of Blair and Labour's growing unpopularity, and the Conservative Party's share of the vote was only 0.5 per cent more than in 2001.

Following Michael Howard's resignation the Conservative leadership contest saw four candidates stand: David Cameron, Kenneth Clarke, David Davis and Liam Fox, with the latter two coming from the right of the Party and the former two more from the centre. Following the votes of MPs the contest saw Cameron (seen by some as a 'moderniser') defeat Davis (generally viewed as a Thatcherite traditionalist), by 68 per cent to 32 per cent in the ballot of Party members. This appeared to mark a break with Thatcherism and was certainly exploited as such in Cameron's presentation of his position as leader.

David Cameron's conservatism

There has been, and will continue to be, much debate about the extent to which the ideas of David Cameron and his leading colleagues and supporters within the Conservative Party, particularly in relation to social policy, are linked with Thatcherite ideas, or more 'compassionate' or 'progressive' approaches (see, for example, Evans, 2008, 2010; Bochel, 2011). While it is not intended to pursue those debates here in any great depth, it is nevertheless important to consider briefly the changing stance of the Conservatives since 2005.

The continued support for Thatcherite ideas within the Conservative Party, whether in Parliament or in the country, had made it difficult for any of Thatcher's successors to make significant changes to the Party's policies and to alter public perceptions of it, although, as Bale (2008) has pointed out, this appeared to be largely based on a failure to separate out her three election victories from 'her far more ambivalent record when it came to public policy and indeed public support' (Bale, p 282). Despite this allegiance to Thatcherism, Cameron almost immediately sought to present the Conservatives in a different way from his predecessors. Early in his leadership he sought to demonstrate a concern for environmental issues (including opposing a third runway at Heathrow Airport), support for the NHS, expressed the view that the Conservatives had a responsibility to support social justice and to tackle poverty (see, for example, Hickson, 2009; Page, 2011), and took a more socially liberal approach to issues such as sexuality. And, at least prior to the financial crisis of 2007 onwards, he appeared to recognise that the Conservatives needed to respond to the electorate's apparent desire for good quality public services, stating that economic stability would take precedence over tax cuts.

Critics noted, however, that there were few new policy initiatives to provide substance to the rhetoric, and pointed out that Cameron had been one of the architects of the Party's relatively hard-line general election manifesto in 2005. They also highlighted his undertaking to remove the Conservatives from the European People's Party grouping in the European Union (EU) Parliament, which resulted in the formation of a new European Conservatives and Reformists group of Eurosceptic Conservatives and parties which favour deregulation and the free market, some members of which appear to hold hard-right views.

It was certainly true that the early years of Cameron's leadership were characterised by broad position statements from the leader rather than by the development of substantive policies. Indeed, there was arguably a much greater emphasis on Cameron's own persona, and on symbolic attempts to differentiate the Party from Thatcherism, than there was on policy. Where policy was concerned, the Conservatives established six policy review groups, drawing on input from people from outside traditional politics, such as academics and practitioners. Several of the groups covered areas relating to social policy, such as 'public services improvement', which included education, health, social care and social housing; 'social justice', which covered topics such as addiction, economic dependency, educational failure, family breakdown and the voluntary sector; and 'globalisation and global poverty'. The work of these groups led to a series of 'policy Green Papers', but these often contained few policy proposals, were sometimes contradictory in their recommendations and generally lacked endorsement or commitment from the Party leadership. Nevertheless, a number of themes could be identified running across them, including a clear commitment to a significant role for not-for-profit and voluntary organisations in the provision of public services, as well as to a considerable degree of private sector involvement; a central role for choice for consumers of public services; and a promise of a reduction in bureaucracy while maintaining mechanisms for audit and inspection.

It is also possible to identify early signs of some of the thinking that would be the basis of the future government's policies, including what would become Cameron's 'Big Society' idea. For example, in the Chamberlain lecture in Birmingham in 2006 Cameron said:

We need a government that is prepared to trust the third sector more. Sometimes that will mean letting go, taking risks, saying sometimes, we're doing a lousy job rehabilitating drug users or helping excluded kids back into school – you have a go.

And it will always mean – before taking any decision, before setting up any new bureaucracy – asking the question: what is the third sector, charities, voluntary bodies and social enterprises already doing and what more can they do? (Cameron, 2006a)

And later that year in his Scarman lecture, he argued that:

The poverty-fighting agenda I have outlined today is a radical one for my Party, because for the first time it commits us to tackling relative, not just absolute poverty.

But it is also a radical agenda for politics in this country, because it involves a dramatic decentralisation, a big shift in emphasis ... from the state to society.

It will empower the individuals and organisations that hold the key to tackling the stubborn poverty that still blights too many communities in Britain. (Cameron, 2006b)

Cameron took up the idea that British society is 'broken', reflecting the ideas of his predecessor, Iain Duncan Smith. After standing down as leader Duncan Smith established The Centre for Social Justice, the ideas and reports from which appeared to correspond with the views of some newer Conservative MPs (Bochel and Defty, 2007; see also Chapter Three by Nick Ellison in this volume). In addition, the ideas contained in *Breakdown Britain* (Social Justice Policy Group, 2006) and *Breakthrough Britain* (Social Justice Policy Group, 2007) fed into the Conservatives' policy reviews and were taken up by Cameron and others, with the result that the notion that society was 'broken', whether in relation to family breakdown, poverty or unemployment, became a major theme for the Conservatives in the period up to the 2010 General Election, chiming also with the view that what was necessary to respond to this situation was not more state involvement, but less, with a greater role for charities, community organisations, social enterprises and the private sector. Cameron also argued, in *The Daily Telegraph*, that social problems could be resolved in much the same way as Britain's economic problems had been solved in the 1980s, with 'the need to give people more freedom and control over their lives, so they can exercise responsibility' (Cameron, 2007).

While the Centre for Social Justice has clearly been influential, other think tanks have also fed into Conservative thinking. These have included those which influenced Conservative policy in the 1980s and 1990s, such as the Adam Smith Institute, the Centre for Policy Studies and the Institute for Economic Affairs, and others, more recently established, such as Policy Exchange, ResPublica and the Social Market Foundation. While it is always difficult to assess the impact of these organisations, they tend to serve not only as suppliers of ideas for the Conservative Party, which can be accepted or not, but perhaps equally importantly, they can help to shape the political and intellectual context in which the Party's ideas are discussed and policies developed. In addition, Cameron's allies within the Conservative Party, such as Michael Gove and David Willetts, added to the debates about poverty, inequality and exclusion, for example in relation to education (Exley and Ball, 2011), reinforcing debates about the extent to which the Conservative Party was moving away from Thatcherite ideas towards a different form of 'compassionate' (Willetts, 2005a), 'progressive' (Katwala, 2009) or 'modern' conservatism (Page, 2010).

There can also be little doubt that under David Cameron the Conservatives benefited from Labour's grip on the policy agenda loosening following their 2005 General Election victory, from Labour's internal travails and from a relatively easy ride from the media in relation to scrutiny of the Conservatives' ideas and policies. However, the financial crisis of 2007 onwards appeared to pose significant challenges for the Conservatives as well as for the government, with the rapid increase in the budget deficit which arose from the effective nationalisation of some major banks, combined with the Labour government's use of public expenditure to reduce the impact of the recession on parts of the economy and on jobs. In particular it raised questions about the size and approach of the UK's financial sector, and, just as significantly in political terms, how to deal with the rapid increase in public borrowing. The Conservatives' response was to blame the Labour government for its mismanagement of the economy, and, in common with the other parties, bankers for their role in bringing about the crisis. They also took a significantly harder line than the Liberal Democrats, and particularly Labour, on the scale and timing of reduction of the deficit.

However, despite the softer line on much domestic policy, the emphasis on the environment, the attempt to recruit more women and minority ethnic candidates for parliamentary seats and other rebranding of the Conservative Party, including a new logo, surveys of voters suggested that many were still unsure of what the Conservatives stood for, perhaps because of the lack of a clear philosophy, a contrast with the Thatcher period, or even New Labour's 'Third Way'. As a result it was arguable that:

> The party, under Cameron, had succeeded in neutralising the negatives, but had not received a positive lead in a range of important respects. The result was that both main parties entered the election almost neck and neck on many competence judgments, despite Gordon Brown's unpopularity and despite the financial crisis and recession. (Green, 2010, p 678)

The 2010 General Election

At the start of the Conservatives' 2010 general election campaign it was apparent that the idea of the 'Big Society' was intended to provide a philosophy of participation and responsibility to underpin the Conservatives' policies, and this was reflected in the title of the manifesto, *Invitation to join the government of Britain*. The 'Big Society' was contrasted with the 'big government' that the Conservatives saw as having failed, and sought to combine decentralisation, and lower taxation and public expenditure with the idea that individuals, the voluntary sector and social enterprises would play a major role in providing public services and addressing Britain's 'broken society'.

In the event, the Conservative manifesto reflected traditional Conservative concerns as well as the efforts made by David Cameron to develop new policy strengths, with sections on longstanding Conservative topics, such as 'Fight back against crime' and 'Raise standards in schools', alongside newer themes such as 'Back the NHS' and 'Build the Big Society'. Among specific pledges were those to increase spending on the NHS in real terms every year (although, as critics pointed out, given the Conservatives' commitment to massive cuts in public expenditure, this implied bigger reductions in funding for other services), the creation of a Big Society Bank, funded from unclaimed bank assets (although with no real indication of how much this would deliver), the provision of an additional 4,200 Sure Start health visitors and a rather vague pledge to 'recognise marriage and civil partnerships in the tax system' (Conservative Party, 2010, p 41).

Despite the Conservatives having entered the general election campaign with the hope that they might achieve a majority in the House of Commons, it became clear that the Party remained unable to increase its share of the vote significantly above the level of the three previous elections. In addition, the Big Society, intended to lie at the heart of the campaign, proved to be problematic and, instead of differentiating the Conservatives from their rivals, created confusion. If it was indeed offering a new way of doing things, its launch only weeks before Election Day seemed strange, and for many, it appeared ambitious, unclear and unrealistic. Conservative candidates reported that voters were confused about what it meant. As a result, rather than being the centrepiece of the campaign, the Big Society was relegated to a minor role.

The election campaign was also thrown into turmoil by the televised leadership debates. In particular the presence of Nick Clegg in the debates, on equal terms with Gordon Brown and David Cameron, and his performance in the first debate, which was seen by many as overshadowing those of his rivals, appeared to lead to a surge in support for the Liberal Democrats as measured by opinion polls. This became the 'story' for much of the media coverage of the remainder of the campaign, making it difficult for the other parties to get their messages to the top of the news agenda.

Although changing patterns of political participation and support make comparisons with past elections problematic, the Conservative Party did not perform particularly well at the 2010 General Election. Faced by a Party that had been in government for 13 years, led by an unpopular Prime Minister, in a country emerging from perhaps the worst economic crisis since the 1930s, the Conservatives polled 36.1 per cent of the vote, only 3.8 per cent more than under Michael Howard's leadership in 2005 and 4.4 per cent more than under William Hague in 2001. As a result, although the Conservatives won 306 seats, gaining 97, they remained short of the 326 MPs required to achieve a majority in the House of Commons. With Labour having won 258 seats and the Liberal Democrats 57, some sort of agreement was necessary to form a new government. After five days, on Tuesday 11 May, a deal on a coalition between the Conservatives and the Liberal Democrats was finally announced.

The Coalition

Initially set out in a short paper under 11 headings, the Coalition's approach was fleshed out somewhat in *The Coalition: Our programme for government* (Cabinet Office, 2010) on 20 May. This contained a mixture of policies drawn from the manifestos of each of the two parties, together with some proposals for political reform that had been in neither. While the decision of the Liberal Democrats to join the Conservatives in government came as a surprise to many, this was to some extent perhaps because the Liberal Democrats had been subject to significantly less media and public scrutiny than the other parties. While previous leaders, such as Charles Kennedy and Menzies Campbell, were arguably drawn from the social democratic side of the Party, a group of Liberal Democrats set out, in *The Orange Book: Reclaiming liberalism* (Marshall and Laws, 2004), something of a different approach, suggesting, for example, that Liberals and Liberal Democrats had sometimes lost sight of some of the 'fundamental principles' of liberalism (Laws, 2004, p 19) and that there had been 'the development of a well-meaning "nanny-state liberalism", in which respect for personal rights and freedoms has at times been compromised by the pursuit of other, no doubt well-intentioned, objectives' (Laws, 2004, p 24). Although *The Orange Book* did not necessarily form a coherent and consistent set of arguments, there was considerable emphasis on the strengths of economic liberalism and the need for the Liberal Democrats to utilise choice, competition, consumer power and the private sector. Under the leadership of Nick Clegg many of *The Orange Book* Liberal Democrats had come to prominence by 2010, and they were perhaps more comfortable sharing power with the Conservatives than their predecessors might have been.

Examination of the Coalition agreement and the *Programme for government* helps to highlight that in some policy areas there were significant levels of overlap between the Conservative and Liberal Democrat parties prior to the election, including many aspects of civil liberties, greater freedom for schools, linking increases in the state pension to earnings, and the idea (although not necessarily the size) of the 'pupil premium'. In other areas the Liberal Democrats were successful in including their policies in the agreement; notably the Party's (expensive) commitment to the raising of personal tax allowances was retained. The Liberal Democrats also did well in terms of ministerial appointments, with five members of the Cabinet and a further 11 MPs and two Peers in ministerial posts.

However, in many areas, including social policies, the Conservatives' approach clearly took precedence. For example, in education, the Academies Act was rushed through Parliament despite concerns about its possible impact, including on children with special educational needs. In terms of welfare to work, again Conservative policies appeared to dominate the Coalition's thinking. In relation to immigration, rather than the Liberal Democrats' proposal for an amnesty for immigrants, the Coalition took up the Conservatives' idea of a 'cap' on non-EU immigration, although tensions remained with the Business Secretary, Vince Cable, a Liberal Democrat, saying that the way that the government's policy was being applied was damaging British business (*The Financial Times*, 17 September 2010). On health, despite the Liberal Democrats previously opposing increasing spending on the NHS in real terms because of its implications for other areas of public expenditure, they accepted the Conservatives' plans, and despite the *Programme for government* promising 'We will stop the top-down reorganisations of the NHS that have got in the way of patient care' (Cabinet Office, 2010, p 24), only two months into the new government the Health Secretary, Andrew Lansley, announced a major restructuring of the NHS, proposing to give general practitioners (GPs) control of much of the budget (DH, 2010). Public health was to be the subject of a separate White Paper later in 2010. Neither Party's manifesto said much about benefits, and this was reflected in the *Programme for government*, although it was clear early in the life of the Coalition that there were to be significant reductions in the benefits budget, with £11 billion of cuts announced in the Emergency Budget and further reductions of around £7 billion set out by the Chancellor, George Osborne, in the Spending Review in October 2010 (HM Treasury, 2010). These early cuts tended to focus on people of working age, with pensioners much less affected.

Some areas were clearly problematic for the Coalition, with the approach to higher education in the *Programme for government*, where the parties had very different approaches to the funding of universities, continuing to rely on the Browne review, although Cable suggested the possibility of a graduate tax in July 2010 before rejecting it himself in September the same year (Baker, 2010). Along with Conservative proposals to introduce transferable tax allowances for married couples, this was an area where the Coalition agreement allowed Liberal Democrat MPs to abstain in a vote in the House of Commons. Similarly, the funding of long-term care continued to be a major issue, with the problem passed on to the Commission on Funding of Care and Support which was not due to report until July 2011, although the Spending Review promised an extra £2 billion for social care over four years while at the same time announcing major cuts in local authority budgets. On crime and policing the Conservatives' proposals for the direct election of local police commissioners, replacing the indirectly elected police authority, survived the Coalition agreement, but with the Justice Secretary, Kenneth Clarke, questioning the 'prison works' orthodoxy (Clarke, 2010), the direction of criminal justice policy remained unclear.

In some ways perhaps more importantly than any particular policy, given its implications for public expenditure and consequently for public services as a whole, the Conservatives' approach to cutting the deficit has been dominant, so that policy since May 2010 has been driven by Conservative priorities, accepted by the Liberal Democrats' leadership following the election, in terms of the speed and depth of cuts in public expenditure, with the measures arising from the Emergency Budget in June 2010 being widely criticised for being regressive and for hitting households of working age (see, for example, Browne and Levell, 2010) and women (Stratton, 2010). The depth of cuts foreshadowed in the June Emergency Budget clearly had implications for other policy areas, but even following the Spending Review in October 2010, which set out the proposed expenditure for government departments up to 2014–15, it was often not clear what the impact of these would be in detail.

While the bulk of this chapter has been concerned with areas that fall within the remit of the Westminster Parliament, it is important to remember that substantial areas of social policy are subject to the powers of the devolved legislatures in Northern Ireland, Scotland and Wales. In each of those devolved administrations political control is now different from that at Westminster and both political control and approaches to policies may diverge further in the next few years. The Coalition's acceptance of the proposals of the Calman Commission in Scotland (including shifting partial responsibility for the level of income tax to the Scottish Parliament) and the agreement to 'introduce a referendum on further Welsh devolution' (Cabinet Office, 2010, p 28) suggests recognition of the realities of devolution. Nevertheless, there will be significant implications from decisions made by the Coalition government, not least because cuts in public expenditure will be passed on to the devolved governments which will then have to make decisions about how to implement them in their domains.

An early assessment

There are clearly a variety of different ways in which the development of Conservative social policy under Cameron's leadership can be characterised. For some it is largely a continuation of Thatcherite approaches, albeit perhaps with a slightly different emphasis and a somewhat more caring face. This view has gained credence for many from the enthusiasm with which the Coalition government has sought to reduce public expenditure, which is reminiscent of the Thatcher governments' views, including that 'Public expenditure is at the heart of Britain's economic difficulties' (HM Treasury, 1979, p 1) and the wish to roll back the frontiers of the state, with a perception that in the same way as the notion of 'crisis' was used to justify attacks on the welfare state in the 1980s, so too is the financial deficit in the current period.

However, for others it has been seen as a more 'compassionate' or 'progressive' form of conservatism, which, despite identifying individuals and individual choices as lying at the heart of many social problems, also sees a role for governments in responding to these issues. This would accord with the acceptance of Labour's commitment to end child poverty and the recognition of poverty and inequality as problems. It is also possible to see the Conservatives as having taken on New Labour's ideas in some areas, in the same way as in 1997 Labour was seen as having accepted many of the ideas of Thatcherism.

Nevertheless, the implications of severe public expenditure cuts, combined with the suggestions of a new relationship between individuals and society and the state, are likely to mean change to public services on a massive scale and imply a significant reduction or even residualisation of the welfare state in many areas. In addition, despite the apparent commitment to the reduction of poverty and associated social ills, for Cameron and other 'progressive Conservatives', the answer to these problems is generally seen as less government with more of a role for individuals, the local community, the voluntary sector and social enterprises, with the 2010 Spending Review emphasising the redistribution of power 'away from central government' and the 'opportunities and funding available to the voluntary and community sector' (HM Treasury, 2010, p 8). While this might fit well with much Conservative thinking, and the views of many *Orange Book* Liberal Democrats, there will be others within the Liberal Democratic Party who may feel much less comfortable with both the policies and the ideas underpinning them, while the realities, including in terms of public opinion and election results, may be even less palatable.

In addition, the future of Cameron's 'Big Society' remains uncertain. While it potentially offers a contrast with Labour's 'big government' and Thatcherism's individualism, it is far from clear whether it can make the transition into practice. Rather than the state or the market, it appears to rely on a sense of duty or responsibility on the part of individuals and communities to respond to social problems (see Chapter Three by Nick Ellison and Chapter Four by Ruth Lister, this volume). The question of whether a 'Big Society' can be developed to replace many of the welfare functions of the state, let alone without high levels of state support, remains open, while issues over regulation and quality assurance are also likely to be significant as the state withdraws from or reduces its role in many areas of provision.

There are also marked inconsistencies in the ideas which underpin the Coalition's proposals, frequently reflecting the development of Conservative policy under Cameron's leadership. In areas such as work and benefits, and certainly the economy, much of the emphasis appears to be on individuals as rational actors. Yet the commitment to state funding of the NHS and education, and to some extent to social justice, would appear to sit uneasily with such a philosophy. And in education the depth of spending cuts proposed by the Coalition would appear to sit uneasily with plans for hundreds of new 'free schools'.

Despite the attempts to modernise the Conservative Party, the efforts to change the Party's image, new policy developments, a more popular leader, an unpopular Labour leader, a financial crisis and a recession, the Conservatives' electoral progress under David Cameron was limited up to the 2010 General Election. As a result the Party was forced into a coalition with the Liberal Democrats. In the early months of the Coalition the Conservative Party in Parliament appeared the more disciplined of the two. However, having achieved power, the longevity of the Coalition and even the shape of its policies are likely to be affected by the economy, ideology and by electoral calculations for both parties, and it is difficult to predict how these will develop in the coming months and years.

References

Baker, M. (2010) 'Graduate tax ruled out as "unworkable"', *Times Higher Education*, 23 September.

Bale, T. (2008) '"A bit less bunny-hugging and a bit more-bunny-boiling"? Qualifying Conservative Party change under David Cameron', *British Politics*, vol 3, no 2, pp 270-99.

Bochel, H. (2010) 'One Nation conservatism and social policy, 1951–64', *The Journal of Poverty and Social Justice*, vol 18, no 2, pp 123-34.

Bochel, H. (ed) (2011) *The Conservative Party and social policy*, Bristol: The Policy Press.

Bochel, H. and Defty, A. (2007) *Welfare policy under New Labour: Views from inside Westminster*, Bristol: The Policy Press.

Bosanquet, N. (1983) *After the New Right*, London: Heinemann.

Browne, J. and Levell, P. (2010) *The distributional effect of tax and benefit reforms to be introduced between June 2010 and April 2014 – A revised assessment*, London: Institute for Fiscal Studies.

Cabinet Office (2010) *The Coalition: Our programme for government*, London: Cabinet Office.

Cameron, D. (2006a) Chamberlain lecture, 14 July.

Cameron, D. (2006b) 'Tackling poverty is a social responsibility', Scarman lecture, 24 November.

Cameron, D. (2007) 'What makes me Conservative', *The Daily Telegraph*, 8 September.

Clarke, K. (2010) 'The government's vision for criminal justice reform', Speech to the Centre for Crime and Justice Studies, 30 June.

Conservative Party (2010) *Invitation to join the government of Britain*, London: Conservative Party.

DH (Department of Health) (2010) *Equity and excellence: Liberating the NHS*, London: The Stationery Office.

Driver, S. and Martell, L. (2006) *New Labour*, Cambridge: Polity Press.

Evans, S. (2008) 'Consigning its past to history? David Cameron and the Conservative Party', *Parliamentary Affairs*, vol 61, no 2, pp 291-314.

Evans, S. (2010) '"Mother's boy": David Cameron and Margaret Thatcher', *British Journal of Politics and International Relations*, vol 12, no 3, pp 325-44.

Exley, S. and Ball, S.J. (2011) 'Something old, something new: understanding Conservative education policy', in H. Bochel (ed) *The Conservative Party and social policy*, Bristol: The Policy Press, pp 97-117.

Friedman, M. (1962) *Capitalism and freedom*, Chicago, IL: Chicago University Press.

Green, J. (2010) 'Strategic recovery? The Conservatives under David Cameron', *Parliamentary Affairs*, vol 63, no 4, pp 667-88.

Harris, R. and Seldon, A. (1979) *Over-ruled on welfare*, London: Institute of Economic Affairs.

Hayek, F. (1944) *The road to serfdom*, London: Routledge.

Hayek, F. (1976) *Law, legislation and liberty*, Vol 2, London: Routledge.

Hickson, K. (2009) 'Conservatism and the poor: Conservative Party attitudes to poverty and inequality since the 1970s', *British Politics*, vol 4, no 3, pp 341-62.

HM Treasury (1979) *The government's expenditure plans 1979/80 to 1982/83*, London: HMSO.

HM Treasury (2010) *Spending Review 2010*, London: The Stationery Office.

Katwala, S. (2009) 'In Maggie's shadow', *Public Policy Research*, vol 16, no 1, pp 3-13.

Laws, D. (2004) 'Reclaiming Liberalism: A liberal agenda for the Liberal Democrats', in P. Marshall and D. Laws (eds) *The Orange Book: Reclaiming liberalism*, London: Profile Books.

Marshall, P. and Laws, D. (eds) (2004) *The Orange Book: Reclaiming liberalism*, London: Profile Books.

Page, R.M. (2010) 'David Cameron's modern Conservative approach to poverty and social justice: towards one nation or two?', *The Journal of Poverty and Social Justice*, vol 18, no 2, pp 147-60.

Page, R.M. (2011) 'Clear blue water? The Conservative Party's approach to social policy since 1945', in H. Bochel (ed) *The Conservative Party and social policy*, Bristol: The Policy Press, pp 23-39.

Powell, M. (ed) (1999) *New Labour: New welfare state? The 'third way' in British social policy*, Bristol: The Policy Press.

Seawright, D. (2009) *The British Conservative Party and One Nation politics*, London: Continuum.

Seldon, A. and Snowdon, P. (2005) 'The Conservative Party', in A. Seldon and D. Kavanagh (eds) *The Blair effect 2001-5*, Cambridge: Cambridge University Press, pp 131-56.

Social Justice Policy Group (2006) *Breakdown Britain*, London: Social Justice Policy Group.

Social Justice Policy Group (2007) *Breakthrough Britain*, London: Social Justice Policy Group.

Stratton, A. (2010) 'Women will bear brunt of budget cuts, says Yvette Cooper', *The Guardian*, 4 July.

Willets, D. (2005a) 'Compassionate conservatism and the war on poverty', Speech to the Centre for Social Justice, 6 January (www.davidwilletts. co.uk/2005/01/06/compassionate-conservative/).

Willets, D. (2005b) 'A new conservatism for a new century', Speech to the Social Market Foundation, 2 June (www.davidwilletts. co.uk/2005/06/02/new-conservatism/).

TWO

Something old and blue, or red, bold and new? Welfare reform and the Coalition government

Jay Wiggan

It's time for something different, something bold – something that doesn't just pour money down the throat of wasteful, top-down government schemes. The Big Society is that something different and bold. (Cameron, 2010b)

Introduction

Despite previous indications that investment in public services would be safe in their hands, the onset of recession in 2008 provided an opportunity for Conservative politicians to advocate austerity in public spending and an intensification of market-led public service reform (Evans, 2010, p 13; HM Treasury, 2010a). It would be wrong, however, not to acknowledge the shift in language and focus of the Conservative Party prior to the 2010 General Election. Keen to develop a framework which permitted a commitment to economic liberalism, the reinvigoration of self-reliance and a concern for social justice, leading modernisers drew on the work of leading civic conservatives (Letwin, 2003; Willetts, 2005b) to self-style themselves and their policies as representing a progressive conservatism. A key idea within this progressive Conservative narrative is its emphasis on reanimating the institutions of civil society to provide an alternative to state services, but also a buttress against market failure. The progressive conservative milieu of David Cameron's project of renewal has also thrown up the complementary, yet arguably more radical interpretation, of what modernisation should entail in the Red Tory agenda of Phillip Blond. Blond (2010) concurs with the civic conservative emphasis on civil society and a reduced role for the state, but is more circumspect as to whether the empowerment of communities and individuals will occur unless the neoliberal orthodoxy is challenged and ownership of assets and wealth among low-income families is improved (Blond, 2008, p 89, 2009b, 2010). What makes Red Toryism of interest is that it implicitly offers an alternative to the vision of progressive conservatism promoted by the Conservative Party leadership. From within the framework of Conservative thinking it attempts to break conservatism from neoliberalism by establishing that the latter is not the champion of free markets, but of monopolistic big business (Coombs, 2010). Similarly Red Toryism draws attention to how social inequality shapes opportunity and poverty, yet remains critical of hierarchical and state-led policy responses (Coombs, 2010, p 3).

This chapter argues that, while Conservative Party politicians and government ministers have on occasion echoed the rhetoric of Red Toryism, their approach to welfare reform shows a continuation of neoliberal orthodoxy (Cabinet Office, 2010a; Conservative Party, 2010a, 2010c). Rather than the radical shift in priorities implied by Red Tory analysis and policy proposals, the Coalition's welfare reforms are suggestive of what Soss et al (2009), in their examination of US welfare reform, refer to as neoliberal paternalism. Under neoliberal paternalism, welfare reform brings together new public management practices of contracting out and performance management with a coercive paternalism that strives to strengthen labour discipline among benefit recipients. Unemployed individuals are presumed to be responsible for their unemployment and lack the competence or willingness to alter their situation. It falls to policy to instil an understanding of market rationality and what constitutes 'good' behaviour, which is represented as the moral obligation of benefit recipients to work and manage their and their family's affairs competently (Soss et al, 2009, p 4). Meanwhile, the existence of large numbers of benefit claimants is taken, not as evidence of market failure, but as demonstrating the limited effectiveness of public employment services, thereby justifying further economic liberalisation. Underpinned by ideological commitments to neoliberalism and historic antipathy to equality, the Conservative-led Coalition has utilised a civic conservative narrative to express disquiet about poverty while harnessing concerns regarding the size and scope of the state with populist social policy (Gough, 1983, p 154). The outcome is that users of social welfare services are portrayed as irresponsible and incompetent individuals, rather than as citizens entitled to support (Gough, 1983, p 154). In contrast to the proposals of Red Toryism, welfare reform is not breaking with economic liberalism or promoting wider distribution of asset wealth.

Rather it helps re-regulate employment and social security provision on terms favourable to the expansion of the scope, penetration and organising principles of market forces (Soss et al, 2009, p 2).

Seizing the progressive baton? The modern Conservative critique of the welfare state

Elected as leader in 2005, David Cameron recognised that voters perceived the Conservative Party as advocates of individualism and representatives of the wealthy and big business, with little interest in the poor and public services (Evans, 2008, p 9; Quinn, 2008, p 190). Senior Party members sought to reframe public perceptions by showing an acceptance of social liberalism and emphasising the collective as well as the individual (Cameron, 2009a, 2010a, p 293; Osborne, 2009). In a piece of neat political footwork, Cameron (2009b, p 7) sought to distance the Party from perceptions of self-interest, by arguing that a sole emphasis on economic growth and rolling back the state would not empower communities and individuals, redistribute opportunity or address poverty. Acknowledging poverty as an unacceptable social problem, Cameron accepted relative definitions of poverty, setting him apart from some of the sceptical views expressed by Conservative politicians in the 1980s (Lister and Bennett, 2010, p 86; Page, 2010, p 153). Yet these developments were framed within traditional Conservative attitudes to the state. Alluding to Thatcher's infamous dictum, that there was no such thing as society, only individuals and families, Cameron noted that society existed, but that it was not synonymous with the state (Evans, 2008, p 9). In making this distinction, Cameron implicitly drew on civic conservative ideas articulated by Conservative politicians such as David Willetts and Oliver Letwin (Hickson, 2009, p 357), who at the time of writing (2011) are Minister for Higher Education and Minister of State in the Cabinet Office (see also Chapter Three by Nick Ellison, this volume). The civic conservative perspective accepts that tension exists between market and society, but suggests that the disinterest of Conservatives in the collective good of society has been overstated and misrepresented. Being in favour of economic liberalism does not mean the disavowal of collective action to address social problems (Willetts, 2005b, 2008). The collective institutions of society are a necessity for a functioning liberal market economy, but in turn the free market is a necessity for generating prosperity (Letwin, 2008, p 75). The contentious issue is what form collective action should take, how it is situated within the relationships and dispersal of power between the state, civil society, communities, families and individuals (Letwin, 2003; Willetts, 2008). Conservative modernisers characterise the pursuit of social justice by New Labour as an example of how state intervention, for noble purposes, displaces civil society and traditional family support that promoted and sustained self-reliance. As a consequence, independence and responsibility are discouraged, exacerbating social problems, while an unresponsive state bureaucracy, lacking incentives to pursue efficiency and innovation, is created. Civic Conservatives instead advocate less state intervention, preferring instead to strengthen the bonds of society. Through fostering trust and reciprocity and building up civil society it is assumed that people will be better prepared, in the event of market failure, to rely on themselves and their families, or will turn to charities and community organisations to tackle social problems at the local level (see Letwin, 2003; Willetts, 2005a, 2005b, 2008).

> So we must engage people at the local level and recreate the neighbourly society. We will do this only if we recognise that communities are networks or relationships that turn collections of people into responsible individuals. Active communities with strong relationships foster social trust – shared respect and decency between individuals. To foster those relationships, to create that sense of community, we need to give impetus to every institution across the country that makes it possible. We must give succour to every neighbourhood across the country which, instead of waiting for the state to solve a problem, is getting together to produce home-grown solutions. (Letwin, 2003, p 52)

The Conservative Party commitment to a Big Society of individuals and communities empowered to take control over service delivery is an expression of this vision. The state is transformed from provider and controller of services to a dependent population to that of the facilitator of independence and funder of a decentralised plurality of service providers (Conservative Party, 2010c, p 37; see also Chapter Three by Nick Ellison and Chapter Four by Ruth Lister, this volume). Its advocates argue that, unlike New Labour's regime of performance targets, the Big Society will free public sector staff from bureaucratic interference, give power to service users and harness the private and third sector to improve efficiency, innovation and effectiveness (Cameron, 2010b). Similar sentiments are echoed in the Red Tory strand of progressive conservatism, although it is also more wary of the private sector and market forces (Blond, 2009e; Blond, 2010).

The RedTory challenge: something (a little bit) different

One of the most striking ideas within contemporary Conservative thinking is Phillip Blond's Red Tory reworking of the Conservative tradition to offer a route out of the supposed impasse created by Labour and Conservative governments (see ChapterThree by Nick Ellison, this volume). Blond divides the 65 years since 1945 into two periods of consensus in political economy, the welfare state and the market state.The welfare state is characterised as Keynesian economic policy, corporatism and state-led welfare provision. Centralised state policies are portrayed as undermining the independence and mutualist aspects of working-class self-reliance and organisation by replacing them with services and assistance, managed by the professional middle classes. Meanwhile the focus on individual freedoms brought about by the liberation movements of the 1960s and 1970s is said to have disrupted the traditional family and promoted a moral relativism among the middle and working classes. The forces of individualism unleashed by these developments ushered in the neoliberal reforms of the 1980s and the market state (Blond, 2008, 2009a). Under the auspices of free market modernity, the market state liberalised the economy, promoted the free movement of capital, flexible labour markets and new public management ideas in public services. For Blond, some of these reforms were necessary but they did not lead to the empowerment and wealth promised, particularly for the poor. Instead, monopolistic and speculative practices took root, as the powerful captured the gains of liberalisation and crowded out small businesses and opportunities for distributing wealth to poorer sections of society (Blond, 2009a, 2009b, 2009c, 2010, p 18).

> The great paradox of the neo-liberal account of free markets that has dominated discussion and determined practice and indeed economic reality for the past thirty years is that in the name of free markets the neo-liberal approach has presided over an unprecedented reduction of market diversity and plurality. It has reduced the type of provision available and the numbers of providers. In the name of freedom we have produced economic concentration and in a number of areas monopoly dominance or indeed something very much like it. (Blond, 2009c, p 2)

The promotion of individualism meanwhile resulted in the atomisation of communities and a decline in trust and commitment to the public good. As a consequence, contractual relationships came to define social and economic interaction and the bureaucratic state expanded to enforce compliance (Blond, 2009d, 2010, p 58). The Red Tory position shares with civic conservatism a belief in reducing the scope of the state in order to foster responsibility, reciprocity and restore civil society. Yet for Blond, it is economic liberalism, as well as the state, which is responsible for undermining the intermediary structures, such as the church, family and mutual organisations that make up civil society (Blond, 2008, 2010). The link Blond makes between unemployment, welfare 'dependency', inequality and economic liberalism is where he seeks to detach social conservatism from neoliberal economics (Coombs, 2010). In this, Red Toryism breaks from leading Conservatives, who do not accept a contradiction between neoliberalism and the good society (Willetts, 1992, 2005a; Letwin, 2003; Osborne, 2009). The Red Tory position critiques the trend towards ever greater liberalisation of the economy and the privileges given to big business. Instead a civic economy premised on trust, reciprocity and sustainability is promoted. The presumption is that this will facilitate self-regulation, reduced compliance costs and less state intervention, creating truly free markets and stimulating investment and growth (Blond, 2009a, 2009b, 2009c). The speech given by David Cameron to the World Economic Forum in Davos in 2009 alluded to the Red Tory critique of monopoly capitalism and its indifference to various aspects of social and economic life:

> So it's time to place the market within a moral framework – even if that means standing up to companies who make life harder for parents and families. It's time to help create vibrant, local economies – even if that means standing in the way of global cultural juggernauts. And it's time to spread opportunity and wealth and ownership more equally through society and that will mean, as some have put it, recapitalising the poor rather than just the banks. (Cameron, 2009c)

The problem that arises is that the Red Tory critique of monopoly capitalism and economic liberalism suggests the prioritisation of localism and economic protectionism (Coombs, 2010, p 4). This would require, as Coombs (2010, p 5) eloquently notes, 'the elite to go precisely against their own self-interest as a class determinately situated in the capitalist production process: whether financial or industrial'. The leading members of the Coalition certainly share socio-cultural experiences and economic interests that mark them out as part of the elite. Of the 23 ministers appointed to Cabinet, 15 attended either the University of Oxford or Cambridge and a majority attended independent schools (Doble, 2010). According to *The Sunday Times*, 18 of the ministers appointed to the post-election Cabinet were also millionaires, drawing their wealth from a mixture of industry, finance, property and inheritance (Milland and Warren, 2010). Despite the occasional rhetorical flirtation with Red Toryism, leading Conservatives show little enthusiasm for policy that might undermine their historic class interest or their ideological advocacy of economic liberalism. The Big Society, when examined through the lens of welfare reform, is premised on the familiar principle of less eligibility together with a restructuring of public services to bear down on the 'social wage' (Gough, 1983), while ensuring that what remains is organised according to market principles. The outcome is, then, that spending restraint is coupled with the expansion of opportunities for business to profit from the commodification of inactive labour, first through benefit reforms, designed to bring more individuals into the labour market at a price acceptable to employers, and second by contracting out systems, advantageous to large for-profit providers (Grover, 2009, p 488; Soss et al, 2009, p 20).

Unleashing the Big (market) Society in welfare to work

One Big Society idea is for public sector employees, including those working in organisations such as Jobcentre Plus, and/or citizens, to be given the option to form and run services as a cooperative (Stratton and Sparrow, 2010). The suggestion is that such cooperatives could eliminate many of the hierarchical and centralising tendencies of welfare provision, helping to reinvigorate civil society and improve community and staff control. The concern is that these proposals occur within a framework of public service reform shaped by neoliberal commitments to market rationality in the form of competitive contracting. It seems that staff or citizen cooperatives would be subject to a payment by results contract and a competitive tendering process prior to any contract renewal (Conservative Party, 2010b, p 5). Potentially this facilitates the gradual withdrawal of the state from provider of services to that of arm's-length purchaser of private sector services, as cooperatives would risk losing out to better resourced private sector organisations during successive tendering rounds. For Conservative modernisers the expansion of market forces is not incompatible with the delivery of social welfare or the strengthening of society and so this is not an issue (Willetts, 1992, 2005a, 2005b). Yet it raises the question whether the Big Society is merely cover for persisting with the type of new public management reforms that have shaped public services since the 1990s (Griffiths, 2009, p 102). The Coalition government's welfare to work scheme, the Work Programme (Freud, 2007; DWP, 2008; Cabinet Office, 2010a, p 23; Conservative Party, 2010c, p 15), does not suggest a new approach to labour market policy, but rather an intensification of existing trends towards marketisation (see Chapter Seven by Dan Finn, this volume). The Work Programme expands the opportunities available for private and third sector providers and strengthens market rationality by reinforcing the link between provider payment and client job outcomes. Contestability, however, potentially requires a trade-off between achieving economies of scale, lower transaction costs and maintaining greater stability or realising greater competition, diversity and innovation. Ministers have indicated a preference for 'well capitalised and well resourced' groups to function as 'prime' contractors in the Work Programme (Barker and Timmins, 2010; Freud, 2010), suggesting a preference for greater stability. A danger is that, far from creating a plurality of providers, the expansion of marketisation will result in dominance by a few private sector organisations. Under New Labour, of the 14 prime contractor organisations delivering phase one of Flexible New Deal (introduced in 2009), 12 were drawn from the private sector, with one from the third sector and one from the public sector (DWP, no date). The Work and Pensions Committee (2010, p 43) subsequently expressed concern that prime contractors could dictate delivery in their area and squeeze out smaller providers, or pass on financial risks by sending them the hardest to help clients. The Work Programme, despite allusions to the potential for third sector involvement and improved employment outcomes for clients, risks creating the private monopolistic practice that Phillip Blond (2009a) warns is a consequence of neoliberalism.

The emphasis on 'results' has also raised concerns from providers regarding the feasibility, in the midst of a weak labour market, of any attempts to weight the payment structure too heavily towards job outcomes (Timmins, 2010). A failure to sufficiently and appropriately incentivise job outcomes, however, risks exacerbating the opportunities in such programmes for providers to cherry-pick the most job-ready clients and park the least job ready (Davies, 2007, p 152). The Work Programme attempts to balance these challenges by paying providers in three stages: an attachment fee to help with initial start-up costs; a job outcome fee for moving a client into employment; and a sustainment fee for keeping a client in employment (DWP, 2010c, p 6). The inclusion of a sustainment fee is recognition that many benefit claimants move between low pay and unemployment. Of course, incentivising providers to keep clients in the labour market via post-employment contact also demonstrates how the state is reshaping support. Market mechanisms are used to extend a paternalistic supervisory reach into the labour market to better regulate client adherence to behaviour that complies with market-orientated notions of what constitutes (economic) independence (Soss et al, 2009, p 17).

Tackling 'dependency': retrenchment and conditionality in social security

While civic conservatism has provided the theoretical backdrop for justifying a reduction in direct state provision of welfare services in order to achieve social justice goals, much of the work underpinning welfare reform was initiated prior to the election by The Centre for Social Justice think tank, established by the current Secretary of State for Work and Pensions, Iain Duncan Smith (Page, 2010, p 149; and see Chapter Three by Nick Ellison and Chapter Eight by Tina Haux, this volume). The Centre for Social Justice has produced detailed research analysing poverty and suggesting social security reform (see Lister and Bennett, 2010; Page, 2010). It argues that the tax and benefit system is helping to create a 'broken society' because it is poor at instilling work expectations, weak in the application of conditionality and actively discourages employment through perverse financial incentives, which fosters welfare dependency (Social Justice Policy Group, 2007, p 5, 2009). It is not surprising then, that the Coalition identifies welfare dependency and worklessness, perceived as key indicators of a 'broken Britain', as a priority, or that the focus for reform is individual behaviour and the benefit system (Cabinet Office, 2010b; DWP, 2010a, 2010b). As Lister and Bennett (2010, p 88) note, the notion of a broken society and its attendant welfare dependency is a useful hook for the Conservatives to hang almost any policy prescription on, and helps to legitimise an emphasis on the reciprocal obligations of the poor, over their entitlement to welfare as citizens (Fitzpatrick, 2005, p 16). Linking poverty to 'disordered' behaviour is, as Soss et al (2009, p 8) point out, a useful means for transforming the welfare state. In an era of fiscal restraint, the social security budget is an attractive target for retrenchment and restructuring, particularly when little public support exists for extra spending on the workless (Barnes and Tomaszewski, 2010, p 196).

The failure of individuals to act in a manner the government deems responsible, and indeed argues is positively harmful, can be used to justify a more punitive and less generous form of provision. The 2010 Emergency Budget announced spending reductions on welfare of £11 billion by 2014-15 (HM Treasury, 2010a, p 40), and the October 2010 Spending Review announced an additional £7 billion of savings (HM Treasury, 2010b, p 68). Coalition ministers argue there is no alternative, as to do nothing about the cost of social security is simply unaffordable (Duncan Smith, 2010). The Chancellor of the Exchequer, George Osborne, justified the tax and benefit changes announced in the 2010 Emergency Budget as ensuring resources target those most in need (Osborne, 2010). The Institute for Fiscal Studies suggests, however, that the new Budget measures are largely regressive and will disproportionately affect low-income households (Browne and Lovell, 2010, p 2). Over the period of the Parliament, the value of working-age benefits and tax credits will be eroded by a switch in the measure of inflation used to up-rate them each year. Rather than the retail price index (RPI) or Rossi index, benefits will now rise in line with the consumer price index (CPI) that tends to increase at a slower rate than the measures it replaces. To achieve savings of £775 million a year by 2014-15 the value of Childcare Tax Credit from 2011 will be limited to 70 per cent of childcare costs rather than its current 80 per cent. Low-income couples with children will also now be required to work at least 24 hours between them, with one partner working at least 16 hours per week, in order to qualify for Working Tax Credit (HM Treasury, 2010b, p 68). The rate at which support through the tax credit system is withdrawn as income rises is also being raised, so that support tapers off more quickly (HM Treasury, 2010a, p 34). Together with the announcement that, from 2013, Child Benefit will be withdrawn from families with higher-rate tax payers (HM Treasury, 2010b, p 68), it is clear that the Coalition is pursuing the residualisation of social security. Divesting wealthier households of a stake in the social security system isolates those who continue to receive support, making the application of punitive policy more politically and socially acceptable. It marks a notable break with New Labour's 'progressive universalism' which sought to encourage solidarity by concentrating resources on low-income families, while maintaining or extending eligibility for limited support through the benefit and tax credit system to higher income families (see Chapter Nine by Kitty Stewart, this volume).

A more punitive approach is also evident in out-of-work benefits, with the Coalition seemingly seeking to strengthen work incentives and/or encourage self-reliance through reductions in benefit levels and a tightening of conditionality. Eligibility for the contributory-based employment and support allowance (ESA) will now be time limited to 12 months for sick and disabled people in the work-related activity group (those judged to be capable of, and engaged in, a journey back into paid work) of ESA. Claimants who reach the time limit may be able to claim the income-based version of ESA, but this applies an income and savings means test, thereby limiting claimant eligibility to the very poorest. Jobseeker's Allowance (JSA) claimants receiving Housing Benefit face a 10 per cent cut in the amount they receive if they are in receipt of JSA for longer than 12 months (HM Treasury, 2010a). Meanwhile, lone parents whose youngest child is aged five or above will, during 2011–12, become ineligible for Income Support and will instead need to claim either JSA or ESA, both of which have more stringent work-related activity requirements (HM Treasury, 2010, p 33; and see Chapter Eight by Tina Haux, this volume). The Coalition is, it seems, determined to strengthen the principle of less eligibility and, as a consequence, lone parents and other out-of-work benefit recipients face being squeezed by limited employment opportunities, tighter benefit conditionality and reductions in the generosity of in-work benefits.

The Red Tory thesis accepts the notion of welfare dependency and its implied role in creating a broken atomistic society (Blond, 2010, p 76). What separates Blond's approach is that his analysis links dependence on benefits to a growing concentration of wealth and asset ownership in Britain, from which the poorest in society are excluded (Blond, 2010, p 206; see also Wind-Cowie, 2009, p 17). A lack of assets means poor individuals have neither a cushion against unforeseen risks nor the opportunity to invest in themselves, their families or communities. For Red Toryism, while moving people into work is necessary, it will not on its own strengthen individual or community independence as low-paid employment is unlikely to alter patterns of wealth distribution. New routes out of poverty are needed that use asset-based welfare to spread ownership and wealth to low-income communities and therefore enhance their autonomy and opportunities. Without this, the reanimation of reciprocity, responsibility and autonomous organisation within the poorest sections of society (see Blond, 2009f; Wind-Cowie, 2009, p 24) will be difficult to achieve.

Interestingly, the New Labour government's Child Trust Fund (CTF) is an example of a tentative step into asset-based welfare. The CTF guaranteed that, for all children born on or after September 2002, the state would pay £250 into a tax-free CTF account upon its opening, with a top-up payment when the child reached seven years of age. The Coalition, in contrast, signalled its lack of enthusiasm for asset-based welfare when it announced in the June 2010 Emergency Budget that state contributions to the CTF would be gradually discontinued. The antipathy of the Coalition to the CTF was forewarned in the run-up to the 2010 General Election. The Liberal Democrats pledged to end state payments into the CTF altogether (Liberal Democrats, 2010, p 16), while the Conservative Party promised to cut state contributions to the CTF for all but the poorest one third of families and disabled children (Conservative Party, 2010c, p 8). The Saving Gateway was due to roll out from July 2010 and New Labour hoped it would encourage personal savings among low-income families by topping up every £1 of personal savings with 50p from the state. It has also been cancelled by The Coalition Government (HM Treasury, 2010a, p 35). The prospects for the Red Tory vision of a more equitable distribution of wealth and assets (Blond, 2010, p 206) appear forlorn. Perhaps this is not surprising, as measures which may reduce inequality have long been regarded by the New Right and One Nation wing of the Conservative Party as misguided, given perceptions of the necessity of inequality for ensuring incentives to hard work and to stimulate investment (Hickson, 2009, p 353). A strengthening of the autonomy of low-income individuals through the provision of assets might also diminish their reliance on the labour market. Such a development would undermine the very flexibility of the low wage sector of the labour market which current welfare reform seeks to enhance.

The reduction in the value of working-age benefits indicates the Coalition is determined to strengthen the principle of less eligibility and make existing outside of the labour market more difficult. Yet to ensure that benefit recipients regarded as lacking the competence or capacity to understand what is good for them or good for society get the message, the state is also increasingly turning to greater coercion (Soss et al, 2009, p 7). The thinking underpinning such developments is encapsulated in the work of US academic Lawrence Mead. During the summer of 2010, Mead visited 10 Downing Street and advised the Coalition to tie benefit entitlements more closely to work requirements. Mead argued this was needed to change public perceptions of social security as a 'lifestyle' option (Helm et al, 2010). Leaving aside the accuracy or not of this observation, such advice flows from Mead's contention that the principle obstacle to employment participation among the workless is the attitude, behaviour and competency of the workless themselves. For Mead, many of the unemployed are unwilling or unable to meet the demands of employers and the stricture of the working environment (Mead, 1997, p 61). The problem of unemployment then, is located in a breakdown in the work discipline of the poor and the gap between their stated desire to work and their capacity to do so (Mead, 1997, p 24). Mead believes a combination of 'help and hassle', grounded in personalised support and monitoring of client behaviour by welfare advisers, together with mandated activation and threat of sanction, is needed to instil and maintain work discipline (Mead, 2007).

In the UK the notion of 'help and hassle' permeates debates around social security, irrespective of whichever party is in power. Under New Labour the requirements that benefit recipients participate in active labour market schemes and work-related activity were gradually intensified and expanded (Dwyer, 2008, p 202) to encompass not only unemployed jobseekers, but also claimants previously categorised as economically inactive. Even in the midst of the recession New Labour, through the Welfare Reform Act 2009, legislated for a pilot 'work for your benefit' scheme targeting benefit recipients who had been unemployed for two or more years (Welfare Reform Act 2009, section 1). The pilot workfare scheme sought to steal a march on Conservative proposals that all JSA claimants unemployed for more than two years during a three-year period should be required to join a community work scheme (Conservative Party, 2008a, p 31; Conservative Party, 2008b, p 12). The need for a stronger conditionality regime to promote work obligations was reiterated in the Coalition's *Programme for government* (Cabinet Office, 2010a, p 23) and the subsequent Green Paper, *21st century welfare* (DWP, 2010a, p 18). The 2010 White Paper *Universal Credit: Welfare that works* (DWP, 2010b) provides some detail of what this entails, announcing a sharper series of penalties in JSA and ESA that escalate each time a client fails to meet job search or work-related requirements. JSA clients who fail to comply with directions by a Jobcentre Plus adviser to apply for a job, refuse a job offer or fail to take part in a mandatory work activity will experience a loss of benefit. For a first 'offence' benefits will be stopped for three months, while a third failure to comply will result in the total loss of JSA for three years (DWP, 2010b, p 31).

Conclusion

The language and ideas drawn on by leading Conservatives to fashion a 'progressive conservatism' owes much to the 'broken society' analysis promoted by The Centre for Social Justice and civic conservative thought, regarding the importance of civil society for mitigating the disruptive effect of free markets (Evans, 2008, p 299; Crisp et al, 2009). The Red Tory thesis is superficially complementary to Cameron's project of modernisation, but Blond's analysis actually provides a damning critique of the prevailing neoliberal orthodoxy, with radical implications for socioeconomic policy (Blond, 2010). The self-defined progressive conservatism of leading Conservative Party politicians, however (Cameron, 2009a, 2010a, p 287; Osborne, 2009), is a useful concept precisely because it does not necessitate a break with neoliberalism. The core tenets of progressive conservatism provide the means and political space for the Conservative-led Coalition to voice concerns about poverty and social justice, while pursuing welfare reforms based on traditional Tory commitments to self-reliance, independence and the market. The Conservative governments of the 1980s and 1990s sought the restoration of capital's pre-eminence, through the development of a neoliberal state. At the core of this was, and continues to be, the promotion of flexibility in labour markets, the free movement of capital and an antipathy to all forms of solidarity as a potential source of countervailing power (Harvey, 2004). There is little evidence of a recent change in the Conservative Party's historic acceptance of inequality (Hickson, 2009) or preference for a more limited social welfare system. Research into the views held by Conservative Members of Parliament (MPs) in the last Parliament, for example, indicated a lack of support for the redistribution of wealth and a tendency to favour welfare as a safety net (Bochel and Defty, 2010, p 80). Similarly, the Conservatives remain committed to policies, such as those on corporate taxation, that reduce the share of taxation paid by big business (Conservative Party, 2010a, p 13). Given the existing constellation of Conservative Party ideological and class interests, it seems unlikely that Red Toryism will marshal support for its vision of how to reshape the UK's political economy from within Conservatism itself. Indeed, the welfare reforms of the Conservative-led Coalition, far from breaking with neoliberalism, are consistent with its intensification. The consequence is an evolving neoliberal paternalist model of welfare, where provision is reshaped to expand the scope of market forces and to ensure benefit recipients acquiesce to its mode of rationality (Soss et al, 2009).

References

Barker, A. and Timmins, N. (2010) 'Coalition takes early axe to Labour job schemes', *Financial Times*, 9 June (www.ft.com).

Barnes, M. and Tomaszewski, W. (2010) 'Lone parents and benefits: an obligation to look for work', in A. Park, J. Curtice, K. Thomson, M. Phillips, E. Clery, and S. Butt (eds) *British Social Attitudes: The 26th report*, London: Sage Publications, pp 194-216.

Blond, P. (2008) 'Red Tory', in J. Cruddas, and J. Rutherford (eds) *Is the future Conservative?*, London: Lawrence & Wishart, pp 79-90 (www.lwbooks.co.uk/conservative.pdf).

Blond, P. (2009a) 'Rise of the Red Tories', *Prospect*, February, pp 32-6.

Blond, P. (2009b) *The civic state: Remoralise the market, relocalise the economy, recapitalise the poor* (www.demos.co.uk/files/File/Phillip_Blond_-_The_Civic_State.pdf).

Blond (2009c) 'The future of conservatism', Speech to the launch of ResPublica, 26 November (www.respublica.org.uk/articles/future-conservatism-0).

Blond, P. (2009d) *From spend to investment: Essential welfare reforms for the 21st century*, 2 November (www.respublica.org.uk/articles/spend-investment).

Blond, P. (2009e) 'David Cameron's "philosopher king" explains how his party will help those betrayed by Labour', *The Daily Mail*, 13 October (www.dailymail.co.uk).

Blond, P. (2009f) 'The new conservatism can create a capitalism that works for the poor', *The Guardian*, 2 July (www.guardian.co.uk).

Blond, P. (2010) *Red Tory: How the right and left have broken Britain and how we can fix it*, London: Faber & Faber Ltd.

Bochel, H. and Defty, A. (2010) 'Safe as houses? Conservative social policy, public opinion and parliament', *The Political Quarterly*, vol 81, no 1, pp 74-84.

Browne, J. and Lovell, P. (2010) *The distributional effect of tax and benefit reforms to be introduced between June 2010 and April 2014: A revised assessment*, Briefing Note BN108, London: Institute for Fiscal Studies (www.ifs.org.uk/bns/bn108.pdf).

Cabinet Office (2010a) *The Coalition: Our programme for government* (www.cabinetoffice.gov.uk/sites/default/files/resources/coalition_programme_for_government.pdf).

Cabinet Office (2010b) *State of the nation report: Poverty, worklessness and welfare dependency in the UK*, London: HM Government (http://umbr4.cabinetoffice.gov.uk/media/410872/web-poverty-report.pdf).

Cameron, D. (2009a) 'Making progressive conservatism a reality', Speech to the launch of the Progressive Conservatism project, Demos, 22 January (www.demos.co.uk/files/File/David_Cameron_Making_progressive_conservatism_a_reality.pdf).

Cameron, D. (2009b) 'The Big Society', Speech given for the Hugo Young memorial lecture, 10 November (www.conservatives.com/News/Speeches/2009/11/David_Cameron_The_Big_Society.aspx).

Cameron, D. (2009c) 'We need popular capitalism', Speech given to the World Economic Forum in Davos, 30 January (www.conservatives. com/News/Speeches/2009/01/David_Cameron_We_need_popular_ capitalism.aspx).

Cameron, D. (2010a) 'Social responsibility is the essence of liberal conservatism. This is the Britain we want to build', in D. Jones, *Cameron on Cameron: Conversations with Dylan Jones* (4th edn), London: Fourth Estate, pp 275-98.

Cameron, D. (2010b) 'Big Society Speech' by the Prime Minister, 19 July (www.number10.gov.uk/news/speeches-and-transcripts/2010/07/ big-society-speech-5357272).

Conservative Party (2008a) *Work for Welfare: Real welfare reform to help make British poverty history*, Policy Green Paper No. 3, www.conservatives. com/Policy/Responsibility_Agenda.aspx

Conservative Party (2008b) *Making British poverty history: Report for the Conservative Party*, April (www.conservatives.com).

Conservative Party (2010a) *A new economic model: Eight benchmarks for Britain* (www.conservatives.com).

Conservative Party (2010b) *Power to public sector workers* (www. conservatives.com).

Conservative Party (2010c) *Invitation to join the government of Britain*, Conservative Party Manifesto (www.conservatives.com).

Coombs, N. (2010) 'The political theology of Red Toryism', Paper presented to the Political Science Association Annual Conference, Edinburgh, 31 March–1 April (www.psa.ac.uk/journals/ pdf/5/2010/1296_1499.pdf).

Crisp, R., Macmillan, R., Robinson, D. and Wells, P. (2009) 'Continuity or change: what a future Conservative government might mean for regional, housing and welfare policies', *People, Place & Policy Online*, vol 3, no 1, pp 58-74.

Davies, S. (2007) 'Contracting out employment services to the third and private sectors: a critique', *Critical Social Policy*, vol 38, no 2, pp 136-64.

Doble, A. (2010) *Who know who: The Coalition cabinet*, Channel 4 News, 13 May (www.channel4.com).

Duncan Smith, I. (2010) 'Welfare for the 21st century', Speech by the Secretary of State for Work and Pensions, 27 May (www.dwp.gov.uk).

DWP (Department for Work and Pensions) (no date) *Phase one Flexible New Deal suppliers* (www.dwp.gov.uk/docs/fnd-phase-1-suppliers.pdf).

DWP (2008) *No one written off: Reforming welfare to reward responsibility*, Cm 7363 (www.dwp.gov.uk/welfarereform/noonewrittenoff/ noonewrittenoff-complete.pdf).

DWP (2010a) *21st century welfare*, Cm 7913, London: The Stationery Office (www.official-documents.gov.uk/document/cm79/7913/7913. pdf).

DWP (2010b) *Universal Credit: Welfare that works*, Cm 7957, London: The Stationery Office (www.dwp.gov.uk/docs/universal-credit-full-document.pdf).

DWP (2010c) *The Work Programme prospectus – November 2010* (www.dwp.gov.uk/docs/work-prog-prospectus-v2.pdf).

Dwyer, P. (2008) 'The conditional welfare state', in M. Powell (ed) *Modernising the welfare state: The Blair legacy*, Bristol: The Policy Press, pp 199-218.

Evans, S. (2008) 'Consigning its past to history? David Cameron and the Conservative Party', *Parliamentary Affairs*, vol 61, no 2, pp 291-314.

Evans, S. (2010) '"Mother's boy": David Cameron and Margaret Thatcher', *British Journal of Politics and International Relations*, vol 12, issue 3, pp 325-43.

Fitzpatrick, T. (2005) 'The fourth attempt to construct a politics of welfare obligations', *Policy & Politics*, vol 33, no 1, pp 15-32.

Freud, D. (2007) *Reducing dependency, increasing opportunity: Options for the future of welfare to work*, Department for Work and Pensions, London: Corporate Document Services (www.dwp.gov.uk/publications/dwp/2007/welfarereview.pdf).

Freud, D. (2010) 'Address to welfare providers', Speech by Minister for Welfare Reform, 2 June, Church House (www.dwp.gov.uk).

Gough, I. (1983) 'Thatcherism and the welfare state', in S. Hall and M. Jacques (eds) *The politics of Thatcherism*, London: Lawrence & Wishart, pp 148-68.

Griffiths, S. (2009) 'Cameron's Conservatives and the public services', in S. Lee and M. Beech (eds) *The Conservatives under David Cameron: Built to last?*, Basingstoke: Palgrave Macmillan, pp 97-108.

Grover, C. (2009) 'Privatising employment services in Britain,', *Critical Social Policy*, vol 29, no 3, pp 487-509.

Harvey, D. (2004) *Neo-liberalism and the restoration of class power* (www.princeton.edu/~sf/workshops/neoliberalism/classrestore.pdf).

Helm, T., Asthana, A. and Harris, P. (2010) 'How Britain's new welfare state was born in the USA', *The Observer*, 7 November.

Hickson, K. (2009) 'Conservatism and the poor: Conservative Party attitudes to poverty and inequality since the 1970s', *British Politics*, vol 4, no 3, pp 341-62.

HM Treasury (2010a) *Budget 2010*, HC61, London: The Stationery Office Ltd (www.hm-treasury.gov.uk/junebudget_easyread.htm).

HM Treasury (2010b) *Spending Review 2010*, Cm 7942, London: The Stationery Office Ltd (www.hm-treasury.gov.uk/spend_sr2010_easyread.htm).

Letwin, O. (2003) *The neighbourly society: Collected speeches 2001-2003*, London: Centre for Policy Studies (www.cps.org.uk/cps_catalog/CPS_assets/101_ProductPreviewFile.pdf).

Letwin, O. (2008) 'Oliver Letwin MP interviewed by Alan Finlayson. From economic revolution to social revolution', in J. Cruddas and J. Rutherford (eds) *Is the future Conservative?*, London: Lawrence & Wishart, pp 71-8 (www.lwbooks.co.uk/ebooks/conservative.pdf).

Liberal Democrats (2010) *Liberal Democrat Manifesto 2010* (www.libdems.org.uk/our_manifesto.aspx).

Lister, R. and Bennett, F. (2010) 'The new "champion of progressive ideals"? Cameron's Conservative Party: poverty, family policy and welfare reform', *Renewal*, vol 18, no 1/2 (www.lwbooks.co.uk/journals/renewal/articles/Spring10ListerBennett.pdf).

Mead, L. (1997) 'Welfare employment', in L. Mead (ed) *The new paternalism: Supervisory approaches to welfare*, Washington, DC: Brooking Institution Press, pp 39-89.

Mead, L. (2007) 'Towards a mandatory work policy for men', *The Future of Children*, vol 17, no 2, pp 43-72.

Milland, G. and Warren, G. (2010) 'Austerity Cabinet has 18 millionaires', *The Sunday Times*, 23 May (www.timesonline.co.uk/tol/news/politics/article7133943.ece).

Osborne, G. (2009) 'Progressive reform in an age of austerity', Speech to Demos, Tuesday, 11 August (www.conservatives.com).

Osborne, G. (2010) Budget statement by the Chancellor of the Exchequer, 22 June (www.hm-treasury-gov.uk/junebudget_speech.htm)

Page, R. (2010) 'David Cameron's Modern Conservative approach to poverty and social justice: towards one nation or two?', *Journal of Poverty and Social Justice*, vol 8, no 2, pp 147–60.

Quinn, T. (2008) 'The Conservative Party and the "centre ground" of British politics', *Journal of Elections, Public Opinions and Parties*, vol 18, no 2, pp 179-99.

Social Justice Policy Group (2007) *Breakthrough Britain: Ending the costs of social breakdown, Vol 2: Economic dependency and worklessness* (www.centreforsocialjustice.org.uk/client/downloads/economic.pdf).

Social Justice Policy Group (2009) *Dynamic benefits: Towards welfare that works*, A policy report by the Economic Dependency Working Group (www.centreforsocialjustice.org.uk).

Soss, J., Fording, R.C. and Schram, S.F. (2009) 'Governing the poor: the rise of the neoliberal paternalist state', Paper presented to the Annual Meeting of the American Political Science Association, Toronto, Canada (www.uky.edu/~rford/SossFordingSchram_APSA2009.pdf).

Stratton, A. and Sparrow, A. (2010) 'Tories renew pledge to allow public sector workers to form co-operatives', *The Guardian*, 15 February.

Timmins, N. (2010) 'Huge cuts put back to work drive in peril', *The Financial Times*, 16 September.

Welfare Reform Act 2009, c 24, London: The Stationery Office (www. legislation.gov.uk/ukpga/2009/24/pdfs/ukpga_20090024_en.pdf).

Willetts, D. (1992) *Modern conservatism*, London: Penguin.

Willetts, D. (2005a) 'Compassionate conservatism and the War on Poverty', Speech to the Centre for Social Justice, 6 January (www. davidwilletts.co.uk/2005/01/06/compassionate-conservative/).

Willetts, D. (2005b) 'A new conservatism for a new century', Speech to the Social Market Foundation, 2 June (www.davidwilletts. co.uk/2005/06/02/new-conservatism/).

Willetts, D. (2008) *Renewing civic conservatism*, The Oakeshott Lecture, London: London School of Economics, 20 February.

Wind-Cowie, M. (2009) *Recapitalising the poor: Why property is not theft*, London: Demos (www.demos.co.uk/publications/recapitalising-the-poor).

Work and Pensions Committee (2010) *Management and administration of contracted employment programmes*, Fourth Report of Session 2009-10, HC101, House of Commons, London: The Stationery Office.

THREE

The Conservative Party and the 'Big Society'

Nick Ellison

Introduction

Despite continuing scepticism 'on the doorstep', enthusiasm for the 'Big Society', at least among key elements of the Conservative Party, appears to be increasing. This chapter first looks at the changing context of Tory politics and specifically the origins and nature of the Big Society as set out by contemporary Conservative thinkers – and think tanks. Thereafter the discussion considers how well ideas about the Big Society articulate with the principles that underpin the Coalition government's social policies. In view of the current financial crisis (skilfully transformed by the Conservative–Liberal Democratic Coalition government into a crisis of the public sector), a particular point of concern is how far Big Society thinking might be contributing to new forms of discipline and social control as particular interpretations of individual behaviour and 'responsibility' risk 'redlining' the more deprived sections of the community. A brief concluding section raises some wider issues about the feasibility of the Big Society as a 'project', and poses the rhetorical question as to whether its main legacy could be little more than a renewed authoritarianism.

Changing Conservative politics

Before exploring Conservative thinking about the Big Society itself, it is important to understand how the idea gained influence in the Tory Party. How, in other words, did a conception of society that, on the face of it, promises to decentralise state power, empower local communities and individuals, increase social justice and reduce poverty (see Cameron, 2009, pp 3-4), find purchase in a party that, both before and after New

Labour's election victory in 1997, appeared unable to shake off an embedded image of callous disregard for the victims of free market liberalism and marked intolerance over social and moral issues? One answer to this question could be that the corrosive combination of neoliberalism and moral authoritarianism (Gamble, 1994) that defined the 'Thatcherite' Conservative Party in the 1980s and 1990s has *not* been shaken off and the Party continues to pursue the economic and social goals espoused by Margaret Thatcher and her acolytes. On the other hand, it is reasonable to argue that *something* has changed in the Conservative Party, most obviously since David Cameron became leader in 2005. For Bale (2010, p 381), Cameron's swift decision to move to the centre ground of politics was the crucial factor that distinguished him from his ill-fated immediate successors. His election 'was immediately followed by a series of counter-intuitive initiatives and announcements, by the dumping of particularly toxic policies ... by unapologetic raids on Labour and Lib Dem territory, and by action to make the Party look at least a little more like the country whose votes it was seeking'. As Bale (2010, p 381) goes on to state, 'ideology was out and pragmatism in. Thatcherism wasn't so much apologized for as turned into history' (see also Chapter One by Hugh Bochel, this volume).

This modernisation strategy did not proceed unopposed. In fact, disquiet has consistently been expressed by Thatcher loyalists like John Redwood, Graham Brady, Edward Leigh and others over a range of touchstone policy issues such as tax cuts, grammar schools and immigration. Moreover, it is not entirely clear whether the wider Tory Party membership is happy with the strategic direction that has been adopted, and it is not hard to detect a persistent undercurrent of criticism about Team Cameron's modernising agenda emanating from the Conservative Right and those media outlets that support it (see Heffer, 2010). Such criticism is perhaps not surprising in view of the fact that a majority of Tory Members of Parliament (MPs) voted for either David Davis or Liam Fox in the 2005 leadership contest – both individuals being to the right of Cameron himself (Evans, 2008, p 301). Nevertheless, the potential for disruption is such that Cameron and his inner circle cannot entirely rely on the loyalty of Tory MPs – something that was made clear by Barry Legg, a member of the right-wing Bruges Group, immediately after arrangements for coalition with the Liberal Democrats were revealed in May 2010 (Legg, 2010).

The threat of disloyalty within Conservative ranks lends credibility to the view that the shift of focus achieved by Cameron, although real, has been overstated. Evans (2008, pp 305-7), for example, points out that Cameron quickly gave ground on the survival of grammar schools when the issue threatened to divide the Party in 2008, and he also notes that Cameron has maintained a strong anti-European stance since he became leader. William Hague, a noted Eurosceptic, was made Shadow Foreign Secretary in 2006 and has since taken over as Foreign Secretary in the Coalition government. Moreover, although he delayed the move by three years, Cameron nonetheless withdrew Tory Members of the European Parliament (MEPs) from the European People's Party-European Democrats (EPP-ED) group of centre right parties, placing them instead in the nascent (and considerably more right wing) European Conservatives and Reformists (ECR) grouping, a decision that surely has to be regarded as a significant genuflection to the Eurosceptic right. On welfare issues, too, Cameron, Iain Duncan Smith and others who are closely involved with the Party's efforts to develop new ideas about the welfare state have continued to warn against the dangers of 'welfare dependency' in ways reminiscent of Thatcher's US-inspired 'New Right' critique of the post-war welfare state (see below and Prideaux, 2010).

Whatever the precise balance between modernisers and traditionalists, however, the more user-friendly version of conservatism endorsed by Cameron has gained sufficient support in the Party to enable the leadership to pursue its developing vision of the Big Society. Indeed, for 'critical supporters' like Tim Montgomerie, founder of the website ConservativeHome, Cameron has succeeded in drafting 'the most interesting definition of conservatism since the Thatcher-Reagan era', essentially by reconciling elements of economic liberalism with an older more 'social' strand of Tory 'One Nationism' (Montgomerie, 2010, p 30). On evidence of this kind, then, it is important not to assume too readily that the current Tory leadership is essentially comprised of unreconstructed neoliberals, and worth pausing to consider their conception of, and proposals for, the Big Society, alongside the place of social policy within it.

Thinking the Big Society

In terms of immediate pre-history, the Big Society is a recent addition to the Tories' contemporary ideological portfolio. The phrase itself did not make any sustained appearance before David Cameron delivered his Hugo Young Lecture in November 2009. Prior to that event, what were to become key Big Society themes gathered momentum in the form of, inter alia, the 'broken society', the 'responsible society' and the need to effect a shift from the 'welfare state' to the 'welfare society' – all of these terms being framed by the leadership in terms of the positive contribution that 'liberal' or 'progressive' conservatism could make to ameliorating Britain's social ills.

This sense of *society*, broken or not, is significant. However, to understand the specific etymology of the Big Society, it is important to explore how different components of thinking have contributed to what is still a work in progress. Three broad perspectives can be delineated within the Conservative Party: Burkean, pragmatic and compassionate conservatism. There is plenty of common ground among these perspectives, but, for analytical purposes, it is useful to separate them, not least because the lines of division may in time come to constitute the potential fault lines of future disagreements as policy details progressively flesh out what remains a fairly unfocused and heterogeneous 'vision'.

Burkean conservatism

The Burkean perspective is best exemplified in the thinking of David Willetts, currently Minister of State for Universities and Science in the Coalition government. Why Burkean? Willetts' approach, initially set out in his book, *Modern conservatism* (Willetts, 1994), makes it clear that, while he is a convinced free marketeer and an admirer of key New Right thinkers like Friedman and Hayek, he nevertheless sees a need to balance neoliberal ambitions with a civic, 'associative' framework of the kind originally championed by Edmund Burke (see Chapter Two by Jay Wiggan, this volume). Radical though Burke's thinking could be – his support for American independence is well known – he was no friend of Enlightenment thinking and is best remembered for lauding the 'little platoons' of intermediate groups and institutions that he believed sustained the myriad relationships and forms of reciprocity that defined civil society. The point for Conservatives, as Willetts (2005, p 10) has argued, is to 'be followers of Burke not Rousseau' in the sense that attention should be paid to 'roots, understanding and identity' in the context of a flexible, market economy and 'a more cohesive society' (Willetts, 2005, p 9) based on 'partnership' rather than on abstract values grounded, for instance, in a nebulous 'General Will'. For Willetts, as for Burke, and indeed Michael Oakeshott, it is the 'small' allegiances, local networks and the ties induced by custom and kinship that make a society – and, importantly, allow these practices to be passed from generation to generation.

If Willetts has put a 21st-century twist on this Burkean framework, it is his contention, derived from game theory, that there is a need in modern, secular society to find ways of building reciprocity and altruism by supporting institutions 'where people interact with each other sufficiently frequently for co-operation to emerge as a rational strategy' (Willetts, 2008, p 9). The state has a role to play here, but one that moves with the grain of changing societal culture, creating 'the environment in which the social norms and institutions which enable reciprocity can flourish' (Willetts, 2008, p 17). In social policy terms, this perspective makes the case for limited direct interference from the state, arguing that it should not act as a monopoly supplier of services nor seek to impose particular policy 'solutions' before public opinion is ready to accept them. Indeed, for Willetts, 'the real and interesting battleground of politics today is non-state collective action – everything that stands between the individual and the state' (Willetts, 2005, p 6). It is in this space that the Burkean strand of conservatism sees Big Society initiatives developing. However, Willetts sounds a note of caution about their likely costs when he acknowledges that market societies are fractured and fragmented, and that 'social liberalism doesn't come cheap'.

Pragmatic conservatism

The main feature of this Burkean approach to the Big Society is that it locates the idea firmly within a Conservative historical tradition that is not 'anti-state' *per se*. As such, Burkean conservatism is perfectly consistent (although perhaps less engaged in terms of specific policy recommendations) with the more pragmatic, behavioural and policy-focused approaches to the Big Society that are associated with individuals like Greg Clark and Oliver Letwin, respectively Minister for Decentralisation and Minister of State at the Cabinet Office in the Coalition government. If there is any underlying 'rationale' associated with this perspective, it is that 'nudge' theory (see Thaler and Sunstein, 2008) has influenced certain senior ministers and Party officials who are interested in steering the *behaviours* of citizens in ways that lead to favoured outcomes while at the same time preserving 'free choice' (see Chapter Four by Ruth Lister, this volume). Letwin (2008), for example, has stated that 'we've been interested in "nudge economics" because it opens up new possibilities … [in] giving a gentle push to society to move in a direction of greater responsibility, or greater coherence, or more stability, or neighbourliness, or better health'. As *The Guardian* reported (Chakrabortty, 2008), enthusiasm for nudge economics goes beyond Letwin. In June 2008, senior Conservatives, including Steve Hilton, Head of Strategy, James O'Shaughnessy, Director of Research, and Letwin himself, met Richard Thaler to discuss how a Conservative government could work with him to develop policies designed to nudge behaviour in desired directions. They identified public health issues such as binge drinking and obesity as potentially open to nudge tactics, although ambitions for the application of behavioural economics to public policy go well beyond these particular areas.

Since coming to power, the Coalition government has established a 'nudge unit' – formally titled the 'Behavioural Insight Team' – in the Cabinet Office under the leadership of David Halpern, a behavioural economist and one-time member of former Prime Minister Tony Blair's Strategy Unit. Halpern (2010, p 4) is critical of both the neoliberal right and the 'rational "Weberian" welfare state', advocating instead the possibilities offered by developing policies informed by the 'hidden wealth' of the 'world of friendship, care and gift-based exchanges' that formal economics ignores. He believes that 'normal' informal relationships, based on trust, can be stretched 'to reach a little further than [they] might otherwise do', with the intention of building up the 'reservoirs of our collective hidden wealth'. The state's role in this process would be subtle, although tangible nonetheless, using alternative forms of democratic decision making and working with citizens to 'co-produce' public services in order to develop new forms of 'affiliative welfare'.

Compassionate conservatism

This pragmatic perspective differs in tone from the third – and for present purposes most important – strand of Big Society thinking, compassionate conservatism. Embodied in the views of Iain Duncan Smith, Tim Montgomerie and, rather differently, Phillip Blond, this approach brings a distinctly Christian flavour to the analysis of the state of the UK, the nature of the Big Society and the role of welfare (see Chapter Two by Jay Wiggan, this volume). Since the early 1990s committed Christians, although far from numerous in the Conservative Party, have become increasingly influential in Tory policy-making circles. An early example of this rising influence was the founding of the Conservative Christian Fellowship (CCF) at the University of Exeter by Tim Montgomerie in 1990. Montgomerie has said that the aim was to reinstate a moral case for conservatism, the hope being that 'an organised Christian group could reignite the party's compassion' (quoted in Cook, 2010, p 1). The message, however, was a socially liberal one. CCF and its affiliated non-denominational organisation, Renewing One Nation, did not dwell on matters of personal morality such as homosexuality or abortion, but instead advanced ideas and policies that took seriously the need to tackle poverty and increase social justice in ways that appealed to a traditional Christian world view. These objectives were reflected in Duncan Smith's Catholic-inspired desire to do the same.

Following his brief period as Party leader, Duncan Smith, with Montgomerie and others, established The Centre for Social Justice in 2003. Since its launch, there is no doubting the influence that this think tank has had on Party policy making (see Chapter Two by Jay Wiggan and Chapter Eight by Tina Haux, this volume). Although The Centre for Social Justice's claim that it has formulated over 70 Conservative policies may be an exaggeration, two reports commissioned by David Cameron, *Breakdown Britain* (Social Justice Policy Group, 2006a) and *Breakthrough Britain* (Social Justice Policy Group, 2007a), have had a profound impact on the leadership's ideas about social policy and directly contributed to policy proposals set out in the Conservatives' 2010 election manifesto. The ideas underpinning the proposals are echoed elsewhere in the Tory think tank universe. Writing for Policy Exchange, Norman and Ganesh, for example, believe that compassionate conservatism speaks to a need for trust and security in British life, and in particular for a 'huge devolution of power away from Whitehall, towards independent institutions, towards the private and voluntary sectors, and towards local government' (Norman and Ganesh, 2006, p 3; see also Norman, 2010). More explicitly than The Centre for Social Justice, Norman and Ganesh acknowledge that the Thatcher years saw a marked centralisation of the state (Norman and Ganesh, 2006, p 8) that needs to be reversed, although they concentrate the force of their criticism on what they regard as the excessive centralisation of key areas of welfare in the New Labour era.

Phillip Blond, director of the think tank ResPublica, has explored in greater detail this critique of the current state of society in general and the role of the state in particular. Blond is important because he is as scathing about neoliberalism as he is about New Labour and what he labels 'the errors of the left' (Blond, 2010). Combining a demand for the remoralisation of the market with a call for the break-up of central state power, he argues that the neoliberal marketplace has become a site of monopolistic practices and corporate privilege that work to the disadvantage of the poorest sections of society, while the welfare state, in its efforts to protect people from damaging exposure to market discipline, has induced dependency and squeezed out mutualism and community self-help. In place of neoliberalism and welfare statism there needs to be a 'new civil state [which] would restore what the welfare state had destroyed' (Blond, 2009, p 2). With the welfare state much reduced and the marketplace free of corporate monopolies, conditions would be ripe for the emergence of an associative democratic arena in which citizens could 'take over the state in their own areas to either be commissioners of their own services or run them for themselves or each other' (Blond, 2009, p 2). Blond's vision, then, has a potentially radical edge: employee ownership schemes, cooperative ownership, user involvement and citizen participation contributing to a decidedly egalitarian vision of the civil state (Blond, 2010). Conversely, however, his hopes for the types of individual behaviour that would be fostered in such an environment are considerably more traditional and closely mirror the socially conservative diagnoses and solutions advocated by The Centre for Social Justice (see Chapter Two by Jay Wiggan, this volume).

These three strands of Big Society thinking, taken together, form a powerful right-of-centre analysis of the UK's social and economic ills, and provide at least an outline of the Big Society alternative. There is clearly substantial overlap of both personnel and ideas among these perspectives, although each highlights different elements of the case for decentralisation and the rejuvenation of civil society. So, for example, the Burkean approach is decidedly secular and, at least for Willetts, consequently favours methods of encouraging individuals to cooperate by appealing to their self-interest, bounded rationality and capacities for satisficing. Little is said about the moral case for change, and there is also no substantive critique of the workings of the market, which are broadly accepted as an integral element of a free society. Pragmatists would concur with much of this view but concentrate on the 'how' of the Big Society, particularly how state power can be used to shape individual and collective behaviours in the interests of desired social outcomes. Compassionate conservatism, finally, leads with the moral case for social change. The Centre for Social Justice focuses on poverty reduction, social justice and 'responsibilisation', while Blond complements these preoccupations, first, with a more forthright critique of the deleterious effects of markets and, second, with a more idealised vision of the Big Society as a mutualised 'good society'.

Selling the Big Society

Cameron and other Conservative leaders brought elements of these perspectives together in a variety of speeches and publications that have come to reflect the general case for the Big Society. Cameron's Hugo

Young Lecture in November 2009 perhaps stands as the best example of this highly conscious attempt both to change how the Tory Party was perceived in the country and to re-make the case for a particular interpretation of 'One Nation' conservatism. The lecture heavily criticised New Labour's attempt at 'big government' and contrasted this with the new Tory vision of a One Nation Big Society based on decentralisation, neighbourhood and individual empowerment, and largely organised by voluntary organisations, social enterprise and individuals themselves. Blond's critique of the post-war welfare state was used specifically to support the case against big government (interestingly, his critique of the free market was not referred to), while the social conservatism of both Blond and The Centre for Social Justice was much in evidence. Indeed Cameron's rhetoric reflects the key themes of compassionate conservatism:

> When you are paid more not to work than to work, when you are better off leaving your children than nurturing them, when our welfare system tells young girls that having children before finding security of work and a loving relationship means home and cash now ... when social care penalises those who have worked hard by forcing them to sell their home ... when your attempts at playing a role in society are met with inspection, investigation and interrogation, is it any wonder that our society is broken? (Cameron, 2009, p 6)

This broad message – the call for a richer, decentralised civil society, but one rooted in socially Conservative values – was reiterated by Cameron in a number of speeches delivered during the 2010 general election campaign (Cameron, 2010a, 2010b, 2010c, 2010d). In addition, even as he criticised 'big government', Cameron appeared to endorse a role for the state as a vehicle for 'actively helping to create the Big Society, directly agitating for, catalysing and galvanising social renewal' (Cameron, 2009, p 1). Over time, however, and particularly over the course of the election campaign itself, a Burkean 'small state' message emerged that concentrated on how the removal of central controls would lead to the greater empowerment of communities and an increase in voluntary action. Breaking up 'state monopolies' and moving from a 'bureaucratic world ... to a post-bureaucratic world' (Cameron, 2010b, p 2) would allow charities, social enterprises and companies to provide public services in ways that would be more alive to people's needs and so more accountable. Accountability, however, would need to be allied with a greater *responsibility* on the part of citizens to act in particular ways – and here 'nudge politics' is relevant. In a speech delivered in March 2010, Cameron (2010c, p 5) referred to a series of activities, including 'setting up new schools ... taking over the running of parks, libraries and post offices ... holding beat meetings so they could ask police officers what they were doing' as examples of the sorts of socially useful behaviours that would need to be encouraged in the Big Society.

Of course, ideas set out in the run-up to a general election campaign are inevitably simplified for mass consumption and should not be taken as entirely accurate accounts of future policies. Since taking office, however, the Coalition government has moved with some speed to provide governmental impetus to Big Society initiatives of the kind advertised during the election campaign. As Alcock (2010, p 2) has noted, a Minister for Civil Society has been appointed under Francis Maude at the Cabinet Office, while the management consultant Nat Wei, whose social enterprise activities came to the attention of Cameron after he became Party leader, has been ennobled and taken on as a government adviser on Big Society issues. Greg Clark, as Minister for Decentralisation, has been given the task of dismantling what he has referred to as Labour's 'command state' (Clark and Mather, 2003) in favour of the devolution of power to local government and beyond (see Conservative Party, 2008). As an initial step, *Building the Big Society*, a Cabinet Office paper published in August 2010 (Cabinet Office, 2010, pp 1-2), sketched out a set of already agreed policies designed to reduce central government interference and control in certain areas, and to promote local and voluntary activities. According to this paper, not only is local government to be granted more autonomy but communities and neighbourhoods are also to be given more influence in local planning decisions. In addition, new cohorts of community organisers are to be trained to support the creation of neighbourhood groups, and the development of 'mutuals, co-operatives, charities and social enterprises' is also to be encouraged to allow them 'to have much greater involvement in the running of public services' (Cabinet Office, 2010, p 2).

In some ways these putative policy options are beguiling. Setting ideological differences to one side, it is important to remember, pace Burke, that there is a long history of mutualism and cooperative enterprise on the British left, which looks precisely to civil society as an arena that needs to be preserved from encroachments by the state. Early 19th-century British radicalism and later Victorian working-class movements associated with craft unionism, the friendly societies and guild socialism were all sceptical of central state power, and conceived their respective conceptions of socialism accordingly. As noted, however, the twist (one might say 'wrench') given by contemporary Tory thinkers to this civic associationist tradition is the distinctly conservative (in both its 'big C' and 'small c' variants) conceptualisation of social responsibility. This theme is nowhere more prominent than in the social policy recommendations developed by The Centre for Social Justice and its allies – and here it is possible to discern a distinct tension in the overall vision. Put concisely, while it may be that certain sections of society could potentially benefit from greater control of their immediate destinies, should Coalition policies prove 'realistic' (see below and Alcock, 2010, pp 4-5), it is not clear that the most disadvantaged groups in society are likely to benefit to the same degree. Indeed, the opposite could be the case: a reduced state, 'nudge' politics, greater local autonomy and a more active civil society for the majority may need to be bought at the price of greater state interference, 'shove politics' and the increasing enforcement of specific policies for the worst off groups.

This characterisation of a bifurcated 'Big Society', where certain groups will prosper and others fall under the auspices of an 'enforcer state', is likely to be played out differently in the different policies of government ministries. So, for example, how Greg Clark understands Big Society initiatives from the standpoint of his responsibilities for decentralisation at Communities and Local Government, how nudge politics is interpreted by the Cabinet Office in the different areas where individual behaviours are considered to be in need of 'reshaping', or how Lord Wei conceives the Big Society, as it were, 'in the round', and decides which aspects to highlight in terms of political spin, is likely to differ in both idiom and *intent* from how Duncan Smith and his advisers understand welfare issues at the Department for Work and Pensions. This is not to deny that considerable agreement about the general nature of the Big Society exists among Tory 'believers', but differences of tone, emphasis and *task* are important.

Conservative social policy: a Big Society?

Other chapters in this volume deal with welfare issues in more detail. Here, however, it is important to note the degree to which C(c)onservative understandings of the 'broken society' and the role to be played by individual and family responsibility in 'fixing' it have become embedded in the Coalition government's approach to social policy. The Centre for Social Justice, as the most social policy-focused of the Tory think tanks, has played an important role in this process. Put concisely, the architecture of The Centre for Social Justice's first major publication, *Breakdown Britain*, is founded on the contention that there are five 'pathways to poverty' – family breakdown, educational failure, economic dependency, indebtedness and addictions (Social Justice Policy Group, 2006a, p 15). These pathways are essentially 'behavioural' and are interrelated. Moreover, each is held to contribute directly to worklessness and poverty in what is conceived as a uni-directional line of causality (see Lister and Bennett, 2010). On the face of it, remedies take the form of a range of measures designed to alter behaviours in ways that are in keeping with Big Society notions of community empowerment – with a discernible emphasis on various forms of third sector service delivery (see Social Justice Policy Group, 2006b, p 20). However, the acknowledgement of the importance of the third sector is consistently accompanied by calls for greater personal and family responsibility – and here there is little doubt that the balance between the anticipated contribution of 'Big Society welfare' and the moral expectations placed on individuals themselves is weighted towards the latter. In *Breakthrough Britain*, for example, individual responsibility is regarded as the cornerstone of a social policy that is lodged firmly in traditional institutions like marriage and the family – indeed it is stated that 'restoring stability in family life [lies] at the heart of our approach' (Social Justice Policy Group, 2007a, p 12). The point is made starkly in the first volume of *Breakthrough Britain* dedicated to family breakdown where, in the context of a discussion that highlights the decline in marriage rates, the rise in divorce rates and the increase in numbers of single-parent families, it is first made clear that 'our headline policy aim is to build stronger families' (Social Justice Policy Group, 2007b, p 30), and then argued that the preferred path to this end is through rigorous work incentives and the discipline of the marketplace. Any state support that is required 'should be done in a way that ultimately encourages family networks to be self-supporting ...'

Ideas and recommendations of this kind would be less noteworthy had they not been enthusiastically embraced by the Coalition government. While the 'message' about responsibility and incentives has been reinforced by key Conservative thinkers outside the UK (see Helm et al, 2010, pp 32-3), Duncan Smith's appointment as Secretary of State for Work and Pensions provides a clear line of continuity between Centre for Social Justice-inspired policy recommendations and what have now become Coalition government proposals. A significant example of this connection is the White Paper (DWP, 2010) that Duncan Smith introduced in the House of Commons in November 2010. It is clear from this that the desire to break the 'habit' of worklessness, endorsed so explicitly by The Centre for Social Justice, has been embraced by the Coalition in the form of increased conditionality. Building on New Labour's not inconsiderable efforts to impose conditions on benefit receipt for jobseekers (Dwyer, 2000; Dwyer and Ellison, 2009), proposed changes to the benefits system will see a marked tightening of eligibility rules, particularly for groups such as single parents and people with disabilities (see Chapter Eight by Tina Haux, this volume).

Going further, the work incentive and conditionality dimensions of the White Paper chime conveniently with the government's stated desire rapidly to reduce the UK's current budget deficit – with a proposed £17.5 billion of welfare cuts announced by the Coalition government between June and October 2010. The combination is, as it were, 'instructive', with 'work incentive-driven' conditionality and reductions to existing benefits effectively acting as disciplinary measures for the enforcement of the particular understandings of responsibility and individual behaviour recommended by The Centre for Social Justice.

Against this backdrop, it seems that the putative rewards (should they be realised) of greater empowerment and control by individuals over their own lives and by communities over their collective fortunes promised in Big Society rhetoric are not equally on offer to all citizens. Rather, as argued above, admission to the Big Society has to be earned through good behaviour. One difficulty, of course, is whether the resources required to underpin preferred behaviours – the availability of employment for example – will actually be forthcoming in an era of austerity, but there is more to the problem than this. As Alan Deacon has stated recently (Helm et al, 2010, p 33), there is a contradiction at the heart of the Coalition government's welfare policies between 'the authoritarianism of work enforcement through the work programme and the [Big Society] emphasis upon personal freedom and getting government off our backs'. This insight can be extended a little. The Big Society, as conceptualised by Conservative thinkers, has no place for those who, largely for reasons associated with lack of opportunity and the disadvantages resulting from their socioeconomic position, find it hard to 'fit in'. And yet surely the hallmark of a truly 'big' society should be its willingness and capacity to develop public and social policies that are sufficiently generous and resource-rich to embrace those who are most marginalised. Who else, after all, really needs a Big Society?

The Big Society: rhetoric or reality?

To this sceptical account of the likely 'social reach' of the Big Society, further scepticism needs to be added concerning the feasibility of the project as currently outlined by government. The issue is important because the scale of the transition of services hitherto delivered by the state to providers from the voluntary and community sectors, and social enterprise, is such that many groups and communities could be adversely affected should the dynamic new 'civil society' fail to emerge.

Two 'practical' examples and one theoretical 'observation' will suffice to indicate the size of the task ahead. First, there is a resource issue – and here the apparent absence of any serious costing of the state's withdrawal from service provision and the subsequent take-up of delivery by third sector organisations suggests a basic lack of logic among policy makers. According to a recent publication by Anna Coote, Director of Social Policy at the New Economics Foundation, the level of resources provided by government to support Big Society initiatives will be insufficient to guarantee the successful transition of key services from state to third sector and voluntary provision. To date, £470 million has been allocated over four years to help 'community groups build the Big Society'. This money is expected to pay for 5,000 new community organisers, with £100 million being set aside in the 'Big Society Bank' to 'help charities, voluntary groups and social enterprise make the transition'. Conversely, however, the imperative of deficit reduction means that 'charities will lose £4.5 billion as a result of spending cuts' – and this in a context of the recent rise in VAT and an ongoing decline in charitable giving (see Coote, 2010, p 6). Wilding (2010, p 1) makes the additional point that 37 per cent of charitable income comes from statutory sources, so cuts here are likely to have a decisive impact on the nature and extent of third sector activities. A further issue raised by Wilding (2010, p 2) is that charities holding government grants and contracts to deliver public services tend to operate with around four months' worth of free reserves (one third holds no reserves at all), so the loss of income through the proposed cuts could result in the collapse of some organisations.

The second issue relates to the highly diverse nature of the UK third sector. In view of the small sums available for what will inevitably be a major expansion of provision, it is difficult to understand how the organisations involved will have the resources to develop levels of service delivery that are both socially and spatially coherent. Decentralisation and greater local control, in other words, may be bought at the cost of a relative equality of provision with the result that services may differ markedly on cost and quality across England.[1] Significantly, too, it is well known that current funding for charities is skewed in favour of a few large organisations with the bulk of the third sector being characterised by small, or very small, bodies that provide only modest levels of service. Even the Social Justice Policy Group (2006b, p 12) acknowledges that 'smaller charities make up 87% of Britain's third sector but receive just 5.4% of its income', going on to note that 'their income has fallen by 30% over the past 10 years – so much so that the Charities Aid Foundation believes that smaller TSOs [third sector organizations] may become unsustainable'. It is possible, then, that there could be a significant 'failure of supply' if third sector services cannot provide services of sufficient quality and spread to sustain the myriad demands of local communities.

Other potential problems abound and include resource issues of time, expertise and access (see Coote, 2010, pp 16-17). As one unnamed senior government adviser has recently pointed out, the Big Society will 'need an army of people with spare time and lots of energy to set up schools, form patient groups, become police commissioners, help run local services and analyse all the data being published to hold organisations to account' (*The Observer*, 2010). One fear, as the same source has commented, is that 'the idea won't work as not enough people will want to make it happen'. Conversely – and more theoretically – even should a viable network of third sector, mutual and community organisations, and volunteers, materialise, how well would this new model army relate to the prevailing institutional practices and assumptions of the much-championed free market? Harrison (2010, p 33) argues that these organisations, 'rather than being the embodiments of best practice within a "humanised" economic liberal dispensation … [may] seek to offer islands of protection and collective learning within relatively unwelcoming environments'. Certainly concepts of 'ownership', participation and belonging are likely to differ markedly from free market norms and expectations with potential knock-on effects for constructive cooperation and understanding between the two sectors.

Of greater concern, however, despite Blond's optimism about prospects for a moralised mutualism and the stated hopes of Burkeans and pragmatists for a more vibrant and accountable civil society, is the distinct possibility that an under-resourced third sector and voluntary universe will fail to thrive. Inevitably, the consequences of failure will be concentrated on those severely deprived communities where high-quality services and support are most needed and resources at their most scarce. At the time of writing, no statements or proposals have been forthcoming from Coalition policy makers that acknowledge the dangers associated with this sort of bifurcation. So, with this prospect of a two-speed Big Society in mind, and in view of the 'disciplinary' character of current proposals for cuts in welfare benefits, there is every reason to endorse Harrison's (2010, pp 34-5) wariness of 'national political appropriations of ideas on co-ops and mutuality, especially [when] informed by hopes of cost-cutting or a crude responsibilisation agenda'.

Note

[1] As Alcock (2010, p 6) notes, the Big Society is very much an 'English policy environment'. Third sector policies are currently the responsibility of devolved administrations in Northern Ireland, Wales and Scotland.

References

Alcock, P. (2010) *Big society or civil society? A new policy environment for the third sector*, Birmingham: Third Sector Research Centre.

Bale, T. (2010) *The Conservative Party from Thatcher to Cameron*, Cambridge: Polity Press.

Blond, P. (2009) 'The future of Conservatism', Speech to launch ResPublica, 26 November (www.respublica.org.uk/articles/future-conservatism-0).

Blond, P. (2010) *Red Tory: How left and right have broken Britain and how we can fix it*, London: Faber & Faber.

Cabinet Office (2010) *Building the Big Society* (www.cabinetoffice.gov.uk/media/407789/building-big-society.pdf).

Cameron, D. (2009) 'The Big Society', Hugo Young Lecture, 10 November (www.conservatives.com/News/Speeches/2009/11/David_Cameron_The_Big_Society.aspx).

Cameron, D. (2010a) 'Mending our broken society' (www.conservatives.com/News/Speeches/2010/01/David_Cameron_Mending_our_Broken_Society.aspx).

Cameron, D. (2010b) 'From central power to people power' (www.conservatives.com/News/Speeches/2010/02/David_Cameron_From_central_power_to_people_power.aspx).

Cameron, D. (2010c) 'Our "Big Society" plan' (www.conservatives.com/News/Speeches/2010/03/David_Cameron_Our_Big_Society_plan.aspx).

Cameron, D. (2010d) 'Big Society versus big government' (www.conservatives.com/News/Speeches/2010/04/David_Cameron_Big_Society_versus_Big_Government.aspx).

Chakrabortty, A. (2008) 'From Obama to Cameron, why do so many politicians want a piece of Richard Thaler?', *The Guardian*, 12 July.

Clark, G. and Mather, J. (2003) *Total politics – Labour's command state*, London: Conservative Party Policy Unit.

Conservative Party (2008) *A stronger society: Voluntary action in the 21st century*, Responsibility Agenda, Policy Green Paper No 5, London: Conservative Party.

Cook, C. (2010) 'Christian Tories rewrite party doctrine', *Financial Times*, 12 February.

Coote, A. (2010) *Cutting it: 'Big Society' and the new austerity*, London: New Economics Foundation.

DWP (Department for Work and Pensions) (2010) *Universal Credit: Welfare that works*, White Paper (www.dwp.gov.uk/policy/welfare-reform/legislation-and-key-documents/universal-credit/).

Dwyer, P. (2000) *Welfare rights and responsibilities: Contesting social citizenship*, Bristol: The Policy Press.

Dwyer, P. and Ellison, N. (2009) 'Work and welfare: the rights and responsibilities of unemployment in the UK', in M. Giugni (ed) *The politics of unemployment in Europe: Policy responses and collective action*, London: Ashgate, pp 53-66.

Evans, S. (2008) 'Consigning its past to history? David Cameron and the Conservative Party', *Parliamentary Affairs*, vol 61 no 2, pp 291-314.

Gamble, A. (1994) *The free economy and the strong state*, Basingstoke: Macmillan.

Halpern, D. (2010) *The hidden wealth of nations*, Cambridge: Polity Press.

Harrison, M. (2010) 'Property rights, empowerment and "consumer insulation": asset-based welfare systems and the "real third way"', Paper delivered to conference on 'Housing privatisation: 30 years on', Leeds, July.

Heffer, S. (2010) 'Class envy won't win the Tories the next election', *The Daily Telegraph*, 5 October.

Helm, T., Asthana, A. and Harris, P. (2010) 'How Britain's new welfare state was born in the USA', *The Observer*, 7 November.

Legg, B. (2010) 'Cameron has sold out the Tory Party', *The Guardian*, 11 May.

Letwin, O. (2008) 'From economic revolution to social revolution', *Soundings*, Lawrence & Wishart Reading Room (www.lwbooks.co.uk/ReadingRoom/public/letwin.html).

Lister, R. and Bennett, F. (2010) 'The new champion of progressive ideals? Cameron's Conservative Party: poverty, family policy and welfare reform', *Renewal* vol 18, no 1, pp 84-109.

Montgomerie, T. (2010) *Falling short: The key factors that contributed to the Conservative Party's failure to win a parliamentary majority*, London: ConservativeHome.

Norman, J. (2010) *The Big Society*, Buckingham: University of Buckingham Press.

Norman, J. and Ganesh, J. (2006) *Compassionate conservatism: What it is, why we need it*, London: Policy Exchange.

Observer, The (2010) 'Welcome to the ever-diminishing world of the "big society"', 21 November.

Prideaux, S. (2010) 'The welfare politics of Charles Murray are alive and well in the UK', *International Journal of Social Welfare*, vol 19, pp 293-302.

Social Justice Policy Group (2006a) *Breakdown Britain: Interim report*, London: The Centre for Social Justice.

Social Justice Policy Group (2006b) *Denying the vulnerable a second chance: Undervaluing Britain's third sector in the fight against poverty*, Third Sector Working Group, State of the Nation Report, December.

Social Justice Policy Group (2007a) *Breakthrough Britain: Ending the costs of social breakdown. Overview*, London: The Centre for Social Justice.

Social Justice Policy Group (2007b) *Breakthrough Britain: Ending the costs of social breakdown*, vol 1, *Family breakdown*, London: The Centre for Social Justice.

Thaler, R. and Sunstein, C. (2008) *Nudge: Improving decisions about health, wealth and happiness*, London: Yale University Press.

Wilding, K. (2010) 'Funding and the Big Society: evidence for policy makers', Paper delivered at the NCVO/TSRC Big Society Evidence Seminar, 11 October.

Willetts, D. (1994) *Modern conservatism*, Hardmondsworth: Penguin.

Willetts, D. (2005) 'A new conservatism for a new century' (www.davidwilletts.co.uk/2005/06/02/new-conservatism/).

Willetts, D. (2008) 'Renewing civic conservatism', The Oakeshott Lecture, London School of Economics and Political Science, 20 February.

FOUR

The age of responsibility: social policy and citizenship in the early 21st century[1]

Ruth Lister

A few decades ago Maurice Roche concluded an influential book on citizenship with the observation that 'the politics of citizenship has for generations formulated its goals, fought its battles and found its voice in the discourse of rights. In the late twentieth century', he argued, 'it also needs to be able to speak, to act, and to understand itself in the language of citizens' personal responsibility and social obligation, in the discourse of duties as well as of rights' (1992, p 246). Whatever the validity of that statement at the time, the politics of citizenship in the UK has subsequently changed in the direction called for by Roche so that 'the processes of "responsibilization"' have increasingly shaped the ideal citizen of today (Clarke, 2005, p 451). Nevertheless, writing in autumn 2010, as we head into the uncharted waters of coalition government, Prime Minister David Cameron speaks as if Roche's criticism were still apposite. He thereby ignores the persistent drumbeat of responsibility, which provided the soundtrack for both the Blair-Brown and the Thatcher-Major years.

To recap: back in 1988, John Moore, then Social Security Secretary, called for 'correcting the balance of the citizenship equation. In a free society the equation that has "rights" on one side must have "responsibilities" on the other' (1988). In the early days of New Labour former Prime Minister Tony Blair declared that 'duty is an essential Labour concept. It is at the heart of creating a strong community or society'. And he distanced himself from 'early Left thinking' in which the 'language of responsibility [was] spoken far less fluently than that of rights' (1995). Yet, 12 years on, when he became leader, Gordon Brown told Labour's Annual Conference that 'we have not done enough in the last ten years to emphasise that in return for the rights we all have, there are responsibilities we all owe' (2007).

Three years later, on the steps of No 10 Downing Street, Cameron declared 'I want to help try and build a more responsible society here in Britain. One where we don't just ask what are my entitlements, but what are my responsibilities' (2010c). Responsibility is one of the trinity of values guiding the Coalition. In particular, the 'plan to build the Big Society is based on a simple idea: responsibility' (Conservative Party, 2010, p 2), and 'the values implicit in the Big Society [are] duty, responsibility, obligation' (Cameron, quoted in *The Independent*, 19 April 2010). One difference between the Conservatives and New Labour, however, is that in the 'citizenship equation' there is little or no talk now about rights to balance the emphasis on responsibilities.

This chapter begins with a discussion of the dominant discourses of citizenship, informed by the underlying principle of responsibility, some of the policies they have informed and how these reflect the changing role of the state. But social citizenship is not just about the relationship between citizens and state. So we then turn to consider changing social relations of citizenship and how counter-discourses of responsibility have been deployed from outside the state and government.

Dominant discourses of citizenship responsibility

Four politically dominant, sometimes overlapping, discourses of citizenship in the UK in recent years have been those of contractualisation, opportunity and aspiration, consumerisation, and active citizenship. They all, in different ways, place responsibility on the individual citizen. Moreover, they all, to a greater or lesser extent, reflect an 'individual rational actor logic' in which 'citizens behave as rational actors, weighing up alternatives and choosing the one they believe suits them best' as individuals (Taylor-Gooby, 2009, pp 115, 58). We are, however, likely to see a modification of this logic through the 'nudge' approach of behavioural economics, which aims to steer or 'nudge' individuals into changing their behaviour without assuming that they operate as rational actors (Thaler and Sunstein, 2009). David Cameron has set up a 'nudge unit' in the Cabinet Office (see Chapter Three by Nick Ellison, this volume).

Contractualisation

From the outset the New Labour government propounded an explicitly contractual relationship between rights and obligations, notably in 'a new welfare contract' (DSS, 1998). In 2008 successive Work and Pensions

Secretaries spoke of the government's duty 'to keep the contract between the state and the individual under constant review to ensure that the balance between rights and responsibilities is properly maintained' (Hain, 2008), and of the 'need to rewrite the terms of the welfare contract' (Purnell, 2008). During the election campaign, the electorate received 'A contract between the Conservative Party and you', signed by David Cameron, which told us that 'real change only comes when we understand that we are all in this together; that we all have responsibility to help make the country better'. More specifically, Cameron pledged to introduce yet another 'new welfare contract', which 'will draw on the principles of the Big Society', with the threat that 'if you fail to take responsibility then the free ride is over' (Cameron, 2010b). The contract subsequently appeared in a consultation paper on welfare reform. It states that 'by actively putting work at the centre of working-age support we want to create a new contract with the British people. This contract is about a responsible society' (DWP, 2010a, p 39).

For both New Labour and the Tories, the welfare contract involves not just the explicit exposition of the state's contract *with* its citizens but also the contracting *out* of some of its own responsibilities to the private and voluntary sectors. This is most notable with regard to welfare to work, which sits at the heart of the welfare contract. The implications for citizenship of contracting *out* are underlined by Carmel and Papadopoulos: 'such reforms are highly political, as they partially decouple the citizen from the state and political processes by mediating and dispersing the citizen's experience of policy among a range of organisations that are not politically accountable, and whose contract is with the state, rather than with the client' (2009, p 102).

The contractualisation of welfare echoes earlier developments in the US where Fraser and Gordon warned that 'the claims of the poor ... are being weakened by a resurgence of the rhetoric of contract' (1994, p 104). In both the US and the UK the underlying model is an individualised gender-neutral one: 'that of the individual adult worker who makes a contract with the state in respect of his or her rights and responsibilities' (Gerhard et al, 2002, p 123). Yet, as a Social Security Advisory Committee paper points out, it is a 'rather one-sided contract' in which 'the balance of power ... is currently firmly tilted in favour of the state' (Griggs and Bennett, 2009, p 64).

Hartley Dean contrasts these individualistic 'contractarian repertoires' of responsibility with 'solidaristic repertoires ... premised on a collectivist view of the social order in which the priority is to sustain cooperative solidarity' (2007, p 579). Conservative rhetoric that 'we are all in this together' notwithstanding, contractarian repertoires look likely to continue to trump solidaristic ones in the development of social citizenship.

Opportunity and aspiration

Dean argues that 'contractarian understandings will focus on the competitive nature of labour markets and the responsibility of the individual to compete' (2007, p 583). This was made explicit in a Prime Ministerial foreword to one of New Labour's many consultation documents on welfare reform: 'In a globalised world, we simply cannot afford the high price of large numbers of people on benefits. Instead, we need people in work, making the best use of their talents and helping us compete', which in turn requires 'that rights are met with tough responsibilities' (Brown, 2008, p 5). Part of the terms of the welfare contract, outlined by former Work and Pensions Secretary James Purnell, was 'a credible ladder of opportunity from low paid jobs to higher skills and better pay' in return for which 'those who can work will be obliged to work or train for work' (2008). This is an example of how opportunity, which in the form of equality of opportunity displaced equality as a key value for New Labour, was itself made contingent on the responsibility to pursue it. As Blair put it, 'our contract with the people was about opportunity and responsibility going together' (1997).

Increasingly too New Labour spoke the language of aspiration – good citizens aspired to improve their position through their own efforts, taking up the opportunities opened up to them. And in Cameron's foreword to the Conservative manifesto, reference to the belief in responsibility is followed by the statement that 'we believe in enterprise and aspiration' (Cameron, 2010a, p 1). The sentiment is echoed in his joint foreword to the Coalition programme, with Deputy Prime Minister Nick Clegg, in which they promise 'individual opportunity extended' as part of a complete recasting of 'the relationship between people and the state' (Cameron and Clegg, 2010, p 8). As leader of the Liberal Democrats, Clegg had previously established an independent commission on social mobility. In a speech to mark the first 100 days of the Coalition, he spelt out the government's 'determination to create a more socially mobile society' as its 'long-term social policy goal', and announced a new ministerial group, which would develop a social mobility strategy with the help of the former Labour Cabinet Minister, Alan Milburn (Clegg, 2010).

As Stefan Collini observes, in recent years we have been encouraged to see ourselves as an 'aspirational society', which 'expresses a corrosively individualist conception of life'. In doing so, he points out, 'it speaks to individuals' sense of themselves as trying to get on, but hides from them the reality and power of the social patterns that determine their ability to do so' (2010, pp 29, 34).

Consumerisation

New Labour's first welfare reform Green Paper heralded 'the rise of the demanding, sceptical, citizen-consumer' (DSS, 1998, p 16), the spectre of which has driven an agenda of modernisation, marketisation, choice and personalisation of public services. This citizen-consumer also lurks behind the Coalition's promises of empowerment for public service users, which draws on 'Conservative thinking on markets, choice and competition' together with 'the Liberal Democrat belief in advancing democracy at a much more local level' (Cameron and Clegg, 2010, p 8).

Linking choice in public services with increased selectivity of benefits, Taylor-Gooby argues that together they represent a transition to a 'more individual, less solidaristic, citizenship' (2009, p 31). The language of responsibility is less dominant than that of choice in the consumerist policy discourses. Nevertheless, the expectation clearly is 'that the combination [of] "independence" and "choice" [will] produce people who [are] more self-sufficient and less of a cost', and citizen-consumers are expected to 'make "responsible" choices' (Clarke et al, 2007, p 65).

Active citizenship

Citizen-consumers are also increasingly expected to be active citizens in the 'co-production' of welfare. Reform of public services under New Labour suggested 'a new form of collaborative contract between state and citizen based on concepts of responsible and active citizenship' (Newman et al, 2004, pp 205-6).

As well as the individualistic active consumer-citizen, the responsible 'active citizen' comes in a variety of other guises, some of which represent an attempt to temper the individualism of dominant citizenship discourses. Back in the 1980s, the active citizen was invoked to counteract the effects of neoliberal economic and social policies through charitable giving and voluntary activity. It was a top-down model of active citizenship in which the successful were called on to help the unsuccessful through the unregulated and uncertain private arena of charity and good works rather than the regulated public arena of tax-funded benefits and services.

The active citizen continued to figure during the New Labour years, not just as a consumer and paid worker but also in more collective form, particularly through an '"empowered public" discourse' directed at marginalised groups or communities (Barnes et al, 2007, p 10). Through public participation initiatives such groups were now expected to be active citizens themselves rather than the recipients of the largesse of more successful and fortunate citizens.

We can expect a big role for the active citizen in the Big Society (see Chapter Three by Nick Ellison, this volume). One of the Coalition government's first statements heralds the building of the Big Society as 'the responsibility of every citizen'. It promises a voluntary National Citizen Service for 16-year-olds 'to give them a chance to develop the skills needed to be active and responsible citizens' (Cabinet Office, 2010b, p 2). Moreover, Cameron and Clegg explain that the fusion of their plans and philosophies around social responsibility and the role of the state will 'create a Big Society matched by big citizens' (Cameron and Clegg, 2010, p 8).

'Big citizens' and 'active citizenship' have also been promoted by Richard Reeves and Dan Leighton of the think tank Demos as key to what they believe is a 'republican moment', reflected in an increasingly vocal discourse of republicanism on the centre-left (Reeves and Leighton, 2010, p 25).[2] One of the 'republican demands' which they articulate is 'a social world dominated by neither the "big state" nor "big society", but populated by big citizens' (2010, p 24). Reeves and Leighton argue that 'power is the currency of republicanism' (2010, p 25).

Republicans tend to ignore the extent to which time is also a currency – and this has been a feminist criticism of the civic republican tradition of citizenship. Active citizenship takes time, and time is very much a gendered resource for citizenship, which impacts on and is mediated by the public–domestic private divide, with implications for men and women's active citizenship in its various guises. This is particularly the case for those who cannot afford to outsource domestic work to poorer women. The New Economics Foundation warns that 'long hours and low wages undermine a key premise of the "Big Society", which is that social and financial gains will come from replacing paid with unpaid labour' (nef, 2010, p 4). Active citizenship thus raises questions about the gendered division of labour and time and also about the regulation of paid working time, which are unlikely to be on the government's agenda for the Big Society.

Some policy implications

In this section we turn to some examples of how social policy has been used to encourage or require mainly the less powerful to exercise responsibilities and obligations and then contrast these policies with the treatment of more powerful institutions and individuals.

Conditionality

The welfare contract, with its emphasis on responsibility and obligation, has meant that social citizenship, particularly as embodied in the social security system, has become increasingly conditional in many welfare states, irrespective of welfare regime type (Lister, 2009; Nevile, 2010). The principle of conditionality was spelt out in a Department for Work and Pensions (DWP) discussion paper:

> Over the past two decades, the concept of conditionality has become central to welfare policy in the major economies. Conditionality embodies the principle that aspects of state support, usually financial or practical, are dependent on citizens meeting certain conditions which are invariably behavioural.... It also draws on the notion that the welfare system rests on a fair bargain of mutual obligations between citizen and state, in simple terms: "something for something". (DWP, 2008, p 1)

The behavioural conditions, to which the DWP document refers, are primarily (although not exclusively) geared directly or indirectly to labour market 'activation' and, to that end, employability. In a false dichotomy, the new 'active' social citizenship is constantly contrasted with the previous, supposedly 'passive', 'dependency'-inducing model. In fact, benefits for unemployed people have always been conditional on availability for paid work. Nevertheless, over the past three decades the conditions attached to receipt of benefit have been intensified, the sanctions for non-compliance increased and conditionality has been extended to other groups of benefit recipients, notably lone parents, partners and people with disabilities. The importance of conditionality to the new government was signified by the inclusion in the initial coalition agreement of the statement that 'we agree that receipt of benefits for those able to work should be conditional on the willingness to work' (Cabinet Office, 2010a, para 7). This has been translated, in the welfare reform White Paper, into 'tougher sanctions to ensure recipients meet their responsibilities' (DWP, 2010b, p 24; and see Chapter Two by Jay Wiggan, this volume).

While work obligations have been intensified for citizens, since 2002 asylum seekers have been denied the civil or economic right to work, described by T.H. Marshall as 'the basic civil right' in the economic field (1950, p 15). At the same time, they have been afforded reduced, or in the case of those refused asylum any, social rights to income or housing support, leading to destitution in all too many cases (Joint Committee on Human Rights, 2007). This is one example of how social citizenship has also become increasingly exclusive of outsiders in many advanced welfare states. Another example, which also represents a further extension of conditionality and contractualisation, is the introduction by New Labour of 'earned citizenship' for immigrants. Access to most benefits and services will be subject to a probationary period of a minimum of six years. John Flint comments that the concept of 'earned' citizenship 'reconfigures the idea of a "right" to citizenship ... and provides an additional mechanism of conditionality for classifying potential citizens' (2009, p 89).

The regulation of behaviour

The use of social citizenship as a disciplinary tool to promote behavioural change and regulate behaviour has not been confined to the sphere of paid work. In 2004, the Prime Minister's Strategy Unit published *Personal responsibility and changing behaviour*. It observes that 'a range of factors suggest that greater focus on behaviour change ... is timely and important'; one of these factors is the 'powerful moral and political arguments for protecting and enhancing personal responsibility' (Halpern and Bates, 2004, p 5). According to Perri 6 et al, 'New Labour's efforts in behavioural change were indeed central to its domestic policy programme. These efforts were extensive and ambitious' (2010, p 445).

With its preoccupation with personal responsibility (and also, in the case of the Conservatives, encouraging marriage), the Coalition government also wants to shape the behaviour of citizens. With echoes of the Strategy Unit report (indeed its co-author now heads the government's new 'nudge unit'), Cameron and Clegg dismiss the assumption that 'central government can only change people's behaviour through rules and regulations'. Instead, they claim, 'our government will be a much smarter one, shunning the bureaucratic levers of the past and finding intelligent ways to encourage, support and enable people to make better choices for themselves' (2010, pp 7-8). This is a clear hint of the government's enthusiasm for 'nudge' although it appears to be happy to apply the same old 'bureaucratic levers' to benefit recipients.

New Labour used social citizenship both to encourage desirable behaviour and discourage undesirable behaviour (Lister, forthcoming). A key example of the former is savings (including for pensions). Martin Hewitt suggested that 'saving is being elevated from a private aspiration of the prudent individual to a core duty of the good citizen supported by government' (2002, p 189). The Coalition government's first Budget announced tax-benefit measures 'to encourage people to take personal responsibility for their actions by rewarding those who work hard and save responsibly for the future' (HM Treasury, 2010b, p 3).

Other examples of New Labour's attempts to promote responsible behaviour through conditional social citizenship rights include the reform of the maternity grant and introduction of a new 'health in pregnancy' grant (now abolished), both tied to health checks; and the establishment of statutory educational maintenance allowances conditional on attendance, with bonus payments for effort (also now abolished).

Housing Benefit reform has been used both to encourage and discourage forms of behaviour. The DWP explained that an 'overarching purpose [of the new local housing allowances] is to transform passive housing support into an enabling provision that places responsibility and choice firmly in the hands of tenants' (DWP, 2006, p 86). Further legislation has brought Housing Benefit into the criminal justice net. It permits a Housing Benefit sanction:

> ... where a person has been evicted for anti-social behaviour and refuses to address their behaviour using the support and help offered to them. This measure is ... about getting people to change their behaviour.... The right to housing benefit must and will carry a responsibility to be a decent neighbour. (DWP, 2006)

As Peter Squires observes, 'the broader responsibilization of social networks' involved in policies to combat anti-social behaviour 'is reminiscent of the "micro-physics" of power described by Foucault or disciplinary relations at the capillary level' (2006, p 153). Commenting on the expansion of the criminal justice system in relation to anti-social behaviour, Nixon and Prior write that 'these new politics of conduct reflect notions of self-regulation and responsible citizenship, with associated political rationalities saturated with a normalising moral discourse in which the law-abiding citizen is differentiated from the irresponsible' (2009, p 71).

Asymmetrical responsibility

One of the main conclusions reached by Perri 6 et al's analysis of behavioural change policies was that 'the strong (more coercive) tools are markedly concentrated on initiatives targeting the poor and low-income working strata' (2010, p 427). Back in 1998, Will Hutton, while accepting a link between rights and obligations, complained that 'most of the obligations that accompany rights in a New Labour order are shouldered by the bottom of society rather than those at the top, which is let off largely scot-free' (*The Observer*, 5 July 1998).

Indeed, as Anthony Giddens observes more recently, in an otherwise positive review of New Labour's record, 'the idea that Labour should be "intensely relaxed about people getting filthy rich" [as Peter Mandelson infamously put it] not only exacerbated inequalities, but also helped to create a culture of irresponsibility. Bosses protected themselves from the risks they asked their employees to bear' (2010, p 26). The irresponsible behaviour of those in the City and the boardroom, driving high risk, bonus-crazy, irresponsible capitalism, led to the credit crunch, the impact of which was borne by people less powerful than themselves. Similarly, the cost of the ecological irresponsibility of the rich, with their conspicuous consumption and gas-guzzling cars, private jets and yachts and even submarines, is borne disproportionately by people living in poverty both domestically and globally. Furthermore, many of the better off have avoided and evaded the citizenship responsibility of paying their due taxes and act as if it were their right not to pay their dues. New Labour colluded in the idea that taxation is an unwelcome burden and failed to make the case, articulated by the Commission on Taxation and Citizenship, that 'taxpaying is a civic duty'. The Commission made clear that 'those who have benefited more from the distribution of income and wealth in the market have a duty to contribute more in return' (2000, p 94).

Yet it was only in New Labour's dying days that it increased taxation on those who have benefited enormously from the market and started talking about the need for the 'rights and responsibilities agenda' to 'go all the way to the top' (interview with Ed Miliband in *The Guardian*, 20 March 2010). So the manifesto, too late, called for 'responsibility from all, including at the top' (Labour Party, 2010, para 0.4).

At the same time, regulation of individual behaviour was matched by deregulation of the financial sector and the labour market. As Reeves puts it, 'they regulated the economy too little and the people too much' (2010). In their manifesto, the Conservatives claim that they will not 'allow irresponsibility in the private sector to continue unchecked' (2010, p viii). However, as Mike Marqusee argues, the massive spending cuts agenda can be understood as 'a transfer of responsibility, moral and fiscal, from speculators and manipulators of debt to the general public' (2010, p 50). Moreover, it is difficult to believe that the Coalition government will be willing to use the state to check the market in any significant way. An early example is its 'new vision for public health', which, according to the Health Secretary, Andrew Lansley, involves 'a new "responsibility deal" with industry that is not built on regulation, but on social responsibility' and on individuals showing responsibility in their eating habits (Lansley, 2010; *The Independent*, 8 July 2010).

The changing role of the state

This is consistent with the critique of the state or 'big government', which has been a central theme of Cameron's 'progressive conservatism'. 'Why is our society broken?', he asked the 2009 Party Conference. 'Because government got too big, did too much and undermined responsibility', was his answer (2009b). Cameron looks to the 'Big Society' and in particular the voluntary and informal sectors, rather than 'the large, clunking mechanism of the state' (2006) as the main drivers of social progress. It is a position that chimes with that held by the economic liberal side of the Liberal Democratic Party. Thus Cameron and Clegg write in their programme for government that 'we share a conviction that the days of big government are over' (2010, p 7).

Cameron's stance has been described as 'a third way in relation to the state, combining hostility with a qualified recognition that it has a vital role to play' (Richards, 2009). In some ways the rhetoric echoes New Labour's third way position on the state, even if the inflection is different, reflecting much greater hostility towards the state and much more qualified recognition of its role. Proponents of the third way, such as Blair and David Miliband, also talked about a more limited state in partnership with the private and voluntary sectors. Back in 2001, Brown promised that 'the role of government will shift even more from the old "directing and controlling" to enabling and empowering voluntary action' (2001).

There are two issues at stake here: the nature of the state and the boundaries of responsibility between the state and the citizen. Blair spelt out his vision of the 'modern popular welfare state' in his Beveridge lecture: 'The state becomes an enabler, not just a provider', providing 'a hand-up not a hand-out' in line with the principle of 'mutual responsibility' (1999, p 13). While New Labour to some extent rehabilitated the state after the assault of Thatcherism, the regulating, target-setting managerial state, operating in certain spheres through quasi-markets, lived on.

The third way also promoted the 'social investment state'. The term was initially coined by Giddens who set the guideline as 'investment in *human capital* wherever possible, rather than direct provision of economic maintenance' (1998, p 117, emphasis in original). New Labour's embrace of social investment meant the strengthening of social citizenship in some spheres, most notably through policies designed to tackle child poverty and develop a childcare strategy. However, the social investment philosophy was essentially instrumental to the demands of global competitiveness, as social policy was still treated as the 'handmaiden' of economic policy (Titmuss, 1974, p 31), and children were constructed as citizen-workers of the future rather than child-citizens in the here and now (Lister, 2003).

Jane Jenson has 'documented a convergence in Latin American and European ideas about social citizenship, following from the adoption and deployment of ideas about the social investment perspective' (2009, p 464). This has meant the reconfiguration of what she terms 'the responsibility mix' (2009, p 452). According to Dobrowolsky, the 'responsibility mix has shifted as a result of both marketization and securitization' (2007, p 646). Securitization refers to the retreat of states from 'broader, liberal ideas of "human security"' as embodied in the notion of social security – a term that has practically been expunged from the lexicon of government in the UK – to narrower 'more traditional, realist-inspired "national security" preoccupations', involving greater coercion (2007, p 630). 'Marketization and securitization mean', she suggests, 'open borders for trade and labor-capital mobility; open borders for certain (in demand) workers; but closed borders to refugees and asylum seekers, and a clamp down on terrorists' (2007, p 650). One casualty has been a number of civil citizenship rights including, in the UK, the unfettered right to peaceful protest (although the Coalition government has pledged to restore this).

Carmel and Papadopoulos bring out the implications for social security: 'The new consensus is that social security should not provide protection but, rather, support…. Social-security-as-support is a "hollowed out" security; its essence – protection – has been changed. In this vision, social security is not primarily about protection from failures of socioeconomic conditions that state action can alter. Rather it is a "helping hand" so that an individual can alter their own behaviour to match the demands arising from these conditions' (2009, p 97). Moreover, if the individual fails to alter her or his behaviour in the appropriate fashion, the light-touch enabling state has not shrunk from playing a directly coercive and intrusive role in enforcing responsibility as part of the welfare contract.

It is premature to suggest how the *nature* of the state might evolve under the Coalition government. In his Hugo Young Lecture, Cameron argued for a 're-imagined role for the state'; his 'alternative to big government is not no government' or even 'smarter government' but government that uses 'the state to remake society' and 'help stimulate social action' (2009a). This perhaps suggests yet another variant of the enabling state, albeit significantly pared back. The *Spending Review framework* makes clear that 'the scale of the challenge presents an opportunity to take a more fundamental look at the role of government in society', with the aim of 'a smaller state' (HM Treasury, 2010a, pp 7, 5). As already indicated, it is clear that the Conservatives intend to continue along the path set by the Thatcher government of shifting responsibility for welfare further from the state to individuals, families, communities and civil society. As one political commentator warned after the Coalition government's first budget, 'Osborne hopes to re-cast the state and to do so in ways that make it politically impossible for future governments to reverse' (Richards, 2010).

The 'social investment state' is vulnerable to the cuts heralded in the framework document, with the Child Trust Fund identified as an early victim. Nevertheless, Iain Duncan Smith, in his first speech as Work and Pensions Secretary, advised that he would be guided 'by this one question – does what we are doing result in a positive Social Return on Investment? [The capitalisation suggests its use as a management tool rather than a political philosophy.] In short, does this investment decision mean a real life change that will improve outcomes and allow an individual's life to become more positive and productive?' (2010).

Social relations of citizenship

Citizenship is not just about relations between citizens and the state. Recent work on 'recasting the social in citizenship' has also emphasised the 'social relations' of citizenship (Isin et al, 2008). A focus on the social relations of citizenship offers another perspective on the institutions through which social citizenship is substantiated. It also opens up the wider politics of citizenship in which constructions of responsibility are contested and it is to these alternative perspectives we now turn.

Welfare institutions as shapers of social relations

Increased selectivity in the social security system represents another shift in social citizenship in recent years in many welfare states. In an important report, which echoes Bo Rothstein's (1998) analysis of welfare institutions, the Fabian Society reasserts the case for universalism as a vital element of citizenship, using arguments that emphasise social relations. One of its premises is that 'the way in which policy divides up a population can actually *constitute* and *shape* the social relationships' between individual citizens (Horton and Gregory, 2009, p 89, emphasis in original). Universal institutions, it argues, both express and strengthen 'the common bonds of membership' of society, 'based on the normative principle that we are all equal citizens' (2009, p 136). As these universal institutions are likely to be eroded yet further, so the common bonds of citizenship are threatened, the more so in the current context of massive inequality.

Social relations of citizenship are also shaped by forms of governance of welfare institutions. User involvement has been promoted to a greater or lesser extent in a range of services. However, as Griggs and Bennett note, 'there are very few opportunities for proactive, sustained or more comprehensive input from claimants about the design and delivery of the benefits system'. Yet, 'empowerment and agency are very important issues in a system in which the balance of power is so unequal' (2009, pp 44, 62). Elsewhere, Bennett suggests that 'giving claimants a role in shaping the benefits system should be seen as relevant to the rights and responsibilities agenda – an extension of rights for claimants and responsibilities for the state' (2008, p 17).

Alternative discourses of responsibility

Bennett's observation serves as a reminder that there are alternative constructions of citizenship responsibility to those that dominate political debate. This brings us to another aspect of Isin et al's interrogation of the 'social in citizenship', which involves 'drawing attention to the process-oriented and contested character of citizenship' (2008, p 11).

Citizenship may function as a disciplinary tool but it also represents an emancipatory concept for marginalised groups and social movements.

John Hoffman describes it as a 'momentum concept'. Such concepts, he explains, '"unfold" so that we must continuously rework them in a way that realizes more and more of their egalitarian and anti-hierarchical potential' (2004, p 138). 'Citizenship is', he contends, 'an on-going struggle with no stopping point' (2004, p 13). Feminism and the environmental movement provide two examples of how this struggle opens up alternative constructions of citizenship responsibility. Indeed, according to Roche, both are 'concerned with the politics of morality and duty' (1992, p 52).

Feminists have challenged dominant constructions of obligation and responsibility at both a philosophical level and with regard to their implications for social policy. Nancy J. Hirschmann, for instance, criticises the construction of obligation associated with social contract theory, rooted in individual consent and choice. She suggests an alternative conceptualisation, which begins 'with connection' and which 'does not depend on explicit choice and takes care and responsibility as central elements of a moral schema that has existed at least as long as the social contract' (1996, pp 170, 162-3).

Selma Sevenhuijsen (1998) has articulated such a conceptualisation more specifically in relation to citizenship, grounded in the ethic of care, developed too from a social policy perspective in the work of Fiona Williams (2001). 'The feminist ethic of care', writes Sevenhuijsen, 'takes the idea of self-in-relationship as a point of entry for thinking about responsibility and obligation' (2000, p 10). Here the emphasis is very much on the social relations of citizenship as located in the private domestic as well as the public sphere. Sevenhuijsen offers her approach as a corrective to the dominance of paid work as the primary citizenship obligation in many welfare states. The question of the relative value accorded to paid work and care as citizenship obligation or responsibility is at the heart of debates in recent years around the extension of conditionality to lone parents claiming benefits, including debates between feminists who place differing emphasis on paid work and care.

Environmentalism echoes the critique of paid work as the primary citizenship obligation. It is through the notion of 'ecological citizenship', in particular, that environmentalists have developed an alternative understanding of obligation and responsibility. According to Andrew Dobson, the concept of ecological citizenship 'deals in the currency of non-contractual responsibility' and 'the idea of obligation ... is central to … a defensible articulation of ecological citizenship' (2003, pp 89, 85). 'The principal ecological citizenship obligation is to ensure that ecological footprints make a sustainable … impact…. Ecological footprints are an expression of the impact of production and reproduction of individuals' and collectives' daily lives on strangers near and far. It is these strangers to whom the obligations of ecological citizenship are owed' (2003, pp 118-19). Moreover, 'the obligations of the ecological citizen extend through time as well as space, towards generations yet to be born' (2003, p 106). The spatial dimension of ecological citizenship overlaps with notions of global citizenship. It underpins claims, in the name of global justice, that global climate agreements must place greater obligations on the global North in recognition of the climate debt, which they owe to countries of the global South (Jones, 2010).

Finally, a Joseph Rowntree Foundation study (Donald and Mottershaw, 2009) indicates how the deployment of a human rights discourse among some poverty activists might be interpreted as, in part, a reaction against dominant constructions of social citizenship, which emphasise personal responsibility and work obligations and which treat social citizenship as instrumental to economic ends. This is especially the case in the US where the formation of a campaign for economic human rights by anti-poverty groups was, according to Cox and Thomas, 'a response to welfare reform' (2004, p 26). The representation of poverty as a human rights issue works to counter the 'othering' of people in poverty and it has mobilised people who might otherwise be unwilling to accept the label of poverty (Lister, 2004). A human rights approach to poverty also shifts the onus of responsibility back from individuals to the state (Goddard and Kazantzis, 2008). It can be used to make the case for adequate benefits sufficient to ensure human dignity. Moreover, it is worth recalling in this context the Beveridge Plan's articulation of the 'aim … to abolish want by ensuring that every citizen willing to serve according to his powers has at all times an income sufficient to meet his responsibilities' (Beveridge, 1942, para 444).

Conclusion

The greater part of this chapter has focused on some of the ways in which social citizenship has become increasingly conditional, exclusive and selective in recent years. This broad message accentuates the continuity of approach between New Labour and the Coalition government. The four overlapping citizenship discourses of contractualisation, opportunity and aspiration, consumerisation and active citizenship together with the preoccupation with changing behaviour, which marked the New Labour years, are reflected also in the Coalition's approach. However, the latter's more hostile stance towards the state is reflected in the absence of any talk of social rights to balance responsibilities and points to an acceleration in the shift towards greater conditionality, exclusivity and selectivity in these rights (at least for those of working age and their children). With regard to selectivity, the ending of universal Child Benefit has been described as 'a symbolic moment for Britain's welfare state' (Timmins, 2010).[3] The Coalition has also indicated its preference for a greater use of 'nudge' and market incentives rather than the law to change behaviour.

Despite citizenship's increasingly disciplinary quality, it retains its emancipatory potential. As such it has been deployed by marginalised groups and social movements to stake their claims, sometimes using the language of human rights rather than citizenship as such. The 'age of responsibility' is thus marked by a growing disjuncture between citizenship 'from above' and citizenship 'from below' – a disjuncture that is in part articulated through contested meanings of responsibility.

There is also a disjuncture or asymmetry between the obligations imposed on the powerless and the failure to require the powerful to fulfil their responsibilities to society in a context of unacceptable levels of inequality. Half a century ago, in a tract on 'the irresponsible society', Richard Titmuss wrote of 'the need to expose the growth of irresponsible power, private and public' (1959/2001, p 141). He suggested that 'in the decades ahead, we shall need all the social inventiveness, democratic skills and sense of responsibility which we can mobilise if we are to begin to close the gap of national inequalities' (1959/2001, p 146). As we face an even wider gap in overall inequality today, as well as a diminution of state action, these words ring in our ears, together with Titmuss's warning that a 'retreat from government' represents 'a retreat into irresponsibility' (1959/2001, p 156).

Notes
[1] An earlier, shorter, version of this chapter was presented as a plenary paper at the 2010 Social Policy Association conference. I am grateful to Adrian Sinfield for his suggestions for strengthening the paper and to the editors for their helpful comments on the first draft.
[2] Reeves has since left Demos to work for the Deputy Prime Minister, Nick Clegg.
[3] In addition, contributory Employment and Support Allowance will be paid for only one year to those deemed capable of work. Yet the

Coalition has also floated the idea of a flat rate pension above the level of means-tested support for future pensioners.

References

6, Perri, Fletcher-Morgan, C. and Leyland, K. (2010) 'Making people more responsible: the Blair government's programme for changing citizens' behaviour', *Political Studies*, vol 58, no 3, pp 427-49.

Barnes, M., Newman, J. and Sullivan, H. (2007) *Power, participation and political renewal*, Bristol: The Policy Press.

Bennett, F. (2008) 'Celebrating sixty years of the welfare state?', *Poverty*, no 131, pp 12-17.

Beveridge, W. (1942) *Report on Social Insurance and Allied Services*, Cmnd 6404, London: HMSO.

Blair, T. (1995) 'The rights we enjoy reflect the duties we owe', Spectator Lecture, London, 22 March.

Blair, T. (1997) 'Why we must help those excluded from society', *The Independent*, 8 December.

Blair, T. (1999) Beveridge Lecture, Toynbee Hall, London, 18 March [reproduced as 'Beveridge revisited: a welfare state for the 21st century', in R. Walker (ed) *Ending child poverty*, Bristol: The Policy Press, pp 7-18].

Brown, G. (2001) 'Let the people look after themselves', *The Times*, 11 January.

Brown, G. (2007) Speech to Labour Party conference, Bournemouth, 24 September.

Brown, G. (2008) 'Foreword', in Department for Work and Pensions, *No one written off: Reforming welfare to reward responsibility*, London: Department for Work and Pensions, pp 5-6.

Cabinet Office (2010a) *Conservative-Liberal Democrat coalition agreement*, London: Cabinet Office.

Cabinet Office (2010b) *Building the Big Society*, London: Cabinet Office.

Cameron, D. (2006) Scarman Lecture, London, 24 November.

Cameron, D. (2009a) 'The Big Society', Hugo Young Lecture, London, 10 November.

Cameron, D. (2009b) 'Putting Britain back on to her feet', Speech to Conservative Party Conference, Manchester, 8 October.

Cameron, D. (2010a) 'Foreword', Conservative Party, *Invitation to join the government of Britain* (Election Manifesto), London: Conservative Party.

Cameron, D. (2010b) 'Ending the free ride for those who fail to take responsibility', Speech, 20 April.

Cameron, D. (2010c), Speech outside 10 Downing Street, 11 May.

Cameron, D. and Clegg, N. (2010) 'Foreword', *The Coalition: Our programme for government*, London: HM Government, pp 7-8.

Carmel, E. and Papadopoulos, T. (2009) 'Governing social security: from protection to markets', in J. Millar (ed) *Understanding social security*, Bristol: The Policy Press, pp 93-109.

Clarke, J. (2005) 'New Labour's citizens: activated, empowered, responsibilized, abandoned?', *Critical Social Policy*, vol 25, no 4, pp 447-63.

Clarke, J., Newman, J., Smith, N., Vidler, E. and Westmarland, L. (2007) *Creating citizen-consumers*, London: Sage Publications.

Clegg, N. (2010) Speech on social mobility, 18 August (www.libdems. org.uk/speeches).

Collini, S. (2010) 'Blahspeak', *London Review of Books*, 8 April, pp 29-34.

Commission on Taxation and Citizenship (2000) *Paying for progress*, London: Fabian Society.

Conservative Party (2010) *A new welfare contract*, London: Conservative Party.

Cox, L. and Thomas, D.Q. (2004) *Close to home. Case studies of human rights work in the United States*, New York: Ford Foundation.

Dean, H. (2007) 'The ethics of welfare to work', *Policy & Politics*, vol 35, no 4, pp 573-90.

Dobrowolsky, A. (2007) '(In)security and citizenship', *Theoretical Inquiries in Law*, vol 8, no 2, pp 629-61.

Dobson, A. (2003) *Citizenship and the environment*, Oxford: Oxford University Press.

Donald, A. and Mottershaw, E. (2009) *Poverty, inequality and human rights*, York: Joseph Rowntree Foundation.

DSS (Department of Social Security) (1998) *New ambitions for our country: A new contract for welfare*, London: The Stationery Office.

Duncan Smith, I. (2010) 'Welfare for the 21st century', Speech, London, 27 May.

DWP (Department for Work and Pensions) (2006) 'Action to tackle nuisance neighbours', Press release, 5 June.

DWP (2008) *More support, higher expectations: The role of conditionality in improving employment outcomes*, London: DWP.

DWP (2010a) *21st century welfare*, Cm 7913, London: The Stationery Office.

DWP (2010b) *Universal Credit: Welfare that works*, Cm 7957, London: The Stationery Office.

Flint, J. (2009) 'Subversive subjects and conditional, earned and denied citizenship', in M. Barnes and D. Prior (eds) *Subversive citizens*, Bristol: The Policy Press, pp 83-98.

Fraser, N. and Gordon, L. (1994) 'Civil citizenship against social citizenship?', in B. van Steenbergen (ed) *The condition of citizenship*, London: Sage Publications, pp 90-107.

Gerhard, U., Knijn, T. and Lewis, J. (2002) 'Contractualization', in B. Hobson, J. Lewis and B. Siim (eds) *Contested concepts in gender and social politics*, Cheltenham: Edward Elgar, pp 105-40.

Giddens, A. (1998) *The Third Way*, Cambridge: Polity Press.

Giddens, A. (2010) 'The rise and fall of New Labour', *New Statesman*, 17 May, pp 25-7.

Goddard, C. and Kazantzis, M. (2008) 'Human rights and human rights based approaches', in *Human Rights and Tackling UK Poverty*, Report of roundtable meeting, 17 January, London: British Institute for Human Rights.

Griggs, J. and Bennett, F. (2009) *Rights and responsibilities in the social security system*, London: Social Security Advisory Committee.

Hain, P. (2008) *House of Commons Hansard*, 7 January, col 54.

Halpern, D. and Bates, C. (2004) *Personal responsibility and changing behaviour*, London: Prime Minister's Strategy Unit.

Hewitt, M. (2002) 'New Labour and the redefinition of social security', in M. Powell (ed) *Evaluating New Labour's welfare reforms*, Bristol: The Policy Press, pp 189-209.

Hirschmann, N.J. (1996) 'Rethinking obligation for feminism', in N.J. Hirschmann and C. Di Stefano (eds) *Revisioning the political*, Boulder, CO: Westview Press, pp 157-80.

HM Treasury (2010a) *The Spending Review framework*, Cm 7872, London: The Stationery Office.

HM Treasury (2010b) *Budget 2010*, HC 61, London: The Stationery Office.

Hoffman, J. (2004) *Citizenship beyond the state*, London: Sage Publications.

Horton, T. and Gregory, J. (2009) *The solidarity society*, London: The Fabian Society.

Isin, I., Brodie, J., Juteau, D. and Stasiulis, D. (2008) 'Recasting the social in citizenship', in I. Isin (ed) *Recasting the social in citizenship*, Toronto: University of Toronto Press, pp 3-19.

Jenson, J. (2009) 'Lost in translation: the social investment perspective and gender equality', *Social Politics*, vol 16, no 4, pp 466-83.

Joint Committee on Human Rights (2007) *The treatment of asylum-seekers*, London: The Stationery Office.

Jones, T. (2010) 'Climate indebted', *Red Pepper*, dec/jan, pp 24-7.

Labour Party (2010) *A fair future for all, The Labour Party manifesto*, London: Labour Party.

Lansley, A. (2010) Letter to *The Observer*, 25 July.

Lister, R. (2003) 'Investing in the citizen-workers of the future', *Social Policy & Administration*, vol 37, no 5, pp 427-33.

Lister, R. (2004) *Poverty*, Cambridge: Polity Press.

Lister, R. (2009) 'Poor citizenship: social rights, poverty and democracy', in A. Kessler-Harris and M. Vaudagna (eds) *Democracy and social rights in the 'two Wests'*, Torino: Otto editore, pp 43-65.

Lister, R. (forthcoming) 'Social citizenship in New Labour's new "active" welfare state', in A. Evers and A. Guillemard (eds) *Social policy and citizenship*, Oxford: Oxford University Press.

Marqusee, M. (2010) 'Busting the straitjacket', *Red Pepper*, dec/jan, pp 50-1.

Marshall, T.H. (1950) *Citizenship and social class*, Cambridge: Cambridge University Press.

Moore, J. (1988) 'The end of the line for poverty', Speech to Greater London Area CPC, 11 May.

nef (New Economics Foundation) (2010) *Ten big questions about the Big Society*, London: nef.

Nevile, A. (ed) (2010) *Human rights and social policy*, Cheltenham: Edward Elgar.

Newman, J., Barnes, M., Sullivan, H. and Knops, A. (2004) 'Public participation and collaborative governance', *Journal of Social Policy*, vol 33, no 2, pp 203-33.

Nixon, J. and Prior, D. (2009) 'Disciplining difference – introduction', *Social Policy and Society*, vol 9, no 1, pp 71-5.

Purnell, J. (2008) Speech to 'Ready to Work, Skilled for Work' Conference, London, 28 January.

Reeves, R. (2010) 'Labour's puritans should let us live our lives', *Financial Times*, 9 February.

Reeves, R. and Leighton, D. (2010) 'The republican moment', *New Statesman*, 26 April, pp 22-5.

Richards, S. (2009) 'Size should not be everything in Cameron's vision of a modern state', *The Independent*, 13 November.

Richards, S. (2010) 'The beginning of the end of the state', *The Independent*, 23 June.

Roche, M. (1992) *Rethinking citizenship*, Cambridge: Polity Press.

Rothstein, B. (1998) *Just institutions matter*, Cambridge: Cambridge University Press.

Sevenhuijsen, S. (1998) *Citizenship and the ethic of care*, London and New York: Routledge.

Sevenhuijsen, S. (2000) 'Caring in the third way. The relation between obligation, responsibility and care in third way discourse', *Critical Social Policy*, vol 20, no 1, pp 5–37.

Squires, P. (2006) 'New Labour and the politics of antisocial behaviour', *Critical Social Policy*, vol 26, no 1, pp 144–68.

Taylor-Gooby, P. (2009) *Reframing social citizenship*, Oxford: Oxford University Press.

Thaler, R.H. and Sunstein, C.R. (2009) *Nudge*, New York and London: Penguin Books.

Timmins, N. (2010) 'Symbolic moment for Britain's welfare state', *Financial Times*, 4 October (www.ft.com/cms/s/0/86295be6-cf9e-11df-a51f-00144feab49a.html).

Titmuss, R.M. (1959/2001) 'The irresponsible society', in P. Alcock, H. Glennerster, A. Oakley and A. Sinfield (eds) *Welfare and wellbeing. Richard Titmuss's contribution to social policy*, Bristol: The Policy Press, pp 141–58.

Titmuss, R.M. (1974) *Social policy*, London: Allen & Unwin.

Williams, F. (2001) *Rethinking families*, London: Calouste Gulbenkian Foundation.

FIVE

Debating the 'death tax': the politics of inheritance tax in the UK

Rajiv Prabhakar

Introduction

This chapter looks at recent debates about inheritance tax in the UK. Politicians have often seemed reluctant to make the case for inheritance tax, and I consider how discussions of this tax have changed in the aftermath of the global financial crisis as well as the new governing coalition between the Conservatives and Liberal Democrats. Although politicians are still wary of arguing for an increase in inheritance tax, centre-left politicians were more willing to resist Conservative calls to cut this tax. Liberal Democrat politicians were able to get the Conservatives to drop their plans to weaken inheritance tax as part of their agreement to form a coalition government, although they in turn had to drop proposals for a property tax. This chapter looks at some of the constraints and opportunities facing efforts to make a political case for inheritance tax.

Wealth inequality is a topic of growing policy concern in the UK. In 2008, Harriet Harman, then Labour Minister for Women and Equality, convened a National Equality Panel to report on inequality in the UK. Chaired by Professor John Hills, this Panel provided a comprehensive map of inequality in the UK, looking for example at income, wealth and education. Its final report notes that: 'For many readers, the sheer scale of the inequalities in outcome which we present will be shocking' (National Equality Panel, 2010, p 2). The report states that household wealth is far more unequally spread than household income in the UK, although the figures are not unusual when compared to the experience of other countries. It notes that the top 10 per cent of households have total wealth (which covers personal possessions, financial assets, pensions and housing) above £853,000, while the bottom 10 per cent of households have wealth less than £8,800. The top one per cent of households have total wealth above £2.6 million (National Equality Panel, 2010). Similar findings are reported in other recent studies of inequality (Wilkinson and Pickett, 2009; Dorling, 2010).

Reducing wealth inequality is also a key theme of recent Conservative writing (Wind-Cowie, 2009; Blond, 2010; Willetts, 2010). Blond (2010) calls for the creation of a 'progressive conservatism' that tries to shape a new politics out of the left and right. An important part of this focuses on 're-capitalising the poor'. Blond says that in 1976, the bottom half of the population owned 12 per cent of the country's liquid wealth, but this fell to one per cent in 2003. If property is included in the definition of wealth, then the bottom half of the population had seven per cent of wealth. Blond argues that reducing wealth inequality is needed to extend real opportunity. Willetts (2010) argues that a neglected topic is wealth inequality between the generations. He contends that a generation of 'baby-boomers' born between 1945 and 1965 enjoy an unfair share of wealth when compared with younger generations, and there is a need for policy to address this inequality.

Taxing wealth is one way of reducing wealth inequality. Although there may be alternatives to this (such as encouraging those with little or no assets to build wealth), wealth taxes feature prominently in proposals to address wealth inequality (Maxwell and Vigor, 2005; O'Neill, 2007; Prabhakar et al, 2008). However, politicians are often wary of arguing for wealth taxes for fear of courting public disapproval. Goodin writes that: 'Inheritance taxes have long been the "third rail" of tax policy, touch them, and you are dead, politically' (Goodin, 2003, p 70).

This rule appeared to be confirmed by the then shadow Chancellor George Osborne's promise at the 2007 Conservative Party Conference to more than triple the threshold of paying for inheritance tax, from £300,000 to £1 million.[1] This pledge was widely credited as reviving Conservative Party fortunes as well as prompting the Labour government to rush through its own proposals to weaken inheritance tax (Prabhakar et al, 2008).

Economic events seemed to change this situation. A banking crisis began in December 2007, and the Labour government eventually had to bail out banks such as Northern Rock and the Royal Bank of Scotland. The UK economy went into recession and the national debt began to rise. The Office for Budget Responsibility's forecast at the June 2010 Emergency Budget notes that, excluding the money spent on financial intervention, the public sector net debt as a percentage of national income rose from 44 per cent in 2008–09 to 53.5 per cent in 2009–10. Public sector net borrowing for 2009–10 was projected to rise to £154.7 billion (Office for Budget Responsibility, 2010).

The debate between the political parties began to focus increasingly on the steps needed to reduce the deficit. Although the extent to which the deficit poses a problem for the UK economy has been questioned by some (Arestis and Sawyer, 2009), the debate between the parties nevertheless focuses currently on the combination of spending cuts and tax rises needed to close the deficit. The way that the deficit is to be reduced is a controversial matter. The bailouts for the banks in effect have meant a transfer of funds from the average taxpayer to those in the financial sector. The way the new Conservative–Liberal Democrat Coalition government has decided to reduce the deficit is through a package of around 80 per cent public spending cuts with 20 per cent tax rises. Polly Toynbee (2010) notes that this mix is regressive, as spending cuts as well as other cuts in welfare payments will hit poorer members of society hardest. She says that emphasising tax rises rather than spending cuts would be more progressive (Toynbee, 2010). The particular tax rises chosen are also important. In his Emergency Budget on 22 June 2010, Chancellor George Osborne announced that value added tax (VAT) would rise from January 2011 from 17.5 per cent to 20 per cent. This tax tends to be regressive, and analysts have questioned Osborne's claim that the Budget was a progressive package (Browne, 2010).

The recession changed the way that inheritance tax was debated. Although politicians still generally avoided calling for inheritance tax to be raised, they began to argue that now was not the time to cut this tax. During the 2010 General Election campaign, Labour and Liberal Democrat leaders Gordon Brown and Nick Clegg criticised the Conservative promise to cut inheritance tax during the televised debates between the Party leaders. They argued that in an 'age of austerity' it was perverse that the Conservatives should be offering a tax cut that would benefit the wealthiest estates in the country. There were also attempts to make a positive case for a capital levy in the run-up to the 2010 General Election by linking this to debates about the long-term funding of social care.

The 2010 General Election resulted in a 'hung' Parliament, with the Conservatives having the largest number of seats. A coalition between the Conservatives and Liberal Democrats was eventually agreed. One of the concessions that the Liberal Democrat negotiating team gained from the Conservatives was an agreement to drop its pledge to raise the inheritance tax threshold. Conversely, the Liberal Democrats had to drop their 'mansion tax' proposals to tax property worth over £2 million, although there was an initial agreement between the parties to raise capital gains tax from its rate of 18 per cent (HM Government, 2010a).

This chapter focuses on the unfolding debate about wealth tax, in particular inheritance tax. Focusing on inheritance tax is important because it is probably the most widely discussed wealth tax in the UK. Indeed, the Conservative plans to reduce inheritance tax were an issue in the 2010 General Election. Examining inheritance tax can perhaps provide some lessons or clues for the likely fate for other types of wealth tax. A study of inheritance tax is also interesting because it provides a glimpse into the changing fortunes of the political parties.

This chapter is organised as follows. First, I sketch out what is understood by wealth taxation. Second, I outline the initial opposition to inheritance tax voiced by George Osborne in 2007. I note how Labour reacted to this with their proposals on inheritance tax. Third, I record how the debate in the parties developed in the aftermath of the global recession as well as the run-up to the 2010 General Election. Fourth, I look at the controversy about the funding of social care. Fifth, some concluding thoughts are offered as to what this means for politicians trying to boost wealth taxes today.

What are wealth taxes?

Wealth taxes can take many forms (Atkinson, 1972; Boadway et al, 2010). Wealth is usually understood to refer to a 'stock' of assets and is usually contrasted with a flow of income. Wealth can cover physical assets such as housing as well as financial wealth such as savings or pensions. Taxing wealth can involve several things. First, this could mean taxing underlying holdings of wealth. For example, one might impose an annual tax on the amount of wealth that a person owns. Second, wealth might give rise to a flow of income, and one might tax these streams of income. For example, a landlord may gain rental income from a property that they own and one could tax these rents. Third, taxes could be placed on transfers of wealth. A person might transfer wealth to a child, say, and one could tax such transfers. Different taxes can be developed depending on whether a tax is placed on the donor or recipient of such a transfer. For a transfer at death, then, a tax placed on the recipient is an inheritance tax. If this tax also applies to the gifts a person receives, then this can be fashioned as a capital receipts tax. Capital receipts taxes can also be shaped in different ways depending on whether such a tax is applied over a person's life or annually. If a tax is placed on the donor, then this is an estates tax. Atkinson (1972) notes that it is important when examining taxes to consider the tax system as a whole. Tax systems can vary widely, and so wealth taxes can be combined with other taxes in many ways.

In this chapter I focus mainly, although not exclusively, on inheritance tax. In the UK, inheritance tax is a misnomer as this tax is placed on the estate rather than the amount that a person inherits. Consequently, it is more properly called an estates tax. However, public debates refer to this as inheritance tax, and I shall use the same label here for convenience.

The following two tables are taken from official statistics on inheritance tax published by HM Revenue and Customs. Table 5.1 shows the receipts from inheritance tax between 2002–03 and 2008–09, while Table 5.2 highlights inheritance tax as a percentage of overall tax revenue. For the purposes of comparison, figures are also included for income tax and VAT as a percentage of the overall tax take (income tax is the single biggest contributor to tax revenue).

The tables show that inheritance tax has played a minor role in public finances over the past decade. Although Table 5.1 shows that the tax raises a modest sum, Table 5.2 highlights that this is only a small percentage of the overall tax take. Inheritance tax thus occupies a place on the

Table 5.1: Inheritance tax receipts in the UK (£million)

	2002–03	2003–04	2004–05	2005–06	2006–07	2007–08	2008–09
Net cash receipts	2,354.1	2,504.0	2,921.9	3,259.1	3,545.2	3,823.7	2,839.2

Source: HM Revenue and Customs (2009)

Table 5.2: Selected taxes as a percentage of total tax revenues

Year	Inheritance tax	Income tax	VAT
2001–02	0.7	33.6	19.0
2002–03	0.7	33.7	19.5
2003–04	0.7	33.1	20.1
2004–05	0.8	33.1	20.0
2005–06	0.8	32.8	18.3
2006–07	0.8	33.8	18.3
2007–08	0.9	32.7	17.9
2008–09	0.7	33.7	17.9

Source: Author calculations from HM Revenue and Customs (2010)

fringes of tax policy. Despite this, this tax attracts considerable public comment. Part of this may be because inheritance tax brings together competing arguments about taxation. Parents may feel that natural justice demands that they should be allowed to pass wealth on to their children. Inheritance tax could be viewed as contradicting this 'natural right'. An offsetting argument is that merit means that wealth transfers should be taxed. Atkinson (1972) argues that merit means it is fairer to tax unearned rather than earned income or wealth. A person receiving an inheritance has not earned it themselves and so this should be taxed. Inheritance tax is a site for these (and other) arguments and this perhaps helps explain why it prompts so much controversy.

The election that never was

In 2007, Gordon Brown became Prime Minister after being elected unopposed as Labour leader after Tony Blair stepped down. Conservative leader David Cameron had a more uncomfortable time. During the summer in 2007, the UK suffered from a bout of flooding and Cameron was criticised in the newspapers for making a trip to Africa at the same time that his own Witney constituency was flooded (Merrick and Ballinger, 2007).

The period before the Party conferences in the autumn was thus marked by growing Labour confidence and Conservative unease. There were rumours that Brown was considering going to the polls and calling a snap general election in October. At the Conservative Party Conference, however, George Osborne made a promise that appeared to change political fortunes. He stated: 'The next Conservative Government will raise the inheritance tax threshold to £1 million. That means we will take the family home out of inheritance tax' (Osborne, 2007).

Osborne's promise had parallels, and was perhaps inspired in part by the campaign against the 'death tax' in the US. In 2001, a coalition of Republican activists and small businesses managed to spearhead a movement that helped repeal estate tax. This campaign energised US conservatives. Although estates tax was paid by only two per cent of estates, critics were able to mobilise public opinion against this tax. One of the features of this campaign was the labelling of estates tax as a 'death tax'. This loaded estates tax with negative meanings (Graetz and Shapiro, 2005; Rowlingson, 2008). Conservatives in the UK began increasingly to pick up on this 'death tax' term and, as we shall see below, they used this when discussing Labour proposals for paying for the long-term care of the elderly.

For the Conservative Party, Osborne's announcement seemed to galvanise their grassroots support (Webster, 2007). Although some Conservatives are sympathetic to inheritance tax, for example believing that inheritances erode a work ethic (Stelzer, 2007), more seem to favour cutting this tax. Arguably more important, however, was the effect on the Labour government. It is likely that the fear that the Conservative pledge would cost votes in marginal constituencies was a key factor that deterred Gordon Brown from calling a general election. This episode damaged Brown's credibility as a decisive leader. Furthermore, instead of defending inheritance tax, the Labour Party tried to pre-empt Conservative plans by making their own changes to inheritance tax. In his pre-budget report in 2007, Labour Chancellor Alistair Darling said that unused parts of a nil rate allowance could now be transferred between married couples or civil partners. A person whose spouse or civil partner had died could now claim the unused part of the nil rate band of their former partner. Darling stated that these changes would come into immediate effect, and would apply whether or not their partner or spouse had passed away. This meant that the combined tax-free allowance for married couples or civil partners would now be £600,000 rather than £300,000, and that by 2010 this combined allowance would rise to £700,000 (HM Treasury, 2007).

Financial crisis

At the start of 2008, the prospects for boosting inheritance tax looked bleak. The 'election that never was' created pressures to cut rather than raise inheritance tax. Although Labour's stance drew criticism from policy activists and other commentators keen to defend inheritance tax (Prabhakar et al, 2008), the government showed little sign of defending inheritance tax. Indeed, its own proposals on the transfer of nil band allowances suggests it was scared of making a case for inheritance tax. This situation changed with the arrival of the global financial crisis later in the year. In the US, problems in the 'sub-prime' housing market helped to spark a global financial crisis and global recession. A key event was the collapse of Lehman Brothers in September 2008. In the UK, there was a slump in the housing market that had knock-on effects on banks such as Northern Rock and the Royal Bank of Scotland, and the government eventually had to intervene to protect the financial system, using public funds to bail out the banks.

The financial crisis created a different climate for discussing inheritance tax. Rawnsley (2009) suggests that changed times meant that the promise had gone from an asset to a liability: 'two years is a very, very, very long time in politics. The cut to inheritance tax doesn't look so smart at all in the utterly changed political atmosphere of recessionary Britain. George Osborne's pledge has gone from being a lifesaver into an albatross around the necks of him and David Cameron' (Rawnsley, 2009).

Having been reluctant initially to defend inheritance tax, Labour politicians were now more willing to criticise Conservative proposals. Providing an inheritance tax cut to the richest estates seemed out of step with an economy trying to cope with a financial crisis, particularly when much of this crisis appeared to the public to be caused by the actions of one of the most well-paid professions, that is, investment bankers. On 2 December 2009, Gordon Brown joked in the House of Commons that the Conservative inheritance tax policy: 'seems to have been dreamed up on the playing fields of Eton' (reported in Treneman, 2009). Labour politicians increasingly began to attack the Conservative promise, and this became one of the features of their general election campaign. The Labour stance towards inheritance tax had changed between the phoney and real elections.

The debate about social care

Arguing against cuts in inheritance tax is not the same as calling for this tax to be strengthened. Labour politicians were keener to oppose Conservative cuts than to call for increases in inheritance tax. Although the recession altered the way that inheritance tax was debated, the impact of this should not be overstated. This would suggest that the 'third rail rule' was bent but not broken.

I now look at one attempt to create a more positive case for a discussion of a capital levy. A capital levy is relevant for inheritance tax debates because it is a levy on the wealth or assets owned by an individual. The discussion of a capital levy ties in with attempted reforms of the system of social care in England. The long-term funding of social care has been recognised as an important policy issue for some time. Demographic changes are one of the key pressures on the costs of providing such care. In particular, there is an ageing of the population, with a rise in the numbers of the very old (Gheera, 2010). The Office for National Statistics notes that between 1983 and 2008 the fastest population increase was for those aged 85 or over. In 1983 there were 600,000 people in the UK aged 85 or over and this rose to 1.3 million in 2008. In 2033, this figure is expected to double again, to 3.2 million, or five per cent of the population. Between 1983 and 2008, those aged

65 and over rose from 15 per cent to 16 per cent of the population, while those aged 16 or under fell from 21 per cent to 19 per cent of the population. In 2033, just under a quarter of the population is projected to be 65 or over while those aged 16 or under will be 18 per cent (ONS, 2009). Gheera (2010) notes that this ageing of the population has been combined with less willingness of family to provide informal care for elderly relatives. This means increased demand for social care. Spending on social care is projected to rise by more than 300 per cent in real terms between 2005 and 2041. Although the funding of social care was therefore already an issue before the recession, the financial crisis arguably raised its profile because of the tighter constraints now placed on public spending.

On 14 July 2009, the Labour government published a Green Paper on reforming the care and support system for people in England. The consultation ran until 13 November 2009. The government argued that the reform of the care system was needed to help cope with the rising costs of care driven by factors such as increased life expectancy. A guiding theme in the Green Paper and later White Paper was a need to create a National Care Service to complement the National Health Service (HM Government, 2010b). This focuses on a division between health and social care. In particular, the Green Paper suggests that while a National Health Service arose to provide people with a universal health service free at the point of delivery, a similar system has not arisen for the provision of social care. Under the current system, government pays for social care for those on low incomes. People are allowed to keep up to £23,000 in savings or other assets, but anything beyond this has to be used to pay for their social care. This might mean that a person has to sell their family home to pay for their care. The Labour government argued that this seemed unfair to many people.

The Department of Health also had a 'Big Care debate' that involved events in different parts of England that aimed to engage the public and different parts of the social care community on the future of the care system. Paying for social care was an important theme of the reform process. Five main options were outlined in the Green Paper. First, pay-for-yourself, where people would be responsible for paying for all of their social care. Second, a partnership approach – government would pay for a proportion of care costs, ranging from a quarter to two thirds depending on income level and then people would pay the remainder. Third, an insurance system, which is similar to partnership, with government paying a percentage of care costs, but then helping people to get insurance to pay the rest. Fourth, a comprehensive policy, where everyone over retirement age would be required to pay into a state insurance scheme. People would make an insurance payment and the state would then pay for social care. Fifth, a fully tax-funded system in which the taxpayer would pay for all social care costs. The Green Paper ruled out the first and the last of these options, saying respectively, that many people would not be able to afford to pay for their social care and that paying it through taxes would be too expensive. The partnership route was the government's favoured option.

Andy Burnham, then Labour Health Secretary, tried to build a consensus for reforming social care. Part of this had involved secret discussions between the political parties aimed at forging consensus. The Conservatives, however, withdrew from these discussions, saying that Labour was trying to smuggle in a death tax. The then Conservative shadow Health Secretary Andrew Lansley argued: 'Behind closed doors Ministers are secretly planning a death tax of up to £20,000 per head which would be levied on the estates of grieving families' (BBC News, 2010). This statement referred to an idea that if people were prepared to pay a £20,000 levy from their estate, then government would guarantee to pay for the rest of their social care needs.

The 'death tax' charge echoed criticisms of wealth taxes in US debates, and became a theme of Conservative Party commentary on Labour plans for social care (Cameron, 2010; Lansley, 2010). On 30 March 2010, the Labour government published a White Paper on building a National Care Service. The White Paper said the comprehensive payment option had the greatest public and stakeholder support and so was Labour's preferred option for paying for social care. This proposal was aimed at striking a balance between the responsibilities of citizens and the state in paying for social care. While the Conservatives recognised a need to involve both government and individuals, they wanted a system to be voluntary and not compulsory. In the run-up to the 2010 General Election they proposed a voluntary one-off £8,000 payment in exchange for free care, although care groups questioned whether this would be enough to pay for social care needs (Gheera, 2010).

The coalition agreement between the Conservatives and Liberal Democrats stated it would establish a commission to examine funding options, which would include looking at the idea of a voluntary levy option (HM Government, 2010a). In July 2010, the Health Secretary Andrew Lansley announced the establishment of the Commission on Funding of Care and Support chaired by Andrew Dilnot (DH, 2010). This Commission is to report by the end of July 2011 and it is exploring a range of funding options. Its terms of reference include the best way of paying for care as a result of partnership between the individual and the state and how individual assets can be protected against the cost of care (http://carecommission.dh.gov.uk/our-role/). The Commission might outline a capital levy as part of its recommendations. Of course, the Coalition government is not committed to accepting any or all of the recommendations from the Commission. Perhaps some clues of the likely stance of government to such a proposal might be gleaned by how it has approached wealth taxes so far.

The Coalition government

The Conservatives dropped their promise to cut inheritance tax as part of the coalition agreement with the Liberal Democrats (HM Government, 2010a). Arguably the Coalition offered the Conservatives a convenient excuse with which to abandon a promise that they increasingly saw as an electoral liability. The Coalition agreement also involved the Liberal Democrats giving up their proposals for a 'mansion tax'. This was their plan to place a one per cent levy on properties worth over £2 million.

The Coalition government has embarked on a series of other measures relevant for debates about wealth inequality. One area that the Liberal Democrats did insist on in their Coalition agreement was to raise the rate of capital gains tax. This is a tax placed on any gains people enjoy on the capital that they own. The Liberal Democrats want capital gains to be treated in a similar way to the taxation of higher incomes. Capital gains are taxed at around 18 per cent, while the top rate of income tax is 50 per cent. The Liberal Democrats argue that fairness should be central to any tax reforms. They probably hold that the 'income rich' are also 'asset rich' and so income and assets should be taxed similarly.

Conservatives are more opposed to increasing capital gains tax (Davis, 2010). Liberal Democrats such as the Business Secretary Vince Cable argue that the commitment to raise capital gains tax is an essential part of the Coalition agreement (BBC News, 2010b). In his Budget on 22 June 2010, Chancellor Osborne announced that capital gains tax was to rise from 18 per cent to 28 per cent for those people with income and taxable gains above the higher rate threshold (HM Treasury, 2010). In the same Budget in 2010, Osborne also stated his intention to introduce a bank levy from January 2011. He said that this would be set at a rate of 0.07 per cent, with an initial rate of 0.04 per cent.

Encouraging those on low incomes to build assets is an alternative way of reducing wealth inequality. However, the Coalition government reduced the scope for this particular path with the axing of the previous

Labour government's policies on asset-based welfare. One of the first acts of the Coalition government was to stop government payments into Child Trust Funds (CTF). The CTF policy provided a £250 endowment for all babies born from September 2002 into a special 18-year savings account, with children from lower-income families qualifying for a £500 payment. On 24 May 2010, the then Chief Secretary to the Treasury David Laws announced that from August 2010 government contributions to the CTF would fall to £50 for higher-income families and £100 for lower-income families. From January 2011, government contributions to the CTF would cease (BBC News, 2010c). Osborne also announced in his June Budget that the Saving Gateway scheme would not go ahead. This was a savings scheme aimed at low-income individuals and was due to be rolled out nationally from July 2010. Savings by those on low incomes were supposed to attract matching funds from government. Osborne declared that the scheme was now unaffordable.

What does this tell us about the prospects for wealth taxation?

Concern has been voiced across the political spectrum about levels of wealth inequality in the UK. This ranges from 'progressive Conservatives' to centre-left commentators such as the Fabian Society. Although there is growing consensus about the need to tackle wealth inequality, there is disagreement about how this might be done. What lessons might be drawn from the above for those keen to use wealth taxes to reduce wealth inequality?

Perhaps the first issue to address is why we should focus on wealth taxes at all. Table 5.2 shows that as a proportion of total tax, inheritance tax is a minor tax. More important taxes for most people are things such as income tax or VAT. One might be tempted to dismiss wealth taxes as a serious route for promoting wealth equality on that basis. Of course, the fact that wealth taxes such as inheritance tax have played a small role in the past does not mean that they have to continue to do so. Part of the problem with wealth taxes might be that it is easier for people to evade inheritance tax than other taxes such as VAT. Although this might explain part of the reason why inheritance tax has played a smaller role when compared with other taxes, it is likely that the tax has also been shaped by deliberate policy choices. In particular, previous governments have avoided stressing wealth taxes. Different policy choices might result in inheritance tax playing a more significant role.

Of course, governments might have avoided using inheritance tax because of a correct perception that the public is more opposed to inheritance tax than other taxes. In this sense, when seeking to raise taxes, governments act opportunistically by picking those taxes that are less likely to provoke public disquiet. Indeed, the nature of the inheritance tax debate seems to show that even in the aftermath of a recession it may be easier to defend a tax against cuts rather than call for its increase. While stopping a cut might be seen as an achievement in itself for those campaigning for wealth taxes, the small role that inheritance tax plays in current tax policy means that preventing a cut will have a limited effect on reducing wealth inequality. A more serious effort to reduce wealth inequality would seem to need higher wealth taxes.

Does this then mean that those wanting higher wealth taxes face an impasse? One of the lessons from the above examination of inheritance tax is that politicians are often keen to shy away from wealth taxes, and efforts to widen the debate can provoke a strong reaction from political opponents. However, the campaign against inheritance tax in both the UK and the US suggests that politicians might be able to shape as well as react to public opinion. In particular, opponents of inheritance tax helped manipulate public debates by developing favourable stories. Public attitudes are not fixed and might be crafted in different directions. Graetz and Shapiro (2005) suggest that it is open to defenders of wealth taxes to develop an alternative vision based on notions such as fairness.

Do politicians then have more room to make a case for higher wealth taxes among the public? I have noted above that politicians have tended to avoid wealth taxes because of a belief that this triggers greater ire among the public than other taxes. There are studies that show public unhappiness with inheritance tax (Hedges and Bromley, 2001; Lewis and White, 2006). For example, in a survey for the Fabian Society Commission on Taxation and Citizenship, Hedges and Bromley found that 51 per cent of respondents thought that inheritance tax should be abolished, while around 20 per cent thought that the threshold at which inheritance tax starts should be raised from its then level of £250,000 to at least £500,000 (Hedges and Bromley, 2001).

One issue with these studies, however, is that they tend to treat inheritance tax in isolation from other taxes. One might suggest that most taxes provoke disquiet, not just inheritance tax. Indeed, the Labour government elected in 1997 faced a serious threat to its authority to govern by a series of protests from lorry drivers and farmers protesting over fuel duty. The issue then for inheritance tax is whether this tax provokes more public unhappiness than other taxes. This can be discovered by directly comparing inheritance tax with other taxes. However, there is limited evidence on this issue. In some initial work on this topic in a focus group study I conducted on public attitudes to inheritance tax, I asked people to trade off cuts in income tax with inheritance tax, and vice versa. I found that while there was unhappiness with both sorts of taxes, some in the groups were willing to back a package of inheritance tax rises and income tax cuts. Admittedly, this is a small study and care should be taken not to exaggerate the findings. Nevertheless, there are grounds to suggest that politicians might have more room than they think to shape public opinion (Prabhakar, 2009).

Liberal Democrat proposals on a mansion tax point to one way that this might be done. For example, politicians may be able to use the fact that instabilities in the housing market were one of the chief causes of the recession to make a case for property taxation. In particular, a house price boom is often thought to have fed a period of excess borrowing, and so when house prices fell this had wider implications for finance and the economy (Watson, 2008). One might use the boom, say, to present an argument for property taxation. Politicians might argue that as property speculation is at the heart of the house price boom, and this cycle of boom and bust in the housing market is not good for the UK economy, then steps should be taken to dampen down house prices. One might do this through a property tax. Of course, this is just one suggestion and does not rule out other arguments for property taxes. However, it highlights ways that politicians might use current conditions to argue for wealth taxes.

It might be easier for politicians to argue for certain types of wealth tax over others. I noted above that wealth taxes can be shaped in a variety of ways. The focus group study I conducted on public attitudes to wealth taxes suggested that public support seemed to be more forthcoming for land or property taxation over inheritance tax (Prabhakar, 2009). One could also seek to have a combination of different wealth taxes. The Coalition government plans to engage the public over spending cuts to public services might also be extended to cover debates about the future role of taxation.

Conclusion

Wealth inequality in the UK is widely seen to be a growing policy problem. Wealth taxes seem to be an obvious tool for reducing wealth inequality. This chapter has looked at political debates surrounding perhaps the most prominent wealth tax, inheritance tax. The recession seems to have had an impact on these debates insofar as it has made it harder to press the case for inheritance tax cuts today. A key question is whether this can also be used to make an argument for rises in wealth taxes. The debate about the funding of social care seems to suggest that this is unlikely to be easy. However, it might be possible to mobilise an increase in public support, particularly if politicians embed debates about wealth taxes in wider discussions of tax policy and tie this in with the recession of 2008 to 2009.[2] Without a more concerted effort to make an argument for wealth taxes, levels of wealth inequality in the UK are likely to be untouched. This could become more important if the Coalition government's plans to cut public spending worsen wealth inequality.

Acknowledgement

The research in this chapter was funded by the Economic and Social Research Council (ESRC) as part of a project on 'Assets, Financial Education and Inequality' (RES 189-25-0002). I am very grateful for this funding. Thanks also to Chris Holden for helpful comments on an earlier version of the chapter. All remaining errors are my own.

Notes

[1] Information about inheritance thresholds can be found at www.hmrc.gov.uk/rates/iht-thresholds.htm
[2] Information on when the UK fell into recession can be found at www.parliament.uk/business/publications/research/key-issues-for-the-new-parliament/economic-recovery/recovery-from-recession/

References

Arestis, P. and Sawyer, M. (2009) 'The future of public expenditure', *Renewal*, vol 17, no 3, pp 32-42.
Atkinson, A.B. (1972) *Unequal shares – Wealth in Britain*, London: Penguin.
BBC News (2010a) 'Inheritence levy to pay for social care denied' (http://news.bbc.co.uk/1/hi/health/8505821.stm).
BBC News (2010b) 'Capital gains tax: no coalition split says Vince Cable' (http://news.bbc.co.uk/1/hi/uk_politics/8707931.stm).
BBC News (2010c) 'Child Trust Funds to be scrapped' (http://news.bbc.co.uk/1/hi/business/10146734.stm).
Blond, P. (2010) *Red Tory. How left and right have broken Britain*, London: Faber & Faber.

Boadway, R., Chamberlain, E. and Emmerson, C. (2010) 'Taxation of wealth and wealth transfers', in J. Mirrlees, S. Adam, T. Besley, R. Blundell, S. Bond, R. Chote, M. Gammie, P. Johnson, G. Myles and J. Poterba (eds) *Dimensions of tax design*, Oxford: Oxford University Press, pp 737–836.

Browne, J. (2010) *Personal taxes and distributional impact of budget measures* (www.ifs.org.uk/budgets/budgetjune2010/browne.pdf).

Cameron, D. (2010) 'Our pensioner pledge' (www.conservatives.com/news/speeches/2010/03/david_cameron_our_pensioner_pledge.aspx).

Davis, D. (2010) 'Raising capital gains tax is unfair, won't work and will punish the hard-working middle classes', *Mail Online*, 28 May (www.dailymail.co.uk/debate/article-1281755/Capital-Gains-Tax-rise-punish-middle-classes.html).

DH (Department of Health) (2010) *First step to sustainable care and support system* (www.dh.gov.uk/en/MediaCentre/Pressreleases/DH_117636).

Dorling, D. (2010) *Injustice: Why social inequality persists*, Bristol: The Policy Press.

Gheera, M. (2010) *Funding social care. Key issues for New Parliament 2010* (www.parliament.uk/documents/commons/lib/research/key%20issues/Key%20Issues%20Funding%20social%20care.pdf).

Goodin, R.E. (2003) 'Sneaking up on stakeholding', in K. Dowding, J. De Wispelaere and S. White (eds) *The ethics of stakeholding*, Basingstoke: Palgrave-Macmillan, pp 65–78.

Graetz, M. and Shapiro, I. (2005) *Death by a thousand cuts. The fight over taxing inherited wealth*, Princeton, NJ: Princeton University Press.

Hedges, A. and Bromley, C. (2001) *Public attitudes towards taxation: The report of research conducted for the Fabian Commission on Taxation and Citizenship*, London: Fabian Society.

HM Government (2010a) *The Coalition: Our programme for government* (www.cabinetoffice.gov.uk/media/409088/pfg_coalition.pdf).

HM Government (2010b) *Building the National Care Service* (www.dh.gov.uk/prod_consum_dh/groups/dh_digitalassets/documents/digitalasset/dh_114923.pdf).

HM Revenue and Customs (2009) *Inheritance tax: Analysis of receipts* (www.hmrc.gov.uk/stats/inheritance_tax/table12-1.pdf).

HM Revenue and Customs (2010) *HM Revenue and Customs annual receipts*, Table 1.2 (www.hmrc.gov.uk/stats/tax_receipts/table1-2.pdf).

HM Treasury (2007) *Meeting the aspirations of the British public: The 2007 pre-budget report and comprehensive spending review*, Cm 7227, London: The Stationery Office.

HM Treasury (2010) *Budget 2010* (www.hm-treasury.gov.uk/d/junebudget_complete.pdf).

Lansley, A. (2010) 'Death tax is alive and kicking', PoliticsHome (www.politicshome.com/uk/article/7315/lansley_death_tax_is_alive_and_kicking.html).

Lewis, M. and White, S. (2006), 'Inheritance tax: what do people think? Evidence from deliberative workshops', in W. Paxton, S. White and D. Maxwell (eds) *The citizen's stake: Exploring the future of universal asset policies*, Bristol: The Policy Press, pp 15-35.

Maxwell, D. and Vigor, A. (ed) (2005) *Time for land value tax?*, London: Institute for Public Policy Research.

Merrick, J. and Ballinger, L. (2007) 'Cameron's unity pleas as he flies in to face Tory flak', *Mail Online*, 26 July (www.dailymail.co.uk/news/article-470440/Camerons-unity-plea-flies-face-Tory-flak.html).

National Equality Panel (2010) *An anatomy of economic inequality in the UK. Report of the National Equality Panel* (www.equalities.gov.uk/pdf/NEP%20Report%20bookmarkedfinal.pdf).

Office for Budget Responsibility (2010) *Budget forecast June 2010* (http://budgetresponsibility.independent.gov.uk/d/junebudget_annexc.pdf).

O'Neill, M. (2007) '"Death and taxes": social justice and the politics of inheritance tax', *Renewal*, vol 15, no 4, pp 62-71.

ONS (Office for National Statistics) (2009) *Ageing: Fastest increase in the 'oldest old'* (www.statistics.gov.uk/cci/nugget.asp?ID=949).

Osborne, G. (2007) 'It's time for aspiration', Speech at Conservative Party Conference, 1 October (www.conservatives.com/News/Speeches/2007/10/George_Osborne_Its_Time_for_Aspiration.aspx).

Prabhakar, R. (2009) 'How can opposition to inheritance tax be weakened?', *Public Policy and Administration*, vol 24, no 3, pp 227-44.

Prabhakar, R., Rowlingson, K. and White, S. (2008) *In defence of inheritance tax*, London: Fabian Society.

Rawnsley, A. (2009) 'Gordon Brown's favourite Conservative policy pledge', *The Observer*, 29 November.

Rowlingson, K. (2008) 'Is the death of inheritance tax inevitable? Lessons from America', *The Political Quarterly*, vol 79, no 2, pp 153-61.

Stelzer, I. (2007) 'Listen to Adam Smith: inheritance tax is good', *Spectator*, 20 October (www.spectator.co.uk/essays/all/269796/listen-to-adam-smith-inheritance-tax-is-good.thtml).

Toynbee, P. (2010) 'Cuts will hit the poor hard. Tax rises would be far fairer', *The Guardian*, 12 June.

Treneman, A. (2009) 'Brown finds his voice and gets Cameron in a right old Eton Mess', *The Times*, 3 December (www.timesonline.co.uk/tol/news/politics/article6941540.ece).

Watson, M. (2008) 'Constituting monetary Conservatives via the "savings habit": New Labour and the British housing market bubble', *Contemporary European Politics*, vol 6, no 3, pp 285-304.

Webster, P. (2007) 'We will raise inheritance tax threshold to £1 million, says George Osborne', *The Times*, 2 October (www.timesonline.co.uk/tol/news/politics/article2570329.ece).

Wilkinson, R. and Pickett, K. (2009) *The spirit level: Why more equal societies almost always do better*, London: Allen Lane.

Willetts, D. (2010) *The pinch: How the baby boomers have stolen their children's future – And why they should give it back*, London: Atlantic.

Wind-Cowie, M. (2009) *Recapitalising the poor: Why property is not theft*, London: Demos.

SIX

The debate about public service occupational pension reform

Edward Brunsdon and Margaret May

Introduction

Public service occupational pensions, covering some 20 per cent of the UK population, are currently under considerable pressure.[1] Journalists and politicians have been voluble in claiming that they are 'unaffordable', 'unfair', 'gold-plated' and the privileged element of a 'pensions' apartheid' (see, for example, Cameron, 2008; Cable, 2009; Brummer, 2010). In more measured tones, academics, business lobbyists, think tanks and financial analysts have argued that they are in urgent need of reform. The Blair-Brown administrations accepted there were concerns and secured a number of negotiated adjustments to arrangements for new entrants. The changes now being advocated constitute a more radical agenda involving the restructuring of pension design and funding for both new and existing members.

Such proposals are not without criticism, however. Unions, academics and other observers have cast doubt on the quality of the reformists' case, claiming many of their revisions are based on poor analysis and unsound evidence. They question whether further amendments are necessary, ask why they are being discussed without consideration of broader social security issues, and wonder whether the proclaimed need for 'affordable' pensions is actually a Trojan horse for a further concerted effort to roll back state provision. The Coalition government's programme of fiscal consolidation and appointment of the Independent Public Service Pensions Commission (IPSPC), with an affordability, fairness and savings remit, has reified these concerns. The Commission's final report was due before the 2011 Budget, but the interim report, published in October 2010, concluded that a continuation of present arrangements was not tenable (IPSPC, 2010a).

This chapter provides a background to the Commission's appointment, outlining the case that has been made for and against further reforms by a range of analysts. It begins with a summary of Labour's amendments before looking at why change proponents ('reformists') think more radical revisions are necessary and what they are proposing. It then examines the ('critics") counter-position before briefly considering the issues emerging from the debate.

Labour's reforms

When it came to power in 1997, Labour inherited an array of public service pension schemes that differed markedly in membership, eligibility, entitlements, funding and governance (illustrated in Table 6.1). Constituted by statute, they comprised three groups:[2]

- centrally run, multiple employer, schemes: the Principal Civil Service Pension Scheme (PCSPS), Armed Forces Pension Scheme (AFPS), Teachers' Pension Scheme (TPS) and NHS Pension Scheme (NHSPS);[3]
- programmes for single authorities or groups, for example, the Research Councils Pensions, UK Atomic Energy Authority Superannuation, Judicial Pension Schemes and Members of Parliament (MPs') Parliamentary Contributions Fund;
- the Local Government Pension Scheme (LGPS), the Police and the Firefighters' Pension Schemes, which were centrally regulated but locally administered.[4]

All apart from the AFPS were contributory and, with the main exception of the LGPS, operated as pay-as-you-go (PAYG) plans.[5] They were principally defined benefit (final salary) rather than defined contribution schemes and thus protected their membership from the investment, annuity and longevity risks associated with the latter.[6]

For much of the post-war period they ran in tandem with private sector schemes that were also predominantly defined benefit. In both instances they reflected a general belief that occupational pensions were key aspects of organisational strategy contributing to recruitment, retention, reward and exit management (May and Brunsdon, 1999). They also served to compensate for relatively low pay in state agencies and operated as icons of supportive workplaces, setting standards for other employers. Buoyed by macro-economic conditions, union pressure, a minimal state pension and government policy, active membership rose from 6.2 million in 1953 (3.1 million in each sector) to 12.2 million in 1967 (8.1 million in the private and 4.1 million in the public sector). Private sector membership subsequently declined to 5.7 million by 2000. By contrast and in spite of Conservative retrenchment in the 1980s and 1990s, public service coverage continued to grow, reaching 4.5 million (GAD, 2003).

By the late 1990s, however, mounting expenditure on both state and public service pensions was causing concern. There were also additional anxieties about declining coverage in the private sector and the drift from defined benefit to less expensive defined contribution plans (typically involving reduced employer contributions and benefits). Labour's election gave it an opportunity to review provision. Its tack was to address and reform the state, private and public service occupational and personal pension pillars independently. Proposals for public services plans centred on raising the normal pension age (NPA) – a key means of reducing future expenditure. In the case of the major PAYG plans (the NHS, Civil Service and Teachers' Pensions Schemes) this involved a rise from 60 to 65 years for new entrants, only agreed after strike threats, lengthy negotiations with the union and concessions on other aspects of the schemes. Any hopes the government held of extending the initiative to existing members were quashed by the nature and strength of this resistance.

Negotiations concerning the LGPS followed a slightly different path. It already had an NPA of 65 but a special clause, the 'Rule of 85', permitted members to retire with a full pension at 60 provided their length of service and age added up to at least 85. Again following protracted discussions, industrial action and the offer of concessions, the government succeeded in getting this rule abolished for new entrants. It continued to recognise the need for lower NPAs in the Uniformed Service Pension Schemes necessitated by the physical demands of the work, but nonetheless secured increases from 50 to 55 for the Police Pension Scheme and from 55 to 60 for the Firefighters' Pension Scheme; it also increased the NPA to 65 for all Uniformed Service Pension Scheme members who left employment early.

Further reforms were negotiated and implemented on a scheme-by-scheme basis, reflecting their varied and complex nature. There was some cross-scheme leverage as in the cost capping and sharing agreements with the unions representing the four main programmes,[7] but there were also separate settlements with individual nuances (see Table 6.1). In general, apart from the new entrants' NPA and cost sharing, the main changes can be summarised as: increases in members' contribution rates (varying by scheme and tiered in some instances); changes to the accrual rates for new entrants (with scheme differences); removal of the additional lump sum payment other than through commutation; tighter ill health rules; and enhancements to survivors' pensions.[8] Labour also implemented a number of actuarial changes, including: the use of SCAPE methodology ('superannuation contributions adjusted for past experience') for determining employer/employee contributions in PAYG plans; ensuring compliance with international accountancy standards; and new codes of practice on investment and governance for the LGPS.[9]

Labour claimed the reforms made public service arrangements more sustainable and attractive. But with the average value of pensions in the main schemes only falling from 24 per cent to 21 per cent of salary (PPI, 2008), others were unconvinced, viewing them as a wholly 'unsatisfactory compromise' (Record et al, 2009). With increasing numbers of retirees (and dependents) drawing pensions (3.9 million in 2009), and burgeoning government deficits, both the Liberal Democrats and the Conservatives called for a review similar to the 2004 Turner Inquiry on private sector pensions. This was realised in the Coalition agreement and the appointment in June 2010 of the IPSPC chaired by Lord Hutton. It was an expedient move by the new government, particularly given the surge in reports and articles questioning the effectiveness of Labour's amendments.[10]

The case for further reform

Most analyses make the case for additional reform by focusing on evidence-based assessments of the major PAYG schemes.[11] Substantively, there are those that focus on particular facets of provision with others offering more broad-based appraisals. Many combine this with a revelatory critical style in which disclosures about 'hidden' or 'disguised' costs and inequities are blended with warnings about the urgent need for change. Collectively, their arguments centre on three key themes: increasing longevity costs; transparency, liabilities and contributions; and issues of fairness.

Increasing longevity costs

The reasoning here is straightforward: longer periods spent in retirement are raising public service pensions costs to the point where they are becoming unaffordable (Small, 2009). Building on a combination of demographic and financial data, it is suggested that people in the UK

Table 6.1: Public service pension scheme reforms (2006–10)[a]

	NHS[b]	Teachers	Civil Service	LGPS	Armed Forces	Police	Fire
Eligibility							
Normal pension age	60-65	60-65	60-65	Unchanged 65; rule of 85 abolished for new entrants (with transitional protection)	Unchanged 55	50 with 25 years' service (below 50 with 30 years) to 55 (57/60 for higher ranks)	55 (from 50 after 25 years' service) to 60
Entitlements							
Pension basis	Unchanged: final salary	Unchanged: final salary	Final salary to career average	Unchanged: final salary	Unchanged: final salary	Unchanged: final salary	Unchanged: final salary
Accrual rate	80ths to 60ths	80ths to 60ths	60ths to 43rds	80ths to 60ths (all members)	69ths (91ths after 22 years) to 70ths[c]	60ths (30ths after 20 years) to 70ths	60ths (30ths after 20ths) to 60ths
Additional lump sum	3 × pension to optional in exchange for reduced pension	3 × pension to optional in exchange for reduced pension	Optional in exchange for reduced pension	3 × pension to optional in exchange for reduced pension (all members)	No change: 3 × pension	Commutation to 4 × pension	60ths (30ths after 20 years) to 60ths
Draw down option	Yes	Yes (all members)	Yes (all members)	Yes (all members)	No	No	No

continued

	NHS[b]	Teachers	Civil Service	LGPS	Armed Forces	Police	Fire
Late retirement enhancement	Introduced	Introduced	Introduced	Introduced (all members)	No	No	No
Secondary benefits							
Survivors' pensions	Extended to include non-legal partners and payable for life						
Survivor's pension on death in retirement	Unchanged: 160th of member's pension	Unchanged: 160th of member's pension	160th to 3/8ths of member's pension	Unchanged: 160th of member's pension	50% to 62.5% of member's pension	Unchanged: 50% of member's pension	Unchanged: 50% of member's pension
Ill health benefit	1-tier to 2-tier	1-tier to 2-tier	Unchanged: 2-tier	1-tier to 3-tier	1-tier to 2-tier	1-tier to 2-tier	Unchanged: 2-tier
Funding							
Employee contribution rates[d]	6% (5%) to 5%–8% (all members)	6% to 6.4% (all members)	Unchanged: 3.5%	6% (5%) to 5.5%–7.5%	Unchanged: non-contributory	11% to 9.5%	11% to 8.5%
Employer contribution rates	14% (England and Wales)	14.1% (England and Wales)	16.7% 24.3%	13.2%	29.4%	24.2%	26.5%
Cost sharing and capping	Introduced	Introduced	Introduced	Introduced	No	No	No

Notes: [a] Adapted from PPI (2008, Table 1) and IPSPC (2010a, Table B1); changes apply to new scheme entrants only unless otherwise specified.
[b] Salaried staff scheme; self-employed staff have a career-average scheme.
[c] For 'other ranks', officers have higher rates.
[d] Where a range is shown, contributions vary with pay.

are living longer – men 20 years beyond 65 and women slightly longer, and in 50 years' time this could rise to 30–35 years. Moreover, the ratio of pensioners (people 65+) to workers (those 20–64) is also projected to increase from 27 per cent to between 47 and 49 per cent in 50 years' time, leaving fewer workers to meet the tax burden of escalating pension costs (PSPC, 2010). Annual payments to PAYG public service retirees were £25.4 billion in 2009-10 and are estimated to increase to £79 billion by 2059-60. The claim that this increase is unsustainable is supported by figures expressing the 'accrued pension liabilities'[12] as a proportion of gross domestic product (GDP). PSPC (2010), for instance, suggests that at 31 March 2008, accrued liabilities of PAYG schemes were estimated at between £770 billion and £1,176 billion, that is, between 53 per cent and 81 per cent of 2008 GDP. Adding to the consternation, the Audit Commission (2010) reported that English LGPS funding levels fell from 84 per cent in 2007 to 72 per cent in 2010, primarily due to poor investment returns.

Transparency, liabilities and contributions

Whether operating independently or used to strengthen longevity concerns, the lack of 'transparency' in pension reporting is also an issue for reformists. The PAYG schemes are again the focus of attack, the argument being that governments have disguised the size of their liabilities and subsidies either by not presenting financial information in a clear and accessible way or by not communicating the 'true costs'. The former charge is largely unelaborated, the latter more complex issue centres on the discount rates employed in: (a) the measurement of accrued PAYG liabilities and (b) the setting of employer pension contributions.

Like the funded LGPS and private sector plans, the PAYG schemes provide estimates of accrued liabilities in their annual resource accounts. To present their cost in today's monetary values involves utilising a discount rate.[13] The government currently employs a rate based on AA corporate bonds (of an appropriate term and currency) that keeps it in line with the financial reporting standards required in company statutory accounts. Reformists, however, feel this is inappropriate. They argue that a more pertinent measure would be the current market rate for index-linked gilts, that is, the rate related to the cost of government borrowing (Record, 2008). In July 2010, the real yield on index-linked gilts was 0.8 per cent above retail price index (RPI) inflation and was substantially less than AA bond yields of 1.8 per cent (3.2 per cent in

2009). Given that the lower the yield, the higher the estimated future liabilities, the change proponents' use of index-linked gilts means, in their valuation, that the government in 2009–10 underestimated the real cost of pension liabilities by between £240 billion and £406 billion (PSPC, 2010).

In the calculation of PAYG pension contributions, the Treasury charges employers (and employees) the proportion of salary that it believes covers pension payments many years into the future. It then pays out whatever the contractual obligations are to current pensioners. At present it uses SCAPE methodology to estimate contributions normally over a three- to four-year period. This combines a number of variables in making its estimates, for example, mortality trends, employment projections, future earnings and inflation rates. Also embedded in the calculation is a discount rate derived from the Treasury's social time preference analysis (STPR).[14] It is this aspect of the methodology – a rate of 3.5 per cent after price inflation – that reformists oppose. In Treasury terms, it is an appropriate long-term rate based on historical patterns of returns on gilts. For change proponents, it is artificial, underestimates the true annual cost of providing pensions and allows: 'the government to fool both itself, and its employers and employees, into thinking that pensions are cheaper than they actually are' (Record et al, 2009, p 39).

Again, they maintain that the market rate for index-linked gilts should be used in calculating employers' pension contributions. Their reasoning is that, if there were no contributions, the government would have to meet its PAYG pension commitments by issuing gilts. Pension contributions are thus a means of deferment. As 'gilts would have been issued at the market rate, such a deferral can be seen as an investment in gilts ... also at the market rate' (Record, 2007, p 27). The significance of this argument is in the subsequent valuation of the contributions. PSPC (2010) estimates, for example, that whereas civil servants were receiving 58 per cent of salary on pre-reform benefit scales and new entrants will receive 43 per cent, the combined employee and employer contribution rates are much less – between 18.6 per cent and 30 per cent. Similar discrepancies between benefit and contribution levels apply in the other major PAYG schemes. While new entrants' pensions are worth around 45 per cent of salary, employees and employers are jointly paying around 20 per cent of salary in contributions. It is the Treasury (and ultimately the taxpayer) that is required to meet the cumulative shortfall, to which public sector employers and employees remain largely oblivious (CBI, 2010).

Fairness

Adding to the pressure for change are concerns about the lack of 'fairness' in current arrangements. Of the several dimensions to this notion that could be addressed, reformists focus on cross-sector inequities and unfairness in the distribution of contributions and benefits within particular schemes. Dealing with them sequentially, they maintain that there is an: 'enormous and growing divide between the quality of pensions on offer to the 20% of the workforce in the public sector and ... the remaining 80%' (PSPC, 2010, p 30) in the private sector which, they argue, is 'unfair' if not 'discriminatory'. They support this contention using two key types of data: selective detail from individual public service schemes and cross-sector comparisons based on intra-sectoral generalisations.

The former are typically employed in the populist press and pressure group reports to attack the pension benefits of senior managers in particular schemes, as in claims that: 'One in three mandarins has a £1 million pension and retires years earlier than private sector staff' (Barrow, 2010) or 'Record numbers retire on £1 million NHS pension pots' (TaxPayers' Alliance, 2008). More general commentaries highlight: 'staggeringly generous' benefits; 'munificent' accrual rates of particular post-reform schemes; low normal retirement ages; low employee contribution rates; and 'benevolent' secondary benefits. While much is made of these illustrations, there is little recognition of historical and contractual scheme diversities, the extent to which pensions were negotiated in broader reward settlements or the degree to which such factors might dilute their comparative value.

The same can be said of the intra-sector generalisations. Particular change proponents acknowledge the complexity of generalising only to ignore its impact on the comparisons they subsequently make. Unfettered by problems of inference, they see increasing unfairness evidenced in differences in:

- *Coverage:* which has continued to fall in the private sector, with just 42 per cent of male and 31 per cent of female employees in schemes in 2008 and only five per cent in micro businesses (five or less employees) compared to 85 per cent in public services.
- *Pension design:* while public service defined benefit schemes have grown over the last decade, many companies have replaced defined benefit with defined contribution plans for both new and existing members.

- *Entitlements:* typically, private sector defined contribution plans have lower levels of employer and employee contributions and realise less certain and lower levels of retirement income. Moreover, in spite of Labour's reforms, some 56 per cent of public scheme members still have an NPA of 60 compared with 25 per cent in the private sector.
- *Labour market conditions:* the disparities in pension opportunities distort mobility and competition; beyond this, under Fair Deal provisions, when public services are outsourced, private and third sector employers have to provide matching pensions for public service transferees at the full not subsidised cost (CBI, 2008; Record et al, 2009; Small, 2009; PSPC, 2010).

It is these inequities that form the basis of a pensions apartheid that is: 'real, unfair and urgently in need of change' (Taylor, 2009, p 21).

Within public service schemes, reformists concentrate on two further inequities: the uneven entitlements between new entrants and existing members consequent on Labour's reforms and those deriving from the design of final salary, defined benefit, pensions. In the case of the first, they do little more than identify the inequities and recommend harmonisation largely through extending new entrants' terms to existing members (for future benefit accrual). They devote much more attention to the imbalances generated by the final salary scheme design itself and the key factors in the pension calculation – the length of pension membership and real salary growth.

What they have argued is that final salary designs are more generous as a percentage of salary to those whose earnings increase quickly and who remain in the scheme for longer. So, for example, employees with regular promotions and associated salary increases not only obtain higher working incomes and pensions than those with flatter career paths but also receive a higher proportion of their pension contributions (Record et al, 2009). Similar examples of disparity arise when comparing those with continuous scheme membership as against early leavers, those who take career breaks (for example, to raise children) or switch between defined benefit and defined contribution plans when moving jobs across the sectors. In effect, the inequities amount to forms of cross-subsidy between different members of the same scheme.

The proposed reforms

The modifications advanced by reformists, like their arguments, vary in magnitude and depth (see Table 6.2). Some look for changes within defined benefit schemes, others their replacement, while many incorporate both within a catalogue of options. Underwriting these proposals are the general objectives of increasing parity within and across the sectors and, crucially, making pensions more affordable. Much less attention is paid to transitional strategies or, with notable exceptions, transitional costs.[15]

The prerequisite for most is full transparency in financial reporting which, as previously indicated, means using the market rate for index-linked gilts as the discount rate. Once the true costs become clear, the need for further change will, they suggest, be indisputable. Seeking sustainability, they have proposed reforms to eligibility and entitlements that take in further increases in NPA in line with rises in the state pension age, changes to accrual rates and benefit adjustments. The last includes increasing fairness and reducing costs by replacing final salary with career average schemes, spreading 'cap and share' across the sector, reductions in secondary benefits, capping pensionable pay and a permanent pension cap.

Benefit modifications have been accompanied by proposals to change scheme funding as well. These range from general calls to rectify the 'imbalance' between employer, employee and taxpayer payments to recommendations for fully tiered contributions. On grounds of parity, there have been demands for employers and employees to meet the full annual costs of pensions and, further, that both PAYG and funded schemes should be contracted into the State Second Pension. In terms of the LGPS, there are arguments for unitised or cross-scheme investment arrangements and even the amalgamation or merger of funds which, it is held, would cut costs, lead to greater parity and create a stronger investment portfolio.

Those advocating more fundamental reforms do so through scheme redesign. In their eyes, final salary, defined benefit schemes should be replaced because the possible adjustments within that design cannot secure the required cost reductions or overcome cross-sector inequities. Indeed there is even doubt about the career average option being effective (CBI, 2010). Greater credence is given to a shift to defined contribution schemes as: 'the only way of bridging the pensions' apartheid and ensuring the sustainability of public finances' (Taylor, 2009, p 21). Caution is expressed, however, about the particular arrangements that would be suitable.

Switching to conventional defined contribution schemes would bring multiple benefits, particularly: the transfer of longevity risk to employees; greater employer cost control; savings for taxpayers; and greater

Table 6.2: Proposals for future public sector pension reform

Proposal	Rationale
Accountability and reporting	
Full transparency in establishing/reporting the 'true' costs of PAYG and funded schemes, and their value to employees	Prerequisite for other reforms; requires use of the market rate for index-linked gilts as the discount rate in calculating outstanding liabilities and employer and employee's annual contributions; ensures stakeholders' cognisance of scheme costs and benefits
Eligibility and entitlements	
Increase NPA for new and existing PAYG and funded scheme members and update in line with state scheme	Helps meet rising longevity costs; parity with state and private sector pensions
Tighten accrual rates for new and existing PAYG and funded scheme members/close future accruals for existing members	Affordability/cost savings; equity; accords with increases in NPA
Benefits	
• Replace final salary with career average provisions	In-scheme fairness; cost savings (average earnings and hence pension over a career typically lower than the final salary)
• Permanent salary ceilings	Affordability/cost savings (higher earners' pension only accrued on part of salary)
• Permanent pension caps	Affordability/cost savings
• Increase lump sum component commutation	Affordability/cost savings
• Further reductions in secondary benefits	Cost savings; incentivises self-provision
• Conditional indexation	Affordability/cost savings
Funding	
Contributions	
• Increase employee contributions	Eases funding pressures; demonstrates value of pension
• Fully tiered contributions	Affordability; greater in-scheme equity
• Increase high earners' contributions	Affordability; greater in-scheme equity
• Employers and employees to meet full annual costs of pensions	Extends risk-sharing; affordability; parity with private sector
• Removal of contracting out from state pension	Parity with other schemes; short-term savings
Funded schemes only	
• Unitised/group investment arrangements	Economies of scale; stronger investment profile; equity across LGPS
• Merger of funds	Ditto

Table 6.2: continued

Proposal	Rationale
Design	
• More sustainable defined benefit schemes (via changes in funding and/or benefits – see above)	Affordability: low transition costs
• Cross-scheme harmonisation	Cross-scheme parity; simplification; economies of scale
• Notional defined contribution scheme	Shifts longevity risks to employees, lowering tax burden; remains PAYG, protecting members from some of the risks of conventional defined contribution plans
• Collective defined contribution scheme	Similar to conventional defined benefit schemes, but investment risks spread across membership generations and away from taxpayers
• Cash balance scheme	Remains PAYG and therefore fewer transition costs; reduces investment risks of conventional defined contribution accounts as guaranteeing notional growth in line with general economic indicators; transparent; contributions adjusted annually to ensure sustainability
• Hybrid schemes	Combine core (but less generous) defined benefit plan with optional funded or notional defined contribution add-ons; taxpayer savings; greater employee choice/flexibility/self-provision through defined contribution options
• Switch from PAYG to funded defined contribution arrangements for new accrual	Taxpayer savings, employee choice/flexibility
• Complementary/flexible workplace savings schemes (eg corporate ISAs)	Enabling employees to 'top up' pension savings; cost savings
Governance	
• Independent agency to administer PAYG schemes	Economies of scale; increased accountability

portability, transparency and cross-sector parity. It is also held to be better attuned to contemporary organisational needs and employee lifestyles. But it could also lead to significant problems. To maintain benefit levels would involve large rises in employer and employee contributions, while reducing benefits could lead to significant numbers leaving schemes. Moreover, if the PAYG schemes were switched to funded defined contribution arrangements then employee and employer contributions would need to be invested in individual employee accounts rather than, at present, being used to pay the pensions of retired members. The government/employers would therefore have to find additional money, entailing higher taxation, additional borrowing or spending reductions to carry on paying existing pensioners and accrued entitlements. Estimates suggest that the cost could be as much as £20 billion a year and would only decline gradually over the century.[16]

Unwilling to absorb such costs, the more radical change proponents have considered other defined contribution options and a range of hybrid plans. The most favoured is a notional defined contribution scheme for current PAYG plans. Here employer and employee would pay contributions credited to individual accounts. Unlike other funded schemes, the money would not be invested in financial markets but in: 'independently-managed, ring-fenced funds, separate from [other] public funds and budgets' (CBI, 2010, p 11) that could be drawn on to provide benefits for current pensioners. The value of the employee accounts would increase in line with selected benchmarks, for example, government gilt yields and/or the consumer price index (CPI). At retirement, the accumulated value would be used to buy an annuity out of the funds. This is seen as a way of overcoming the issue of double payment; eliminating the financial uncertainty of market investment; providing more predictable pension outcomes; and, because of its simplicity, encouraging greater employee understanding and involvement.

The case against further reform

It is fair to say that in pointing to the costs of inaction, reformists have not dwelt on the possible upheavals that their proposals could trigger or the resistance they might meet. They have sought to develop a picture of the dangers of current arrangements and explain why their urgent overhaul is necessary. Although not always in the detail or terms in which the case was originally made, the critics challenge the descriptions, calculative processes and supposed evidential support of these arguments and go beyond this to question the assumptions, 'oversights' and 'absences' in their analyses.

Increasing longevity costs

Critics have generally accepted the government's longevity projections and focused instead on the question of whether, in the light of these, the Blair–Brown amendments are sufficient to manage the rising costs. Here many employers as well as unions held with the Trades Union Congress (TUC) (2010a), which, drawing on National Audit Office (NAO, 2010) data, argues they are appropriate and proportionate particularly when added to more recent public service pay freezes and planned job cuts.

Transparency, liabilities and contributions

Change proponents accused the Treasury of disguising the size of PAYG liabilities and subsidies either by (a) unclear presentation or not making financial information accessible, or (b) not communicating their 'true costs'. Critics are genuinely puzzled by (a), particularly given the improvements in reporting over the last decade (Keogh, 2008). They point to the scheme data now disclosed in annual financial statements and the valuation reports used to set employers' contribution rates. From these, analysts could gather: the valuation of scheme liabilities; current service costs; the level of required contributions; and the cash outflows to meet pension payments. The valuation reports show the demographic and financial assumptions used to underpin the contributions setting process. There is also a supplement of Treasury budgetary data detailing short- and medium-term financial forecasts for these schemes. If this criticism can be upheld at all, it is that not all the information is consolidated and published to an annual timetable and some of it is in a form that might be difficult for scheme members and/or taxpayers to comprehend.

The second, more fundamental, complaint concerns the choice of discount rate. Critics maintain that the use of market rates for index-linked gilts is impractical as it involves employing a potentially volatile rate that, on a day-to-day basis, could lead to large variations in the estimates of liabilities and required contributions. More importantly, however, they think market discount rates are a 'distraction' (Stanley, 2010a) whose relevance is overstated in the cost and contribution calculations. Citing the NAO (2010) in support, they claim that 'projected cash payments' is the more relevant calculation for costing

PAYG schemes. It is a measure that focuses on annual cash requirements rather than aggregate payments, includes pensions to be earned in the future (rather than just liabilities accrued), can be expressed as a proportion of GDP in terms of its affordability and is unaffected by discount rates. It is basically an issue of cash flow addressing the future call on the budget and on borrowing.

It is this difference of calculation that underpins the diverse views on whether PAYG pensions are affordable. Change proponents using aggregate liability figures valued in terms of gilt market rates argue that they are 'out of control' or, in extremis, run the risk of causing national bankruptcy (Silver, 2010). Their critics feel this is a massive distortion. Employing NAO-projected cash payment figures, expenditure on the four main PAYG public service schemes are forecast to rise from 1.7 per cent of GDP to 1.9 per cent between 2018–19 and 2033-34 before falling back below 1.7 per cent by 2059–60 (TUC, 2010a). While these are substantial fluctuations in costs, they are a far cry from the extremely negative scenario painted by reformists.

Is there greater strength in the complaint about the rate used to set employer/employee contributions? Critics think not. Current gilt rates would be equally impractical and as much a distraction. The discount mechanism used by the Treasury is a long-term rate based on historical patterns of returns on gilts. What is more, changing it would either involve removing the calculation from current Treasury guidance used in estimating a wide range of revenue, capital and regulatory projects or, more radically, requiring the Treasury to rethink what has been a comprehensive and effective method of evaluation.

Fairness

Addressing the issues around fairness, much of the critical attention has involved responses to the 'myths' (GMB, 2010a) 'peddled by the right-wing press' and politicians (UNISON, 2009). Employing a range of empirical sources, employers, unions and academics have argued that far from being gold-plated, most public service pensions are quite modest (LGA, 2010). Half of all NHSPS pensioners receive less than £4,000 a year (GMB, 2010b), and only 2.5 per cent receive a pension of more than £40,000 (NAO, 2010). The average payment in the LGPS is £4,033 a year, that for women only £2,600 (GMB, 2010a). In the TPS it is less than £10,000 (NUT, 2010), with 0.2 per cent receiving over £40,000. Civil servants' pensions average £6,500 (TUC, 2009), with just 1.8 per cent getting over £40,000. Critics thus deny that pension payments are out of control or unaffordable and contend that the notion of a pensions apartheid, if not distasteful hyperbole, is empirically and theoretically inaccurate.

A related line of criticism concerns the ease with which reformists make cross-sector comparisons. Cutler and Waine (2010) have argued that drawing differences between public (defined benefit) and private (defined contribution) sectors or between privileged (public) and underprivileged (private) is ill conceived. Not only is there a continuing population of active, deferred and pensioner members in private sector, defined benefit schemes but, like public service plans, there is also a wide variety of eligibility, entitlement and funding differences. When these are coupled with the multiplicity of private sector defined contribution schemes, it becomes clear why critics see the construction of a dichotomous universe as a gross oversimplification only made possible by the suppression of empirical diversity.

This diversity is also exploited in disputing particular inequities identified by reformists. So, for instance, on the NPA comparison the GMB argues there is a difference between the 'formal' NPA (60 for members of the 1995 section of the scheme) and 'actual' NPA which is an average of 62 years (GMB, 2010a). Again, contribution rates cannot be seen in general terms as there are major variations within both sectors that defy the uniform descriptions used by change proponents. In the case of the umbrella LGPS, for example, there are 100 pension funds each with its own actuary setting employer contribution rates; these range from 14 per cent to 25 per cent. In the NHSPS there are now two sectors to the scheme (1995 and 2008) with potentially different levels of employer costs and, also, different levels of benefits.

Little is said about the incongruities *within* public service schemes but whether this is because critics feel vulnerable or because the same issues beset the private sector as well, is not clear. They do, however, pick up on two other inequities that are absent from reformist analyses, namely, the cross-sector differences between the low paid and the disparities between the pensions of private sector directors and senior managers and the rest of the workforce. The first is seen as a consequence of pension coverage and design; only 20 per cent of private sector workers earning between £100 and £200 a week are members of pension plans (and it is likely to be a defined contribution scheme) whereas 70 per cent in the public sector are in defined benefit schemes (TUC, 2009). The second is an inequity initiated by private sector executives. Unlike senior managers in the public services who are in the same schemes as other employees, the TUC PensionWatch survey (2010b) reveals that many company directors are in defined benefit schemes to which the rest of their workforce are denied access. What is more, these provide sizeable benefits. Of the 102 leading UK companies analysed, 63.5 per cent offered defined benefit schemes to at least some of their directors. Their average pension pot was £3.8 million, the annual pension payment £227,726 and their NPA was 60. For directors in defined contribution schemes, the average company contribution was £134,760 a year and the average contribution rate was 19 per cent, about three times that typically available to other employees in the sector. Given the way in which these figures are presented in annual accounts, the TUC argues that if there is a case for greater transparency, it is here.

Beyond these analytical gaps, critics pose a more general question. Why seek to run down public service pensions when the real issue is the lack of coverage and inadequate defined contribution schemes in the private sector? While the question is genuine, it is also geared to provoking reformists into revealing underlying agendas. With the Coalition government it appears relatively clear – they want to 'justify' reforms as one cost-cutting arm of an austerity strategy. Some (see, for example, Stanley, 2010b) also suspect that scale-backs are part of its planned outsourcing of public services to a plurality of alternative providers, a move that requires the modification of Fair Deal guidance and more compatible pension arrangements (ACEVO, 2010).[17]

The specific reform proposals have largely been ignored by critics, presumably on the grounds that if they can undermine the case for change they do not need to consider the detail. They have, however, challenged one key proposition, namely, the suggested replacement of PAYG defined benefit with notional defined contribution schemes. They view this in a similar way to conventional schemes, that is, to retain equivalent benefit levels is likely to mean further large increases in employee contribution rates and the exit of current, low-paid members. If, on the other hand, current contribution levels were maintained, it would lead to reduced benefits and, given the public sector pay structure, presage increasing demand for social security payments (TUC, 2010a).

Emerging issues

Public service schemes are clearly at a crossroads. To listen to change proponents they are in need of radical reform. To heed their critics, Labour's modifications dealt with the concerns about the schemes' affordability and most of the issues regarding transparency. For them, the question of fairness is one of improving private sector provision rather than redesigning public services arrangements. When the debate is relocated to a broader politico-economic landscape, however, it takes on a different complexion. Here it is not just a matter of weighing up the intellectual quality of the arguments on both sides as the extent to which the case for reform resonates with the wider political agenda. Where the government stands is evident from its commitment to expenditure cuts and the reshaping of the state's role, its revision of pension indexation from 2011 – thereby reducing average pension value by around 15 per cent (HM Treasury, 2010) – and the acceptance of IPSPC's recommendation of a three per cent increase in employee contributions (apart from the AFPS).

Indeed, there was concern that the interim report might favour the governmental and reformist agendas with its endorsement of the need to alter the balance between employer, employee and taxpayer contributions, its request that government reconsider discount rates and the recognised unfairness inherent in final salary arrangements. However, its dismissal of some of the change proponents' arguments, recognition of the 'modest' nature of public service pensions, awareness that cross-sector disparities are largely the result of declining private sector provision, and doubts about conventional defined contribution plans left critics feeling that the Commission had navigated a clever, if uncertain, path between the extremes of the debate. Whether they will feel the same way after the final report is, at the time of writing, a matter of speculation. From its call for evidence (IPSPC, 2010b), it will be looking at options for structural reform. Given its continuing concerns about fairness and the management of risk, and the government's desire to both increase mobility between the public and private sectors and to reduce barriers to different ways of providing public services, the end result could well involve significant changes in scheme design and funding.

Moving beyond how the Commission might act, there are other issues that do not appear to be within its remit, notably: the role of pensions in reward packages; their impact on recruitment and retention in public services; the possible effects of the National Employment Savings Trust (NEST); and the repercussions of the pay freeze and of changing pension taxation. But these matters pale in significance against a much broader concern. Why is the government continuing the tradition of its predecessors and appointing a Commission whose terms of reference are confined to a specific sector of pension provision? The debate and the IPSPC's interim report both give strong indications that a more holistic view of occupational pensions is required and, to provide an integrated strategy, it should also include state pensions and personal savings. Only once this is done will government have an opportunity of overcoming the fragmented pension policies and piecemeal changes of the recent past.

Notes

[1] This comprises 5.4 million active (contributing) members, 3.9 million receiving pensions and 3.5 million with deferred entitlements (ONS, 2010).

[2] This analysis excludes what are often termed 'quasi-public' schemes in which the government owns all or part of the pension-sponsoring company (for example, the Civil Aviation Authority, the Post Office and the Royal Bank of Scotland and Lloyds Banking Groups) or where it underwrites all or part of the pension plans for ex-nationalised industries (for example, British Telecom and British Coal). Such arrangements differ in their constitution, regulation and management from those discussed here.

[3] AFPS is UK-wide. The Civil Service has separate schemes for Great Britain and Northern Ireland. The NHSPS and TPS have a scheme for England and Wales, and separate schemes for Scotland and Northern Ireland.

[4] There are 89 LGPS funds in England and Wales, 11 in Scotland and one in Northern Ireland that are administered, managed and funded at a local level.

[5] In PAYG schemes, contributions from current employees and their employers are used to pay today's pensions, with the Treasury making or receiving balancing payments to cover the difference. By contrast, funded schemes, for example, LGPS, are financed from investments built up from employer and employee contributions.

[6] In defined benefit schemes, the rules specify the rate of benefits to be paid. The most common are salary-related schemes in which benefits are based on the number of years of pensionable service, the accrual rate and either final salary or career average calculations. In defined contribution (or 'money purchase') arrangements, the amount of pension received usually relies on the level of contributions paid into a fund, the investment performance of the fund and the annuity rate that converts the fund into an income for life. Whereas investment risks in defined benefit schemes are the responsibility of the employer, in defined contribution plans these, along with annuity and longevity risks, are borne by the employee.

[7] The cost sharing and capping mechanism was introduced in order to transfer, from employers to employees, the risk of future additional costs

resulting from changes in factors such as pensioners living longer than previously expected. The mechanism is designed to be used at routine actuarial valuations.

[8] The MPs funded pension scheme (PCF) was subject to a separate review process, which recommended a move from a final salary to career average provisions with a cap on Exchequer contributions at 15.5 per cent of payroll and a floor of 5.5 per cent (RBSS, 2010).

[9] See note 14.

[10] Of particular note here is the report published just weeks before the appointment of the Hutton Inquiry – by the Public Sector Pensions Commission (PSPC, 2010). Published by the Institute of Directors, its contributors included many of the leading reformists such as: Ros Altmann, Philip Booth, Andrew Lilico, Neil Record, Malcolm Small and Corin Taylor.

[11] Much less attention is given, either directly or through implication, to the funded schemes.

[12] Accrued liabilities is a measure of the value, in today's money, of all pension entitlements to be paid in the future that have been earned to date.

[13] Pension liabilities are normally less than the total projected future payments because money set aside now is expected to benefit from income and capital growth. The annual rate by which a future payment is reduced to give its present value is the 'discount rate'. The higher the discount rate, the lower the sum needed to meet future pension commitments. See IPSPC (2010a, p 73) for a fuller explanation.

[14] For more details on SCAPE and the social time preference analysis see HM Treasury (2003).

[15] The noted exceptions are PSPC (2010) and, to a lesser extent, CBI (2010).

[16] The estimated costs were drawn from IPSPC (2010a). Similar concerns arise for the LGPS. On moving to a conventional defined contribution format, contributions currently employed to pay existing pensions as well as the £4 billion to £5 billion a year investment for future retirement liabilities would be invested in individual defined contribution accounts, thus leaving a major gap in terms of who pays for current pensioners (LGA, 2010). If, however, the costs for existing pensioners could be met by selling pension fund assets or raising contributions, then a shift might become financially feasible if not politically acceptable.

[17] Under the Treasury's Fair Deal guidelines and related LGPS measures, employers are required to provide public sector transferees with a pension

broadly comparable to that which they would have received as public sector employees.

References

ACEVO (Association of Chief Executives of Voluntary Organisations) (2010) 'Letter to Lord Hutton ...', 1 September (www.acevo.org.uk).

Audit Commission (2010) 'Local government pensions in England: an information paper', 29 July, London: Audit Commission (www.audit-commission.gov.uk).

Barrow, B. (2010) 'One in three mandarins has a £1 million pension and retires years earlier than private sector staff', *Mail Online*, 1 January (www.mailonline.co.uk).

Brummer, A. (2010) 'The scandal of the pensions' apartheid: how public sector pension pots soared while everyone else suffered', *Daily Mail*, 19 April.

Cable, V. (2009) *Tackling the fiscal crisis: A recovery plan for the UK*, London: Reform.

Cameron, D. (2008) Question and answer session at the Manchester Chamber of Commerce, 27 November, reported by A. Barker (http://blogs.ft.com/westminster/2008/11).

CBI (Confederation of British Industry) (2008) *Clearing the pensions fog: Achieving transparency on public sector pensions costs*, Brief, December, London: CBI (www.cbi.org.uk/pensions).

CBI (2010) *Getting a grip: The route to reform of public sector pensions,* Brief, April, London: CBI (www.cbi.org.uk/pensions).

Cutler, T. and Waine, B. (2010) *Moral outrage and questionable polarities: The attack on public sector pensions,* Working Paper No 80, Manchester: Centre for Research on Socio-Cultural Change, University of Manchester.

GAD (Government Actuary's Department) (2003) *Occupational pensions schemes 2000: Eleventh Survey by the Government Actuary,* April, London: GAD (www.gad.gov.uk).

GMB (2010a) 'Myths exposed', *GMB Pensions Update,* September (www.gmb.org.uk).

GMB (2010b) 'NHS pension scheme England and Wales: ten key facts', *GMB Pensions Update,* April (www.gmb.org.uk).

HM Treasury (2003) *The green book: Evaluation in central government*, London: HM Treasury.

HM Treasury (2010) *Spending review 2010*, Cm 7942, London: The Stationery Office.

IPSPC (Independent Public Service Pensions Commission) (2010a) *Interim report*, 7 October, London: The Stationery Office (www. pensions.commission@hmtreasury.gsi.gov.uk).

IPSPC (2010b) Call for evidence for final report, 1 November (www. pensions.commission@hmtreasury.gsi.gov.uk).

Keogh, N. (2008) 'Public sector pensions'"perceived" transparency gap' (www.publicservice.co.uk).

LGA (Local Government Association) (2010) 'Councils respond to TaxPayers' Alliance pension report', LGA Press Release, 4 March (www.lga.gov.uk).

May, M. and Brunsdon, E. (1999) 'Commercial and occupational welfare', in R.M. Page and R. Silburn (eds) *British social welfare in the twentieth century*, Basingstoke: Macmillan, pp 271-98.

NAO (National Audit Office) (2010) *The cost of public service pensions*, London: The Stationery Office.

NUT (National Union of Teachers) (2010) 'Gold plated pensions: the government must be joking', *NUT News*, 10 July (www.nut.org.uk).

ONS (Office for National Statistics) (2010) 'Membership of occupational pension schemes is 27.7 million', *Statistical Bulletin*, 28 October (www. ons.gov.uk).

PPI (Pensions Policy Institute) (2008) *An assessment of the government's reforms to public sector pensions*, London: PPI (www.pensionspolicyinstitute. org.uk).

PSPC (Public Sector Pensions Commission) (2010) *Reforming public sector pensions: Solutions to a growing challenge*, London: Institute of Directors.

RBSS (Review Body on Senior Salaries) (2010) *Review of the Parliamentary Contribution Pension Fund 2010*, Cm 7926, Report No 72, London: The Stationery Office.

Record, N. (2007) 'Public sector pensions', *The Actuary*, May, pp 26-7 (www.the-actuary.org.uk).

Record, N. (2008) 'Sir Humphrey's Legacy: an update', *IEA Current Controversies*, Paper 27, London: Institute of Economic Affairs (www. iea.org.uk).

Record, N. and Smith, J.M, edited by Kay, L. (2009) *Public sector pensions: The UK's second national debt*, London: Policy Exchange.

Silver, N. (2010) *A bankruptcy foretold 2010: Post-financial-crisis update*, London: Institute of Economic Affairs (www.iea.org.uk).

Small, M. (2009) *Roadmap for retirement reform 2008*, IoD Policy Paper, London: Institute of Directors (www.iod.com).

Stanley, N. (2010a) 'The CBI on public sector pensions', *Touchstone Blog*, 16 April (www.touchstoneblog.org.uk).

Stanley, N. (2010b) 'The big scary numbers in the IoD report', *Touchstone Blog*, 6 July (www.touchstoneblog.org.uk).

TaxPayers' Alliance (2008) 'Record numbers retire on £1 million NHS pots', 24 February (www.taxpayersalliance.com).

Taylor, C. (2009) *Pensions apartheid: The problem, the cost and the tough choices that need to be made*, IoD Policy Paper, London: Institute of Directors.

TUC (Trades Union Congress) (2009) *Decent pensions for all*, London: TUC (www.tuc.org.uk).

TUC (2010a) 'TUC evidence to the independent public service pensions commission', 30 July (www.tuc.org.uk).

TUC (2010b) *Pension Watch 2010: A TUC report on directors' pensions in the UK's top companies*, London: TUC (www.tuc.org.uk).

UNISON (2009) 'Pensions scheme closures disastrous', *UNISON News*, 5 September.

SEVEN

Welfare to work after the recession: from the New Deals to the Work Programme

Dan Finn

Introduction

Over the past decade there has been a radical change in the British welfare state. In addition to its traditional role in assessing eligibility for and paying cash benefits, the social security system is now expected to play a far greater role in preparing working-age people for, and connecting them to, the labour market. The objective has been to create an active benefit system that reinforces work incentives and reduces costs and 'welfare dependency'.

There were three core components of the welfare to work strategy pursued by the previous Labour government. The first element involved the creation of an 'employment first' system where most working-age people who claim benefits were expected to engage, at least initially, with employment-related services. The second component was to 'make work pay' through tax credits, a national minimum wage and a variety of other services to assist with childcare and the transition into work. The final element involved reforms to employment programmes and services and to the institutions and agencies that delivered them.

Throughout the economic downturn and despite increased unemployment, the Labour government continued to implement its strategy for increasing work-related requirements in the benefit system. Between 2008 and 2010 job search requirements were gradually extended to lone parents with children aged over seven, and from 2008 a new employment and support allowance (ESA), with a stricter work capacity assessment (WCA), replaced earlier disability benefits for new and repeat claimants. Over the same period front-line job centres coped with marked increases in the number of people seeking jobs and claiming benefits and the Department for Work and Pensions (DWP) introduced a succession of employment and training programmes targeted at those most at risk from the recession – those made redundant and young people entering the labour market.

Following the 2010 General Election the Coalition government has also placed welfare reform at the heart of its plans for reducing worklessness and public expenditure. The strategy will involve 'transformational change' to a welfare state now represented as 'a vast, sprawling bureaucracy that can act to entrench, rather than solve, the problems of poverty and social exclusion' (DWP, 2010a, p 9). Planned activation reforms will continue but the Coalition is replacing Labour's employment programmes. New activation requirements will be integrated with the Coalition's own distinctive policies, which comprise a Universal Credit, to replace all working-age benefits, and the introduction of a single Work Programme where contracted providers will be paid for securing job outcomes.

This chapter considers the activation and employment programme reforms introduced as part of the Labour government's welfare to work strategy and analyses the impacts they had. It also assesses the reforms that will now be taken forward by the Coalition government that will shape the welfare to work system over the next decade.

Unemployment and working-age benefit claimants

After recovery from the Second World War the UK enjoyed at least two decades of full employment. This started to change in the 1970s and the impact of the recessions that the UK experienced in the early 1980s and early 1990s was to shake out large population groups from secure employment, contributing to rising unemployment *and* economic inactivity. The data in Figure 7.1 illustrate that the number of people claiming unemployment benefits responded more or less speedily to the economic cycle, but the total number of people claiming all types of working-age benefits increased after each recession.

There has been much debate about the factors driving these changes but from the 1980s evidence emerged suggesting that, among other things, the organisation and delivery of unemployment insurance and other benefits for working-age people was weakening work incentives and increasing unemployment durations (Layard and Nickell, 1998). What became apparent was that at each turn of the economic cycle long-term unemployment had been 'ratcheting' upwards. In the late

1960s, for example, the proportion of those unemployed for over a year averaged 17 per cent; by the mid-1980s it increased to 40 per cent. The 'risk' of unemployment had increased only slightly but it had become 'a much more serious event because it takes so much longer, on average, to get back into work' (Nickell, 1999, p 22).

This increase in long-term unemployment was attributed in part to earlier institutional reforms and cuts in staffing in the public employment service implemented by the first Thatcher government. It was suggested that organisational priorities in the benefit system and in separate 'high street' job centres meant that job matching, monitoring and employment assistance were not linked to receipt of benefit or targeted at claimants. The combined effect was to make the system 'passive', allowing people to drift into long-term unemployment.

From the 1980s a new consensus emerged among UK policy makers about the need to activate the benefit system initially for the unemployed but more recently for lone parents and people with health conditions and/or disabilities. By the 1990s the concern with long-term unemployment was also enmeshed in another narrative that linked the passivity of the benefit system to a wider increase in 'welfare dependency'.

Figure 7.1: Trends in main out-of-work benefits, 1979–2009

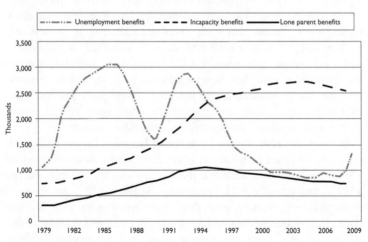

Source: Office for National Statistics, online DWP statistics

Activating the unemployed, lone parents and people on disability benefits

A new approach to 'activation' emerged in a series of reforms introduced by Conservative governments from the mid-1980s. These initially created a 'stricter benefit regime' and culminated in 1996 in the replacement of Unemployment Benefit with Jobseeker's Allowance (JSA) (Price, 2000). Unemployed claimants have since been required to enter an individual Jobseeker's Agreement, specifying the steps they intend to take to look for work, provide fortnightly evidence of job search, and take other steps to improve their employability including participation in job search programmes or training schemes, with sanctions likely for those who fail to comply.

Lone parents, by contrast, had not been required to look for work until their youngest child was aged 16, and people claiming disability benefits were required only to show they were incapable of regular employment. While the flow into these benefits was relatively steady from the 1980s, the average duration of such benefit claims increased, reaching nine years for those on disability benefits (Anyadike-Danes and McVicar, 2008). Most people claiming such 'inactive' benefits had little contact with employment-related services.

In 1997 the Labour government commenced a decade-long programme of incremental reform. Mandatory 'work-focused interviews' (WFIs) for *all* working-age claimants when first claiming a benefit were introduced in 2001. Subsequently ministers increased the frequency with which targeted groups had to attend such WFIs and required participants to develop an 'action plan' with a personal adviser (PA). Most people are now not paid benefit until they attend an initial WFI at a job centre and a person on an 'inactive' benefit who fails to attend subsequent interviews may have their benefit reduced. In 2008 further activation reforms were implemented with JSA job search requirements extended to lone parents, initially for those with children aged over 12, but by 2010 for those whose youngest child was aged over seven.

In 2008 the ESA replaced Incapacity Benefit for new and repeat claimants. During a 13-week assessment phase people who wish to claim ESA are paid the same benefit as JSA, during which they must undergo a WCA and attend a WFI. Those who qualify for ESA are allocated either to a 'support group' or work-related activity group, with the latter currently required to complete an 'action plan' and attend a further five WFIs with a PA. Those in the support group, with the most severe health conditions and/or disabilities, are not subject to activity requirements and are paid a higher rate of weekly benefit. Between October 2008 and November 2009 six per cent of the 686,500 claims assessed by the WCA qualified for the support group, 14 per cent entered the work-related activity group, 39 per cent were found fit for work and 37 per cent left ESA before completing the assessment. Another four per cent were still in the assessment process (DWP, 2010b).

New Deals, Employment Zones and Pathways to Work

Labour's activation reforms were introduced alongside a variety of New Deal employment programmes. The core principle of the programmes for the unemployed was that individuals were 'guaranteed' intensive employment assistance after a particular duration of unemployment, and at that point JSA claimants had to be placed in a job, leave benefit or participate in a full-time employment activity. From 1998 young people aged between 18 and 24 had to enter the New Deal for Young People (NDYP) after six months' unemployment and, from 2001, those aged between 25 and 50 years had to participate in the 'New Deal 25 plus' after 18 months (ND25+). The only alternative for the unemployed involved Employment Zones (EZs), which were introduced in 15 high unemployment areas in 2001. Zones were wholly delivered through contracted organisations that were largely paid by results.

Between 1997 and 2001 the government introduced a succession of voluntary but less comprehensive New Deal employment programmes aimed at lone parents, people with disabilities and unemployed people aged over 50. The most significant programme development for those on inactive benefits was, however, the introduction of Pathways to Work in 2003. This was targeted at people claiming disability benefits and combined PA support, employment and some health assistance, with a series of six mandatory WFIs. The programme was extended nationally in 2008 and targeted in particular at those claiming the new ESA. 'Pathways' was first delivered through job centres in 40 per cent of the country but the subsequent national expansion was contracted out to external providers. Providers were awarded contracts that made a significant proportion of their income dependent on placing participants in jobs sustained for longer than 13 weeks.

Governance and delivery of activation and the New Deals

New Labour's benefit reforms experienced some parliamentary opposition but there was less critical scrutiny of organisational reforms, with Labour ministers seeking to create a 'single work-focused gateway' to the benefit system. An experimental phase culminated, in 2001, in the creation of Jobcentre Plus (JCP). At the same time departmental reform created DWP. Together these organisations were responsible for integrating vacancy matching, job search support and the administration of benefit payments for working-age people.

JCP became operational in April 2002. Within two years most claims were administered through a network of 'contact' and 'benefit delivery' centres and benefits paid directly into bank accounts. Employment services and the monitoring and enforcement of activity requirements were handled through integrated job centres. The structure and layout of the offices were redesigned to reinforce the principle that everyone has an obligation to support themselves, in particular through paid employment. The office integration process was completed in 2008, at a cost of just under £2 billion, when the last of over 800 front-line job centres was opened (NAO, 2008).

JCP is accountable to DWP ministers who 'steer' the agency through annual performance targets. The agency is expected to process and pay benefits accurately and promptly, and to fill employer vacancies, but its primary task is to 'activate' claimants through an 'employment first' approach, and job outcomes are a core measure of success.

Until 2007 JCP had responsibility for awarding and managing most contracts with external providers apart from those that were part of the then government's 'contestability' strategy, where the DWP contracted directly with providers to deliver EZs and private sector-led New Deals (covering about 10 per cent of provision). There was much dissatisfaction with JCP control of the contracting process and the poor performance of external providers. In 2007 all procurement of contracted-out employment programmes was transferred to the DWP.

Over a 10-year period the British employment assistance system had undergone a transition from a highly centralised bureaucracy providing standard services to a more complex public–private delivery network 'steered' by ministers and DWP policy makers through performance targets and contracts.

Impact of the New Deals and EZs

The DWP commissioned impact assessments of activation reforms and each of the New Deals. Such evaluations were typically undertaken within the first three to five years of programme implementation. The studies reported overall positive impacts of moderate size with, for example, NDYP raising outflows into work by five percentage points (a 20 per cent increase) with the costs (net of benefit payments) being outweighed by the measurable savings (van Reenen, 2004). The New Deal for Lone Parents was also found to have doubled the employment chances of participants and increased the proportion of lone parents exiting benefits by between 20 and 25 percentage points (Cebulla et al, 2008).

Impact evaluations of the ND25+ were undertaken as part of studies that compared their effectiveness with EZs. The findings suggested that both interventions increased employment transitions but that EZs appeared to be more effective, with the final study reporting that eight per cent more 25- to 50-year-old participants started jobs in the EZs, and 10 per cent more retained those jobs at 13 weeks, than in comparable New Deal areas (Griffiths and Durkin, 2007).

The comparative success of EZs was given policy significance as it suggested that contractors who were given greater operational flexibility and paid on job placement results produced better outcomes. An assessment of the findings concluded that where EZ provision differed 'most sharply is not so much in the content of provision but in the quality, intensity and customer orientation of services, including the flexibility and continuity of adviser support into employment, the amount of practical assistance available, the extent of employer engagement and the degree of discretion and experimentation possible' (Griffiths and Durkin, 2007, p 34). Less attention was given, however, to the finding that EZs were more expensive or to other evaluations that suggested JCP delivery could be more effective, as in the smaller Action Teams for Jobs programme (Casebourne et al, 2006).

Studies of the New Deals and EZs found that they worked best for those with a better employment record and were least effective for those who had few qualifications, were unemployed longer and had an unstable pattern of employment. Another important finding was that in both EZ and New Deal areas, many of the jobs that had been sustained for over 13 weeks 'had not lasted in the longer term' (Hasluck et al, 2003, p 1).

These more negative findings were amplified in other independent and less favourable assessments of the employment impact of the New Deals.

Some suggested that the reduction in JSA long-term unemployment prior to the recession simply reflected the strength of the economy, and others pointed out that many of those who participated did not get jobs and a significant minority of those who got jobs did not retain them. Poor performance was greatest in older industrial areas, inner cities and social housing estates, and this was attributed to the interplay between local labour market conditions, the characteristics of participants and the weaker capacity of local delivery systems (EEC, 2000; Sunley et al, 2005).

Problem of employment retention and skills

By 2005 overall job entry rates from the New Deals had started to decline and, with unemployment continuing to fall, PAs and programme providers struggled to place clients with more complex barriers into employment. At the same time there was increased concern about the 'recycling' of a significant number of people who had now participated in New Deal programmes several times. This was part of a broader concern with the more general issue of 'repeat claims', where data revealed that of the 2.4 million new JSA claims each year, around two thirds, or 1.6 million, were repeat claims, and that one third of all JSA claims each year were repeat claims from those with low or no qualifications (Leitch, 2006, p 118).

With JSA unemployment falling to levels not seen since the early 1970s policy attention began to focus on the issue of employment retention and the 'low pay, no pay' cycle. There was concern also that while employment rates had increased, so had in-work poverty, and there appeared to be limited opportunities for progression. The Leitch Report (2006), a review of the skill needs of the UK economy, highlighted the poor integration of skills policies with the 'employment first' welfare to work system. It found that a significant cohort of claimants had few transferable skills or qualifications and had 'become trapped in low paid, entry-level work' (Leitch, 2006, p 118). The report also pointed out that there were poor levels of employer engagement so that much of the welfare to work system was not responding to the market effectively, and this seemed to be one cause of the deteriorating performance of the New Deals.

These combined trends reinforced pressure for a 'fresh start' for the New Deals and for a new approach to tackling the combined issues of job placement and employment retention for working-age benefit claimants.

Labour's welfare to work strategy and the welfare market

Between 2006 and 2008 the Labour government announced new objectives and commissioned a series of high-level reviews of its welfare to work and employment policies (see, for example, Harker, 2006; Leitch, 2006; Gregg, 2008). The renewal of the government's strategy involved further changes in the design and delivery of welfare to work programmes; the activation of more working-age claimants through a 'personalised conditionality regime'; improved integration of employment and skills provision; and some devolution of the design and delivery of programmes seeking to improve the ways in which national services could be adjusted to fit local circumstances.

One significant element of the renewed strategy involved the creation of a 'managed welfare market'. The Freud report (2007) proposed a major restructuring of employment programmes and the benefit system and recommended that job search requirements be extended to lone parents and intensified for people on disability benefits. It suggested little change to JCP-delivered work first services for the short-term unemployed but radical change for the longer-term unemployed and 'harder to help' groups who should be transferred to and assisted by external organisations.

The report stressed, however, that existing contracting arrangements were inadequate. They too often specified process rather than outcome, and the contracts had restrictions on recruitment and expenditure that prevented providers from expanding provision or being rewarded for overachievement. Contracts were small scale, had a multiplicity of requirements and start and finish dates, and were too short, discouraging providers from making longer-term investment in their service delivery capacity. The report proposed instead a different performance-based model based in part on the lessons from EZs.

The basic principle of the proposed contracts was that the government and providers would share the savings in benefits over a three-year period that accrues when a participant obtains employment. Phased payments would be made for sustained employment for up to three years, with the possibility of additional payments for pay progression and the achievement of vocational qualifications. Successful providers would be awarded long-term regional contracts, subcontracting as they wished with smaller providers. These 'multi-billion pound' contracts would encourage larger for-profit and non-profit organisations to borrow and invest in advance, knowing they would have an income stream from outcome fees over an extended period. The proposed sequence of outcome payments would also ensure that providers had an incentive to invest in improving the skills and longer-term employability of participants and some of the risks associated with investment in employment assistance could be shifted from government to the private sector.

The government welcomed Freud's proposals and subsequently the DWP (2008) published an overall commissioning strategy outlining how the welfare market would be reformed, with the Department procuring future employment programmes through 'prime providers' on contracts that would last for five years, with the possibility of two-year extensions. Implementation commenced with the Flexible New Deal that started to replace New Deal and EZ provision for the JSA unemployed in 2009. Labour ministers were more wary, however, about longer-term outcome payments and funding employment programmes directly from benefit savings, simply announcing that the approach would be tested through pilot schemes in 2011.

Welfare reform and the recession

The recession and subsequent increases in unemployment added new pressures to the delivery system, although it was significant that the then government continued to implement its activation policies. JCP in particular had to manage the administrative burdens created by the increased influx of unemployed claimants and adapt its service delivery strategy to cope with the effects. At its peak, in February 2009, the number of JSA claimants entering the system increased to 95,000 a week, compared with 45,000 a week prior to the recession. Paradoxically, as the number of claimants flowing into job centres increased, so did the number of job placements secured by JCP, enabling the agency to meet its targets and ministers to emphasise the importance of maintaining the focus on speedy transitions back into employment.

The previous Labour government had also introduced a range of provisions targeted at the newly unemployed and those at risk of redundancy. This combined additional resources for JCP, investment in the 'rapid redundancy service' and new job search courses and training programmes. Other measures were targeted at those groups experiencing the most severe impacts, especially young people and areas with existing high levels of joblessness. The most significant was the counter-cyclical Future Jobs Fund that created community benefit projects offering temporary minimum wage jobs primarily to young unemployed people.

The cumulative impact of JCP employment first practices, the additional programmes and the flow of JSA claimants off benefits and into work was that prior to the UK 2010 General Election, the number of people claiming JSA fell for five months, by nearly 100,000, to 1.51 million in April 2010. The Labour government argued that the combination of its employment interventions and wider economic stimulus package meant that the 2008/09 fall in employment and increase in unemployment was less severe than that which followed the recessions of the early 1980s and 1990s, even though the fall in economic output was swifter and greater (DWP, 2009). Such relative success did not, however, mask the fact that unemployment had increased significantly and did not help Labour avoid defeat in the 2010 General Election.

Conservative and Liberal Democrat policies in opposition

As New Labour reformulated its welfare to work strategy the main opposition Conservative Party was developing its own proposals. In two policy documents, released in 2008 and 2009, the Conservatives articulated their critique of the government's strategy, especially the perceived failure of the New Deals, the inability to reduce the number of people claiming disability benefits and the weakening of work and family formation incentives, in particular through the impact of what it called the 'couple penalty' in the benefit and tax credit systems. The Conservatives embraced Labour's plans to increase employment requirements and related sanctions, but argued they were more capable of delivering the outcomes desired (Conservative Party, 2008, 2009).

The Conservatives fully embraced the proposals in the Freud report and, in a minor political 'coup', they recruited the author, ennobled him, and he was subsequently appointed Minister of Welfare Reform in 2010. The Conservatives now supported the use of prime contractors to work with the longer-term unemployed and those on disability benefits, and these contractors were to be paid by results from future benefit savings. In contrast with their earlier policy of privatising JCP, job centres were to be retained to deliver benefit administration and initial employment assistance (Conservative Party, 2001).

This development work culminated with the publication of *Get Britain working* at the Conservative Party Conference in 2009. This outlined proposals to reduce the number of people claiming disability benefits, increase sanctions and introduce a single Work Programme. There would also be specific emergency measures to tackle increased unemployment. The proposals were included in the 2010 manifesto.

Another development concerned the prominence attached to the proposals emanating from The Centre for Social Justice, the policy think tank established in 2004 by Iain Duncan Smith, a former Conservative Party leader (see Chapter One by Hugh Bochel and Chapter Three by Nick Ellison, this volume). The Centre for Social Justice combined policy analysis and development with support for projects tackling poverty and social exclusion.

In 2006, just after he became leader of the Conservatives, David Cameron commissioned the Social Justice Policy Group, hosted by The Centre for Social Justice, to formulate policy proposals on key social problems, including 'economic dependency'. The subsequent report criticised the poor targeting of Labour's employment programmes, 'weak and ineffective work expectations' and undue complexity and disincentives in the benefit system (Social Justice Policy Group, 2007). The report called for a radical simplification of the benefit system and was followed, in 2009, by the publication of *Dynamic benefits* (The Centre for Social Justice, 2009). This proposed the introduction of a Universal Credit that would replace existing benefits and, by increasing earnings disregards and creating a unified withdrawal rate of 55 per cent, provide greater work incentives. The report estimated that Universal Credit would produce long-term savings but would require £2.7 billion for implementation. In the run-up to the election the Conservative leadership were careful not to commit to implementing these proposals.

The remaking of Liberal Democrat policies was first signalled in the publication of *The Orange Book* in 2004, a collection of 'modernising' essays contributed by many of those who entered ministerial office in the Coalition, including Nick Clegg (Marshall and Laws, 2004). Among other things the publication was seen as marking a turn towards a more market-oriented approach to public sector and welfare state reform.

The Party's approach to welfare reform was more fully articulated at their 2007 Annual Conference. The policy proposed a series of tax and benefit reforms to reduce means testing and poverty alongside major reforms to working-age benefits and the delivery of employment assistance services. The Party proposed the introduction of a single working-age benefit that, with greater employment assistance, would seek to 'halve' the number of people on Incapacity Benefits by 2020. They also proposed that JCP be replaced with a 'slimmed down First Steps Agency', which would assess and pay benefits and be responsible for claimants during the first three months of unemployment. At that point responsibility for providing employment assistance would be contracted out and delivered by 'local, voluntary and private' organisations. There was also to be a 'spend to save' mechanism that paid providers out of future benefit savings but, unlike the Conservatives, the Liberal Democrats appeared to favour locally based commissioning rather than the prime contractor model. The Party acknowledged also that a 'powerful system of monitoring and sanctions/rewards for providers' would be needed to ensure high quality provision (Liberal Democrats, 2007, p 21).

The subsequent Coalition agreement was perceived as reflecting only Conservative proposals but the Liberal Democrats' policy trajectory also dovetailed with the proposed approach to welfare reform and the Work Programme.

Welfare reform, expenditure cuts and Universal Credit

The Coalition agreement put welfare reform at the heart of the new government's programme. The ambition is to further transform the welfare system by making work pay, implementing stricter WCAs, reinforcing the conditional nature of jobseeker benefits and paying welfare to work providers from the benefit savings they generate by getting people into sustained employment. By 2011 the DWP will have implemented the Work Programme, and by 2013 the first people are expected to be claiming Universal Credit, with the full transition to the new system taking around five years to complete (DWP, 2010c).

The legislation to create the Universal Credit will transition through Parliament in 2011. It will create a single integrated working-age credit comprised of a basic allowance, with additional elements for children, disability, housing and caring. The aim is to incentivise work with no one facing a marginal deduction rate of over 70 per cent, with financial adjustments ultimately being made in 'real time' if proposed reforms to IT systems deliver the anticipated functionality. There will also be a stronger system of conditionality and sanctions, with jobseekers expected to follow a 'claimant commitment' or face escalating financial penalties. Sanctions will also be applied to lone parents and people with disabilities in the work-related activity group, as had been proposed by the previous government. There is also a commitment that no one will experience an immediate reduction in cash entitlement at the point of transition to Universal Credit, and £2 billion has been set aside to fund full implementation (DWP, 2010c).

In the meantime continued implementation of Labour's reforms means that by April 2011 all lone parents on Income Support whose youngest child is seven will be transitioned to JSA or other benefits. They will also now be followed by those whose youngest child is aged over five who will be transferred between January and July 2012. At the same time couples with children whose youngest child has reached the age of five, and where neither partner has a disability or has a health condition which prevents them working or is a carer, will need to make a joint claim to JSA, requiring both partners to actively seek work.

Another change concerns reassessment of an estimated 1.5 million people receiving disability benefits to determine who is capable of work and who qualifies for ESA. The process will commence in April 2011 and up to 10,000 people a week will face reassessment over the following three years. This will overlap with the introduction of more stringent assessments for the personal independence payment that will begin to replace disability living allowance (DLA) from 2013/14. About half of those claiming out-of-work disability benefits also receive DLA. There have already been many criticisms of the accuracy of the WCA, undertaken by Atos Healthcare, the sole DWP contractor (Harrington, 2010). Implementation of both these assessment processes is likely to be punctuated by controversy, with many appeals.

The impact of these reforms will also be shaped through the expenditure reductions announced in the 2010 Emergency Budget and subsequent Comprehensive Spending Review. The cumulative impact of benefit cuts will reach an annual £18 billion by 2014/15, and the impact on poorer people will be compounded as they rely more on the public services that are also being reduced. The benefit changes include myriad measures, with the most significant impact likely to be felt by those claiming Housing and Council Tax Benefits, such as those long-term claimants of JSA who will lose 10 per cent of their rent assistance from April 2013. Other cuts will impact on those claiming ESA for over a year, who will lose entitlement unless they satisfy a means test, and young people who lose the education maintenance allowance. These reductions have been partly balanced by increased child tax credits for those on lowest earnings and by a reduction in income tax.

Employment assistance and implementing the Work Programme

The new activation and benefit regime will be implemented by a smaller JCP and an expanded welfare to work industry. By mid-2011 a network of prime contractors or consortia will deliver services through the core Work Programme. This 'core' is being supplemented by additional *Get Britain working* measures, including 'work clubs', 'work for yourself' and other initiatives targeted at the young unemployed. Additionally, a Community Work Experience programme will be mandatory for those unemployed for over two years.

The Work Programme will recruit primarily the young and long-term unemployed who would previously have entered the New Deals. It will cater also for those disability benefit claimants who are transitioned into JSA and those who receive ESA and are subject to work activity requirements. Some will participate on a voluntary basis but most will be mandated to attend and will have to undertake the activities specified by the advisers they engage with.

Prime contractors will have flexibility in designing personalised support and will set their own minimum standards that will subsequently be monitored by DWP. Successful contractors will have been selected on a combination of criteria, including price and quality. These organisations will be funded largely on the basis of securing sustained employment comprised of an initial attachment fee, job outcome payments and then longer-term sustainment payments. The DWP expects to let 40 Work Programme contracts across 18 package areas, covering Great Britain, with at least two providers in each area. Individual contracts will be worth between £10 and £50 million a year and it is estimated that in total between two and three million people will participate over the five-year contract period (DWP, 2010d).

Work Programme contracts transfer the risk of placing long-term claimants in sustained employment to prime contractors. They also require these organisations to be responsible for managing their own supply chains, with the future for most specialist and locally based third and public sector providers being as subcontractors.

Conclusion

The evidence suggests that during a period of sustained economic growth Labour's combination of activation, New Deal and 'make work pay' programmes contributed to falling unemployment and poverty reduction. Progress was undermined, however, by the instability of many entry-level jobs and because many of those who secured sustained employment found they had joined the working poor. In the subsequent period of increased unemployment the welfare to work delivery system proved resilient and, in combination with the stimulus package and new employment measures, the increase in unemployment was less severe than that experienced in earlier recessions.

The Coalition government represents both continuity and change. It will continue implementation of activation reforms that will see most working-age benefit recipients required to engage in employment assistance. It has ended some employment programmes, such as the Future Jobs Fund, faster than Labour anticipated, and has terminated the New Deals. The replacement Work Programme is, however, based on the outsourcing principles developed under Labour, albeit the scale and pace of implementation has been accelerated.

The greatest change concerns implementation of the Universal Credit that will replace existing benefits and tax credits with the aim of reducing complexity and increasing work incentives. The ambition is laudable but the design and implementation problems will be formidable, as earlier Labour experience illustrates, for example, when delivery problems mired the relatively more simple integration of means-tested support for children in an employment-oriented tax credit system (Ombudsman, 2007; Finn et al, 2008). Also, although there is a commitment that there will be no immediate losers in the transition to the new system, it will be introduced alongside significant reductions in varied out-of-work benefits. In combination the proposed reforms and cuts will have mixed impacts, improving assistance and work incentives for some, while reducing out-of-work incomes for many (Browne and Levell, 2010).

There are also risks to the wider implementation of the Coalition's strategy. The welfare to work delivery system has been under intense pressure and is likely to be stretched further when simultaneously implementing activation reforms, a new benefit system and the Work Programme. There is, in the short term, likely to be disruption as JCP adjusts to spending cuts and employment programme delivery is negatively affected both by the transitional and early service delivery problems associated with major recontracting exercises and by the impact of increased caseloads at a time when securing job outcomes may be more challenging.

Work Programme prime contractors may subsequently deliver the outcomes anticipated but there could be other consequences for service delivery. Evidence from studies of welfare markets in Australia and the Netherlands suggest that cost-efficiency gains and increased transitions into employment have, at least in part, been offset by high transaction costs and reductions in service quality (Finn, 2008). In both countries, incentive-based contracts have been associated with 'parking' harder to help service users, where providers focus most effort on those closest to the labour market.

A distinctive contributory factor to such parking has been price competition – now abandoned in Australia and the Netherlands. The risk of using price competition in the Work Programme is that it is likely to encourage unrealistic cost estimates that will limit provider capacity, stifle innovation and encourage parking.

Another risk concerns the potential for implementation or market failure, where providers either reduce services, go out of business or seek to withdraw from unprofitable contracts, and government has no choice but to intervene and ensure service continuity. The British Pathways contracts, which induced providers to 'bid low and promise high', were undermined both by poor design, the impact of the recession and the speed with which ministers sought implementation, and the DWP had to change funding rules to ensure their viability (NAO, 2010). There is a danger that the speed of Work Programme implementation may reproduce such problems.

Finally, the government is likely to be implementing complex work-focused reforms in a context where job vacancies are harder to secure. Although employment will recover following the return of economic growth, it will be some time before employers start to recruit again in large numbers, and the early years of recovery will be vitiated by recruitment freezes and redundancies in the public sector. In this context Work Programme providers may struggle to place their service users into sustained employment and to maintain investment in the new service delivery systems they are expected to create.

References

Anyadike-Danes, M. and McVicar, D. (2008) 'Has the boom in Incapacity Benefit claimant numbers passed its peak?', *Fiscal Studies*, vol 29, no 4, pp 415-34, Oxford: Blackwell Publishing.

Browne, J. and Levell, P. (2010) *The distributional effect of tax and benefit reforms to be introduced between June 2010 and April 2014: A revised assessment*, IFS Briefing Note BN 108, London: Institute for Fiscal Studies.

Casebourne, J., Davis, S. and Page, R. (2006) *Review of action teams for jobs*, DWP Research Report No 328, London: Department for Work and Pensions.

Cebulla, A., Flore, G. and Greenberg, D. (2008) *The New Deal for lone parents, lone parent work focused interviews and Working Families Tax Credits: A review of impacts*, DWP Research Report No 484, London: Department for Work and Pensions.

Centre for Social Justice, The (2009) *Dynamic benefits: Towards welfare that works*, Executive Summary, London: The Centre for Social Justice.

Conservative Party (2001) *Britain works*, London: Conservative Party.

Conservative Party (2008) *Work for welfare: REAL welfare reform to help make British poverty history*, London: Conservative Party.

Conservative Party (2009) *Get Britain working: Conservative proposals to tackle unemployment and reform welfare*, London: Conservative Party.

DWP (Department for Work and Pensions) (2008) *Department for Work and Pensions commissioning strategy*, Cm 7330, London: The Stationery Office.

DWP (2009) *Building Britain's recovery: Achieving full employment*, Cm 7751, London: The Stationery Office.

DWP (2010a) *21st century welfare*, Cm 7913, London: The Stationery Office.

DWP (2010b) *Employment and support allowance work capability assessment: Official statistics*, July, London: DWP.

DWP (2010c) *Universal Credit: Welfare that works*, Cm 7957, London: The Stationery Office.

DWP (2010d) *The Work Programme prospectus*, London: DWP (www.dwp.gov.uk/docs/work-programme-prospectus.pdf).

EEC (European Economic Community) (2000) *Employability and jobs: Is there a jobs gap?*, Education and Employment Committee, Fourth Report, Session 1999-00, Volumes I and II HC 60-I and 60-II, London: The Stationery Office.

Finn, D. (2008) *'Welfare markets': Lessons from contracting out the delivery of welfare to work programmes in Australia and the Netherlands*, York: Joseph Rowntree Foundation.

Finn, D., Mason, D., Rahim, N. and Casebourne, J. (2008) *Problems in the delivery of benefits, tax credits and employment services*, York: Joseph Rowntree Foundation.

Freud, D. (2007) *Reducing dependency, increasing opportunity: Options for the future of welfare to work*, An independent report to the DWP, London: Department for Work and Pensions.

Gregg, P. (2008) *Realising potential: A vision for personalised conditionality and support*, London: The Stationery Office.

Griffiths, R. and Durkin, S. (2007) *Synthesising the evidence on Employment Zones*, Research Report No 449, London: Department for Work and Pensions.

Harker, L. (2006) *Delivering on child poverty: What would it take? A report for the Department for Work and Pensions*, Cm 6951, London: The Stationery Office.

Harrington, M. (2010) *An independent review of the work capability assessment*, London: Department for Work and Pensions.

Hasluck, C., Elias, P. and Green, A. (2003) *The wider labour market impact of Employment Zones*, Warwick: Institute for Employment Research, University of Warwick.

Layard, R. and Nickell, S. (1998) *Labour market institutions and economic performance*, Paper No CEPDP0407, London: Centre for Economic Performance, London School of Economics and Political Science.

Leitch, S. (2006) *Prosperity for all in the global economy: World class skills*, Final Report, Leitch Review of Skills, London: HM Treasury.

Liberal Democrats (2007) *Freedom from poverty, opportunity for all*, London: Liberal Democrats (http://s3.amazonaws.com/ld-migrated-assets/assets/0000/9363/Policy_Paper_80_-_Freedom_from_Poverty.pdf).

Marshall, P. and Laws, D. (eds) (2004) *The Orange Book: Reclaiming liberalism*, London: Profile Books.

NAO (National Audit Office) (2008) *The roll-out of the Jobcentre Plus Office network*, London: NAO.

NAO (2010) *Support to Incapacity Benefits claimants through Pathways to Work*, London: NAO.

Nickell, S. (1999) 'Unemployment in Britain', in P. Gregg and J. Wadsworth (eds) *The state of working Britain*, Manchester: Manchester University Press.

Ombudsman (2007) *Tax credits: Getting it wrong?*, Parliamentary and Health Service Ombudsman, London: The Stationery Office.

Price, D. (2000) *Office of hope: A history of the Employment Service*, Policy Studies Institute, London: University of Westminster.

Social Justice Policy Group (2007) *Breakthrough Britain: Ending the costs of social breakdown, economic dependency and worklessness*, Vol 2, London: The Centre for Social Justice.

Sunley, P., Martin, R. and Nativel, C. (2005) *Putting workfare in place: Local labour markets and the New Deal*, Oxford: Blackwell Publishing.

van Reenen, J. (2004) 'Active labour market policies and the British New Deal for the young unemployed in context', in R. Blundell, D. Card and R. Freeman (eds) *Seeking a premier economy: The economic effects of British economic reforms, 1980–2000*, Chicago, IL: Chicago University Press.

EIGHT

Lone parents and the Conservatives: anything new?

Tina Haux

Lone parents – still a policy issue

The phenomenon of lone parenthood continues to challenge policy makers for three main reasons: the high levels of benefit dependency and poverty and the potentially negative outcomes for children (Bradshaw, 2003). The response of past governments has differed over the past 30 years according to their respective ideological approaches, changes to the characteristics of lone parents, broader economic conditions as well as more general attitudinal changes in society. Under the last Conservative government lone parents 'have been characterised not just as a social problem, but as a social threat, in terms of the amount of public money that is spent on them' (Lewis, 1997, p 50) while the previous Labour government focused more on moving lone parents into paid work (Millar, 2003) as well as on their responsibility as parents (Williams and Roseneil, 2004). The position of the Conservative Party today contains all three themes – the policy proposals in the area of welfare to work and parenting are quite similar to those of the previous Labour government. Yet the emphasis on marriage and stable families as the 'better' family form that should receive more support both financially and in terms of services raises concerns about the perception and support of other family forms such as lone parenthood.

Lone parents in Britain today

Of the 7.6 million families with dependent children in the UK in 2009, 2 million were headed by a lone parent (that is, 27 per cent) (National Statistics, 2010, p 16). In other words, just over one in four families with dependent children is headed by a lone parent in the UK today, having stayed constant since 2000 (National Statistics, 2010).The majority of lone parents were either single or cohabiting (58 per cent) prior to becoming a lone parent, or married (40 per cent). Only a small percentage of lone parents are widowed (three per cent; see Maplethorpe et al, 2010, p 24, table 2.2, Maplethorpe et al's calculations). And while Britain has one of the highest teenage pregnancy rates in the world, the median age of lone parents is 37 years (Gingerbread, 2010). The vast majority of lone parents are women, with less than 10 per cent of lone parents being lone fathers (Gingerbread, 2010; Maplethorpe et al, 2010). Lone fathers tend to differ from lone mothers in a number of aspects, namely lone fathers tend to be older than lone mothers by approximately 10 years and have fewer and older children (Maplethorpe et al, 2010; National Statistics, 2007, p 8, figure 1.8).

Compared to couple families, lone-parent families tend to be slightly smaller (1.7 children on average compared to 1.8 children) and are more likely to live in urban areas, specifically in the most populous regions of the UK (ONS, 2007). However, the most striking and persistent difference between lone-parent families and couple families is income: 47 per cent of lone parents are in the lowest income quintile compared to only seven per cent of couple families (Maplethorpe et al, 2010, p 22, table 2.1). Looking at income over time, a higher proportion of lone-parent families are persistently on low income (defined as at least three consecutive years on low income) compared to couple families although the overall proportion of lone parents on persistent low income has fallen (DWP, 2010a). Still, lone parents have the higher entry rate to (together with pensioners) and lower exit rate from persistent low income than any other group (DWP, 2010a).

Lone parents under the previous Labour government

The previous Labour government (1997–2010) started their first term in office with a controversial piece of legislation regarding lone parents, namely the abolition of the lone parent top-up on Income Support in 1998. However, this controversial policy was in many ways uncharacteristic of the overall direction of the Labour government. Rather than being singled out and accused of being part of a welfare dependency culture as under the preceding Conservative government, lone parents were part of the much broader, more neutral discourse and policies centred on work being the best route out of poverty for a range of inactive groups. The Labour government had introduced a range of policies to enable lone parents to move into work such as the

National Childcare Strategy, new tax credits, the New Deal for Lone Parents and work–life balance policies (see Millar, 2005, among others). And while the Income Support top-up for lone parents was abolished, money subsequently channelled to all children of low-income families has compensated for it (Brewer et al, 2010). Therefore, a more accurate representation of the policies towards lone parents of the last Labour government is that of Jane Millar, who argues that the policies 'not only add up to a substantial investment in resources and money, but they also represent a significant change in policy direction' (2005, p 25).

As discussed by Kitty Stewart in Chapter Nine, this volume, the policies to address child poverty have not been sufficient to meet the child poverty targets the Labour government had set itself of halving child poverty by 2010 and abolishing it altogether by 2020, despite substantial progress. By 2009 relative child poverty had fallen by 16 per cent, absolute poverty by 50 per cent and deprivation by 18 per cent (Waldfogel, 2010). The story of substantial progress despite failed targets is the same when looking at the changes to the employment rate of lone parents during the Labour government's term in office. The employment rate of lone parents currently stands at 57 per cent (Cabinet Office, 2010a, p 32), which means that the 70 per cent lone parent employment target for 2010 has clearly been missed. This is despite the employment rate of lone parents having increased by an 'unprecedented' 12 per cent from 1996 to 2006 (Freud, 2007, p 30; see also Gregg et al, 2006), which is much more than the employment rate of other groups, such as older workers or workers with a disability and poor districts during that period (Gregg et al, 2006, p 41). This increase took place in a time of economic growth, which is likely to have facilitated much of the increase (Millar, 2005; Gregg et al, 2006). However, five per cent of the increase in the employment rate of lone parents is attributed to policy changes (Gregg et al, 2006), mostly due to the more generous package of financial support, with only a small percentage increase being due to compulsory work-focused interviews (WFIs) mentioned further below (Gregg et al, 2006).

While the overall focus with regards to lone parents was on enabling lone parents to move into work, the Labour government also introduced and strengthened compulsion for lone parents on Income Support. First, compulsory WFIs were introduced for Income Support recipients. Then, from November 2008, lone parents on Income Support whose youngest child was 12 years or older were transferred to (income-based) Jobseeker's Allowance (JSA). This was gradually extended to include lone parents whose youngest child was 10 or over in October 2009 and to those whose youngest child was seven or older in October 2010 (Bell, 2009). Prior to 2008, lone parents had been eligible for Income Support until their youngest child reached the age of 16, that is, they were not required to actively seek and be available for work until then. In most other countries social assistance eligibility for lone parents ends when the child is much younger, or is generally time-limited (Bradshaw and Finch, 2002; OECD, 2007). The transfer to JSA is intended to signal that being a lone parent is no longer sufficient reason to claim income-replacement benefits (Haux, 2010). Instead lone parents with older children are now treated like the unemployed, although there are a number of exceptions for lone parents such as being able to look for part-time work only, shorter 'acceptable' travel to work times and consideration of childcare availability (Bell, 2009).

Transferring lone parents with older children from Income Support to JSA was controversial and concerns were raised in a number of areas:

- whether the infrastructure to support lone parents in work was in place and operating well (see, among others, House of Commons, 2008);
- the reform having been introduced in the middle of a major recession (Gloster et al, 2010);
- lone parents with older children no longer having the same choice to be full-time parents as mothers in couples (House of Commons, 2008; Deacon and Patrick, 2011);
- the focus on eliminating child poverty being in danger of overlooking the needs of the parents involved (Lister, 2006);
- whether lone-parent families were really going to be better off in work given that many lone parents were moving into low-paid work (House of Commons, 2008; Deacon and Patrick, 2011), and given the high job exit rates of lone parents identified by Evans et al (2004); and
- whether the age of child by itself was a good indicator of ability to work of lone parents (Gregg et al, 2006; Gregg, 2008; Haux, 2010).

In any case, the likely impact of lone parents with older children having to look for work remains to be seen as the final stage of the reform has only just come into effect. Early feedback suggests that the transition from Income Support to JSA is not always going smoothly and that some lone parents are struggling with pressure, stigma and the complexity of the rules and conditions of JSA (Peacey, 2010). A dislike of having to sign on every fortnight has prompted some lone parents to look for work (Gloster et al, 2010), which suggests that some of the early effects of the reform are as intended by the Labour government.

The Labour government was more accepting of different family forms, such as lone parenthood, than previous governments (Driver and Martell, 2002; Williams and Roseneil, 2004). While its preference for stable, married family as the bedrock of society drew accusations of 'social conservatism' from some quarters, Driver and Martell (2002) argue that the 'support for the traditional family by the government competes with, and is tempered by, a more progressive family policy agenda that recognizes the diversity of contemporary family forms and that fits more comfortably with the social and cultural changes which have taken place in gender relations over the past decades' (2002, p 54). More importantly, one of the main issues with regards to lone parents has been the primacy of paid work as the main role of citizens as it undermines the value of caring: 'As good citizens they should be in paid work ... as good mothers they should be at home preventing their children from misbehaving' (Williams and Roseneil, 2004, p 187). The responsibility of (lone) parents therefore included both being in work and being an effective parent. As with paid work, the Labour government had introduced both more support for parents, for example, through funding a helpline (Williams and Roseneil, 2004), as well as sanctions, for example, parenting classes.

In terms of the overall verdict then, the support and investment to enable lone parents to move into paid work has frequently been described as 'unprecedented'. However, the focus on work as the core citizenship duty for parents has been problematic as it has clashed with expectations of parenting and this is exacerbated by the fact that both carry sanctions.

The Conservative Party in 2010 and lone parents

When comparing the content and origin of the policy proposals of the Conservative Party with regards to lone parents then, two things are noticeable immediately: the similarity of their welfare to work proposals to those of the previous Labour government and the prominence given to family breakdown. Both these issues are examined in more detail below.

Continuing welfare to work reform: the case of lone parents

The Conservatives claim that their welfare to work policies mark a new departure from those of the previous Labour government, promising 'REAL' reform (Conservative Party, 2008, original emphasis). Yet the policy programme put forward by the Conservatives seems very similar to that of the previous Labour government, both in rhetoric and content (Deacon and Patrick, 2011). The emphasis that welfare is a 'hand-up not a hand-out' (Conservative Party, 2010), the focus on workless households, work being perceived as the best route out of poverty and the aim to privatise the delivery of welfare to work could have (and have) all been in a Labour manifesto. Although there are some new elements such as combining all New Deals into a single Work Programme and tougher sanctions (Conservative Party, 2010; Deacon and Patrick, 2011), McKay and Rowlingson (2011) argue that these proposals are an 'intensification of existing policies rather than a new direction'. This assessment also applies to welfare to work policies of the Conservatives focusing on lone parents. Like the previous Labour government, the Conservatives accept the principle underlying this decision, namely that 'the transition from worklessness to work has beneficial effects for both parents and children alike' (Conservative Party, 2008, p 35). The last Conservative government (1979–97) had been neutral regarding lone parents and employment (Lewis, 1995). This is no longer the case. Instead lone parents whose youngest children are of school age, that is, five years old, are expected to work part time and to work full time when their children reach secondary school age (Conservative Party, 2008). This policy will bring Britain more in line with other countries where the age of child is frequently linked to childcare provision or school starting age (Carcillo and Grubb, 2006).

However, one of the key differences with regards to lone parents and activation between the Conservatives and Labour is their view on when lone parents should be preparing to move into work. The previous Labour government wanted lone parents to engage in WFIs once the youngest child was one and to engage in work-related activities once the child was three (Bell, 2009). The Conservatives have argued that young children benefit from having their parents around and have therefore vowed to change the activity requirements for lone parents with children below school age (Conservative Party, 2008). This fits with the emphasis placed by the Conservatives on parenting during the early years but also hints at an underlying 'ideal' lone parent biography, that is, lone parents should be full-time parents while the youngest child is not yet in primary school, should be working part time when the youngest child is in primary school and full time when in secondary school (Conservative Party, 2008). This 'ideal' biography does not leave room for the needs of parents or children at different points of their life. Nor does it fit with a manifesto statement that 'making Britain more family-friendly means helping families spend more time together' (Conservative Party, 2010, p 42).

Where does the focus on family breakdown leave lone parents?

The policies towards the family of the Conservative Party focusing on early years development, reducing child poverty and on helping parents combine work and parenting are quite similar to those of the previous Labour government (Conservative Party, 2010; Daniel, 2011). Yet the extent to which marriage is favoured and supported by the Conservatives goes beyond that of the previous Labour government. According to the Conservatives, marriage is the glue that holds societies together and they therefore propose to redress the balance in the tax and benefits system in favour of marriage as 'this will send an important signal that we value couples and the commitment that people make when they get married' (Conservative Party, 2010, p 41). Daniel (2011) argues that Cameron agreed to be pro-marriage and thereby enter the potentially poisonous territory of moralising families for two reasons: first, in order to delineate his family policy proposals from those of the previous Labour government, and second, in order to appeal to the more conservative supporters of his party.

The pro-marriage stance of the Conservative Party is based on the perceived negative consequences of family breakdown. Family breakdown was one of the most prominent themes of the Conservatives in the 2010 election campaign (Daniel, 2011): 'broken families' were seen as the main cause for the 'broken Britain' of today. The Centre for Social Justice, a think tank set up by Iain Duncan Smith, has been highlighting the level and effect of family breakdown (see Chapter Two by Jay Wiggan and Chapter Three by Nick Ellison, this volume). Commissioned by David Cameron 'to make policy recommendations to the Conservative Party on issues of social justice' (The Centre for Social Justice, 2006, p 2), Centre for Social Justice has published a series of *State of the Nation* reports, for example, on fractured families. The Centre has been very influential in shaping the thinking of the Conservatives as is evident when looking at the number of policy suggestions from the *State of the Nation* reports that have been included in the manifesto, for example, to abolish the marriage penalty in tax credits and introduce a married couple allowance into the tax system, more funding for relationship support and Sure Start centres focusing on the most 'disadvantaged and dysfunctional' families with additional Sure Start workers supporting families from birth until the child moves to school (Conservative Party, 2010).

The initial report by The Centre for Social Justice, *The State of the Nation report: Fractured families* (2006), 'shows more clearly than ever the destructive effects of family breakdown upon millions of children, as well as the links between family breakdown and addictions, educational failure and serious personal debt' (Foreword by Iain Duncan Smith, in Centre for Social Justice, 2006, p 5). The consequences of family breakdown are described in pretty stark terms in the report: the cost of family breakdown is estimated to run to £20 billion per year. Family breakdown is said to be leading to an increase in mental health problems, higher teenage pregnancy rates, lower educational attainment, children entering a life of crime and increased levels of addiction among the children affected, and is likely to affect the following generation, that is, produce the next generation of unstable families (Centre for Social Justice, 2006). The causes of family breakdown are identified as being both individual and structural. Individual causes named in the report are the lack of experience of successful marriages in own childhood, mental health problems and lower educational background. Structural factors identified in the report are poor housing conditions and being housed far away from family support networks, poverty and financial worries adding additional stress, lack of employment opportunities for men and the incentive structure of the tax and benefit system penalising marriage (Centre for Social Justice, 2006).

The analysis laid out in the second report on 'fractured families' forms the basis of the policy recommendations of the follow-up report called *Breakthrough Britain: Ending the costs of social breakdown: volume 1: Family breakdown* (Social Justice Policy Group, 2007). The main policy recommendations focus on increasing the service provision for families, supporting couple and parental relationships, removing the marriage penalty in the tax and benefit system, creating a 'genuine choice' for parents in terms of work and childcare and giving access to better housing by re-invigorating right-to-buy schemes (Social Justice Policy Group, 2007).

The two reports on family breakdown raise three issues: first, the analysis identifies structural factors such as the lack of local employment opportunities and the impact of financial worries. Yet suggestions for structural reforms do not feature in the policy proposals. Instead, the policy proposals are limited to supporting marriage and parenting (preferably within marriage) with additional money and through tailored service provision. Second, while the Conservatives are no longer waging 'war on single parents' (Daniel, 2011), the focus on marriage as the most desirable family form and on the far-reaching negative consequences of family breakdown as well as the negative language of these arguments is far from an endorsement of family diversity. More clearly than in the area of welfare reform, there seems to be an underlying notion of an 'ideal' family not just with regards to work hours but also with regards to family structure. Finally, and perhaps most importantly, there is some dispute over the consequences of family breakdown and whether they are indeed as detrimental to families and children as described in the various Centre for Social Justice reports (Mooney et al, 2009). Based on a review of existing evidence, Mooney et al make three points in counteraction to the claims of The Centre for Social Justice reports:

- 'while family transitions place children at an increased risk of negative outcomes, the evidence shows that relatively few children and adolescents experience enduring problems';
- 'family functioning has a greater impact on outcomes than family structure'; and
- the role of financial hardship as a contributor to and consequence of family breakdown cannot be taken out of the equation (Mooney et al, 2009, pp 1, 2).

Overall then, the policies of the Conservative Party with regards to welfare to work can be described as an intensification of those of the previous Labour government. However, while many policy proposals in the area of family policy are similar to those of the previous government, there is a distinct focus on the negative consequences of family breakdown and the superiority of marriage as a stable family form that is better for children and for society.

Policy development since forming a Coalition government

The Conservatives did not win an outright majority at the election in May 2010 and formed a Coalition government with the Liberal Democrats. The Coalition agreement does not contain much detail (Cabinet Office, 2010b). The Conservative Party seems to be the senior partner in the Coalition in terms of numbers of Members of Parliament

(MPs), Cabinet secretaries, overall number of ministers and importance of the respective portfolios. Iain Duncan-Smith, founder of The Centre for Social Justice, is now Secretary of State at the Department for Work and Pensions. In this role, he published a report called *State of the Nation report: Poverty, worklessness and welfare dependency in the UK* (Cabinet Office, 2010a) that draws heavily on the work by The Centre for Social Justice. It highlights the changes in family composition, the link between lone-parent families and poverty, and discusses the evidence on the effect of family breakdown on child outcomes, arguing that there is 'strong evidence linking the experience of family breakdown and dysfunction to poorer outcomes for both adults and children', and that this highlights the importance of 'family structure and home environment for policy' (Cabinet Office, 2010a, p 53). The report does not refer to marriage as the most desirable family structure but 'intact couple families', in quotation marks. This is presumably a nod to the Coalition partners who, before the election, seemed less convinced by the healing role of marriage (Daniel, 2011).

Since coming to office there has been a flurry of policy announcements, particularly in the Emergency Budget in June 2010 and the Comprehensive Spending Review (CSR) in October 2010. Starting with the June Emergency Budget and how the announcements are going to affect lone parents, one of the key announcements was that lone parents whose youngest child turned five would be required to look for work from 2011–12 onwards, bringing an estimated 15,000 lone mothers into work (HM Treasury, 2010a, p 33). While this is the logical extension of the welfare reform introduced by the Labour government, it goes against the argument made at the time for setting the cut-off point two years after children enter primary school to give them time to settle in (see DWP, 2007). Furthermore, the objections to the initial welfare reform still stand and it therefore remains to be seen whether the anticipated employment increase will indeed take place. While a further reduction of the age limit does not seem likely as 'the Government does not think that lone parents with children under school age should be required to seek work' (HM Treasury, 2010a, p 33), it has since been announced the lone parents are required to stay in touch with the job centre once their youngest child is one (Grice, 2010). In addition to this, the Emergency Budget contained a number of changes to family benefits such as a substantial increase in the Child Tax Credit, Child Benefit rates being frozen, the abolition of tax credits for very young children and further means testing of the family element of tax credits. The most controversial policy, however, is the planned change to Housing Benefit to set maximum rents. While there is some disagreement as to the extent of the impact, some argue that it will mean Housing Benefit recipients currently living in areas with high rents such as central London having to move much further out (Tapsfield, 2010). With 43 per cent of lone parents not in work and lone parents generally concentrated in urban areas, this change is likely to affect a substantial proportion of lone parents.

As expected, the CSR in October 2010 contained more detailed policy announcements than the Emergency Budget (HM Treasury, 2010b). The most radical announcement is the planned introduction of a Universal Credit to replace the current benefit system (HM Treasury, 2010b), championed by Iain Duncan Smith while at The Centre for Social Justice (Centre for Social Justice, 2009). Further details about the design of the Universal Credit have been published in a subsequent White Paper called *Universal Credit: Welfare that works* (DWP, 2010b). The aims of the Universal Credit are to simplify the benefit system by reducing the number of benefits and to increase the work incentive by slightly reducing the withdrawal rate and keeping it constant at 65 per cent of net earnings (HM Treasury, 2010b). The new Universal Credit will combine the three main income replacement benefits (Income Support, income-related JSA and income-related employment and support allowance) and tax credits, together with Housing and Council Tax Benefit, and is thereby likely to be claimed by the majority of lone parents. Part of the new design of the Universal Credit is access to PAYE (pay-as-you-earn) records, which means that assessments of changes to income and therefore changes to tax credit entitlements can be done more frequently than is currently the case (DWP, 2010b). However, the current design of Universal Credit is leaving out many disability benefits, Child Benefit and all insurance-related benefits such as unemployment benefit and Pension Credit. All of these benefits will still have to be calculated separately and many households on low income are likely to be receiving Universal Credit plus at least one other benefit, thereby blurring the desired simplicity of the new benefit and clear work incentive (Toynbee, 2010). According to official estimates, the new Universal Credit will reduce the number of workless households in Britain by 300,000 (around eight per cent), 'could' lift as many as 350,000 children out of poverty (around nine per cent; see DWP, 2010b, pp 52ff), and provide guaranteed work incentives for low-earning workers. However, the proposed Universal Credit is very ambitious both in its design and its delivery, and the full impact will only become apparent once it has been implemented. It has already been suggested that it seems an expensive exercise given that it will only bring together a relatively small number of benefits (Toynbee, 2010; and see Chapter Seven by Dan Finn and Chapter Nine by Kitty Stewart, this volume).

Perhaps the most controversial policy change in the CSR, however, was to introduce means testing to the previously universal Child Benefit based on the income of one parent rather than the household. This effectively punishes couples where one partner earns £44,000 per year or more (that is, a higher rate taxpayer) and the other earns substantially less as they will be no longer eligible, even though their total household income may well be lower than that of a couple where both earn just below the £44,000 threshold who will continue to be eligible (Mulholland and Wintour, 2010). In response to the furore over this new policy, the Conservatives have announced that a marriage tax break is going to be introduced before the next election (Mulholland and Wintour, 2010).

Other changes that are affecting lone parents directly in the CSR are: the extension of 15 hours of free childcare per week to all 'disadvantaged' two-year-olds by 2013, the above-inflation increase of Child Tax Credit (worth £30 in 2011-12 and £50 in 2012–13) and the cap of £500 per week of household benefits payments to lone parents and couples (HM Treasury, 2010b, pp 27ff). A number of measures announced in the CSR such as the ring-fencing of Sure Start centres and additional money for Sure Start health visitors are likely to stem from The Centre for Social Justice reports (2006, and Social Justice Policy Group, 2007) discussed earlier.

Taken together the measures announced in the CSR will have no 'measurable impact' on child poverty over the next two years, according to official estimates (HM Treasury, 2010b, p 29). However, independent estimates suggest that the changes introduced in the June 2010 Emergency Budget and the 2010 CSR are regressive (Brewer, 2010). Furthermore, it is argued that the changes are likely to hit families with children hardest although initially more families in work than those out of work due to the changes to Working Tax Credit and Child Benefit (Brewer, 2010). Hence, lone parents on the whole are likely to be worse off as a result of the CSR as they are relying heavily on the Childcare Tax Credit when in work, which has been reduced, are likely to be affected by the changes to Housing Benefit given that they are more likely to live in urban areas, and by the cuts in public services that are likely to take place over the next couple of years (see Chapter Nine by Kitty Stewart, this volume).

However, this is unlikely to be the end of policy making in this area. Already further proposals that may affect lone parents are being discussed by policy makers, such as harsher sanctions for job seekers refusing job offers (Wintour and Ramesh, 2010), a proposal contained in the Conservatives' manifesto. In addition, a review on Poverty and Life Chances, a Committee on Social Justice and a Taskforce on Childhood and Families have been set up by the Coalition government and their reports will give an indication of the direction of policies towards lone-parent families under the Coalition government.

Summary and conclusions

In summary then, the policy proposals of the Conservatives seem a continuation and 'intensification' (McKay and Rowlingson, 2011) of those of the previous Labour government in the area of welfare to work reform in particular (Deacon and Patrick, 2011; McKay and Rowlingson, 2011), especially with regards to lone parents. The proposal to remove the right to claim social assistance from lone parents once their youngest child is five is a direct continuation of the recent welfare reform of the previous Labour government. This reform had been controversial and most of the objections to the principle, the design and the timing of the reform still hold.

The similarities between the policies of the Conservatives and the previous Labour government also, to a large extent, apply to the area of family policy (Daniel, 2011). The main exception with regards to family policy is the emphasis on the negative consequences of family breakdown for both individuals and society as a whole. The overall effects of the policy announcements in the Emergency Budget and the CSR this year are likely to leave lone parents worse off financially. At the same time, tax breaks for married couples are going to be introduced before the next election. What impact Universal Credit, the most ambitious project of the Coalition, will have on lone parents in general, and their poverty risk in particular, remains to be seen.

How the ideological differences between the Coalition partners with regards to the family will be resolved will become clearer when the numerous reviews that have been commissioned in the area of family policy, social justice and child poverty have reported. However, concerns remain whether the discourse around families of the Conservatives, which is portraying family breakdown as one of the main causes of many social ills, will at some point include lone parents explicitly.

Finally, in these early stages of the Coalition government the agenda with regards to welfare reform and family policy seems to be very much determined by Iain Duncan Smith, and he is implementing many of the policy proposals put forward during his time at The Centre for Social Justice. Many of his predecessors did not stay in the post very long. If he were to move on, the emphasis in policy may well shift as well.

References

Bell, K. (2009) 'Benefits for single parents: the permanent revolution', *Journal of Poverty and Social Justice*, vol 17, no 3, pp 285-88.

Bradshaw, J. (2003) 'Lone parents', in P. Alcock, A. Erskine and M. May (eds) *The student's companion to social policy* (2nd edn), Oxford: Blackwell, Chapter IV.

Bradshaw, J. and Finch, N. (2002) *A comparison of child benefit packages in 22 countries*, DWP Research Report 174, Leeds: Corporate Document Services.

Brewer, M. (2010) *Welfare savings*, London: Institute for Fiscal Studies (www.ifs.org.uk/budgets/budgetjune2010/brewer.pdf).

Brewer, M., Browne, J., Joyce, R. and Sibieta, L. (2010) *Child poverty in the UK since 1998–99: Lessons from the past decade*, IFS Working Paper 10/23, London: Institute for Fiscal Studies (www.ifs.org.uk/publications/5303).

Cabinet Office (2010a) *State of the nation report: Poverty, worklessness and welfare dependency in the UK*, London: HM Government.

Cabinet Office (2010b) *The Coalition: Our programme for government* (www.cabinetoffice.gov.uk/media/409088/pfg_coalition.pdf).

Carcillo, S. and Grubb, D. (2006) *From inactivity to work: The role of active labour market policies*, OECD Social, Employment and Migration Working Papers 36, Paris: Organisation for Economic Co-operation and Development.

Centre for Social Justice, The (2006) *The State of the Nation report: Fractured families*, London: The Centre for Social Justice.

Centre for Social Justice, The (2009) *Dynamic benefits: Towards welfare that works*, London: The Centre for Social Justice.

Conservative Party (2008) *Work for welfare: REAL welfare reform to help make British poverty history*, Policy Green Paper 3, London: Conservative Party.

Conservative Party (2010) *Invitation to join the government of Britain, The Conservative Manifesto 2010*, London: Conservative Party.

Daniel, P. (2011) 'Conservative policy and the family', in H. Bochel (ed) *The Conservative Party and social policy*, Bristol: The Policy Press.

Deacon, A. and Patrick, R. (2011) 'A new welfare settlement? The Coalition government and welfare to work', in H. Bochel (ed) *The Conservative Party and social policy*, Bristol: The Policy Press.

Driver, S. and Martell, L. (2002) 'New Labour, work and the family', *Social Policy and Administration*, vol 36, no 1, pp 46-61.

DWP (Department for Work and Pensions) (2007) *Ready for work: Full employment in our generation*, Cm 7290, Norwich: The Stationery Office.

DWP (2010a) *Low-income dynamics 1998 to 2008 (Britain)* (http:// statistics.dwp.gov.uk/asd/hbai/low_income/LID_tech_note.pdf).

DWP (2010b) *Universal Benefit: Welfare that works*, Cm 7957, Norwich: The Stationery Office.

Evans, M., Harkness, S. and Ortiz, R.A. (2004) *Lone parents cycling between work and benefits*, DWP Research Report 217, Leeds: Corporate Document Services.

Freud, D. (2007) *Reducing dependency, increasing opportunity: Options for the future of welfare to work: An independent report to the Department for Work and Pensions*, Leeds: Corporate Document Services.

Gingerbread (2010) *Gingerbread factfile*, London (www.gingerbread.org. uk/content/365/Gingerbread-Factfile).

Gloster, R., Casebourne, J., Culshaw, S., Mavra, L., O'Donnell, A. and Purvis, A. (2010) *Lone parent obligations: Early findings of implementation as well as experiences of the Income Support and Jobseeker's Allowance Regimes*, DWP Research Report 645, Leeds: Corporate Document Services.

Gregg, P. (2008) *Realising potential: A vision for personalised conditionality and support, An independent report to the Department for Work and Pensions*, London: The Stationery Office.

Gregg, P., Harkness, S. and Smith, S. (2006) *Welfare reform and lone parents in the UK*, CMPO Working Paper, Bristol: University of Bristol.

Grice, A. (2010) 'Single parents should "prepare for work" when child is a year old', *The Independent*, 12 November (www.independent.co.uk/ news/uk/politics/single-parents-should-prepare-for-work-when-child-is-a-year-old-2131808.html).

Haux, T. (2010) *Activation of lone parents: An evidence-based policy appraisal of the recent welfare-to-work reform in Britain*, ISER Working Paper 2010-29, Colchester: Institute for Social & Economic Research, University of Essex.

HM (Her Majesty's) Treasury (2010a) *Budget 2010*, HC61, London: The Stationery Office.

HM Treasury (2010b) *Spending Review 2010*, Cm 7942, London: The Stationery Office.

House of Commons (2008) *Alleviating deprivation, improving social mobility and eradicating child poverty*, HC42-1, Department for Work and Pensions Committee: Second report of the session 2007–8, volume 1, London: The Stationery Office.

Lewis, J. (1995) *The problem of lone mother families in twentieth century Britain*, London: London School of Economics and Political Science.

Lewis, J. (ed) (1997) 'Lone mothers: the British case', in J. Lewis (ed) *Lone mothers in European welfare regimes: Shifting policy logics*, London: Jessica Kingsley, ch 2.

Lister, R. (2006) 'Children (but not women) first: New Labour, child welfare and gender', *Critical Social Policy*, vol 26, no 2, pp 315-35.

McKay, S. and Rowlingson, K. (2011) 'Social security and welfare reform', in H. Bochel (ed) *The Conservative Party and social policy*, Bristol: The Policy Press.

Maplethorpe, N., Chanfreau, J., Philo, D. and Tait, C. (2010) *Families with children in Britain: Findings from the 2008 Families and Children Study (FACS)*, DWP Research Report 656, Leeds: Corporate Document Services.

Millar, J. (2003) 'The art of persuasion: the British New Deal for Lone Parents', in R. Walker and M. Wiseman (eds) *The welfare we want? The British challenge for American reform*, Bristol: The Policy Press, ch 5.

Millar, J. (2005) 'Work as welfare? Lone mothers, social security and employment' in P. Saunders (ed) *Welfare to work in practice: Social security and participation in economic and social life*, Aldershot: Ashgate, pp 23-42.

Mooney, A., Oliver, C. and Smith, M. (2009) *Impact of family breakdown on children's well-being: Evidence review*, DCSF Research Report 113, London: Department for Children, Schools and Families.

Mulholland, H. and Wintour, P. (2010) 'Government set to introduce tax break for married couples', *The Guardian*, 8 October (www.guardian. co.uk/politics/2010/oct/05/government-tax-break-married-couples).

National Statistics (2007) *Focus on families*, S. Smallwood and B. Wilsom (eds), London: HMSO.

National Statistics (2010) *Social Trends no 40*, Newport (www.statistics. gov.uk/downloads/theme_social/Social-Trends40/ST40_2010_FINAL.pdf).

OECD (Organisation for Economic Co-operation and Development (2007) *Babies and bosses: Reconciling work and family life: A synthesis of findings for OECD countries*, Paris: OECD.

Peacey, V. (2010) 'Signing in or stepping up? Single parents' experience of welfare reform', *Journal of Poverty and Social Justice*, vol 18, no 1, pp 100-1.

Social Justice Policy Group (2007) *Breakthrough Britain: Family breakdown*, London: The Centre for Social Justice.

Tapsfield, J. (2010) 'Government says housing benefit cap will go ahead', *The Independent*, 27 October (www.independent.co.uk/news/uk/politics/government-says-housing-benefit-cap-will-go-ahead-2117787.html).

Toynbee, P. (2010) 'No losers – really? Soon they will emerge by the million', *The Guardian*, 12 November (www.guardian.co.uk/commentisfree/2010/nov/12/cuts-losers-will-emerge-by-the-million).

Waldfogel, J. (2010) *Britain's war on poverty*, New York: Russell Sage Foundation.

Williams, F. and Roseneil, S. (2004) 'Public values of parenting and partnering: voluntary organizations and welfare politics in New Labour's Britain', *Social Politics*, vol 11, no 2, pp 181-216.

Wintour, P. and Ramesh, R. (2010) 'Unemployed claimants to face loss of benefits for refusing work', *The Guardian*, 11 November (www.guardian.co.uk/politics/2010/nov/11/welfare-unemployment-benefits-tougher-rules).

NINE

A treble blow? Child poverty in 2010 and beyond

Kitty Stewart

Introduction

The aim of this chapter is to review developments that affected child poverty in 2010, and there is no shortage of things to say. Let us start with the good news. In March 2010 the UK took the unusual step of legislating to eradicate child poverty, placing a duty on the Secretary of State to meet four child poverty targets by 2020/21 (including a relative low income target), and requiring the UK government to produce a regular child poverty strategy as well as annual progress reports. After a general election during which all the major parties agreed on at least the aspiration of eradicating child poverty by 2020, the new Prime Minister David Cameron confirmed in Parliament in July 2010 that his Coalition administration was 'absolutely committed to meeting the child poverty targets' (see *Hansard* records, 7 July 2010). Also encouraging is the fact that the most recent data shows a reduction in child poverty between 2007/08 and 2008/09 – the first such decline since 2005 (Joyce et al, 2010).

On the other hand, in 2008 the UK entered a recession that the Office for National Statistics has described as the longest and deepest since the Second World War (*The Guardian*, 22 December 2009), with worrying implications for children in families living close to the poverty line, especially those with one earner perhaps in precarious employment. In addition, the country faces a structural deficit that would have made cuts in public spending inevitable whichever Party had won the 2010 General Election. The outlook has been exacerbated by the election of a Conservative–Liberal Democrat Coalition government which has pledged to cut further and faster than many had expected (or think necessary), and has indicated that it will do so in ways which may have more serious consequences for poor children than alternative strategies, in terms of the consequences for both income distribution and long-term investment in children's services. Further, there are signs that the measurement of child poverty may itself come under review, with more emphasis on indicators of parenting and family environment and a reduced focus on income-based measures as a result of the recommendations in Frank Field's Independent Review on Poverty and Life Chances (Field, 2010).

At the time of writing in late 2010 it is early to assess the implications for child poverty of any of these developments – the Child Poverty Act 2010, the recession, the structural deficit and the Coalition. This chapter draws where possible on available data, and also discusses the likely impacts of some of the policies announced by the new government. The chapter begins with a brief review of the legacy Labour left in May 2010 before turning to consider the recession, the spending cuts and the Coalition.

Labour's impact

It is a key part of Labour's legacy that the UK has a set of child poverty targets at all, let alone that these targets are now enshrined in law in a way that commits the incoming government both to monitor child poverty and to develop realistic strategies for reducing it. It is of further significance that the headline poverty measure uses a relative poverty line (as is standard in the European Union [EU]), rather than a fixed income line, uprated only for prices (as is the practice in the US). A relative poverty line is more generous because it shifts upwards each year with median living standards, reflecting a concept of need which is linked to social norms rather than survival. It is also more ambitious: progress against a fixed income target can be delivered by any degree of income growth, even if this growth is far outstripped by that for middle and higher incomes, while progress against a relative line requires faster growth at the bottom than in the middle of the distribution.

The Child Poverty Act, which was passed with cross-party support in March 2010, set four UK-wide targets defining the 'eradication' of child poverty (see Kennedy, 2010). By 2020/21, it is a legal requirement that there are:

•   fewer than 10 per cent of children living in households with income below 60 per cent of the equivalised median before housing costs (the relative poverty measure);

- fewer than five per cent of children in households with income less than 70 per cent of the median and also suffering from material deprivation (the combined low income and material deprivation measure);
- fewer than five per cent of children in households with income below 60 per cent of the 2010–11 median (the 'absolute' poverty measure);
- fewer than a certain percentage of children living in persistent poverty, several years at a time – the exact definition and percentage is yet to be specified (the persistent poverty measure).

It will be noted that eradication of child poverty is not understood (on any of the measures) to mean no poverty at all. The Labour government argued that zero poverty would be technically unfeasible because of measurement error in household surveys, along with the fact that snapshot measures of income do not always accurately reflect living standards, for example, among the self-employed (Child Poverty Unit, 2009, para 46). Instead, it proposed a target of between 5 and 10 per cent, as 'an ambitious but technically feasible goal for sustained eradication of child poverty that would put the UK's position on child poverty firmly among the best in Europe' (Child Poverty Unit, 2009, para 53). Certainly in 2008 a relative poverty rate of 10 per cent would have placed the UK third best in the EU, just behind Denmark and Norway, just ahead of Finland, Sweden and the Netherlands, and a very long way from the 24 per cent of children actually recorded as living in poverty in the UK in 2008 using European data.[1] It would be difficult to accuse the Child Poverty Act of lack of ambition.

In addition to laying down targets, the Act also requires the UK government and the Scottish and Northern Irish ministers to publish a regular strategy for meeting the targets (every three years), as well as annual progress reports. The first child poverty strategy must be published by 25 March 2011. The Act further establishes a Child Poverty Commission to provide advice, and places new duties on local authorities and other 'delivery partners' in England to work together to reduce child poverty (see Kennedy, 2010).

These actions on targets and measurement are certainly important, and ensure that child poverty will remain on the agenda in the coming decade. But how far were they matched by policies which delivered in practical terms for poor households with children during Labour's time in office? Figure 9.1 shows changes in relative poverty covering nearly the entire Labour period (data for the final year, 2009/10, were not available at the time of writing). The figure shows the official relative poverty measure alongside series that take 50 per cent and 70 per cent of the median (rather than 60 per cent) as the poverty cut-off. This is done because of the rather arbitrary nature of 60 per cent as the dividing line between poor and not-poor, which tends to invite some scepticism as to whether the poverty rate is falling simply because income changes are taking people from just below to just above the line. The 40 per cent series is not shown because of concerns about its accuracy (see, for example, Brewer et al, 2010).

Figure 9.1: Children living in households below various shares of the contemporary median, 1979–2008/09 (before housing costs)

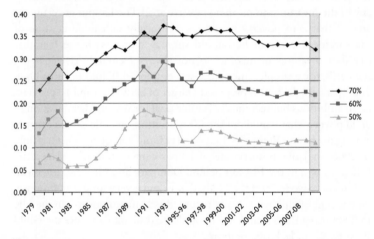

Note: Shading shows periods of recession using the definition in Muriel and Sibieta (2009).
Source: Institute for Fiscal Studies database

Figure 9.1 shows that on all three measures the rate of poverty was considerably lower in 2008/09 than in 1996/97, although for both the 60 per cent and 50 per cent measures most of the progress was achieved in Labour's first term, with 2004/05 (when Labour narrowly missed its first target of cutting child poverty by a quarter) turning out to be the government's finest year in this regard. After that, poverty began to rise slowly, allowing David Cameron to claim accurately that child poverty rose 'under the previous government', if this is taken to mean the last of Labour's three terms. In the final year for which data are available the rates started to fall again, the result of more generous increases in Child Tax Credits and Child Benefit in the 2008 and 2009 Budgets. However, this decrease is not statistically significant (Joyce et al, 2010). Overall, the official child poverty rate fell by 18 per cent between 1998/99 (the baseline year for the child poverty target) and 2008/09, translating as roughly 600,000 fewer children in poverty. Against a moving target this is an impressive achievement – although of course it leaves the government a very long way short of the goal of halving child poverty by 2010/11.

Figure 9.2 shows the same picture for child poverty measured against a set of fixed income poverty lines – shares of the household median in 1998/99, uprated only for prices. Here the story is far more dramatic, with poverty more than halving against the 60 per cent line from the baseline of 1998/99. In a comparison with the impact of President Clinton's policies in the US in the 1990s, Waldfogel (2010) points to the much greater achievements of the Labour government in cutting child poverty against this US-style measure, and calls for the US to look to the UK for lessons in poverty reduction (Waldfogel, 2010). However, once again we see that most progress had been achieved by 2001/02, with stagnation in Labour's third term. It is also interesting to note that poverty fell quite sharply against these fixed income measures even during the Thatcher decade, as a result of strong economic growth which lifted the real living standards of many of those on lower incomes. But during that period those further down the distribution did less well than those towards the middle, as the different slopes of the 50, 60 and 70 per cent lines testifies, and all of those living below any of these lines were increasingly left behind the median, as a glance back to Figure 9.1 shows. In contrast, during the Labour period incomes in the bottom half of the distribution have grown slightly faster than those at the median, resulting in the slow decline of the relative poverty measures.

The discussion to this point has focused on immediate reductions in levels of monetary poverty. Labour's longer-term strategy for eradicating child poverty was two-pronged – to increase household incomes in the short term while also investing in public services to improve life chances and give today's children a better shot at becoming non-poor parents in the future. There is insufficient space here to say much about the impact to date of these policies, which included much greater investment in education (with a stronger focus on disadvantaged areas through Education Action Zones, Excellence in Cities and Ethnic Minority Achievement Grants), early years programmes such as Sure Start and free nursery places and a series of area-based initiatives. But in their summary of the Labour reforms, Hills et al (2009) point to improving educational attainment for the poorest areas and schools and narrowing educational inequalities; significant improvement in indicators of child well-being between 2001 and 2006; near universal participation in early years education at ages three and four and a doubling of formal childcare places; and positive impacts of Sure Start on child development and parenting. These gains are important as a challenge to the Coalition orthodoxy that the structural deficit results from 'years of Labour waste' (George Osborne, 9 July 2010). They are also, of course, important because many successful programmes now face cuts or abolition.

Figure 9.2: Children living in households below various shares of the 1998-99 median, 1979–2008/09 (before housing costs)

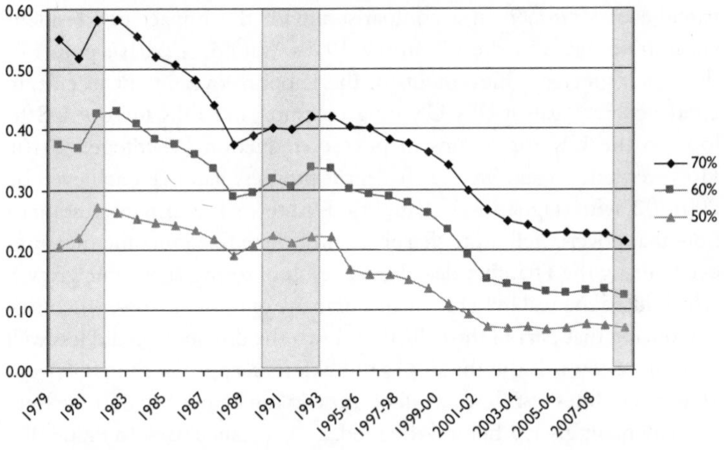

Note: Shading shows periods of recession using the definition in Muriel and Sibieta (2009).
Source: Institute for Fiscal Studies database

Recession

Recession has two conflicting impacts on rates of child poverty measured against a relative poverty line. On the one hand, as parents lose their jobs more families become more heavily reliant on benefits. On the other hand, median household income may fall because of job losses and downward pressure on wages, so benefit recipients may make gains on the median and rates of relative poverty may actually come down. The way these two effects play out against each other will depend in part on the composition of the poor (see, for example, Freeman, 2001). If most families living near the poverty line are already reliant on benefits, relative child poverty is likely to decrease in a recession, but if many working families are hovering just above the line, rising unemployment and cuts to working hours will leave them vulnerable and relative poverty may rise.

It is early to assess the impact of the current recession, but Figure 9.1 shows that poverty fell between 2007/08 and 2008/09 against all three relative poverty lines – the first time since 2003/04 that this had been the case. Figure 9.1 also allows us to compare this to the start of previous recessions. In the early 1990s relative child poverty fell initially and then rose when measured against either the standard poverty line of 60 per cent of median income or the more generous 70 per cent line, while in the early 1980s child poverty rose sharply and then fell back on both measures. In both cases child poverty was higher at the end than at the start of the recession, but as Muriel and Sibieta (2009) point out, these increases were not aberrations but part of a longer-term pattern of steadily increasing child poverty from the late 1970s to the early 1990s. Poverty measured against the more restricted line of 50 per cent of median income is an exception, registering falls during both periods of recession that contrast with rising poverty during the rest of the 1980s. Presumably this is because most people living close to the 50 per cent line were largely reliant on benefits before the recessions took hold and the falling median left this group relatively better off.

The fall in poverty against the strictest poverty line serves as a reminder that using a relative line to measure poverty during a recession can have perverse implications. While relative living standards clearly matter, it is particularly important to keep track of changes in actual living standards when times are tough. As outlined above, a relative measure can underestimate the extent to which living standards are rising during an upturn, and it can equally underestimate the degree to which children are suffering in recession. Figure 9.2 shows that in both the recessions of the early 1980s and early 1990s poverty rose (or at best remained steady) if measured against a fixed income line of 50, 60 or 70 per cent of the 1998/99 median (uprated only for prices). In contrast, between 2007/08 and 2008/09 poverty fell against all three fixed lines. This suggests that recent falls in relative poverty are not artificially reflecting falls in the median but are in fact due to real increases in living standards in low-income households.

How can this be the case? Joyce et al (2010) argue that the recent fall in child poverty is largely explained by falls in the incidence of poverty for families in particular household and employment set-ups (for example, lower rates of poverty for lone parents working part time), rather than by people shifting from one type to another (for example, workless households gaining a worker). In particular, they highlight falls in poverty for children living with two adults, both out of work (from 68.2 per cent to 63.8 per cent between 2007/08 and 2008/09). The only family types that saw poverty rise during this year were children living with a lone parent working full time, or with two parents where one works full time and the other part time or not at all (these are, however, large groups, accounting altogether for nearly half of all children).

Declines in the rate of poverty for households with no worker or only a part-time worker are likely to reflect the above-earnings growth increases in the child element of the Child Tax Credit announced in the 2007 and 2008 Budgets, benefiting those on Income Support or in low-paying jobs, along with real increases in universal Child Benefit. Effective from April 2008 and 2009, these measures came too late to change the poverty figures available before the 2010 General Election but do appear to have had an impact since then, with the Institute for Fiscal Studies predicting that the 2009 increases will show up as a further fall in the child poverty rate in 2009/10, regardless of likely job losses (Joyce et al, 2010). As Figure 9.3 shows, benefit rates for non-working households with children rose as a share of the poverty line after 2007/08 for the first time since 2004/05, giving an overall picture of substantial growth in the relative value of out-of-work benefits for households with children during Labour's time in office. This is a picture that contrasts sharply with the situation for households without children, as Figure 9.3 also illustrates. However, the regular increases in benefits for households with children since 1997 have only just about made up for declines in their relative value during the early 1990s.

Not all households are entitled to these levels of benefit as an automatic right. Couples must claim income-based Jobseeker's Allowance (JSA) rather than Income Support, and from October 2008 this has also applied to lone parents whose youngest child is 12 and who are making a fresh claim, and from October 2010 to lone parents whose youngest child is seven (see the Social Security [Lone Parents and Miscellaneous Amendments] Regulations 2008). The benefit levels under JSA are the same but parents must sign on regularly and show their job centre adviser that they are available and actively seeking work as a condition of receipt. How these reforms have affected individual lone parents in practice is not yet evident, and may become clear only once the economy moves out of recession. A number of amendments made to the regulations as the Welfare Reform Bill passed through Parliament in 2009 introduced some crucial protections for those with sole care of their children: in particular, lone parents need only be available for jobs of 16 hours a week, can suspend their search during the school holidays and can reject

Figure 9.3: Benefit rates for non-working households during two recessions as a share of the poverty line

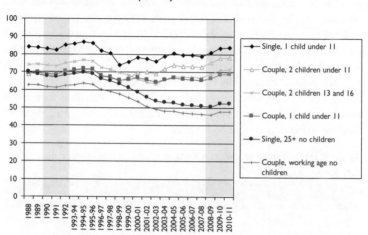

Notes: Shading shows periods of recession using the definition in Muriel and Sibieta (2009). The poverty threshold is 60 per cent of contemporary median income after housing costs, equivalised for household size. The poverty threshold for 2009–10 and 2010–11 is projected from 2008–09 in line with the growth in the (whole economy) average earnings index, following Sefton et al (2009).

Source: Author's calculations using benefit rates reported in DWP (2010) and poverty rates from the Institute for Fiscal Studies inequality and poverty spreadsheet

a job if no suitable childcare is available. Qualitative research will be needed to assess how well these protections work in protecting benefits for those whose childcare responsibilities make many jobs impossible.

It seems, then, that benefit rates for households with children have been holding up during the recession to date, but what has been the impact of job losses? The positive news here is that indications suggest that jobs have – so far – been less affected this time round than in previous recessions. Joyce et al (2010), examining household survey data to 2008/09, point to small decreases in the shares of children living in households with two adults working full time or with a self-employed worker, and increases in the share living with adults working only part time. But they also find a small *fall* (although not statistically significant) in the share of children living in workless households (from 18.4 per cent in 2007/08 to 17.3 per cent in 2008/09). This outweighs the other compositional effects and contributes overall to a further decline in child poverty.

Slightly more recent data from the Labour Force Survey, presented in Table 9.1, indicate that the share of children living in a household without an adult in work did rise sharply between the second quarter of 2008 and the second quarter of 2009, although by much less in lone-parent households than others. The relative protection for lone parents is probably due to the fact that unemployment has risen faster for men than for women during this recession (Muriel and Sibieta, 2009; ONS, 2009). The increase was in any case short-lived for both lone-parent and couple households, falling again between 2009 and 2010 – an indication that the worst may (for now) be over.

Table 9.1: Percentage of children living in workless households: quarterly data for April to June each year

	All household types	Couple households	Lone-parent households
1997	18.6	8.6	57.8
1998	18.4	7.8	56.9
1999	17.6	7.1	55.1
2000	16.4	6.8	52.6
2001	16.1	6.6	51.1
2002	16.5	6.7	50.7
2003	15.9	5.9	50.9
2004	15.8	6.3	49.1
2005	15.4	6.3	47.7
2006	15.3	6.5	46.4
2007	15.3	6.0	48.1
2008	15.2	6.2	47.4
2009	16.7	7.5	48.7
2010	16.1	6.8	48.5

Note: Includes all children under 16 living in households with at least one person aged 16–64.
Source: ONS (2010), Table 3[ii]

In a comparison of the output and employment losses of this and earlier recessions, Gregg and Wadsworth (2010) argue that although this recession has been the worst since the Second World War in terms of lost output, the loss of employment has been much smaller this time, and the period over which employment fell has also been shorter than in the past. They point to a number of factors which may explain this, arguing in particular that, unlike in the early 1980s and early 1990s, the current recession was not exacerbated by tight fiscal and monetary policy aimed at squeezing inflation; instead, both fiscal and monetary policy were loosened quickly and on a large scale to offset the fall in demand. Other factors include the acceptance by employees of lower nominal wage growth, and the relatively good financial shape of many employers as the recession started, which helped avoid job shedding.

The unemployment story is not equally positive across all parts of the UK. Parekh et al (2010) show that while the rise in unemployment in England had tailed off by the second half of 2009, in Scotland and Wales unemployment kept rising into 2010. The authors argue that the sharper increase in unemployment in Scotland explains the fact that child poverty rose by two percentage points in Scotland between 2007/08 and 2008/09 while falling in England (Scotland had until that point been doing better in poverty reduction than other parts of the UK, with a lower incidence of in-work poverty). Among the English regions, Office for National Statistics data show that only Yorkshire and Humberside saw unemployment continuing to rise into 2010.

Some jobs will have been saved because employers opted to keep staff on with reduced working hours. As noted above, household survey data picks up a small increase in the share of children living with part-time workers only – a group at high risk of poverty. Other data sources point to the same phenomenon: the Annual Survey of Hours and Earnings shows small reductions between 2008 and 2009 in the median hours worked per week by both male (1.3 per cent) and female (2.5 per cent) employees. Increases in Child Tax Credit will have offset some but not all of the reductions in earnings for affected lower-income households.

On the whole it seems fair to conclude that children have been reasonably well protected from the worst of the recession so far, by increases in benefits which have helped non-working households with children and those in work but on a low income, and by fiscal and monetary policies which have limited job losses. Both relative poverty and poverty measured against a fixed income line fell between 2007/08 and 2008/09, with the Institute for Fiscal Studies predicting a further fall in relative poverty to 2009/10. What happens next for children in low-income and vulnerable households will depend on whether the Coalition is successful in keeping the economic recovery on track, on the package of cuts in benefits and services and on the government's wider welfare reform strategy.

The Coalition

It is important to remember that public expenditure cuts are not wholly due to the change of government. In 2009/10 public sector borrowing reached 11.1 per cent of national income, with the Treasury estimating that only one third of the total was due to the economic cycle, with two thirds structural (Webb, 2010). This structural budget deficit would need to have been addressed by whichever government had won the election.

However, there can be little doubt that the situation facing low-income families is worse under this government than it would have been under any alternative available in May 2010 other than a Conservative majority. In part this is because it is Coalition policy to cut the deficit more rapidly than Labour or the Liberal Democrats had proposed, with immediate implications for taxes, benefits and services and potentially damaging effects on employment and economic recovery. In part it is because of the (entirely arbitrary) decision that the burden of deficit reduction should fall 80 per cent on public spending and 20 per cent on increased taxation, which itself has distributional consequences (see Sefton, 2002; Horton and Reed, 2010). Then there are the decisions about where exactly public spending cuts should fall. Particularly deep cuts have been made to the welfare bill, with the Chancellor arguing that welfare has been deliberately targeted in order to provide relatively greater protection for spending on education, health and early years provision: £18 billion a year is to be cut from welfare by 2014/15, out of a total spending reduction of £81 billion a year (HM Treasury, 2010b). Thus money is to be removed from the very poorest in society to reduce the burden on public services for the majority.

Three further points are worth making before we consider the detail of the changes to benefits and public spending. First, there is evidence that families with children are no longer considered a priority group for welfare spending (and perhaps more generally) in the way they were under the previous Labour government. Since May 2010 it is only older people who have received exemptions from the cuts, with protection of their universal benefits and more generous uprating rules for Pension Credit and the Basic State Pension than for benefits for working-age households and children.

Second, we appear to be witnessing a shift towards greater targeting of children's benefits, with the abolition of universal Child Benefit and much sharper tapers for Child Tax Credit. This targeted approach is also being extended to some children's services, such as Sure Start (HM Treasury, 2010b). In the short run these changes are progressive and appear logical in a climate in which maximum impact is needed for minimum spending. The blunt way in which the Child Benefit means test will operate (families will lose eligibility if one parent is a higher rate taxpayer) has attracted widespread criticism, but the principle of means testing the benefit has been applauded by some anti-poverty campaigners (see, for example, Narey, 2010). But means testing inevitably has a negative impact on work incentives, while the removal of the principle of universality is also likely to come to seem short-sighted in its implications for the way in which richer people see the benefit system – as a residual safety net meant for others rather than a social insurance-type system which we all pay into when we have no dependants and draw on when our needs are higher. In practice, there is no model for a country that achieves low rates of child poverty by relying on means-tested benefits (Bradshaw and Finch, 2002).

The third point concerns the government's broad approach to reducing child poverty, which is likely to be rather different to that of the previous administration. While supporting the Child Poverty Bill as it went through Parliament, the Conservatives argued that government should focus on the 'underlying causes' of poverty, which Lord Freud (then Conservative Work and Pensions spokesperson) identified as family breakdown, employment, access to drugs and alcohol, and education and skills. These themes were explored by Iain Duncan Smith and The Centre for Social Justice while the Conservatives were in opposition (see, for example, Social Justice Policy Group, 2007), and may be expected to emerge as important planks of anti-poverty strategy under the new administration. While focusing on different causes, Frank Field's recent report has also stressed the idea that tackling poverty is about more than income distribution (Field, 2010). Field, a Labour Member of Parliament (MP), was commissioned by David Cameron to conduct an Independent Review on Poverty and Life Chances shortly after the Coalition took office. His report was published in December 2010 and argues strongly for much greater investment in the foundation years – the years to age five – through high quality childcare and support for better parenting; and also for education in parenting to be incorporated into the curriculum at all levels, to address what Field says is 'a growing indifference from some parents to meeting the most basic needs of children' (2010, p 16).

In a sense this is nothing new: as noted above, the Labour government's strategy for eradicating child poverty was always two-pronged, relying in the short term on income redistribution and in the long term on investment in education and early years services, including parenting, to improve children's chances of becoming effective and self-reliant parents themselves in the future. Policies such as Sure Start and expanded nursery place provision made some headway towards these goals, although there is certainly a strong case that much more needs to be done. But the Field review points not to additional investment overall but to a shift in the balance between the two sets of policies, with a recommendation that resources that would have been spent on increasing tax credits should instead in future be redirected to early years services.

It is inevitable that if this approach is adopted, income poverty rates will increase: benefits and tax credits need to keep rising at the level of average earnings just to keep child poverty at the same rate. Field's position is that lower income poverty is important in the long run, but in the short run the best way to achieve this is to focus on improving children's life chances through services: 'The purpose is not to sideline the goal of abolishing child poverty; it is rather to set out an alternative and broader strategy to achieve this goal' (2010, p 17). To inform and drive this shift he recommends the creation of a new set of life chances indicators to include measures of the home learning environment, positive parenting, quality of nursery care and child development at age three. (The fact that many of these indicators are themselves outcomes to which financial poverty may be a key contributing factor is not discussed.) The indicators are seen as running alongside, not replacing, the existing income poverty measures; replacement would in any case be difficult, given the existence of the Child Poverty Act. But if the Coalition adopts the Field recommendations, the stage is set for some interesting discussions in the future, in which ministers will be required to defend rises in income poverty in the medium term as the best route to cutting child poverty in the long run.

Cuts to benefits and tax credits

As noted, cuts to the welfare bill are central to the Coalition's deficit reduction plan. Many of the changes announced in the June 2010 Emergency Budget and the Comprehensive Spending Review are likely to affect children in low-income families. The most important reforms are listed below (see HM Treasury, 2010a, 2010b):

- Changes to local housing allowances rates, which will particularly affect those in private rented accommodation. Families will be able to claim only up to a weekly limit (from £280 for a one-bed flat to £400 for four or more bedrooms), and maximum rates will also be pegged in all areas with the bottom third of rents locally, rather than the bottom half as at present. The former change will hit families hardest in London and the South East, which may become simply unaffordable for those reliant on Housing Benefit. Housing Benefit will be further reduced to 90 per cent of the initial award for those (including lone parents) claiming JSA for a year.

• The introduction of a benefits cap at £500 a week (£26,000 a year) for workless, non-disabled, non-widowed families. This will primarily affect large families (those with seven or more children), but will also affect those receiving large amounts in Housing Benefit or Council Tax Benefit, which again means particularly those in London and the South East.

• A reduction in the maximum share of childcare costs that can be reimbursed through the childcare element of Child Tax Credit, from 80 per cent to 70 per cent. This will affect all recipients (but the impact will not be reflected in child poverty figures, which are often calculated after housing costs but never after childcare costs).

• The abolition of the baby element of the Child Tax Credit (which doubled the family element in the first year), the abolition of the Health in Pregnancy grant, restriction of the Sure Start Maternity Grant to the eldest child and Child Benefit frozen for three years.

• A slightly steeper withdrawal rate for the Child Tax Credit as earnings rise (up from 39 per cent to 41 per cent), Working Tax Credit frozen for three years from April 2011 and an increase in the qualifying hours for couples from 16 hours to 24 hours from April 2012.

• The decision to uprate benefits and tax credits in the future in line with the consumer price index (CPI), not the retail price index (RPI) or the Rossi index. The CPI is usually lower, meaning this will result in year-on-year real drops in benefits. (The Pension Credit Guarantee and the Basic State Pension are to be the only exceptions, and will be increased in line with earnings.) The Treasury estimates that this little-noticed change alone will save £5.8 billion a year by 2014/15, with savings increasing thereafter – all achieved by reductions in support for the poorest households (HM Treasury, 2010a).

• Still in planning, the introduction of a Universal Credit, to be introduced over two Parliaments. Under this policy, championed by Iain Duncan Smith, the benefit system will be dramatically simplified, making it easier for people to calculate whether or not they will be better off in work. The problem is that simplifying benefits inevitably means being less sensitive to individual circumstances (the number of dependants, housing costs, disability). This in turn will mean either spending more all round to ensure that the new benefit is adequate for a variety of circumstances, or tolerating the fact that some people (those with greater needs) will lose out. This is still one to watch, but given the economic climate the latter approach appears the more likely (see also Chapter Seven by Dan Finn, this volume).

On the other hand:

•   The personal tax allowance is increasing, which will benefit those in work.
•   The child element of the Child Tax Credit will increase above inflation in both 2011 and 2012.

What are these changes likely to mean for child poverty? Chancellor George Osborne claimed that the increases to the Child Tax Credit would be sufficient to prevent child poverty from rising: 'The policies in this Budget, taken together, will not increase measured child poverty over the next two years' (George Osborne's Budget Speech, 22 June 2010). At the same time, Treasury calculations suggested that the impact of the budget would be progressive overall, as long as measures already announced by Labour were also taken into account (HM Treasury, 2010a).

However, as the Institute for Fiscal Studies has pointed out, this analysis did not include the impact of all the benefit changes announced in the Budget, because the Treasury felt that some of these (such as those to Housing Benefit) were too difficult to model. Making what it argues are 'reasonable assumptions', the Institute for Fiscal Studies has modelled the full effect of the reforms and argues that the June 2010 Emergency Budget was regressive among the bottom 90 per cent of the income distribution, and that, combined with the welfare cuts in the Spending Review, 'the overall set of this Government's changes to taxes and benefits is clearly regressive amongst the bottom 90% of the income distribution' (Brewer, 2010, p 3). On child poverty, Brewer argues that whether the increases in Child Tax Credit will dominate other effects will depend on family circumstances – the number of children, housing tenure and rent, working hours and earnings. For some families, certainly until 2012/13, the rise in Child Tax Credit will be enough. But overall the

Institute for Fiscal Studies' view is that 'it would be very surprising if the direct impact of the Government's tax and benefit changes to date on child poverty was neutral by the end of the Parliament' (Brewer, 2010, p 4). Institute for Fiscal Studies analysis indicates that households with children will lose by more than those without children at all parts of the income distribution, and among households with children the losses are regressive, other than for the top decile (Browne, 2010).

Cuts to services

While cuts to welfare are to shoulder the burden of nearly one quarter of total spending cuts, services are only relatively, not absolutely protected. There are two areas in which the Spending Review pledges significant funding increases – the expansion of part-time nursery places to disadvantaged two-year-olds, and the pupil premium for disadvantaged school pupils. Both were key Liberal Democrat election pledges and have been held up by Deputy Prime Minister Nick Clegg as a major part of the justification for Liberal Democrat participation in the Coalition. The Spending Review dedicated £7.2 billion for the two policies – a positive step *if* the funding proves genuinely additional.

However, at the same time, the Spending Review announced that both Sure Start and current spending on education per school pupil are to be protected in cash terms only (small real increases in education spending are due to rising pupil rolls), while schools' capital spending faces a 60 per cent cut by 2014/15. The further education budget will be cut by 12 per cent in real terms through reductions in per capita funding for 16- to 19-year-olds and abolition of the education maintenance allowance (see HM Treasury, 2010b for details).

Horton and Reed (2010) use survey and government spending data to put together a picture of how public spending is distributed across households, estimating the value of services used by different households and adding this to household income. They then examine how the picture is changed by the cuts (see also the update in TUC, 2010). Their conclusion is that those on lower incomes benefit most from public spending, and that (unsurprisingly, given the first finding) the cuts will be highly regressive overall. Among household types, lone-parent households and single pensioners face the greatest losses as a percentage of household income (lone parents losing the equivalent of 18 per cent of income), largely because of particularly severe cuts to the budgets for social housing and social care.

Public sector job losses

The discussion so far has been static in considering only the distributional implications of public spending cuts. However, the cuts may also affect child poverty through further unemployment. The Office for Budget Responsibility (OBR) initially forecast the loss of 490,000 public sector jobs by 2014/15, revised down to 330,000 in November 2010. Opinion on whether growth in the private sector will make up for these losses is divided. Robert Chote, Chair of the OBR, said that the creation of a million jobs in that time would 'more than offset' the public sector losses (BBC, 29 November 2010), but analysis by PricewaterhouseCoopers concluded that the cuts could lead to knock-on private sector losses of almost half a million further jobs (PwC, 2010), and the Chartered Institute of Personnel and Development has estimated that more than 1.6 million jobs will go in total by 2016, with the private sector hardest hit.

The government's anti-poverty strategy is relying heavily on Robert Chote turning out to be right. In its response to the Institute for Fiscal Studies' verdict on the June Emergency Budget the Treasury argued that the Institute's analysis was too narrowly focused on tax-benefit changes and ignored 'the pro-growth and employment effects of Budget measures such as helping households move from benefits into work, and reductions in corporation tax' (*The Guardian*, 25 August 2010). However, if private sector growth fails to materialise quickly, the full impact of the Emergency Budget and the Spending Review could in fact be more, rather than less, regressive than the Institute for Fiscal Studies analysis suggests.

Conclusions

Children in low-income households may be considered to have suffered a treble blow in 2010 – the continuing impact of the recession, the need to reduce the structural deficit and the arrival of a new government committed to particularly steep cuts to public spending and placing a lower priority both on income poverty and on children. In practice, at the time of writing, the measured impact of the recession has not been as bad for child poverty as it might have been: jobs have been less affected than in previous recessions, and benefit increases introduced under Labour have also had a protective effect. Child poverty fell between 2007/08 and 2008/09 and is predicted to have fallen again to 2009/10. However, recent cuts both to the welfare bill and to public spending mean the story gets much more worrying from here. Child poverty looks almost certain to rise from 2010/11, an early challenge to both the spirit and the substance of the Child Poverty Act, and a tragedy with long-term consequences for the children involved.

Note

[1] Data downloaded from the Eurostat website, October 2010. The figures are for the share of under-18s living in households below 60 per cent of national median equivalised income before housing costs, as recorded by Eurostat using EU-SILC data (the European Union Survey of Income and Living Standards). Numbers may differ slightly from those from national data sources but can be more reliably used for cross-national comparison.

References

Bradshaw, J. and Finch, N. (2002) *A comparison of child benefit packages in 22 countries*, DWP Research Report No 174, London: Department for Work and Pensions.

Brewer, M. (2010) 'The Spending Review and children', Presentation to the All Party Parliamentary Group for Children, Monday 29 November.

Brewer, M., Phillips, D. and Sibieta, L. (2010) *What has happened to 'severe poverty' under Labour?*, 2010 Election Briefing Note no 3, London: Institute for Fiscal Studies.

Browne, J. (2010) 'Distributional analysis of tax and benefit changes', Presentation at the Institute for Fiscal Studies 2010 Spending Review briefing, 21 October.

Child Poverty Unit (2009) *Ending child poverty: Making it happen*, London: HM Government.

DWP (Department for Work and Pensions) (2010) *The abstract of statistics for benefits, National Insurance contributions, and indices of prices and earnings* (2009 edn), London: DWP.

Field, F. (2010) *The foundation years: Preventing poor children becoming poor adults*, The report of the Independent Review on Poverty and Life Chances, December, London: HM Government.

Freeman, R. (2001) *The rising tide lifts...?*, NBER Working Paper no 8155 (www.nber.org/papers/w8155.pdf).

Gregg, P. and Wadsworth, J. (2010) *The UK labour market and the 2008–2009 recession*, CEP Discussion Paper no 950.

Hills, J., Sefton, T. and Stewart, K. (eds) (2009) *Towards a more equal society? Poverty, inequality and policy since 1997*, Bristol: The Policy Press.

HM Treasury (2010a) *Budget 2010*, London: The Stationery Office.

HM Treasury (2010b) *Spending Review 2010*, London: The Stationery Office.

Horton, T. and Reed, H. (2010) *Where the money goes: How we benefit from public services*, London: Trades Union Congress.

Joyce, R., Muriel, A., Phillips, D. and Sibieta, L. (2010) *Poverty and inequality in the UK: 2010*, IFS Commentary C116, London: Institute for Fiscal Studies.

Kennedy, S. (2010) 'Child Poverty Act 2010: a short guide', House of Commons Library Standard Note SN/SP/5585.

Muriel, A. and Sibieta, L. (2009) *Living standards during previous recessions*, IFS Briefing Note BN85, London: Institute for Fiscal Studies.

Narey, M. (2010) 'Time to end Child Benefit', *The Guardian*, 4 October.

ONS (Office for National Statistics) (2009) *The impact of the recession on the labour market*, London: ONS.

ONS (2010) 'Work and worklessness among households, 2010', *ONS Statistical Bulletin*, 8 September 2010 (www.statistics.gov.uk/pdfdir/work0910.pdf)

Parekh, A., Kenway, P. and MacInnes, T. (2010) *Monitoring poverty and social exclusion in Scotland 2010*, York: Joseph Rowntree Foundation.

PwC (PricewaterhouseCoopers) (2010) 'Sectoral and regional impact of the fiscal squeeze', 13 October.

Sefton, T., Hills, J. and Sutherland, H. (2009) 'Poverty, inequality and redistribution' in J. Hills, T. Sefton and K. Stewart (eds) *Towards a more equal society? Poverty, inequiality and policy since 1997*, Bristol: The Policy Press, pp 21–46.

Sefton, T. (2002) *Recent changes in the distribution of the social wage*, CASEpaper 62, London: Centre for Analysis of Social Exclusion, London School of Economics and Political Science.

Social Justice Policy Group (2007) *Breakthrough Britain: Ending the costs of social breakdown*, Policy recommendations to the Conservative Party, London: The Centre for Social Justice, July.

TUC (Trades Union Congress) (2010) 'Spending review will hit the poorest 15 times harder than the rich, says TUC', Press release, 22 October.

Waldfogel, J. (2010) *Britain's war on poverty*, New York: Russell Sage Foundation.

Webb, D. (2010) 'The economic recovery and the budget deficit', in *Key issues for the new Parliament 2010*, House of Commons Library Research, London: House of Commons.

TEN

The English NHS as a market: challenges for the Coalition government

Nicholas Mays

Introduction

'We will stop the top-down reorganisations of the NHS that have got in the way of patient care' (HM Government, 2010, p 24). Despite this claim the Coalition government moved swiftly to publish a National Health Service (NHS) White Paper in July 2010 (Secretary of State for Health, 2010), mixing radical structural change with market policy continuity. The radical change involves removal of the customary intermediate tiers in the NHS between the national and local levels, and the replacement of primary care trusts (PCTs) with general practitioner (GP)-led commissioning consortia. Continuity is seen in the government's commitment, echoing its New Labour predecessor, to pursue patient choice and provider competition in the English NHS. The government wants the NHS to develop into a publicly financed universal service delivered through a regulated market replacing the model of a public service delivered through a hierarchy of publicly owned organisations. This chapter assesses the potential consequences of the Coalition's proposals for the NHS – and, given the degree of policy continuity, it begins with a review of New Labour's market changes, as this should provide some indication of the likely effects of the Coalition's proposals.

New Labour's reinvented market in the English NHS

New Labour's *NHS Plan* (Secretary of State for Health, 2000) led to substantial investment in NHS workforce and capacity. Its later market reforms (Secretary of State for Health, 2002; DH, 2005) – represented diagrammatically as in Figure 10.1 – introduced three key changes designed to build on that investment: first, to create the conditions for a more competitive NHS market by increasing the number and range of providers offering services to NHS patients; second, to reward hospitals for attracting NHS patients; and third, to give NHS patients a choice of where to receive elective treatment.

Figure 10.1: Main components of the quasi-market reforms in the English NHS, introduced in 2002–08, including the government's expectations

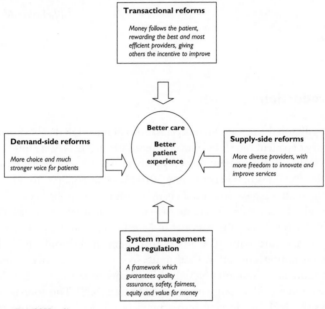

Source: DH (2005, p 9)

The two previous White Papers (Secretary of State for Health, 1997, 2000) had explicitly rejected the use of market forces. However, by 2002, the government believed that its concerns about the performance of the English NHS could not be remedied without expanding the repertoire of policy instruments to include greater supplier competition to provide NHS services. The perceived problems included:

• the system's inadequate responses to increased funding as shown by, for example, persistent variations in performance and productivity;

- the limitations of relying for performance improvement principally on 'top-down' targets driven from Whitehall and Downing Street, backed by strong, hierarchical performance management within the NHS;
- the slow growth of NHS capacity without the involvement of private and other new providers;
- the risk of missing the latest and most demanding waiting-time target of no more than 18 weeks from GP first appointment to treatment.

The main market-related reform mechanisms, introduced in stages that gradually coalesced into a 'reform programme' (see Figure 10.2), comprised:

- Increasing the diversity of providers to the NHS through:
  - Department of Health-led procurement of independent sector treatment centres (ISTCs) providing elective surgery and diagnostics (42 ISTCs opened between 2002 and 2008);
  - encouragement to private hospitals to enter the NHS market from 2002 onwards and later to third sector organisations, particularly 'social enterprises'.
- Additional financial, clinical and managerial autonomy for high performing NHS hospitals, known as NHS foundation trusts (FTs), starting in 2004, with preferential access to the 'payment by results' (PbR) system (see below).
- 'Payment by results' (PbR), a case-based hospital payment system with nationally fixed prices, designed so that money should 'follow the patient' and competition should be on quality not cost, introduced in stages from 2005 (covering 40 per cent of hospital care purchased by PCTs in 2009/10).
- Individual patient choice of four or more hospitals (including a private sector option) for planned care between 2006 and 2008, and the choice of any hospital meeting NHS standards and paid according to the PbR tariff from April 2008, supported by a new system known as 'Choose and Book' for paperless GP referrals and telephone booking of hospital appointments by patients.
- PCTs reduced in number from 300 to 152 in 2006, retaining responsibility for commissioning NHS services from a budget allocated in relation to the relative needs of their populations, but required to devolve some of their commissioning decisions to general practices with indicative budgets (called practice-based commissioning).

Figure 10.2: Staged implementation of the quasi-market reforms in the English NHS, 2002–08

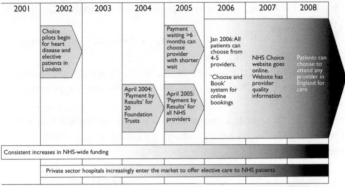

Source: Cooper et al (2010a, Figure 1, p 46)

Two new regulatory bodies were also established in 2004: a financial regulator of NHS FTs known as Monitor and a quality regulator in the form of the Healthcare Commission (now the Care Quality Commission).

The impact of the reintroduction of the market into the English NHS

There is a rapidly accumulating body of research on the impact of the post-2002/03 changes in the hospital sector and various attempts have been made to bring this evidence together to provide overall assessments of the reintroduction of market-related changes in the English NHS (Audit Commission and Healthcare Commission, 2008; Brereton and Gubb, 2010; Brereton and Vasoodaven, 2010). There is also evidence emerging from the programme of studies on the reforms commissioned by the Department of Health itself (http://hrep.lshtm.ac.uk/). The overviews to date tend to conclude that the NHS market has not so far had a major impact, principally because it has not been systematically implemented in the face of numerous barriers to change and because other New Labour policies appear to have had more impact, particularly the increase in overall spending and the setting and enforcement of targets (Propper et al, 2008). By contrast, the most recent studies of specific aspects of the changes tend to demonstrate significant effects in the direction expected by the proponents of reform, but have not, so far, been fully taken into account in the syntheses.

Competition and its effects on quality, equity and efficiency

Did competition increase after the NHS market was reintroduced and, if so, where in the country and for which services? The answer seems to be that while hospital markets in England remained highly concentrated (uncompetitive), particularly for emergency and unplanned use of services, there was an appreciable rise in spatial competition between hospitals after 2003/04, and especially from 2006/07, suggesting that the effect of the changes may have accelerated towards the end of New Labour's period in office (Gaynor et al, 2010). The increase in competitive pressures was most noticeable around the fringes of the main urban areas, not in the conurbations (where presumably there had always been de facto competition). The level of competition between acute hospitals was, not surprisingly, higher for elective (planned) services than for emergency services or for services requiring continuity of care such as maternity.

Brereton and Gubb (2010) used a different approach to conclude that the extent of competition was very limited; they found that few services were reported to have been put out to tender in the period and that most providers retained monopoly power in their localities and were able to dictate to PCTs rather than having to compete for PCT business. It is likely that both reports are correct: there was an increase in competition associated with the reforms around the conurbations, but this had not yet affected large areas of service.

Critics of New Labour's changes had been concerned that increasing competition between hospitals, with fixed prices for different types of cases, would harm the quality of care and increase inequity of access because providers would be encouraged either to skimp on the care of more difficult patients or avoid treating potentially more needy patients in preference to potentially easier cases (so-called 'cream skimming'). The evidence appears to show no such effect in the 2000s. Instead, the increase in inter-hospital competition after 2003/04 was associated with an improvement in clinical outcomes, as measured using acute myocardial infarction (AMI) and all-cause post-hospital death rates (see Figure 10.3), and a fall in length of stay. Between 2003/04 and 2007/08, death rates fell more in hospitals that faced more competition and this did not seem to be explained by any increase in spending per capita or change in admission rates, implying an increase in productivity associated with greater competition (Gaynor et al, 2010). Cooper et al (2010) also

Figure 10.3: 28-day post-hospital mortality rate (all causes) and levels of HHI pre- and post-market reforms

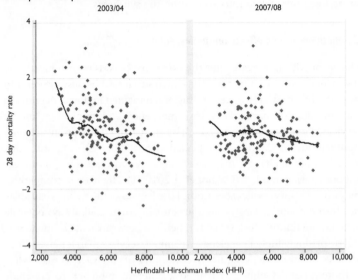

Notes: The Herfindahl-Hirschman Index (HHI) is a measure of spatial competition, in this case based on flows of patients to each hospital from different neighbourhoods. Each point in each figure represents a hospital. The HHI is for all elective services calculated using actual patient flows. The line is the prediction from a locally weighted regression of the mortality rate adjusted for case mix (using the shares of admissions within five-year age-gender bands) on HHI.
Source: Gaynor et al (2010, Figure 1b, p 44)

showed a quicker fall in AMI mortality (that is, emergency care) for patients living in more competitive hospital markets after the January 2006 introduction of patient choice of elective provider. Similarly, Bloom et al (2010) showed that greater spatial competition was also associated with better management practices and, in turn, with better performance. It is unclear why competition should be positive for an outcome such as AMI mortality where the imperative is to reach the nearest hospital as soon as possible and where patient choice and competition are likely to be irrelevant. AMI was chosen for investigation on the grounds that admissions and deaths are relatively frequent and that the infrastructure used to treat AMI cases is common to the other services provided at the same hospital. Thus one interpretation of the findings is that hospitals that do well in treating AMI patients have robust clinical systems that benefit patients more generally. Another related possibility is that hospitals in more competitive areas may have taken steps to improve the quality of their elective services in order to retain market share which, in turn, had effects on the organisation as a whole, including emergency services.

There were also concerns at the outset that competition in the context of PbR might result in lower quality of care since the price for each type of case was fixed in advance regardless of the actual cost of treatment. Although the outcome measures available from routine NHS data are limited, there was no evidence of any negative effect on indicators such as in-hospital all-cause mortality comparing England with PbR and Scotland without (Farrar et al, 2009). Indeed, in a comparison of English NHS FTs with Scottish NHS trusts, 2003/04–2005/06, there was a significant difference in the change in in-hospital mortality, suggesting that quality of care had improved more quickly in England.

The other major concern about competition related to equity of access to NHS services, given that PbR gave hospitals strong incentives to reduce waiting times and length of stay for elective surgery. However, Cookson and Laudicella (2010) found no obvious change in socioeconomic equity of use from 2001/02 to 2008/09 for elective procedures and some signs that equity might have improved slightly since inpatient admission rates rose slightly faster in low-income areas than elsewhere. They also tried to disentangle the equity effects of competition from the potential equity effects of spending growth and other aspects of reform. They found that increased competition between 2003/04 and 2008/09 did not undermine socioeconomic equity in hospital care and, if anything, may have very slightly increased utilisation of elective inpatient care in low-income areas (Cookson and Laudicella, 2010). Finally, Cookson and Laudicella (2011) examined whether hospital patients living in low-income areas of England cost more to treat, to see whether there were a priori grounds to expect 'cream skimming'. Using hip replacement as an example, and using length of stay as an indication of cost, the study showed that patients from the most deprived areas (the lowest 10 per cent) stayed only six per cent longer than other patients (the other 90 per cent) in 2001/02, falling to two per cent by 2007/08. The major determinants of length of stay were age and number of diagnoses. Thus under the NHS fixed price payment system, there were potential incentives for hospitals to 'cream skim' by avoiding very elderly and very sick patients with multiple co-morbidities, but incentives to avoid treating socioeconomically disadvantaged patients were relatively small.

These findings are consistent with another longitudinal study using NHS routine hospital data looking at socioeconomic variation in NHS hospital waiting times for hip replacement, knee replacement and cataract surgery, 1999–2007, covering both the period when New Labour drove reform exclusively through targets and top-down performance management, and later when it reintroduced the quasi-market alongside its other policy instruments (Cooper et al, 2009). These authors found that the deprivation gradient of waiting (that is, people in more deprived areas tending to wait slightly longer than those in less deprived areas) at the beginning of the period had disappeared and may even have slightly reversed by 2002 (the heyday of 'targets and terror') and changed little when the market was reintroduced. Cookson and Laudicella's (2010) findings are also consistent with a further recent study using routine patient level data showing that socioeconomic equity in colorectal, breast and lung cancer procedure use changed little between 1999 and 2006 (Raine et al, 2010).

One explanation for Cookson and Laudicella's (2010) findings is that the effect of pressure to meet waiting-time targets, which began before the market reforms and persisted throughout the reform period, was greater than any effect of private sector entry and/or competition. This is consistent with the findings of local case study research on the impact of the reform mechanisms by Powell et al (2010) and with the Civitas analysis that the NHS market only operated in isolated pockets and only for a small number of services (Brereton and Gubb, 2010). It is possible, therefore, that any inequities associated with market competition did not occur in the 1990s and 2000s, not necessarily because the NHS market was designed to prevent them or even reduce them, but because it was only operating weakly. If true, such an inference has major implications for the future impact of the market given that the Coalition government aims to implement a fully functioning market in the English NHS (discussed later).

Markets and competition are generally justified on efficiency grounds. Here, evaluation has been assisted by the fact that the market reforms were applied to England but not to Scotland, and that the PbR activity-based hospital payment system was also introduced in stages in England. As a result, Farrar et al (2009) were able to compare the impact of PbR over time between countries, and within England between different types of NHS hospital and different types of services. They found that PbR's effect on unit costs was modest, but statistically significant, and in the direction expected from simple economic theory and experience in other similar healthcare systems. For example, a difference-in-difference analysis comparing FTs in England with all hospitals in Scotland between 2003/04 and 2006/07 showed a significantly greater fall in length of stay among FTs, resulting in a unit cost advantage to England (as mentioned earlier, there was no evidence that this fall was associated with poorer quality).Although the growth in measured volume of services was greater in England than in Scotland, the difference was most likely the result of England's waiting-time targets rather than PbR per se.

Impact of greater provider diversity

As well as being a key part of the government's strategy to increase the level of competition in the developing market for NHS services, widening the range of providers offering their services to NHS commissioners and to individual patients under patient choice was seen as a way of encouraging innovations in service delivery that would improve efficiency, quality and responsiveness of care more quickly than would have been possible with publicly owned providers. What evidence is there that such market entry occurred, that the new entrants performed better than their predecessors and that this was attributable to their ownership?

In general, research in this area suggests that the pace and extent of entry of new providers was modest and influenced by the policies of local commissioners as well as the substantial hurdles that potential new providers faced in bidding for NHS work and negotiating contracts (for example, diseconomies of scale in the bidding process disadvantaged smaller, niche providers from the third sector) (Bartlett et al, 2010; Brereton and Gubb, 2010). In addition, private and third sector organisations tended to bid to provide different services (for example, the third sector tended to offer niche expertise in providing services to 'hard-to-reach' groups and mental health, disability, learning difficulties or long-term care) (Allen and Jones, 2011). As a result, the amount of head-to-head competition between NHS-owned, private and third sector providers was very limited, and thus the amount of evidence on the relative quality, outcomes and costs of the same services delivered by different providers remained small.

One aspect of provider diversification that has generated particular controversy and a little comparative research was New Labour's programme to establish both NHS and ISTCs specialising in routine elective surgery alongside conventional NHS hospital provision. ISTCs were introduced in 2002 to provide routine elective surgery and diagnostic procedures for NHS patients.They were intended to increase capacity, raise productivity, increase quality and improve value for money. Indeed, there is qualitative evidence that NHS providers of elective surgery responded to ISTCs by introducing new care pathways and other changes to improve patient experience and improve efficiency (Bartlett et al, 2010). However, New Labour's centralised ISTC procurement was heavily criticised, for example, for leaving public providers with the more difficult cases (Pollock and Godden, 2008).

The main difficulty comparing ISTC provision (and, indeed, that of any alternative provider) with NHS provision is how to ensure like-for-like comparisons when the case mix of patients treated in each sector differs. There are two studies of patient experience. The first, a study by the Healthcare Commission (2007), found that patients in ISTCs rated their care highly (97 per cent rated their overall care as 'excellent' or 'good') and on a number of criteria more highly than NHS organisations. These included time of admission and no change to admission arrangements, involvement in decisions about their care and the provision of information and explanations about their care. In the second study, a multi-variate analysis, Pérotin et al (2010) compared patient experience in terms of aspects of care such as cleanliness of facilities, food quality, explanations provided by medical staff, delays, privacy and dignity. After taking into account the characteristics of the patients, the patient selection process and individual hospital characteristics, there was no difference in the level of quality reported by patients in ISTCs and NHS providers (although patients' experience was different, with some groups preferring NHS providers in some areas of care and ISTCs in others).

The only comparative study of clinical quality, by Browne et al (2008), showed slightly better patient-reported outcomes in ISTCs versus NHS providers of elective surgery, although the differences were not statistically significant. Given the large difference in case mix between the two sectors and within groups of patients receiving the same operation (for example, cataract surgery, hip replacement or hernia repair), all comparative findings must be treated with caution.

Likewise, among different NHS providers, there is no evidence that NHS FTs' superior performance versus other NHS trusts is attributable to their governance status and greater freedoms rather than their pre-FT performance, except perhaps for their greater responsiveness to patients (Healthcare Commission, 2005; House of Commons Health Select Committee, 2008; Allen et al, 2010).

Concerning innovation, Bartlett et al's (2010) qualitative investigation indicated that while the NHS organisations had greater resources to drive innovation in clinical practice, private organisations innovated more in organisational and working practices. An important area of innovation among the third sector providers was to include healthcare services within a broader range of community activities.

Overall, there appears to be no solid evidence internationally or domestically favouring one sector over another in terms of innovation, quality and outcomes of care (Heins et al, 2010). The evidence to date suggests that the main drivers of performance relate to the regulatory environment and market conditions within which providers operate (Allen et al, 2011; Heins et al, 2010).

Impact of patient choice of place of care

Another novel and much debated part of New Labour's reintroduction of market-like mechanisms into the English NHS was the phased introduction of individual patient choice of provider of planned hospital care (Figure 10.2). New Labour had criticised the 1990s market on the grounds that 'patients followed contracts' set by commissioners and resolved, instead, that 'money should follow patients' choices' as far as possible. Although other dimensions of patient choice such as choice of type of treatment were advocated in the reform period, the government's flagship choice policy explicitly related to choice of place of elective care.

This policy raised a number of questions, in particular, how much did NHS patients value the offer of a range of choices of place of planned care, would it be possible to offer this routinely, would choice of provider change patients' destinations, what would drive patients' choices and would choice policy improve the responsiveness, quality and effectiveness of NHS care at reasonable cost?

The best evidence on this policy comes from a project commissioned as part of the health reforms evaluation programme (Dixon et al, 2010), which suggests that the vast majority of patients thought that having a choice of provider was important, particularly older patients and those from minority ethnic backgrounds. This was contrary to the prevailing view of healthcare professionals that patients did not want to be offered a choice of provider. Surveys suggest that about half of elective patients were being offered a choice of provider for their first outpatient appointment by the late 2000s (Dixon, 2010; Dixon et al, 2010), but that GPs were reluctant to offer choice routinely. Most of the patients offered a choice did choose their local provider (69 per cent), but patients offered a choice were more likely to travel to a non-local hospital (29 per cent) than those not (22 per cent) (Dixon et al, 2010). Patients reporting a bad previous experience of a hospital were also more likely to go elsewhere following the offer of choice. Patients with higher levels of education were more likely to be aware that they were entitled to a choice and to go to a non-local hospital after having been offered a choice, suggesting a possible source of inequity generated by the choice policy, at least in its early stages until people became aware of the policy. On the other hand, there were no obvious signs of socioeconomic bias in the offer of choice.

GPs and providers believed that choice was relevant only in urban centres while, in fact, patients living outside urban centres were more likely to be offered a choice and were more likely to choose to travel to a non-local provider. This is consistent with Gaynor et al's (2010) finding that the most marked increase in spatial competition associated with the reintroduction of the market occurred outside the conurbations.

Patients drew on various information sources to help them choose, including their own past experience (41 per cent), and advice from their GP (36 per cent) and from friends and family members (18 per cent). GPs provided little information to their patients (Dixon et al, 2010). Only four per cent of patients had looked at the NHS Choices website and one per cent had consulted other websites. Cleanliness, quality of care and the standard of facilities were the three most important factors that patients said had influenced their choice of hospital (see Figure 10.4). A key policy question is whether shifts in routine elective referrals at the scale reported by Dixon et al (2010) are sufficient to signal to less well performing hospitals that they need to improve their performance, given that most hospital income is derived from unplanned activity and less routine services. At the time of Dixon et al's (2010) study, NHS trusts were receiving high volumes of referrals and the NHS budget was rising unprecedentedly, which limited the clinical and financial threat posed by patients choosing alternative providers. There was some limited competition for patients living at the edge of local catchment areas, but most provider staff perceived individual patient choice as having relatively little impact on flows compared with GPs' decisions. NHS providers also felt little competition from the independent sector and often worked collaboratively with it to treat patients on waiting lists within target treatment times. These perspectives need to be set against the eight per cent of patients offered a choice who opted for a non-local hospital. Although this is a small percentage of all hospital patients, this aspect of the market might well demand more of providers' attention in the future, as commissioners' finances become more restricted.

Figure 10.4: Factors influencing patients' choice of hospital

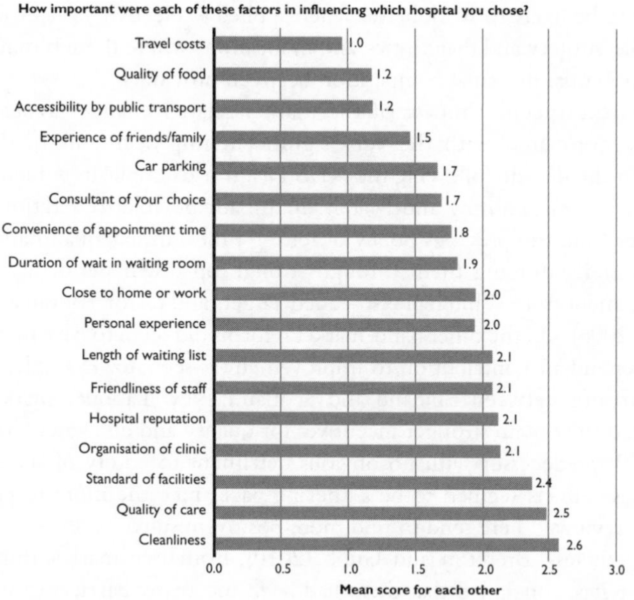

How important were each of these factors in influencing which hospital you chose?

Factor	Mean score
Travel costs	1.0
Quality of food	1.2
Accessibility by public transport	1.2
Experience of friends/family	1.5
Car parking	1.7
Consultant of your choice	1.7
Convenience of appointment time	1.8
Duration of wait in waiting room	1.9
Close to home or work	2.0
Personal experience	2.0
Length of waiting list	2.1
Friendliness of staff	2.1
Hospital reputation	2.1
Organisation of clinic	2.1
Standard of facilities	2.4
Quality of care	2.5
Cleanliness	2.6

Mean score for each other

Note: In this figure, factors rated as 'essential' were scored as 3, 'very important' as 2, 'somewhat important' as 1 and 'not important' as 0. The scores shown are the mean score given by respondents for each factor. Scores for each factor have been rounded to one decimal place. The length of the bar represents the non-rounded score.

Source: Dixon et al (2010, Figure 16, p 70)

Overall verdict on New Labour's reinvention of the NHS market

By the time New Labour left office, the English NHS was still some distance away from functioning as a fully fledged market for publicly financed care, although there was evidence of increasing levels of inter-hospital competition on grounds of quality. Entry and growth of new providers was limited and had been relatively slow, and the hospital market remained fairly concentrated. This was reinforced by GPs' tendency to continue to choose on behalf of their patients, and to choose local providers that they knew. Implementation of the market-related changes varied by specialty and by area, with a strong focus on elective care. PbR still only applied to a minority of the hospital services paid for by PCTs. As Brereton and Gubb (2010, p xii) concluded: 'We found isolated examples of the NHS market delivering the benefits that were anticipated; however, the market, by and large, has failed thus far to deliver such benefits on any meaningful or systemic scale'. The market reforms appear to be likely to work better when applied to elective services, for example, surgery and diagnostics, and in locations where there is much more potential or actual competition between providers.

Thus the specific impact of the market-related changes appears modest compared with the very significant improvements in the NHS in the decade following the *NHS Plan* (for example, in reducing waiting times) (Thorlby and Mabin, 2010), attributable to additional resources and the previous policy of setting time-limited, quantitative targets and enforcing them through strong, top-down performance management from Whitehall – so-called 'targets and terror' (Bevan and Hood, 2006). On the other hand, market reforms did seem to have made an independent contribution to improvement as seen, for example, in comparisons between England and Scotland. New Labour's market appeared to contain stronger incentives for quality and efficiency than its 1990s predecessor with no obvious detriment to equity of access, and these effects seemed to be gathering pace since the more recent studies reviewed here tend to find more positive results.

Nonetheless, Brereton and Gubb (2010), from free market think tank Civitas, concluded that there had been too many barriers to the operation of a market for NHS services under New Labour, rather than a fatal flaw in the concept. The distortions they highlighted were power imbalances between PCT commissioners and providers, particularly ordinary NHS trusts, the lack of a level playing field between NHS and non-NHS providers to the detriment of the latter and perverse incentives under PbR to admit patients who would be better off out of hospital. They further argued that there were still many restrictions to non-NHS providers entering the NHS market and a lack of skills relevant to working in a market among both commissioners and providers.

The Coalition government's NHS White Paper *Liberating the NHS*

Perhaps mindful of Civitas's criticisms of New Labour's market, the Coalition government announced further changes to the governance, organisation and incentive structure of the English NHS in its July 2010 White Paper *Equity and excellence: Liberating the NHS* (Secretary of State for Health, 2010). While Chris Ham of the King's Fund greeted the White Paper by saying, 'Today's White Paper represents one of the biggest shake ups of the health system since the NHS was established' (King's Fund, 2010a), the White Paper can be seen to present remarkable continuity with New Labour's project to transform the English NHS into a fully functioning market for publicly financed healthcare.

The Coalition supported the basic principles of the NHS (general tax finance, universal access, services largely free at the point of use) and offered increases in funding of one per cent above inflation over the five years 2011–15 (relatively generous compared with the cuts in many other areas of public spending set out in the October 2010 Comprehensive Spending Review), but a far lower rate of increase than previously experienced and representing a shortfall estimated at between £15 billion and £20 billion between 2011 and 2014. The government also argued that further major changes were needed for the service to meet rising expectations, technological advances and increasing demand, plus improve its efficiency. It criticised New Labour for sacrificing clinical quality in the pursuit of shorter waiting times, excessive use of targets backed by aggressive performance management from the centre, political meddling, allowing PCTs to be dominated by hospital providers, insufficient clinical engagement in management, particularly of resources, and neglecting productivity improvements by failing to implement market reforms with sufficient vigour. Thus a key reason for the changes was to 'bring together responsibility for clinical decisions and for the financial consequences of these decisions' (Secretary of State for Health, 2010, para 4.4, p 27) and to increase the scope for market forces to apply to the provision of NHS services to improve performance.

The White Paper proposed a significant set of changes:

- giving several hundred groups of GP practices (to be known as GP commissioning consortia) budgets to commission care for their registered patients by 2013;
- abolishing 152 PCTs and strategic health authorities during 2012/13, and cutting NHS management costs by 45 per cent by the end of 2014;
- establishing a statutory NHS Commissioning Board at national level responsible to the Secretary of State for managing within the overall NHS budget, delivering improvements in key outcome areas (but without use of targets and performance management) and commissioning highly specialised care, as well as providing guidance and support to GP commissioning consortia, and holding them to account, by April 2012;
- slimming down (30 per cent reduction in staff) and refocusing the Department of Health on public health and social care policy, and

on leading a new National Public Health Service to be based in local government;

- shifting all NHS trusts to foundation status or social enterprises (mutual organisations owned by their staff) with greater financial independence, by 2013/14;
- abolishing New Labour's performance targets, in particular those related to waiting time reduction, and replacing them with outcome targets by the end of 2014;
- extending the role of Monitor, currently the financial regulator of FTs, to become the economic regulator of the provider market for all services funded by the NHS during 2013/14;
- setting up local 'Health Watch' groups funded by local government to replace Local Involvement Networks to help the public and patients to influence local services with a national Health Watch body within the Care Quality Commission (which remains the quality regulator for all health and social care providers), from April 2012;
- transferring funding for health improvement (public health services) to local authorities which will jointly appoint directors of public health as the local leaders of a new national Public Health Service to be established by 2012;
- extending individual patient choice of hospital to include specific specialists or clinical teams.

Implications for the future

Although the Coalition's plans can be viewed simply as an accelerated continuation of the previous government's gradual implementation of a market for services to NHS patients from 2002/03, if implemented as described, they will decisively turn the delivery of NHS healthcare into a regulated market open to 'any willing provider' regardless of ownership and subject only to the interventions of separate economic (competition) and quality regulators (Black, 2010; King's Fund, 2010b; NHS Confederation, 2010; The Nuffield Trust, 2010). By contrast, the historically weaker commissioning side of the service will remain more conventionally hierarchical, with GP commissioning consortia accountable to the NHS Commissioning Board, and thence to the Secretary of State and Parliament. However, unlike previous incarnations of the NHS, there will be no intermediary organisations at regional level able to help coordinate the investment decisions of autonomous public and private providers with the plans of locally focused, independent-minded GP commissioners. Given that healthcare is prone to market failure, such a structure could lead to inefficient duplication, fragmentation and destabilisation of provision just when financial stringency demanded the best use of resources across the entire system.

The King's Fund (2010b) argued that 'the scope of the government's proposals, the speed with which they have been developed, and the urgency with which they are being implemented mean that they are much more ambitious than previous reforms'. The Fund also questioned whether such extensive further reform was needed on the grounds that the English NHS had made very considerable progress towards being a highly performing system during the New Labour years, initially through the use of targets and performance management and latterly by adding greater supply-side competition (Thorlby and Maybin, 2010). The Coalition has rejected New Labour's use of targets and intends to rely exclusively on regulated market competition.

Furthermore, there are considerable risks inherent in the disruption caused by further restructuring when cutting management expenditure drastically and when the service is required to make £20 billion of cash releasing savings in order to manage with far less generous funding over the next five years. Restructuring will also generate its own costs, putting further pressure on budgets (Walshe, 2010). As a result, PbR prices will have to become less generous when there are already moves in train to extend the range of services paid for under PbR, to pay less for unplanned admissions beyond agreed levels, to widen experiments in quality-adjusted PbR payments and to allow some locally negotiated, market-driven variation in the PbR tariff (eg, where services are tendered for). There is likely to be intensified price competition affecting non-PbR services. Private for-profit and third sector involvement is also set to increase.

Although GP commissioning consortia echo the Conservatives' extensions of GP fund holding in the mid-1990s, the new consortia will have to involve all GP practices and will face far greater pressures since they will be responsible for around 80 per cent of a much less generous NHS budget than their predecessor PCTs. There are big questions relating to the willingness and ability of GPs to lead such organisations (their initial reaction has been sceptical) (King's Fund and Doctors.net.uk, 2010), and how well they will be supported (for example, to assess population needs, handle financial and clinical risk and contract with providers) as management budgets are cut. Will consortia have the levers to influence GPs' behaviour to pursue quality improvements and cost savings given that they will not have responsibility for the contracts of their constituent practices? How will the inevitable conflicts of interest between GPs as both commissioners and providers of services be handled, given the strong likelihood that increasing their role in provision will be a strong motivation for GPs to take part in consortia? How will secondary care specialists respond to resources being controlled by groups of primary care generalists? Will GP consortia be better placed to resist pressures to fund high-cost treatments for small numbers of patients at the expense of services able to generate measurable health improvements at a population level? Will consortia be better able to negotiate service reconfigurations with large acute hospitals than their PCT predecessors?

Taken together, such changes could well mean that the impact of the post-2010 market is more unpredictable than either the 1990s internal market or New Labour's version with administered prices. Will quality continue to be associated with greater competition and will equity continue to be unaffected in a more fluid NHS market with possibly greater price competition and more independent sector involvement? The evidence suggests that socioeconomic equity of access was not harmed by New Labour's market, but a more complete, more competitive NHS market could well have a different effect on equity. Likewise, the evidence suggests that New Labour's market with fixed prices performed better than the Conservatives' 1990s internal market with locally negotiated prices in that under New Labour greater competition was associated with better outcomes of hospital care and the reverse in the 1990s. Allowing more price competition could have negative effects on equity.

References

Allen, P., and Jones, L. (2011) 'Increasing the diversity of NHS providers', in N. Mays, A. Dixon and L. Jones (eds) *Understanding New Labour's market reforms of the English NHS*, London: King's Fund, forthcoming.

Allen, P., Wright, J., Dempster, P.G., Hutchings, A. and Townsend, J. (2010) *Investigating the governance of NHS foundation trusts*, Final report to NIHR Service Delivery and Organisation Programme.

Allen, P., Bartlett, W., Pérotin, V., Zamora, B. and Turner, S. (2011) 'New forms of provider in the English National Health Service', *Annals of Public and Comparative Economics*, vol 332, no 1, pp 77-95..

Audit Commission and Healthcare Commission (2008) *Is the treatment working? Progress with the NHS system reform programme*, London: Audit Commission.

Bartlett, W., Allen, P., Perotin, V., Turner, S., Zamora, B., Matchaya, G. and Roberts, J. (2010) *Provider diversity in the NHS: Impact on quality and innovation*, Report to Department of Health Policy Research Programme.

Bevan, G. and Hood, C. (2006) 'Have targets improved performance in the English NHS?', *BMJ*, vol 332, no 7538, pp 19-22.

Black, N. (2010) '"Liberating the NHS"– another attempt to implement market forces in English health care', *New England Journal of Medicine*, vol 363, no 12, pp 1103-5.

Bloom, N., Propper, C., Seiler, S. and van Reenen, J. (2010) *The impact of competition on management quality: Evidence from public hospitals*, Discussion paper 2010/09, London: Imperial College Business School.

Brereton, L. and Gubb, J. (2010) *Refusing treatment: The NHS and market-based reform*, London: Civitas.

Brereton, L. and Vasoodaven, V. (2010) *The impact of the NHS market: An overview of the literature*, London: Civitas.

Browne, J., Jamieson, L., Lewsey, J., van der Meulen, J., Copley, L. and Black, N. (2008) 'Case mix and patients' reports of outcome in independent sector treatment centres: comparison with NHS providers', *BMC Health Services Research*, vol 8, no 78 (doi:10.1186/1472-6963-8-78).

Cookson, R. and Laudicella, M. (2010) *Effects of health reform on health care inequalities*, Draft final report to the Department of Health Health Reform Evaluation Programme.

Cookson, R. and Laudicella, M. (2011) 'Do the poor cost much more? The relationship between small area deprivation and length of stay for elective hip replacement in the English NHS from 2001/2 to 2007/8', *Social Science and Medicine*, vol 72, no 2, pp 173-84.

Cooper, Z.N., McGuire, A., Jones, S. and Le Grand, J. (2009) 'Equity, waiting times, and NHS reforms: retrospective study', *BMJ*, vol 339, b3264 (doi10.1136/bmj/b3264).

Cooper, Z.N., Gibbons, S., Jones, S. and McGuire, A. (2010) *Does hospital competition save lives? Evidence from the English NHS patient choice reforms*, Working Paper 16/2010, London: LSE Health, London School of Economics and Political Science.

DH (Department of Health) (2005) *Health reform in England: Update and next steps*, London: DH.

Dixon, S. (2010) *Report on the National Patient Choice Survey – February 2010 England*, London: Department of Health (www.calderdale-link. org.uk/wp-content/uploads/downloads/2010/07/dh_117096.pdf).

Dixon, A., Robertson, R., Appleby, J., Burge, P., Devlin, N. and Magee, H. (2010) *Patient choice: How patients choose and how providers respond*, London: King's Fund.

Farrar, S., Yi, D., Sutton, M., Chalkley, M., Sussex, J. and Scott, A. (2009) 'Has payment by results affected the way that English hospitals provide care? Difference-in-difference analysis', *BMJ*, vol 339, b3047 (doi: 10.1136/bmj.b3047).

Gaynor, M.S., Moreno-Serra, R. and Propper, C. (2010) *Death by market power: Reform, competition and patient outcomes in the National Health Service*, NBER Working Paper 16164, Cambridge, MA: National Bureau of Economic Research.

Healthcare Commission (2005) *The Healthcare Commissions review of NHS foundation trusts*, London: Healthcare Commission.

Healthcare Commission (2007) *Independent sector treatment centres: Review of the quality of care*, London: Healthcare Commission.

Heins, E., Price, D., Pollock, A.M., Miller, E., Mohan, J. and Shaoul, J. (2010) 'A review of the evidence of third sector performance and its relevance for a universal comprehensive health system', *Social Policy & Society*, vol 9, no 4, pp 515-26.

HM Government (2010) *The Coalition: Our programme for government*, London: Cabinet Office.

House of Commons Health Select Committee (2008) *Foundation Trusts and Monitor*, Sixth Report of Session 2007-08, London: The Stationery Office.

King's Fund (2010a) 'The King's Fund's response to the NHS White Paper', Press release, 12 July, London: King's Fund (www.kingsfund. org.uk/press/press_releases/the_kings_funds.html).

King's Fund (2010b) *Liberating the NHS: The right prescription in a cold climate?*, The King's Fund response to the 2010 health White Paper, London: King's Fund.

King's Fund and Doctors.net.uk. (2010) *Impact of the health White Paper. What do doctors think?*, London: King's Fund (www.kingsfund.org.uk/ current_projects/the_nhs_white_paper/impact_of_the_health.html).

NHS Confederation (2010) *Equity and excellence: Liberating the NHS. Consultation response from the NHS Confederation, 5 October 2010*, London: NHS Confederation.

Nuffield Trust, The (2010) *The coalition government's NHS reforms: An assessment of the White Paper*, Briefing, London: The Nuffield Trust (www.nuffieldtrust.org.uk/publications).

Pérotin, V., Zamora, B., Reeves, R., Bartlett, W. and Allen, P. (2010) *Does hospital ownership affect patient experience? An investigation into public-private sector differences in England,* under review.

Pollock, A. and Godden, S. (2008) 'Independent sector treatment centres: evidence so far', *BMJ,* vol 336, no 7641, pp 421-4.

Powell, M., Millar, R., Mulla, A., Brown, H., Fewtrell, C., McLeod, H., Goodwin, N., Dixon, A. and Naylor, C. (2010) *Comparative case studies of health reform in England,* Report submitted to Department of Health Policy Research Programme.

Propper, C., Sutton, M., Whitnall, C. and Windmeijer, F. (2008) 'Did "targets and terror" reduce waiting times in England for hospital care?', *B.E. Journal of Economic Analysis & Policy,* vol 8, no 2 (Contributions), Article 5 (www.bepress.com/bejeap/vol8/iss2/art5).

Raine, R., Wong, W., Scholes, S., Ashton, C., Obichere, A. and Ambler, G. (2010) 'Social variations in access to hospital care for patients with colorectal, breast and lung cancer between 1999 and 2006: retrospective analysis of hospital episode statistics', *BMJ,* vol 340, b5479 (doi:10.1136/bmj.b5479).

Secretary of State for Health (1997) *The new NHS: Modern, dependable,* Cm 3807, London: The Stationery Office.

Secretary of State for Health (2000) *The NHS Plan,* Cm 4818-I, London: The Stationery Office.

Secretary of State for Health (2002) *Delivering the NHS Plan – Next steps on investment, next steps on reform,* Cm 5503, London: The Stationery Office.

Secretary of State for Health (2010) *Equity and excellence: Liberating the NHS,* Cm 7881, London: The Stationery Office.

Thorlby, R. and Maybin, J. (eds) (2010) *A high-performing NHS? A review of the evidence 1997–2010,* London: The King's Fund (www.kingsfund. org.uk/publications/a_highperforming_nh.html).

Walshe, K. (2010) 'Reorganisation of the NHS in England', *BMJ,* vol 341, c3843.

Part Two
Education in international context

Gaby Ramia

Introduction

Given the importance of education to life opportunities, it is perhaps surprising that education has not been more prominent in social policy debate. In the contemporary UK context of welfare and general public sector cuts and restructuring, education stands as one of the main weapons against social and economic marginalisation and a means of re-fortifying progressive citizenship. Lest it only be seen in terms of protection against market excesses, however, education is also vital to national economies themselves, in particular to the building of their global competitiveness within the knowledge economy. As the chapters of this section of *Social Policy Review 23* reveal, changes in education at all levels in recent times have reflected a profound questioning and re-definition of traditional conceptions of citizenship, and the most potent conduits for education restructuring have been internationalisation and marketisation. The influence of these two trends is all the greater because of their mutually reinforcing character.

With the themes of citizenship, markets and internationalisation in mind, Part Two begins with Chapter Eleven by Ben Kisby and James Sloam, who focus specifically on 'citizenship education' in the UK and comparable countries. They discuss separately the programmes of England, Wales, Scotland and Northern Ireland, and their analysis also features the US, France and Germany. They view citizenship education in terms of 'promot[ing] political participation in diverse, pluralistic societies'. As they point out, this is an international agenda, with the Council of Europe explicitly seeking to foster 'education for democratic citizenship and human rights'. The chapter explores the varied approaches to citizenship education in secondary schools within the countries of interest, and the authors draw lessons from cross-national comparative discussion, principally with reference to 'four key pillars of good practice': political literacy, experiential learning, appropriate institutional structures and supply-side factors relating to 'the delivery of conventional politics'. They argue that understanding citizenship education programmes in different countries serves governments well in policy learning, particularly given that there is no one recipe for national success and no 'one size fits all'.

Chapter Twelve by Neville Harris also has major implications for citizenship through education but takes a more local approach, focusing on England. Rather than citizenship education, however, he analyses trends in education dispute resolution and rights redress, focusing on 'alternative' methods in the management of disputes between parents and educational and governmental authorities. Harris considers the implications of using alternatives to more 'traditional' (that is, formal-legal) adjudicative processes. His prime example is 'mediation', where a neutral third party – a mediator – meets with the two primary parties to a dispute, individually and collectively to facilitate a 'negotiated settlement'. Supporters of 'alternative dispute resolution' (ADR), as it is called, often argue that it saves public money by diverting cases away from expensive courts and tribunals, and that it can result in more mutually satisfactory outcomes for all parties. Yet, as Harris argues, adopting methods such as mediation alters the form of dispute resolution, but not its essential character, which remains 'combative and narrowly focused, regardless of its social justice implications'. In effect, using his own words in the chapter title, with ADR as with traditional methods, the parent of an aggrieved child must still 'shout' for justice, and those parents more attuned to assertive negotiation stand to fare better than those who are not.

Moving outside the UK, Chapter Thirteen, by Andrew Butcher and Terry McGrath, examines the intersection between international education and foreign policy in the context of New Zealand, a small country of 4.2 million people but one which has seen dramatic growth in international students studying within its shores. With a now long-term strategic focus by government on cooperation with Asia, the region to which New Zealand belongs, Butcher and McGrath identify a major growth in students travelling, first from South East Asia but more recently especially from China, Japan, India and Saudi Arabia. In analysing historical trends in the relationship between foreign policy and international education, they argue that the links between the two are clear to see, even if policy scholars, civil servants and policy makers in the country have yet to realise their significance. The foreign policy objectives of aid and the defeat of communist interests from South East Asia lay behind the first, limited opening up of New Zealand's borders to international students in 1951 under the Colombo Plan. Fees at that stage were minimal or non-existent, but as international education began to grow dramatically from the 1980s, the agenda moved squarely to trade benefits and were linked to the labour market skills and associated migration needs of the country. In terms of fee revenues the technical and tertiary sectors have been the main beneficiaries, although successive governments have also sought to decrease educational institutions' reliance on the public dollar. Student safety from crime and discrimination, and the reputation of major education exporter countries, is also a theme examined.

The realms of public expenditure, market imperatives and the internationalisation of education are also explored in Chapter Fourteen, by Simon Marginson and Erlenawati Sawir. Their context is Australia, New Zealand's closest neighbour and historically the most similar national regime in public and social policy. Rather than foreign policy, Marginson and Sawir's central interest is the link between international education and the human security of international students. After a brief discussion of the concept of human security, their analysis turns to an extensive review of the political economy of growth in the market for international education services. The status of international students in the global market is then discussed, followed by a case study of students' security in Australia, stemming from a programme of 200 in-depth interviews with individuals studying onshore in that country. As the authors make clear, the significance of Australia stems from the fact that, although a relatively small country in global terms, with a total population of 22 million people, it has the world's fourth largest international student enrolment in absolute terms, behind the US, the UK and Germany respectively. In terms of per capita international student enrolment, it is first. The authors argue that international education needs to be 're-normed', principally through re-regulation for student security. This would more effectively cater for the rights of students to safety and social and economic inclusion in their host society.

The final chapter, Chapter Fifteen, by Stephen J. Ball, has a similar focus in dealing with the commercialisation of international education services. However, his focus is on the development and the fragmentation of services which transcend national borders. In his words, this is reflected in 'the growth of multinational education businesses and new policy assemblages'. Ball's usage of 'policy' is broad enough to capture the relationship between international business concepts and strategies on the one hand, and policies and regulations on the other. Corporate philanthropy plays a role in partially addressing equity and access issues in the context of privatisation, the other part being fulfilled by national governments and by new forms of global civil society, such as the Clinton Global Initiative. Key individuals, such as social entrepreneurs and non-traditional academics, he argues, must and do collaborate with organisations in all sectors and at all geographical levels, and with publishers in transnational knowledge networks and epistemic communities of various kinds. In coming to terms with these new and as yet less understood forms of education internationalisation, he argues, 'education policy analysis can no longer sensibly be limited to within the nation state and ... must also extend its purview to include transnational business practices'.

ELEVEN

Citizenship education in international perspective: lessons from the UK and overseas

Ben Kisby[1] and James Sloam

Introduction

Social policy can be viewed as a branch of public policy that is particularly concerned with human welfare or perhaps human 'well-being', since 'well-being is about how well people *are*, not how well they *do*' (Dean, 2006, p 1, original emphasis). It is therefore interested in a whole range of public policies that aim to improve welfare and well-being, for example, through meeting particular needs citizens have or improving their material conditions or seeking to promote certain forms of citizen behaviour, and it includes a wide variety of policy areas, such as social security, healthcare, housing, employment, pensions, social care, crime and education. Education, at a general level, is an important tool of social policy in the UK and elsewhere, concerned as it is with promoting the intellectual and social development of individuals and the socialisation of young people into society through the transmission of particular norms and values.

Much faith has been placed in education as an answer to the problem of how to promote political participation in diverse, pluralistic societies (Barber, 1994; DfEE/QCA, 1998; Carnegie Corporation/CIRCLE, 2003; Kisby and Sloam, 2009a) – especially given the declining participation of citizens in some forms of democratic engagement, which has become a major theme for policy makers and academics in liberal democracies across the western world (Putnam, 2000; Barber, 2004; Macedo et al, 2005; Hay and Stoker, 2009). Citizenship education in schools has provided a specific response to these challenges. Increasing interest in citizenship education is in many ways an international phenomenon, as illustrated by the strong support for 'education for democratic citizenship and human rights' in the Council of Europe (2002, 2010).

This chapter explores the varied approaches to citizenship education in secondary schools in the United Kingdom, the United States, France and Germany. These countries are appropriate for comparison because of their broad similarities as wealthy, industrialised, liberal democratic, western countries that have all developed important initiatives to promote citizenship education since the 1990s. The chapter provides a brief summary of existing provision in these four countries. It then sets out important lessons that can be drawn from these different experiences on the basis of 'desirability' and 'feasibility' (Rose, 1993). The chapter critically analyses the forms of citizenship education advanced in these countries in terms of four key pillars of good practice, which it argues are essential for the promotion of active citizenship: political literacy, experiential learning, appropriate institutional structures and supply-side factors relating to the delivery of conventional politics.

The United Kingdom

The UK's asymmetric form of devolved governance developed significantly after the Labour Party came to power in 1997. In 1998 Labour established a Scottish Parliament, a National Assembly for Wales and a Northern Ireland Assembly. Several important policy-making powers were devolved to these new bodies from the UK central government (see Keating, 2002; Bradbury and McGarvey, 2003). Yet differences in educational structures and approaches pre-date the recent devolution process. Indeed, Wales, Scotland and Northern Ireland already enjoyed a substantial degree of autonomy in relation to education. In Scotland this can be traced back to the establishment of the Union with England in 1707. In Wales, this autonomy was only reasserted in 1987 with the announcement of the creation of a Welsh National Curriculum. In Northern Ireland, the Protestant and Catholic churches historically have played, and continue to play, an extremely important role in educational provision.

England

Labour came to power in 1997 committed to addressing what it perceived as a decline in levels of social capital in Britain, and citizenship lessons were introduced in England principally because of concerns held by a range of actors, including politicians, academics and pressure groups, about this (Kisby, 2006, 2007). The framework for citizenship education in English schools was provided by the report of the Advisory Group on Citizenship (AGC), *Education for citizenship and the teaching of democracy in schools*, published in September 1998 (DfEE/QCA, 1998) and chaired by the late Bernard Crick. As a result, since August 2002 citizenship education has been part of the non-statutory personal, social and health education framework at primary level and a statutory subject at secondary level. Citizenship education in England focuses on promoting both participation in conventional forms of politics (for example, voting) and in engagement in the community. It was initially defined in terms of three strands – 'social and moral responsibility, community involvement and political literacy' (DfEE/QCA, 1998, p 11). It is underpinned by what may be described as a 'republican communitarian' model of citizenship, which emphasises both political participation in the public realm of the state and civil society and the importance of community membership as a necessary prerequisite for such participation (Kisby, 2009).

These communitarian ideas were a strong influence on the philosophy of New Labour – embodied in its mantra of 'rights and responsibilities' (Blair, 1998) – and can also be found in the current Conservative-Liberal Democrat Coalition's concept of a 'Big Society' (Cameron, 2010). Successive Labour governments after 1997 sought to address concerns about political disengagement by citizens through efforts to reduce 'social exclusion' (for example, targets to reduce child poverty) and to increase ties to the state through an emphasis on 'citizenship' and 'Britishness' (Brown, 2004; Goldsmith, 2008). However, this was also tied to concerns about the perceived 'failure' of multiculturalism (and immigration) that increased after the 'race' riots in Bradford in 2001 and the London bombings in July 2005 (Phillips, 2004; Portillo, 2005). In this context, community cohesion became an increasingly important objective of citizenship education, and a new fourth strand on 'identity and diversity: living together in the UK' was introduced in September 2008 (DfES, 2007) to go alongside the three initial strands.

Wales

Citizenship education in Wales is not part of the Welsh National Curriculum. It is not on a statutory footing, nor is it taught as a separate subject. Lessons in citizenship are provided by schools through personal and social education, which became a statutory component of the Welsh curriculum in September 2003 for Key Stages 1 to 4. *Personal and social education framework Key Stages 1–4* (ACCAC, 2000, p 2), a non-statutory framework, was published in 2000 and outlines how schools can seek to foster active citizenship by Welsh pupils. School children are encouraged to be active citizens in local and global contexts. Citizenship education in Wales is driven, in particular, by the interaction of the cross-curricular themes of 'community understanding' and the 'curriculum cymreig'. Community understanding is 'central' to the concept of 'cymreig' (that is, those things such as language, history and culture, for example, that relate specifically to Wales) and 'will need to be developed in every school in Wales, as part of the entitlement of all children' (CCW, 1991, p 3).

Schools are to ensure that pupils are 'encouraged and equipped to demonstrate commitment to community life in participation, service and action which promotes the well-being' of communities and that 'political literacy' is fostered (ACCAC, 2000, p 5). However, schools have a good deal of autonomy in deciding how best to deliver citizenship education, and provision is uneven. The office of Her Majesty's Inspectorate for Education and Training in Wales provided a rather negative assessment of progress so far with regard to the promotion of 'social responsibility' or 'values education', arguing that much more needs to be done: 'Schools do not always plan a whole-school approach to promoting social responsibility. Few teachers have received specific training in promoting social responsibility and as a result, the explicit promotion of social responsibility is often limited to a small number of subjects' (Estyn, 2007, p 4).

Scotland

In Scotland, there is no statutory national curriculum, which is the result of a long tradition of doubts about the efficacy of centralised, hierarchically imposed education initiatives (Paterson, 1996, 2002). As such, responsibility for what is taught lies with local authorities and schools. In Scotland, like Wales, there has been no new subject or curricular area of 'citizenship' introduced into schools. This is not to suggest that citizenship education is not delivered in Scotland. Elements of what can be described as 'education for citizenship' have been provided by schools since the introduction of Modern Studies as an Ordinary Grade or 'O' Grade (roughly equivalent to the old English 'O' Level) qualification in 1962 (Andrews and Mycock, 2007, p 74). Modern Studies (which is not compulsory) combines a range of areas of study, including geography, history, economics, politics and international issues, promoting knowledge of current affairs and political literacy more generally.

Citizenship education in Scotland (as in Wales) also places a greater stress on cultural identity than in England. All subjects are meant to feed into citizenship education, with issues deemed relevant to citizenship taught through whole-school and cross-curricular activities. Citizenship education should therefore pervade through the ethos of schools. For Learning and Teaching Scotland (LTS), the educational national review body, in order for young people to develop the capacities for citizenship, four aspects of citizenship education, in particular, need to be developed: 'knowledge and understanding', 'skills and competencies', 'values and dispositions' and 'creativity and enterprise' (LTS, 2002, p 3). However, as a result of the high degree of autonomy afforded to schools and individual teachers, there is a wide disparity in terms of how citizenship education is delivered (HMIE, 2006a). Her Majesty's Inspectorate of Education, the body responsible for the monitoring of education in Scotland, has emphasised the point that much more effort is needed to turn aspirations into practice at grass-roots level in the transition towards the new Curriculum for Excellence (HMIE, 2006a, 2006b).

Northern Ireland

The education system in Northern Ireland is, in some important respects, not unlike the systems in place in England and Wales – the crucial difference being 'that the administration of schools in Northern Ireland is politicized differently', principally as a result of profound political and religious differences between members of the Protestant and Catholic communities (O'Callaghan and Lundy, 2002, p 16). Lessons in citizenship were previously provided by schools through two compulsory, complementary cross-curricular themes, 'education for mutual understanding' (EMU) and 'cultural heritage', which were formally introduced in all schools in 1992. Both of these themes sought to promote greater cross-community awareness and tolerance (DENI, 1999).

After the Belfast Agreement the Council for the Curriculum, Examinations and Assessment (CCEA) proposed the introduction of citizenship education in secondary schools, to further promote mutual understanding, tolerance and respect. Following the 2003 curriculum review in Northern Ireland undertaken by the CCEA, which raised concerns about the consistency of citizenship education provision, citizenship education was introduced as an explicit statutory entitlement (Andrews and Mycock, 2007, p 76). Since September 2007 citizenship education provision for primary schools has been established as a strand within the personal development syllabus as 'mutual understanding in the local and global community', and is concerned with a range of themes including:'my family and friends','my school','my community' and 'the wider world'. Secondary schools have seen the introduction of 'local and global citizenship' as a statutory component of the revised Northern Ireland Curriculum as part of 'learning for life and work'. Students address four key concepts as part of local and global citizenship. These are: 'diversity and inclusion', 'equality and social justice', 'democracy and active participation' and 'human rights and social responsibility' (see CCEA, 2004, 2005). The syllabus for local and global citizenship provides a comprehensive framework – founded on evidence-based practice in teaching and citizenship education (in some ways similar to the framework for citizenship education in England) – for the achievement of active citizenship (CCEA, 2010).

The United States

While 'citizenship education' in the UK intentionally and explicitly advocates political participation,'civic education' in the US has focused to a greater extent on the citizen's role in the community and on 'civic engagement'; that is, 'working to make a difference in the civic life of our communities and developing the combination of knowledge, skills, values and motivation to make that difference ... through both political and non-political processes' (Ehrlich, 2000, p vi). Citizenship education has not been formalised within a central, common framework as now exists in England. Many schools do provide courses on subjects such as 'American government', 'civics', 'US political system', 'contemporary issues' or 'economic, legal and political system in action' (Ruget, 2006, p 25), but there is a great deal of variety in provision. For example, formal assessment of civic education is encouraged in 30 states but not in the other 20 (National Center for Learning and Citizenship, 2009). Furthermore, implementation of citizenship education is largely determined by each individual district and school board (Torney-Purta and Vermeer, 2004). Efforts have been made by important advocacy groups, such as the Carnegie Foundation and the Center for Information and Research on Civic Learning and Engagement (CIRCLE) (Carnegie Corporation/CIRCLE, 2003), to develop and coordinate a national framework for citizenship education, but they have made little headway in the US federal system.

Although community service is a common feature of school life and levels of volunteering among young people in the US remain comparatively high, 'school-based civic education is in decline' and teachers fear addressing controversial topics (Carnegie Corporation/CIRCLE, 2003, p 7), such as the issue of voter registration (seen to favour the Democratic Party). The US federal system makes it difficult to achieve a unified approach – it allows flexibility in provision (adapting to local circumstances), but makes citizenship education vulnerable to pressure from political and social groups, which have become increasingly aware of the importance of education (for example, advocates of the teaching of 'creationism' in schools). In this context, it is perhaps understandable that schools have been reluctant to promote 'political participation' as opposed to 'worthy' activities in the community.

France

In France, former Education Minister, Jean-Pierre Chevènement, introduced 'civic education' (*'education civique'*) as a compulsory subject in primary schools and the *collège* (lower secondary school for 11- to 15-year-olds) in 1985 to address the perceived problem of increasing cultural diversity (Bergougnioux, 2003, p 56). However, this initiative aimed to teach values and issues rather than discuss them or integrate them more broadly into the curriculum. This problem was directly addressed in 1996, when citizenship education was turned into a cross-curricular subject in lower secondary schools, to be integrated into the ethos of the *collège*. In 1999 a new compulsory subject, 'civic, legal and social education' (*'éducation civique, juridique et sociale'*, or ECJS) was introduced into the *lycée* (upper secondary school for 15- to 18-year-olds; see Starkey, 2000, p 40) amid concerns about the perceived growing indifference of young people towards politics and core social values, and about youth crime and disorder. It was also a reaction to the perceived impact of immigration – in particular, the political and social alienation of young immigrants, dramatically illustrated by the explosion of violence in the Paris *'banlieue'* (suburbs) and elsewhere in France in 2005.

ECJS aimed to address social, economic and political alienation (Ministère de l'Education, 2000). The central aim of ECJS is to enable citizens to develop the capacity for civic engagement, which supposes the formation of reasoned opinion, the ability to express oneself, and acceptance of public debate, and is taught through conceptual reflection

– principally, the discussion of 'democratic values' using knowledge of 'constitutional principles' (taught at the intermediate level) (Tournier, 2006). However, there is something of a tension here between this interactive style of curriculum and educational practice in France, which is oriented towards the teaching of 'scientific' knowledge as opposed to the discussion of current (controversial) political issues. Although there is no community participation element to the programme, citizenship education has been supported by wider changes in the education system. The decentralisation of secondary education after 1998 has meant that schools are increasingly embedded in their communities (Cole, 2005), offering potential for learning beyond the school environment should it become a policy priority.

Germany

'Political education', as it is called in Germany, is treated as a general aim of education and is integrated into all subjects, but it is also taught as a separate subject (although not usually to young people under 12 years of age). Political education is a holistic concept that is taught in most major institutions in German society – from trades unions to sports clubs to the armed services. Democratic engagement is strongly promoted by the Federal Centre for Political Education (BPB) and the Federal Ministry for Family Affairs, Senior Citizens, Women and Youth. The presence of strong regional government (as in the US) does, however, mean that that there is no national framework for citizenship education in Germany. Each of Germany's 16 '*Länder*' (states) has almost complete control of education policy, and this is reflected in the variety of terms used for subjects relating to citizenship education (22 in all! see Edelstein, 2004) – from 'social studies' ('*Sozialkunde*') to 'community studies' ('*Gemeinschaftskunde*') to 'politics and the economy' ('*Politik und Wirtschaft*') (Abs et al, 2006; Lange, 2006). Nevertheless, more effort is made to coordinate education policy than is the case in the US.

Common policies and strategies for education are discussed by state governments three or four times a year at the *Kultusministerkonferenz* (literally 'Culture Minister Conference', a state conference on education and media). In Germany, the teacher traditionally possesses a high degree of autonomy. This offers individual teachers the flexibility to engage with students' different perceptions and experiences. However, a key concern here is that German teachers are trained within individual disciplines rather than in pedagogy per se, and often believe that teaching a discipline is both more important than, and incompatible with, the promotion of broader democratic goals. Thus, recent innovations to promote political participation – in particular, the 'Demokratie Lernen und Leben' ('Learning and Living Democracy') programme set up by the BPB – have met with stiff resistance from social science teachers who usually teach political education classes (Edelstein, 2004; Sliwka et al, 2006).

Discussion: citizenship education and lesson-drawing

The problems of comparison across time and space are well known and include important issues such as the limited number of appropriate cases or countries for comparison, difficulties caused by different cultural understandings of particular concepts, and the need for value judgements to be made in the evaluation of different cultural practices. We agree with Kuhn (2006, p 2), who notes that: 'International comparative studies on civic education are especially difficult because of the lack of a common understanding of what civic education is as a subject and because of different cultural and political traditions or different school systems'. Nevertheless, comparison is possible and instructive.

As we have argued elsewhere (Kisby and Sloam, 2009b), there are four key principles that underlie the successful delivery of citizenship education. First, citizenship lessons must be underpinned by a commitment to political literacy, to provide citizens with the knowledge, skills and values to participate in the democratic life of their polities (Crick, 2004). Second, citizenship education must be underpinned and driven by experiential learning (Dewey, 1916; Kolb, 1984), as connecting learning to students' experiences is essential for both pedagogical and participatory reasons (Sloam, 2008). Third, citizenship education must be supported by appropriate institutional structures that facilitate an open and democratic environment (Gutmann, 1999; Carnegie Corporation/ CIRCLE, 2003; Torney-Purta and Amadeo, 2003); it is essential that citizenship classes must be deeply integrated into the overall school environment (Sliwka et al, 2006). Finally, if active citizenship is to be promoted through citizenship education, we argue that supply-side factors relating to the delivery of conventional politics are also crucial (Kisby and Sloam, 2009b). While these principles are clearly not exhaustive – other factors like specialist teacher training also play a critical role – they offer a sound basis for evaluating citizenship education across different countries. How does current policy and provision in the different countries we examine match up to these criteria?

Political literacy

In terms of political literacy, the frameworks for citizenship education in England and Northern Ireland come closest. In both countries citizenship (or local and global citizenship) classes are statutory, are taught both discretely and across the curriculum and aim to provide students with the knowledge to understand, and the skills to engage in, political activities. In Scotland and Wales, by contrast, commitment to political literacy is patchier. In both countries much attention is focused on issues of national identity (for example, the strong emphasis on cultural, historical and linguistic identity and distinctiveness). Although there is evidence that teaching citizenship education through other subjects rather than as a separate subject may be the most effective way of transmitting relevant knowledge to students (Whiteley, 2008, p 26), the fact that citizenship education in not statutory in Scotland and Wales leaves the door open for significant unevenness in provision. Similarly, in the US and Germany, there are examples of excellent practice, but provision is diverse and sketchy across these federal systems.

On the other hand, a strong national framework and a very prescriptive education system and policies do not guarantee that citizenship education succeeds at ground level. The highly centralised system in England, for example, denies schools and teachers the flexibility to teach citizenship education within their own unique contexts. In France, over-centralisation is accompanied by an imposed identity and hierarchical learning structures, which makes it difficult for students to define citizenship in their own terms. Thus, the tensions between over-centralised, top-down citizenship education (which is unlikely to deliver in practice) and a more decentralised approach (which is unlikely to establish a coherent common framework) are not easily solved.

Yet the picture is not bleak, as innovative initiatives have sometimes established a better balance in both unitary and federal states. At the micro-level, specialist training can give citizenship teachers the tools to overcome these problems themselves. In unitary states, greater freedom can be given to schools and teachers. The Cambridge Primary Review (2009), for example, recommended the scaling back of the National Curriculum in England to 70 per cent, with 30 per cent reserved for a localised 'Community Curriculum'. In federal states, more effective national coordination of citizenship education is a potential solution. In Germany, the BPB is designed to fulfil this role. Although similar institutions exist to support and promote citizenship education in the UK (for example, the Citizenship Foundation, the Community Service

Volunteers, the Association for Citizenship Teaching), in the US (for example, the Center for Civic Education) and in France (for example, the Centre National de Documentation Pédagogique, and the network of Centres Régionals de Documentation Pédagogique), they lack status and/or the resources of the BPB. At the end of 2007, the BPB could boast a staff of 235 and an annual budget of over €35 million (BPB, 2007). The UK, the US and France would, in our view, benefit significantly from the creation of well-resourced, official national-level bodies such as the BPB.

Similarly, the UK, France and Germany could improve support for citizenship education in schools if this was taken seriously in universities and colleges, as in the US (Sliwka, 2006; Sloam, 2008). Quite unlike the other three countries in this study, in the US much of the impetus for the promotion, evaluation and reform of citizenship education comes from higher education, which acts as a centre for advanced research (for example, CIRCLE and the Carnegie Foundation for the Advancement of Teaching) and as laboratories for democratic engagement and citizenship education (for example, Carnegie Foundation/CIRCLE, 2006; Colby et al, 2007). The value of this level of democratic engagement for US universities and US society is significant – as illustrated by the explosion of civic engagement and political participation on campuses in recent years (HERI, 2009).

Experiential learning

To provide effective citizenship education, both experiential learning and an open and interactive learning environment are necessary. This is not to say that learning outcomes are not important, but that student-centred teaching and a school ethos that embraces student participation in decision making are integral features of good citizenship education. As the AGC argued in its 1998 report on citizenship education in England: 'Schools need to consider how far their ethos, organisation and daily practices are consistent with the aim and purpose of citizenship education and affirm and extend the development of pupils into active citizens' (DfEE/QCA, 1998, p 49). The sentiments of the AGC report are also expressed in the Carnegie Corporation/CIRCLE (2003) report on *The civic mission of schools*, as well as the BPB-sponsored 'Learning and Living Democracy' programme in Germany.

Yet with regard to experiential learning, we find a nuanced picture. Although the English and Northern Irish curricula stress the importance of diversity and multiculturalism and the multiple identities that exist within society, the approaches adopted are undermined in different ways by the nature of the respective education systems. In England, students and schools are regularly tested and evaluated on pupils' exam success, and teachers and schools are limited in their autonomy by the rigidness of the National Curriculum (Ball, 2008; Pring et al, 2009). This undermines efforts to promote learning through experience. In Northern Ireland, the continuing very high levels of segregation of pupils into Catholic and Protestant schools helps perpetuate rather than ameliorate deep religious and political divisions in society. Attempting to promote mutual understanding and tolerance between students from one background in a context where very often they have little or nothing to do with students from another background is problematic, to put it mildly.

In France, the centralised education system is also a problem and experiential learning is weakened by the very hierarchical relationship between teacher and student. Citizenship education in Germany suffers from the same problem as France. According to Edelstein (2004, p 5): 'German schools are hierarchical institutions placed in a hierarchically organised ... bureaucratic system with limited traditions of participatory governance'. This has a bearing on instruction, which is oriented towards the behaviourist (transmission) model of teaching (Torney-Purta et al, 2001, p 164). In France and Germany, the existing teaching cultures – in general, behaviourist, hierarchical and transmission-based – are problematic. To improve citizenship education in these countries there is a need for the further development of student-centred teaching (perhaps through more specialised training like the Postgraduate Certificate in Citizenship Education that now exists in England). On the other hand, in England there is still a strong need for greater autonomy for teachers to practice the student-centred approach that is already privileged in existing teacher training. The greater autonomy afforded to schools and teachers in the US, Scotland and Wales, the less exam-oriented nature of their respective curricula (in comparison to England), the greater embeddedness of schools within their communities (Carnegie Corporation/CIRCLE, 2003; Chitty, 2009; Freeman, 2009) and the greater emphasis on community involvement, enhance the possibilities for experiential learning for pupils.

Institutional structures

In addition to the process of teaching and learning, pupil participation in decision making in schools helps to establish a participatory ethos in which citizenship education can thrive. In this respect, we have witnessed much progress in each of the countries studied in this chapter. Despite the hierarchical nature of teaching and learning, French secondary schools are now required by law to have a committee for health and citizenship education, comprised of teachers, students and parents, that contributes to the school action plan. In England, there has also been much improvement in student representation in decision making in schools. All relevant parties – teachers, non-teaching staff, pupils, parents and other members of the community – are now expected to be involved in decision making with regard to the school's operation. Nevertheless, these positive developments in England and France again run up against the constraints of centralisation, which make decision making in schools a largely path-dependent process.

In short, if issues surrounding the curriculum, budget and associated considerations are largely determined by central government, freedom of decision making is restrained, so that student input is severely restricted in a number of crucial areas. In this context, efforts to give teachers and schools more autonomy (as in the US and Germany) are to be welcomed.

Supply-side factors

Finally, if active citizenship is to be promoted through citizenship education, we argue that supply-side factors (see Hay, 2007, pp 39–60) relating to the delivery of conventional politics are also crucial (Kisby and Sloam, 2009a). Here, we tie together the concepts of 'internal efficacy' and 'external efficacy' (Balch, 1974; Pasek, 2009). While the three other pillars of good practice address the internal efficacy of the student, political actors and structures shape external efficacy. The relationship between citizenship education, political agency and the supply of political goods is largely ignored in the existing literature. We argue that these relationships need to be nurtured – in the context of citizenship education, supply-side actors (for example, politicians) must engage with students within relevant institutional contexts. The centralised system in England, for example, shows how political institutions can act as barriers to democratic engagement – all the good work done through citizenship education can be undermined by a political system that reduces incentives for participation through a lack of access (to political influence) and rewards (positive impacts from engagement). In this respect, the devolved Parliament in Scotland, the devolved Assemblies in Wales and Northern Ireland, and the state and district authorities in the US and Germany, are at least closer to the people, that is, they are smaller units of government that, at least in principle, offer more promising avenues for citizens to influence the political process.

The way formal politics is practised impacts on citizens' attitudes to politicians and to the political system, and so it is particularly important for the development of external efficacy. In recent decades, the drop in confidence in political institutions has been widely recognised (for example, Pharr and Putnam, 2000). It is rare for politicians to directly address issues of concern to young people, such as youth unemployment and housing – political parties *rationally* neglect marginalised groups (including young people) that are less likely to vote (Sloam, 2007). This is particularly so with regards to issues of concern to school students below the voting age. If the 'input legitimacy' of electoral politics is worryingly low among young people (in most industrialised democracies voting and party membership has markedly declined in recent decades), 'output legitimacy' is likely to be further weakened by the recent global recession, with young people in industrialised democracies disproportionally bearing the brunt of rising unemployment. According to Organisation for Economic Co-operation and Development (OECD) (2009) figures, 15- to 24-year-olds make up 26.2 per cent of the unemployed in France, 15.6 per cent in Germany, 27 per cent in the UK and 26.4 per cent in the US. Nevertheless, the Obama campaign for the US Presidency shows what can be done if politicians directly address young people and the issues that concern them – the campaign marked a surge in youth engagement, in terms both of campaigning and voting (CBS News, 2008; CIRCLE, 2008a, 2008b).

Conclusion

Citizenship education is vital as a means of providing citizens with the knowledge, skills and values they need to critically appraise ideas, engage in different ways in active participation in society, and to contribute to political debates at personal, local, national and indeed international levels; it should have a role to play within society for both democratic and pedagogical reasons. More specifically, citizenship education in schools – when absorbed into the general curriculum and school ethos – can provide socialisation into democracy, providing students with enough knowledge to make sense of the world (in their own terms). It can enable the development of skills of interaction and engagement, and teach the relevance of political knowledge and democratic skills for a citizen in their everyday lives. In this chapter, we have examined the provision of citizenship education in the UK, the US, France and Germany and have structured our discussion by utilising four key principles that, in our view, underpin the successful delivery of citizenship education: political literacy, experiential learning, institutional structures (in the school and beyond) and supply-side measures relating to the delivery of conventional politics.

We have argued that there are some strengths in terms of the existing provision of citizenship education in each of the countries we have examined, although none of the countries adopts each of the principles of best practice we have identified. We accept that national differences – in terms of both the content and delivery of citizenship education – are important and necessary. We are not advocating a one-size-fits-all approach, and the learning process must pay due attention to the feasibility of new policy initiatives in each of the countries, taking into account the indigenous political systems and teaching cultures. Nevertheless, policy learning about citizenship education initiatives in the UK, the US, France and Germany has the clear potential to strengthen provision and move policy makers closer to achieving their objectives.

Acknowledgements

The authors are grateful to Majella Kilkey and Gaby Ramia for their very helpful comments on an earlier version of this chapter.

Note

[1] The research for this chapter was carried out while Ben Kisby held an Economic and Social Research Council (ESRC) postdoctoral research fellowship – Grant Number PTA-026-27-2023 – that provided the support that enabled him to undertake this work.

References

Abs, H., Schmidt, A., Huppert, A. and Breit, H. (2006) *Context report on civic and citizenship education in Germany*, German Institute for International Educational Research.

ACCAC (2000) *Personal and social education framework: Key Stages 1 to 4 in Wales*, Cardiff: ACCAC.

Andrews, R. and Mycock, A. (2007) 'Citizenship education in the UK: divergence within a multinational state', *Citizenship Teaching and Learning*, vol 3, no 1, pp 73-88.

Balch, G. (1974) 'Multiple indicators in survey research: the concept "sense of political efficacy"', *Political Methodology*, vol 1, no 2, pp 1-43.

Ball, S. (2008) *The education debate*, Bristol: The Policy Press.

Barber, B. (1994) *An Aristocracy of everyone: The politics of education and the future of America*, New York: Oxford University Press.

Barber, B. (2004 [1984]) *Strong democracy: Participatory politics for a new age*, Berkeley, CA: University of California Press.

Bergougnioux, A. (2003) 'L'école et l'éducation civique', *La Revue de l'Inspection Générale 03 ,Existe-t-il un modèle éducatif français?'*, Ministère de l'Education (http://media.education.gouv.fr/file/37/6/3376.pdf).

Blair, T. (1998) *The Third Way: New politics for the new century*, Pamphlet No 588, London: Fabian Society.

BPB (Bundeszentrale für Politische Bildung) (2007) *Jahresbericht: 2006–2007* (www.bpb.de/files/WS9EZP.pdf).

Bradbury, J. and McGarvey, N. (2003) 'Devolution: problems, politics and prospects', *Parliamentary Affairs*, vol 56, no 2, pp 219-36.

Brown, G. (2004) Speech by the Rt Hon Gordon Brown MP, Chancellor of the Exchequer, at the British Council Annual Lecture, 7 July, *The Guardian* (www.guardian.co.uk/politics/2004/jul/08/uk.labour1/print).

Cambridge Primary Review (2009) *Introducing the Cambridge Primary Review* (www.primaryreview.org.uk/Downloads/Finalreport/CPR-booklet_low-res.pdf).

Cameron, D. (2010) 'Big Society speech', Liverpool, 19 July (www.number10.gov.uk/news/speeches-and-transcripts/2010/07/big-society-speech-53572).

Carnegie Corporation (Carnegie Corporation of New York)/CIRCLE (The Center for Information and Research on Civic Learning and Engagement) (2003) *The civic mission of schools*, Carnegie Corporation (www.carnegie.org/pdf/CivicMissionofSchools.pdf).

Carnegie Foundation (Carnegie Foundation for the Advancement of Teaching)/CIRCLE (2006) *Higher education: Civic mission and civic effects*, Carnegie Foundation (www.carnegiefoundation.org/sites/default/files/publications/elibrary_pdf_633).

CBS NEWS (2008) 'Editorial: Youth engagement made difference in election', 10 November.

CCEA (Council for the Curriculum, Examinations and Assessment) (2004) *Local and global citizenship: A KS3 teaching resource* (Part 1), Belfast: CCEA.

CCEA (2005) *Local and global citizenship: A KS3 teaching resource* (Part 2), Belfast: CCEA.

CCEA (2010) *Key Stage 4: Learning for life and work: Local and global citizenship sample learning programme: Encouraging active participation amongst young people* (www.nicurriculum.org.uk/docs/key_stage_4/areas_of_learning/learning_for_life_and_work/ks4_citizenship_programme.pdf).

CCW (1991) *Community understanding: A framework for the development of a cross-curricular theme in Wales*, CCW Advisory Paper 11, Cardiff: CCW.

Chitty, C. (2009 [2003]) *Education policy in Britain*, Basingstoke: Palgrave.

CIRCLE (The Center for Information and Research on Civic Learning and Engagement) (2008a) 'National exit polls report youth represented 18 percent of voters' (www.civicyouth.org/national-exit-polls-report-youth-represented-18-percent- of-voters/).

CIRCLE (2008b) 'Youth turnout rate rises to at least 52%' (www.civicyouth.org/youth-turnout-rate-rises-to-at-least-52/).

Colby, A., Beaumont, E., Ehrlich, T. and Corngold, J. (2007) *Educating for democracy: Preparing undergraduates for responsible political engagement*, San Francisco, CA: Jossey-Bass.

Cole, A. (2005) 'Education and educational governance', in A. Cole, P. Le Galès and J. Levy (eds) *Developments in French politics 3*, Basingstoke: Palgrave, pp 195-211.

Council of Europe (2002) Recommendation Rec(2002)12 of the Committee of Ministers to member states on education for democratic citizenship (adopted by the Committee of Ministers on 16 October 2002 at the 812th meeting of the Ministers' Deputies) (https://wcd.coe.int/ViewDoc.jsp?Ref=Rec(2002)12&Language=lanEnglish&Site=CM&BackColorInternet=9999CC&BackColorIntranet=FFBB55&BackColorLogged=FFAC75).

Council of Europe (2010) Recommendation CM/Rec(2010)7 of the Committee of Ministers to member states on the Council of Europe charter on education for democratic citizenship and human rights education (adopted by the Committee of Ministers on 11 May 2010 at the 120th Session) (https://wcd.coe.int/ViewDoc.jsp?Ref=CM/Rec(2010)7&Language=lanEnglish&Ver=original&Site=CM&BackColorInternet=C3C3C3&BackColorIntranet=EDB021&BackColorLogged=F5D383).

Crick, B. (2004) 'Politics as a form of rule: politics, citizenship and democracy', in A. Leftwich (ed) *What is politics? The activity and its study*, Cambridge: Polity Press, pp 67-85.

Dean, H. (2006) *Social policy*, Cambridge: Polity Press.

DENI (Department of Education, Northern Ireland) (1999) *Towards a culture of tolerance: Education for diversity*, Bangor: DENI.

Dewey, J. (1916) *Democracy and education: An introduction to the philosophy of education*, New York: Macmillan.

DfEE (Department for Education and Employment)/QCA (Qualifications and Curriculum Authority) (1998) *Education for citizenship and the teaching of democracy in schools*, London: DfEE/QCA.

DfES (Department for Education and Skills) (2007) *Diversity and citizenship*, London: DfES.

Edelstein, W. (2004) 'The struggle for citizenship education in German schools', Paper presented at the UK–German education policy seminar on 'Cultural diversity in school education', Berlin, November.

Ehrlich, T. (ed) (2000) *Civic responsibility and higher education*, Phoenix, AZ: Oryx Press.

Estyn (2007) *Values education: An evaluation of provision of education for the promotion of social responsibility and respect for others* (http://estyn.gov. uk/publications/Values_education_an_evaluation_of_provision_of_ education_for_the_promotion_of_social_responsibility_and_respect_ for_others_2007.pdf).

Freeman, M. (2009) 'Education and citizenship in modern Scotland', *History of Education*, vol 38, no 3, pp 327-32.

Goldsmith, P. (2008) *Citizenship: Our common bond*, London: Ministry of Justice (www.justice.gov.uk/reviews/docs/citizenship-report-full.pdf).

Gutmann, A. (1999 [1987]) *Democratic education*, Princeton, NJ: Princeton University Press.

Hay, C. (2007) *Why we hate politics*, Cambridge: Polity Press.

Hay, C. and Stoker, G. (2009) 'Revitalising politics: have we lost the plot?', *Representation*, vol 45, no 3, pp 225-36.

HERI (Higher Education Research Institute) (2009) *The American freshman: National norms for fall 2008* (www.gseis.ucla.edu/heri/PDFs/ pubs/briefs/brief-pr012208-08FreshmanNorms.pdf).

HMIE (Her Majesty's Inspectorate of Education) (2006a) *A portrait of current practice in Scottish schools and pre-school centres: Education for citizenship*, Edinburgh: HMIE.

HMIE (2006b) *Improving Scottish education*, Edinburgh: HMIE.

Keating, M. (2002) 'Devolution and public policy in the United Kingdom: convergence or divergence?', in J. Adams and P. Robinson (eds) *Devolution in practice: Public policy differences within the UK*, London: Institute for Public Policy Research, pp 3-21.

Kisby, B. (2006) 'Social capital and citizenship education in schools', *British Politics*, vol 1, no 1, pp 151-60.

Kisby, B. (2007) 'New Labour and citizenship education', *Parliamentary Affairs*, vol 60, no 1, pp 84-101.

Kisby, B. (2009) 'Social capital and citizenship lessons in England: analysing the presuppositions of citizenship education', *Education, Citizenship and Social Justice*, vol 4, no 1, pp 41-61.

Kisby, B. and Sloam, J. (2009a) 'Revitalising politics: the role of citizenship education', *Representation*, vol 45, no 3, pp 313-24.

Kisby, B. and Sloam, J. (2009b) 'Revitalising democracy: civic education in Europe and the United States', Unpublished paper presented at the 2009 Annual Meeting of the American Political Science Association, Toronto, Canada, September.

Kolb, D. (1984) *Experiential learning: Experience as the source of learning and development*, Englewood Cliffs, NJ: Prentice Hall.

Kuhn, H.-W. (2006) 'European approaches to civic education for the promotion of democracy', Speech delivered at the Conference on Democracy Promotion and International Cooperation, Denver, Colorado, 25-29 September, Center for Civic Education (www.civiced. org/index.php?page=papers_speeches).

Lange, D. (2006) 'Response: Germany 1', *IDEA questionnaire on civic education*, International Institute for Democracy and Electoral Assistance (http://civiced.idea.int/public/viewSurveyResponse. jsp?srId=4345659).

LTS (Learning and Teaching Scotland) (2002) *Education for citizenship in Scotland: A paper for discussion and development*, Glasgow: LTS.

Macedo, S., Alex-Assensoh, Y. and Berry, J.M. (2005) *Democracy at risk: How political choices undermine citizen participation, and what we can do about it*, Washington, DC: Brookings Institution Press.

Ministère de l'Education (2000) 'Éducation civique juridique et sociale enseignement commune: programme applicable à compter de l'année scolaire 2000-2001', *Bulletin Officiel du Ministère de l'Education Nationale et du Ministère de la Recherche*, HS 6, 31 August, Ministère de l'Education (www.education.gouv.fr/bo/2000/hs6/civique.htm).

National Center for Learning and Citizenship (2009) *Citizenship education inclusion in assessment and accountability systems*, Denver, CO: Education Commission of the States (http://mb2.ecs.org/reports/ Report.aspx?id=107).

O'Callaghan, M. and Lundy, L. (2002) 'Northern Ireland', in L. Gearon (ed) *Education in the United Kingdom*, London: David Fulton Publishers, pp 16-28.

OECD (Organisation for Economic Co-operation and Development) (2009) *LFS by sex and age – Indicators*, OECD: Paris (http://stats.oecd. org/Index.aspx?DataSetCode=LFS_SEXAGE_I_R).

Pasek, J. (2009) 'Maligned youth? How exit polls systematically misrepresent youth turnout', Unpublished paper presented at the APSA Annual Meeting, Toronto, Canada, September.

Paterson, L. (1996) 'Liberation or control: what are the Scottish educational traditions of the twentieth century?', in T. Devine and R. Finlay (eds) *Scotland in the twentieth century*, Edinburgh: Edinburgh University Press, pp 230-49.

Paterson, L. (2002) 'Scotland', in L. Gearon (ed) *Education in the United Kingdom*, London: David Fulton Publishers, pp 29-39.

Pharr, S. and Putnam, R. (eds) (2000) *Disaffected democracies: What's troubling the trilateral countries?*, Princeton, NJ: Princeton University Press.

Phillips, T. (2004) 'Multiculturalism's legacy is "have a nice day" racism', *The Guardian*, 28 May.

Portillo, M. (2005) 'Multiculturalism has failed but tolerance can save us', *The Sunday Times*, 17 July.

Pring, R., Hayward, G., Hodgson, A., Johnson, J., Keep, E., Oancea, A., Rees, G., Spours, K. and Wilde, S. (2009) *Education for all: The future of education and training for 14-19 year-olds*, London: Routledge.

Putnam, R. (2000) *Bowling alone: The collapse and revival of American community*, New York: Simon & Schuster.

Rose, R. (1993) *Lesson-drawing in public policy. A guide to learning across time and space*, Chatham, NJ: Chatham House.

Ruget, V. (2006) 'The renewal of civic education in France and America: comparative perspectives', *The Social Science Journal*, vol 43, no 1, pp 19-34.

Sliwka, A. (2006) 'Citizenship education as the responsibility of a whole school: structural and cultural implications', in A. Sliwka, M. Diedrich and M. Hofer (eds) *Citizenship education: Theory, research, practice*, Münster: Waxmann, pp 7-18.

Sliwka, A., Diedrich, M. and Hofer, M. (eds) (2006) *Citizenship education: Theory, research, practice*, Münster: Waxmann.

Sloam, J. (2007) 'Rebooting democracy: youth participation in politics in the UK', *Parliamentary Affairs*, vol 60, no 4, pp 548-67.

Sloam, J. (2008) 'Teaching democracy: the role of political science education', *British Journal of Politics and International Relations*, vol 10, no 3, pp 509-24.

Starkey, H. (2000) 'Citizenship education in France and Britain: evolving theories and practices', *The Curriculum Journal*, vol 11, no 1, pp 39-54.

Torney-Purta, J. and Amadeo, J.-A. (2003) 'A cross-national analysis of political and civic involvement among adolescents', *PS: Political Science and Politics*, vol 36, no 2, pp 269-74.

Torney-Purta, J. and Vermeer, S. (2004) *Developing citizenship competencies from kindergarten through grade 12: A background paper for policymakers and educators*, Denver, CO: Education Commission of the States (www.ecs. org/clearinghouse/51/35/5135.pdf).

Torney-Purta, J., Lehmann, R., Oswald, H. and Schulz, W. (2001) *Citizenship and education in twenty-eight countries: Civic knowledge and engagement at age fourteen*, Amsterdam: International Association for the Evaluation of Educational Achievement.

Tournier, V. (2006) 'Response: France 1', *IDEA questionnaire on civic education*, International Institute for Democracy and Electoral Assistance (www.civiced.idea.int/public/viewSurveyResponse. jsp?srId=4729460).

Whiteley, P. (2008) 'Can voting be taught? Citizenship education and the electoral participation of students', Unpublished paper.

TWELVE

"You're only going to get it if you really shout for it": education dispute resolution in the 21st century in England

Neville Harris

Introduction

Education is a field in which there are underlying tensions between individual rights and public resources. Levels of satisfaction with schools and further and higher education institutions expressed by users seem to be high in England (Ofsted, 2007; Ivens, 2008; HEFCE, 2010) but grievances are common. As education issues can impact directly on the interests of individual children they are especially likely to be viewed as serious by parents, and thus grievances have a tendency to be transformed into disputes (Adler et al, 2006, pp 44-5). Parents will '"fight for the rights" of their children' (Ofsted, 2010, p 6; see also Lamb, 2009). This was true of Ms X, whose comments are quoted in the title to this chapter. She was interviewed for my research in England into dispute resolution and special educational needs (SEN), part of an Anglo-Scottish project (jointly with Sheila Riddell) funded by the Economic and Social Research Council (ESRC) (RES-062-23-0803).

Ms X's child had dyslexia but the local authority initially refused to provide the extra hours of specialist teaching support per week that Ms X sought for her. Ms X decided not to appeal to a special needs tribunal due to the cost of legal representation which she mistakenly thought was essential. In her negotiations, however, she was supported by her "lawyer trained" sister. She refers to "fighting all the way". Although the local authority eventually agreed to make four hours of extra provision per week, Ms X had, in her words, to "really push for it", and she added:

"that's not right, that's not fair is it? Because there's many folks out there that frankly do deserve it".

This highlights several concerns. First, so far as procedural justice is concerned, Ms X's mistaken view as to the necessity for representation shows the existence of potential barriers (due to ignorance) to effective access to formal dispute resolution mechanisms. Second, a just outcome (substantive justice) may depend on the capacity and tenacity of claimants acting privately as much as on the inherent quality of the decision maker. But, at the same time, issues of distributive justice and equity may also arise in such cases, since the granting of some claims could mean that fewer resources are available for allocation to less fortunate but possibly equally meritorious claimants. There is a tension between the subjectively based individual claim for fairness and the objectively fair allocation of resources that is consistent with notions of social and distributive justice.

This chapter assesses the role played by the different dispute resolution mechanisms in the fight for substantive justice in the field of education in England. It considers the implications of using alternatives to formal adjudicative processes, particularly those in which justice is in effect 'negotiated' in a private forum, such as via mediation, where a neutral mediator generally meets with the parties individually and collectively to facilitate a negotiated settlement. This chapter argues that adopting such an alternative for education cases alters the form but not the essential character of dispute resolution, which will remain combative and narrowly focused, regardless of the social justice implications. It begins by considering the place of the right to redress in the bundles of rights that characterise the status of users of public services. It looks at the evolution of dispute resolution mechanisms and the influence of the recently developed policy of 'proportionate dispute resolution', focusing in particular on mediation as the policy preference, before drawing some conclusions about the suitability of the current dispute resolution framework.

Consumerism, citizenship and redress

Many education-related claims centre on substantive rights that are relatively weak and subservient to state authority. Often they are concerned with choice, the 'leading idea of education reform' during the 1980s and 1990s (Brighouse, 2000, p 19) and still a dominant feature. Redress may play a part in the management of choice, whether by legitimating it or by correcting decisions that wrongly deny it. Choice and redress are among the core elements of consumerism, which was engendered by the marketising reforms to public services, intended to generate more efficient provision through the operation of a competitive market. Consumerism continued as a 'generic organizing principle for public sector reform' under New Labour post-1997 (Vidler and Clarke, 2005, p 20), associated with the idea that imbalances of power between state providers and private users of public services need to be redressed to ensure truly effective and accountable services (Stafford, 2009, p 267). But choice and redress also fall within the much analysed paradigm of citizenship, an ambiguous, multilayered and contested concept (Lister, 2007) essentially denoting a relationship with the state founded on rights and responsibilities in which, if enjoyed fully, the citizen has an opportunity to participate effectively in social, economic and political spheres. It connotes, among other things, a degree of 'ownership' of essential services, enhancing democratic principles and making services more responsive to people's needs.

This solidaristic view of citizenship may be contrasted with its more contractarian form in which the exercise of choice is given freer rein and the responsiveness and efficiency of services is the socially beneficial by-product of such individualistic action (Dean, 2002, pp 187-8). Although, under New Labour, the ministerial rhetoric was 'saturated with the language of consumerism', and neoliberalism remained 'part of the mental furniture of the political elite' (Marquand, 2004, p 118), the more collectivist and democratic notion of 'empowerment' was advanced, with, for example, the prospect of 'a school system shaped by parents' (DfES, 2005, p 23). The orientation towards more collectivist notions of 'community' has, if anything, intensified under the new Coalition government as it looks to increase parental participation in decision making 'not just about their children's education but the design and delivery of services' (DfE, 2010b, para 3.1) and the establishment of 'free' schools.

There is a theoretical distinction between the consumer, acting out of private self-interest and unconcerned about the plight of others, and the citizen, whose status is based on rights but also responsibilities to the wider community. However, in reality, people's relationship with the providers of public services has a number of dimensions (Clarke et al, 2007). The idea of the 'consumer-citizen' combines the direct personal engagement of the consumer with the 'less direct' relationship involving 'rights and duties that derive from membership of society' in the citizenship model (Woods, 1988, p 327). There is evidence that in exercising educational choice (Wilkins, 2010, pp 185-6), claiming welfare entitlement (Dean, 2002, p 188; see also Clarke et al, 2007) and accessing education as a student (Ahier et al, 2003), people are driven not only by self-interest but also a sense of community. Similarly, where redress is concerned, some people are seeking a remedy for themselves while others may wish to highlight deficiencies in order to benefit others (see Harris, 2007, p 574).

Under consumerism, redress may be regarded in somewhat instrumental terms, as a means by which users of services can hold providers to account and for upholding users' substantive rights, particularly concerning choice. In this way the operation of the market and the rebalancing of power between users and providers are reinforced. But redress is also a civil right of citizenship, one of the often interdependent classes of such rights – civil, political and social (Marshall and Bottomore, 1992; Fabre, 2000). Civil rights support the realisation of social rights, albeit that the latter tend to be highly contingent, often resource-dependent and difficult to enforce. However, they depend on individual action. Legal aid provision can recognise the need for this to be supported, but (especially with an exclusion of legal aid for education cases currently in prospect) other support may be needed, such as a 'triage plus' approach in which an expert adviser helps citizens make an informed decision about a route to redress (see Adler, 2008).

Support for the realisation of rights has occurred in the field of SEN through parent partnership services (PPS) (DfES, 2001, part 2), which parents have been found to value and perceive as 'empowering' (Rogers et al, 2006, p 48). PPS frequently assist in negotiations with local authorities but tend not to regard their role as including advising parents which dispute resolution option to select or representing them at a tribunal (Harris and Smith, 2008). More recently, the role of 'choice adviser' has been created in connection with schools admissions.[1] The adviser may assist with redress, including preparation of an appeal, accompanying parents to a hearing and, with local agreement, presenting the appeal (DCSF, 2010, Appendix 5, para 18). These specialist forms of support may reduce some of the barriers to redress that people from socially disadvantaged groups are more likely to experience (see below) and which are set to increase given the current proposals to cease public legal aid funding for most non-judicial review education matters (Ministry of Justice, 2010).

Expansion of redress

Rights of redress have featured prominently in education reform over the past three decades. They have supplemented the established administrative justice mechanisms dealing with citizen versus state grievances, such as the Local Government Ombudsman (LGO) and the High Court's judicial review jurisdiction in respect of claims of illegality/irrationality on the part of public authorities, which in fact only deals with a small minority of the education disputes in the UK.

Complaints mechanisms

The development of complaints procedures fitted with the consumerist policy trend as a means of assisting in the management of services by making providers aware of faults needing to be addressed. In a market environment, consumers' complaints are thus seen as helping to 'drive up the quality of services' (Dean, 2002, p 178). As Furedi (2010, p 3) says, 'the complaining pushy-parent is likely to emerge as the hero in the drama of marketisation'. As the Secretary of State for Education was being inundated by increasing numbers of complaints about schools or local authorities – reportedly thousands each month (National Consumer Council, 1992, p 5) – a new localised complaints system was introduced under the Education Reform Act 1988, although only for curriculum and related complaints. Such complaints could not go to the Secretary of State unless they had been through the local process. Unfortunately, parents were often unaware of the arrangements and there was much confusion among schools and local authorities regarding their remit (Harris, 1993). This complaints process was abolished in April 2010.[2] But meanwhile New Labour had introduced a separate school-based system for other complaints, involving arrangements made by the school governing body, having regard to central guidance.[3] Ofsted (Office for Standards in Education, Children's Services and Skills) was subsequently given the power to investigate written complaints by parents once they had been pursued via this school-based procedure,[4] but only complaints about matters relating to the school, such as its quality and standards of education, its leadership and management, and its contribution to pupils' well-being and development and, later, to 'community cohesion'.

A survey has found a significant number of parents to be 'surprised' and 'disappointed' that the Ofsted procedure excludes complaints about an individual child's treatment (Ofsted, 2007, Annex). In 2008 only 1,394 written complaints were made under it and only 25 were investigated; most were ineligible (Henry, 2009). The lack of a remedy for parents is one of the limitations of this route (the availability of a remedy is one of the Parliamentary Ombudsman's core principles of an effective complaints procedure: PHSO, 2009). Nevertheless, Ofsted can convene a meeting with parents at the school and its report is to be sent to the governing body and disclosed to parents. Thus complaints will be more openly discussed and notified to interested parties.

A separate new process that does cover complaints concerning individual treatment has been piloted in selected areas since April 2010.[5] It involves the LGO and covers complaints of an 'injustice' caused by the governing body or headteacher. Admissions matters are excluded. So are matters covered by a right of appeal, a restriction intended to minimise the number of separate routes of redress (DCSF, 2008a, para 83) but one that is considered unnecessary by the Administrative Justice and Tribunals Council (AJTC) (2009). Generally the complaint must have gone first to the governing body and not been resolved satisfactorily. The LGO's investigation must 'be conducted in private'.[6] A mediator may be appointed and paid to assist. On upholding a complaint the LGO may make recommendations to the school to remedy it and to prevent further injustices from similar acts. The governing body has to state what it proposes to do and could be required to publish an 'adverse findings notice'.[7] Publication would thus provide a means by which the public interest in an essentially private process of complaint is to some extent recognised. Although the LGO can only make recommendations, the Secretary of State has a power, enforceable in the courts, to direct compliance with them. The LGO lends independence and considerable complaints handling experience to this new system, and there is likely to be monitoring of complaints whereas there is no central collection of data on complaints handled by schools. Nevertheless, the Coalition government's Education Bill now proposes to end this new LGO role, primarily on cost grounds.

The LGO also retains its long-standing *general* statutory jurisdiction for dealing with complaints of maladministration (such as delays or misapplication of policies or procedures) against local authorities. In 2009–10, 2,136 (or 12 per cent) of these complaints concerned education, predominantly school admissions (approximately 66 per cent of education cases) and SEN (approximately 14 per cent).[8] Remedies, such as compensation, re-running of processes or an apology, may be recommended where an injustice is found (which happens in only a small minority of cases). Complainants in education cases can also refer their case to the Secretary of State once the LGO process has been exhausted. There are therefore three separate complaints processes covering school education, making the system as a whole complex and liable to be somewhat confusing to parents and young people.

In higher education, complaints processes have had consumerist underpinnings, but the emphasis today is on quality assurance. Institutions operate an internal process of up to three stages. Quality Assurance Agency (QAA) guidance (2007a) tolerates the variation found across institutions – for example, in relation to the definition of a complaint, the holding of oral hearings, time limits and sanctioning of legal representation (Harris, 2007; see also Jackson et al, 2010). A student survey has found moderate levels of satisfaction with institutions' procedures: almost half did not regard them as generally meeting the QAA precept of being 'fair, effective and timely' (NUS, 2009, p 32). But students' awareness and understanding of them is uneven. Concern about the lack of independence in the internal process has led to calls for 'campus ombudsmen', as found in US universities (see Harris, 2007, and Evans, 2008). There is also, since 2004, the possibility of subsequent external adjudication by the designated body, the Office of the Independent Adjudicator for Higher Education (OIA), which also offers general guidance. The number of complaints to the OIA has more than doubled since 2005 to 1,007 in 2008-09, of which around 200 were ineligible for investigation, mostly because the internal procedures had not been fully exhausted (OIA, 2010a, charts 1 and 8). The OIA can make similar recommendations (in practice adhered to) to those of the LGO, including compensation; £45,000 was the largest amount recommended in a case in 2009 (OIA, 2010a). A high proportion of complaints (75 per cent in 2009) are rejected. Several OIA rulings have led to judicial review challenges to decisions (20, of which only four have been granted permission).[9] A significant barrier under the internal or external processes is that complaints concerning matters of 'academic judgement', and thus assessment or award decisions, which are the most common grievances, are excluded (OIA, 2010b, p 4).

The QAA also has a 'Causes for Concern' complaints process. It may examine 'any policy, procedure or action implemented or omitted by an institution … which appears likely to jeopardise the institution's capacity to assure the academic standards and quality of any of its HE [higher education] programmes and/or awards' (QAA, 2007b, para 1). However, this is explicitly *not* intended to offer redress to an individual complainant but is linked to the QAA's role in safeguarding standards.

Appeal processes

As part of the policy framework of 'parent power' in the 1980s, local appeal mechanisms were created for school admission and permanent exclusion decisions (Harris, 1999). In 1994 a national Special Educational Needs Tribunal (SENT) was established in place of local and central appeal processes for SEN cases (with a right of further appeal on a point of law to the High Court). By the mid-1990s all these mechanisms offered successful appellants a binding decision. New Labour added an Office of Schools Adjudicator to consider parental and other objections to school admissions policies. Pressure from headteachers to abolish school exclusion appeal panels on the ground that they undermined their disciplinary authority was resisted, but their composition was changed to include people with headteacher experience. Procedural rules and guidance were introduced to improve consistency and fairness.[10] Admission appeal panels were reformed to ensure a more independent membership and they were placed under a statutory duty to have regard to the appeals code of practice (DCSF, 2009).

SEN appeal procedures were also improved, and in 2002 SENT was renamed the Special Educational Needs and Disability Tribunal (SENDisT) when complaints of disability discrimination in schools were added to its jurisdiction.[11] In November 2008 it was merged into the unified First-tier Tribunal. Education appeals increased dramatically during the 1990s.[12] Admission cases quadrupled and peaked at just under 95,000 in 2001–02. SEN appeals more than doubled between 1995–96 and 2002–03 when there were 3,500 lodged. This rapid growth has now ended and numbers have declined a little. SEN appeals totalled 3,400 in 2009–10 (Tribunals Service, 2010, p 139), although there is a high rate of withdrawal or concession.[13] In 2008–09 there were 88,270 admission appeals (30 per cent of the 63,720 heard were upheld) (DfE, 2010a). The fall in exclusion appeals has been sharper (mainly due to a decline in the number of permanent exclusions); the 2008–09 total of 640 (590 heard, of which 25 per cent were upheld) was half that of a decade earlier (DfE, 2010c).

The SEN appeals process is relatively slow. In 2009–10, 25 per cent of cases were still unresolved after 22 weeks (Tribunals Service, 2010, p 142). Parents find it stressful (Lamb, 2009), and local authorities consider it to be biased towards parents (Riddell et al, 2010). Nevertheless, it has been found to operate in a generally fair and professional manner (see, for example, Harris, 1997; Evans, 1998; Penfold et al, 2009). The SEN tribunal is valued for its independence and expertise. Unlike the other education appeal bodies it has a president and panels chaired by tribunal judges. The admission and exclusion appeal panels are less well regarded. There is concern about procedural unfairness and lack of independence (see Harris and Eden, 2000; Council on Tribunals, 2003).

Special guidance has been published (LGO, 2004) and organisational and training reforms proposed (Leggatt, 2001; Council on Tribunals, 2003). Leggatt's (2001) recommendation to include these two bodies in the proposed unified Tribunals Service has not been implemented, but training for panels has now become mandatory. Exclusion and admission appeal bodies continue to be relatively ill-equipped to deal with the complex and challenging task that they face. Moreover, the essentially adversarial nature of the appeal hearing, especially in exclusion cases, is out of step with the trend towards more informal, consensual forms of dispute resolution. It is thus ironic that mediation is available for SEN cases – the one field in which the appeal process is on the whole viewed so positively.

'Proportionate dispute resolution'

Especially since the Woolf (1996) report on civil justice, government and many professionals have increasingly supported the principle of using 'alternative dispute resolution' (ADR) mechanisms instead of courts and tribunals for civil disputes.[14] ADR processes, such as mediation, conciliation or arbitration, are seen as involving less formality and improved access to justice. Mediation has come to dominate, indeed monopolise, official thinking (Genn, 2010a, 2010b). The Master of the Rolls (effectively the head of the civil judiciary in England and Wales) has referred to the goal of making mediation 'litigation's twin' (Neuberger, 2010, para 6). Its use in civil and family cases is well established, but a prediction that the momentum towards ADR 'could draw the concept of "mediate, don't litigate" into public consciousness' (Walsh, 2004, pp 101–2) has not yet proved accurate. Although settlement is the most common means by which judicial review cases are resolved (Bondy and Sunkin, 2009), use of mediation has been low. Nevertheless, it sits well with the idea of 'proportionate dispute resolution' (PDR) proposed in the 2004 Department for Constitutional Affairs White Paper on redress for public service users (DCA, 2004). PDR involves using accessible mechanisms that enable disputes to be resolved 'as quickly and cost effectively as possible' via 'tailored dispute resolution services ... without recourse to the expense and formality of courts and tribunals' (DCA, 2004, paras 2.2, 2.3, 2.11). It is hoped that PDR, combined with improvements in initial decisions by public authorities, may reduce the need for tribunal or court hearings (DCA, 2004, para 10.11). Denying access to formal judicial processes could potentially conflict with Article 6 of the European Convention on Human Rights (supporting the determination of civil rights before an impartial tribunal),[15] so the aim was instead to confine their use to when it was really necessary.

Mediation was already in use for SEN disputes (Hall, 1999) by the time that the SEN and Disability Act 2001 provided for local dispute resolution arrangements, intended to involve mediation (DfES, 2001, part 2) and required to run alongside the right of appeal, although the aim was, over time, to 'reduce the need for recourse to the Tribunal' (DfES, 2002, part 3, para 10). Furthermore, under its rules the tribunal must, in appropriate cases, bring the parties' attention to the availability of ADR and facilitate its use, provided that it would be consistent with the 'overriding objective' (comprising, inter alia, avoidance of delay, effective utilisation of the tribunal's expertise and ensuring the parties' full participation in the proceedings).[16] If this occurs early in the proceedings it could expedite resolution and thereby reduce the number of very late settlements, which lead to inefficiencies for the tribunal. Entry into mediation is, however, by consent, and a requirement that tribunal rules reflect this[17] has been welcomed on the basis that vulnerable appellants would 'not be or feel pressurised by officials into using ADR when what they seek is a hearing before an independent tribunal judge' (House of Lords Constitution Committee, 2006, para 16). In SEN cases parents in fact often appeal to put pressure on the local authority and may not feel optimistic about reaching a settlement via mediation until an appeal is underway (Tennant et al, 2008, pp 52-3).

There is no evidence that the availability of mediation has reduced the rate of appealing to any significant extent. In the ESRC research less than one third of local authorities thought it had reduced appeal numbers. Parents' tendency to pursue an appeal and enter mediation simultaneously could be one factor. Indeed, parents often see an appeal as helping to lever the local authority into mediation (Tennant et al, 2008, pp 52-3). Perhaps more significant, however, is the low take-up: across the ESRC research's local authorities there were in 2006–07 (*n*=54) just 72 mediations and in 2007-08 (*n*=55) only 58, a mean annual rate of just over one per authority. This is lower than the 1.7 rate from mediation provider figures over a similar period in National Centre for Social Research (NatCen) research, which also found that an average of two cases per authority were resolved prior to formal mediation, with the intervention of the mediation provider (Tennant et al, 2008, tables 3.1 and 3.2). Take-up is affected by schools' unawareness of mediation (Tennant et al, 2008, p 30) and a failure by local authorities to publicise or promote it sufficiently. Authorities harbour doubts over its added value given the existing scope for dialogue with parents and the additional cost of mediation where it is paid for on a per case basis. Use of mediation is also hindered by local authority refusal in some cases to participate in it (one in seven of the ESRC authorities had refused at least once). Parents' lack of understanding of the process, doubts about the mediator's independence, and pessimism regarding the prospects of settlement, based on the claimant's past experience or others' views, are also factors. Some parents want a 'day in court' anyway and wish to preserve tactical advantage by not playing their hand early. Some feel that, where negotiations are faltering, an impasse has been reached which only independent adjudication can resolve.

Mediation has been little used for other education disputes. It is, however, seen as having potential in higher education disputes. Recently Foskett J commented in a case arising out of alleged disability discrimination against a student that 'the engagement of a suitable mediator at an early stage could result in a rapid and satisfactory resolution from the point of view of all parties before positions become entrenched'.[18] Some universities have reportedly looked to establish in-house mediation services, while an independent (fee-charging) service has been established, although its caseload to date has been fairly small (Evans, 2004, 2008). In a recent survey, around 70 per cent of complainants would have liked a mediated session or meeting with the OIA and the university to attempt to resolve differences (OIA, 2010b, figure 7). The OIA considers that ADR is likely to be more valuable prior to the exhaustion of the university's internal procedure and is wary of going beyond its 'core role' of adjudication (OIA, 2010b, paras 7.27-7.28).

Why mediation?

Although mediation has not become well established in this field, it remains at the forefront of ideas about modernising dispute resolution. Proponents say it helps to identify and focus on the key issues and to bring about earlier resolutions. It is viewed positively by participants and attracts high levels of compliance. It also assists in the maintenance of good long-term relations, better mutual understanding and effective communication, which are essential to professional–parent partnership approaches (Hall, 1999; Gersch and Gersch, 2003). In SEN cases it is considered by local authorities to be less stressful for parents than the appeal process (Harris and Smith, 2008). By encouraging early dialogue it can reduce the risk of a full-blown dispute (Hall, 1999, para 7.3; Tennant et al, 2008, p 51). It is also said to enable more widely focused, interests-based rather than purely rights-based solutions to be sought (Stilitz and Sheldon, 2007, p 166). The idea that by participating in mediation the parties themselves become 'part of the solution' also chimes well with a participatory model of citizenship.

However, mediation continues to divide opinion (see Genn, 2010b, pp 78-125). In addition to doubts about its cost-effectiveness or capacity to extend the scope for settlement or speed up resolution (see Tennant et al, 2008, p 46) are more fundamental concerns. One of these is about whether the interests of 'justice' are served by a negotiated outcome to a dispute that is essentially about fundamental rights (Supperstone et al, 2006; Stilitz and Sheldon, 2007; Bondy and Mulcahy, 2009). Richardson and Genn (2007) argue that adjudication is needed for citizen versus state disputes concerning issues of liberty and personal status and those which concern entitlement to a material benefit, such as social security, which hinge on legal questions concerned with satisfaction of statutory conditions. In their view, mediation may, however, be suitable in a third category of cases, concerned with 'entitlement to consideration', where rights are less clear cut and are conditioned by wide-ranging resource and other considerations. SEN is identified as one such area. But one could argue that the tribunal is particularly well placed, because of its expertise and independence, to identify on the basis of normative considerations what is needed for the child. Moreover, the right to education is a fundamental right, regardless of the basis and means by which provision is to occur. Provision must be appropriate; a process of negotiation with a brokered outcome may not guarantee it. Furthermore, some SEN appeals are about basic yes/no issues such as whether there should be a formal assessment, where the scope for a mediated settlement is limited.

Another fundamental question is whether mediation can counter the inherent power imbalance between the parties. Adler is sceptical, arguing that it 'would take a very skilled mediator' to achieve this (Adler, 2006, p 978). He sees tribunals as better in this regard because they adopt a proactive and enabling approach. Stilitz and Sheldon (2007, p 165), on the other hand, believe that 'a skilled and robust mediator' can even things out. Evidence from my ESRC survey supports Adler's thesis – only 23 per cent of local authorities (n=60) considered that parents gained from using mediation, as against 55 per cent believing this in respect of the tribunal. A voluntary body representative said that a parent "could be pushed into accepting something they don't want". But a more fundamental concern is whether citizens may settle for less than their true entitlement: seven per cent of local authorities (n=58) and 22 per cent of PPS (n=78) said that in at least one SEN case mediation had in their view resulted in the parents accepting less than a tribunal decision could have given them. A solicitor said that parents should not "go into mediation blindfolded" and needed to "know first what their fundamental rights are". SENDisT statistics for 2007/08 reveal that parents had legal representation in 22 per cent of hearings (legal aid is not available) and were represented by others in 25 per cent of cases. For mediation, however, there is a premise that legal professional assistance is unnecessary and it is positively discouraged. This increases the concern about the inherent 'inequality of arms' likely to prejudice those from more deprived socioeconomic backgrounds. There is a widespread view (for example, Coldron et al, 2002) that middle-class parents benefit most from opportunities to seek redress, and there is no evidence that mediation is an exception to this. With regard to ethnicity, Genn et al (2006) found no evidence that minority ethnic parents were at a greater disadvantage in bringing a SEN appeal than other groups, although in the ESRC research one third of local authorities thought that they were, slightly more than thought this was the case in mediations.

There is also concern about whether there is sufficient attention paid to children's interests, particularly since the law governing dispute resolution in SEN cases does not recognise the child as a party.[19] Mediation is said to be designed to act in the child's best interests, rather than to apportion blame (DfES, 2001, para 2.27), and to have as a 'fundamental principle' that 'the child's welfare and needs are key considerations' (DfES, 2002, section 3, para 8). Article 12 of the United Nations (UN) Convention on the Rights of the Child gives the individual child a right to express a view, to be given due weight in accordance with their age and understanding, and in this regard to be heard in relevant judicial and administrative proceedings. Many professionals acknowledge the importance of this principle but do not put it into practice. Moreover, parents resist children's attendance at mediation meetings because it is not explicitly encouraged, or for protective reasons (Soar et al, 2006).

In the ESRC research mediators commented that age and disability sometimes made the child's attendance inappropriate. However, hearing directly from the child may be important given that 'the parental views of their child's wishes are not always accurate' (Soar et al, 2006, p 154). Few children attend a SEN tribunal hearing despite their right to do so (subject to the tribunal's power to exclude them). Also, the child can not be a party to a SEN appeal. Party status is now being conferred in Wales (under the Education [Wales] Measure 2009), has been under consideration in England and is supported by the Lamb Inquiry (Lamb, 2009, para 5.78). Appellant status could better ensure that there is a focus directly on the child's interests. One partly compensatory factor could be the greater role played by mothers than fathers in the 'fight' for their child's rights; in the ESRC research over 90 per cent of PPS respondents said that mothers were their main clients. No conclusive picture emerged regarding differences between males' and females' advocacy for their children, but in family mediation there appears to be a general tendency for women to be more focused than men on their family and children's interests than on their own (Tilley, 2007).

Using mediation for the other key dispute areas in education is also problematic. Its early use in discipline cases could enable exclusion risk factors to be identified and reduced. Where exclusion has occurred, it might assist in determining the basis for reinstatement or other future arrangements, as it can consider a broader range of issues than an appeal. However, as the power to exclude should not be wielded disproportionately there is also a 'vindication of rights' case for formal adjudication. Using mediation reduces the potential for court or tribunal decisions to reveal deficiencies in practice. Also, it is not clear that a mediated settlement would safeguard the interests of the alleged victims of any misbehaviour. A further difficulty is that the role of mediation is not really to find facts or evaluate evidential matters, often central to exclusion cases. Mediation is unlikely to be suitable for another key dispute area, school admissions, as many disputes concern over-subscribed schools; competing claims for limited places have to be ranked and mediation would not work (cf Stilitz and Sheldon, 2007).

So mediation has both advantages and drawbacks. Most of the problems are concerned with issues of principle to do with the public vindication of rights, the potential risk that compromise poses to entitlement, and recognition of the rights of the child. Mediation is seen as having practical benefits if used at a relatively early stage in a dispute and if the subject matter makes it intrinsically suitable. That it has not proved popular in SEN cases in England is not merely down to judgements about its potential for resolving disputes but also the benefits of alternative strategies, notably an appeal or direct negotiation, in the minds of claimants and their advisers.

Implications and conclusions

Administrative grievances vary in nature and form (Adler et al, 2006). For education, a range of dispute resolution mechanisms diverse in focus, operating methods and remedial powers perhaps fits well with the variety of grievances that people may have. Additionally, there are different modes of decision making.Thus, as Mullen (2010, p 410) argues, 'an administrative system which relies heavily on professional judgment and experience may require a different approach to redress from one in which decisions are made according to detailed rules'. This distinction reflects two of the three models of administrative justice advanced by Mashaw (1983). One is his 'professional treatment' model (pp 26-9), in which decisions are reached on the basis of contextual interpretation, drawing on professional expertise related to the needs of the client; it has the legitimating value of 'service'. Rule-based decision making, on the other hand, accords with Mashaw's 'bureaucratic rationality' model, whose legitimating goals are accuracy and efficiency; it would represent an attempt to 'realize society's pre-established goals' (p 26) by applying rules correctly. The third model, 'moral judgment' (pp 29-31), has as its primary goal conflict resolution over questions of entitlement by a neutral decision maker; adjudication fits this model.

Bureaucratic rationality predominates in some SEN decisions, such as a local authority's classification of SEN in its area, while professional treatment applies to others, such as the determination of the contents of a statement, which draws on a multi-professional assessment.The moral judgment model is applicable to the tribunal's determination based on the interpretation of law and facts and enabling professional discretion to 'be tested according to whether it has delivered their children's rights correctly' (Blair, 2000, p 190).The attempted rationalisation of education decision making through the increased use of rules and practice codes has shifted it further in the direction of bureaucratic rationality. Mashaw (1983, p 40) notes the competitiveness of his three models, so that, for example, bureaucratic rationality may be 'undermined by ... the highly textured search for moral deservedness inherent in traditional adjudication'. Such a tension has been identified in the field of SEN, where local authorities fear that tribunal decisions may distort resource allocations (Riddell, 2003, p 203). However, it may also pull in the opposite direction, as has occurred in the context of social security appeals (Buck et al, 2005, p 220). Riddell (2003) and Adler (2003, 2010) have extended the models to take account of the influence of managerialism, consumerism and markets on administrative justice. 'Consumerism', for example, focuses on active user participation and has a legitimating goal of consumer satisfaction, which seems to fit with the methodology and goal of mediation. 'Managerialism', whose legitimating goal is improved efficiency, involves accountability based on judgements of performance remedied through, among other things, complaints to bodies such as ombudsmen. Managerialism has been increasingly manifest in the field of education through target setting, regulation and various accountability mechanisms – Ofsted, OIA and LGO.

Having alternative arrangements may give complainants more choice of process that will best address their interests. The downside is that it can be confusing for citizens (NAO, 2005, para 1.35), although, as we have seen, some kind of 'triage plus' to guide parents in their selection may be possible. The House of Commons Education and Skills Committee (2006, paras 226-7) has supported the idea of a common dispute resolution system for *all* areas of education. Incorporating mediation could be a problem given its unsuitability for various kinds of dispute. Adapting existing mechanisms would be possible, for example by bringing mediation into the appeal process (rather than simply being encouraged by the tribunal) or importing ombudsman-type techniques into appeal cases (yet Adler, 2006, pp 978-80 and 984-5, argues that this may have very limited potential given the different aims of ombudsmen and tribunal process, although he has separately [Adler, 2010] observed that tribunals have become more inquisitorial and thus ombudsmen-like).

Ultimately, a favourable outcome to an education dispute often rests on a hard fought fight, albeit sometimes with one hand tied behind one's back, which may potentially result in an injustice to others. One can perhaps see the force in Clarke et al's (2010, p 39) argument that the school admissions appeal system may afford an element of procedural justice but 'does not have the ability to deliver "social justice"'. The same must be true of mediation. There remain questions as to whether, with its negotiated outcome, this private process is an appropriate mechanism of accountability in the sphere of public education[20] and whether it can properly safeguard citizens' rights. As Genn says: 'Does it contribute to substantive justice? No, because mediation requires the parties to relinquish ideas of legal rights during mediation and focus, instead, on problem solving ... it is *just about settlement*' (Genn, 2010b, pp 116-17, original emphasis). Moreover, mediation may be less adversarial in approach than litigation or appeal processes, and more conciliatory than complaints processes, but it does not materially alter the underlying character of disputes. Although the forum differs, complainants will still be seeking determinedly to have their claim upheld. The citizen who opts for mediation may still have to 'shout for' the outcome they want.

Notes
[1] Education Act 1996, Section 332A(1), inserted by the SEN and Disability Act (SENDA) 2001, Section 2; School Standards and

Framework Act 1998, Section 86(1A), inserted by the Education and Inspections Act 2006 (the 2006 Act), Section 42.

[2] Apprenticeships, Skills, Children and Learning Act 2009 (the 2009 Act), Schedule 16, part 7.

[3] Education Act 2002, Section 29.

[4] Education Act 2005, Sections 11A and 11B, inserted by the 2006 Act, Section 160; Education (Investigation of Parents' Complaints) (England) Regulations (SI 2007/1089), as amended by SI 2008/1723.

[5] 2009 Act, Part 10, chapter 2.

[6] 2009 Act, Section 209(2).

[7] 2009 Act, Section 212.

[8] LGO (2010, tables 1 and 2); and see the table at www.lgo.org.uk/publications/annual-report/ (accessed 14 September 2010).

[9] OIA (2010a, p 17). The four cases are: *R (Budd) v The Office of the Independent Adjudicator for Higher Education* [2010] EWHC 1056 (Admin); *R (Maxwell) v The Office of the Independent Adjudicator for Higher Education and the University of Salford* [2010] EWHC 1889 (Admin); *R (Arratoon) v Office of the Independent Adjudicator for Higher Education* [2008] EWHC 3125 (Admin); and *R (Siborurema) v Office of the Independent Adjudicator* [2007] EWCA Civ 1365, CA.

[10] The Education (Pupil Exclusions and Appeals) (Maintained Schools) (England) Regulations 2002 (SI 2002/3178).

[11] Under SENDA 2001, Part 2, chapter 1.

[12] Statistics are drawn from the SENDisT President's annual reports and official DfES/DCSF/DfE annual statistics as per DfE (2010a) and DfE (2010c).

[13] Annual statistics show that around 40 per cent of appeals are withdrawn and 30 per cent are conceded.

[14] See, for example, Lord Chief Justice Woolf's comments in *R (Cowl) v Plymouth City Council* [2001] EWCA Civ 1935 at paras 1-3 and 27.

[15] This view regarding Article 6 is contested: see Genn (2010b, pp 102-3).

[16] The Tribunal Procedure (First-tier Tribunal) (Health, Education and Social Care Chamber) Rules 2008 (SI 2008/2699), rules 2 and 3.

[17] Tribunals, Courts and Enforcement Act 2007, Section 24.

[18] See *Maxwell*, note 9 above, at para 84.

[19] Education Act 1996, Section 332B.

[20] It is acknowledged that the tribunal hearing will normally also be held in private: note 16 above, rule 26(2) and (3). It may only be held in public if that is 'in the interests of justice'.

References

Adler, M. (2003) 'A socio-legal approach to administrative justice', *Law and Policy*, vol 25, no 4, pp 323-52.

Adler, M. (2006) 'Tribunal reform: proportionate dispute resolution and the pursuit of administrative justice', *Modern Law Review*, vol 69, no 6, pp 958-85.

Adler, M. (2008) 'The idea of proportionality in dispute resolution', *Journal of Social Welfare Law*, vol 30, no 4, pp 309-21.

Adler, M. (2010) 'Understanding and analysing administrative justice', in M. Adler (ed) *Administrative justice in context*, Oxford: Hart, pp 129-59.

Adler, M., Farrell, C., Finch, S., Lewis, J., Morris, S. and Philo, D. (2006) *Administrative grievances: A developmental study*, London: National Centre for Social Research.

AJTC (Administrative Justice and Tribunals Council) (2009) *Department for Children, Schools and Families. A new way of handling parents' complaints about school issues*, London: AJTC.

Ahier, J., Beck, J. and Moore, R. (2003) *Graduate citizens? Issues of citizenship and higher education*, London: RoutledgeFalmer.

Blair, A. (2000) 'Rights, duties and resources: the case of special educational needs', *Education and the Law*, vol 12, no 3, pp 177-93.

Bondy, V. and Mulcahy, L. with Doyle, M. and Reid, V. (2009) *Mediation and judicial review: An empirical research study*, London: The Public Law Project.

Bondy, V. and Sunkin, M. (2009) *The dynamics of judicial review. The resolution of public law challenges before final hearing*, Colchester: University of Essex.

Brighouse, H. (2000) *School choice and social justice*, Oxford: Oxford University Press.

Buck, T., Bonner, D. and Sainsbury, R. (2005) *Making social security law*, Aldershot: Ashgate.

Clarke, J., McDermont, M. and Newman, J. (2010) 'Delivering choice and administering justice: contested logics of public services', in M. Adler (ed) *Administrative justice in context*, Oxford: Hart, pp 25-45.

Clarke, J., Newman, J., Smith, N., Vidler, E. and Westmarland, L. (2007) *Creating consumer-citizens: Changing identities in the making of public services*, London: Sage Publications.

Coldron, J., Stephenson, K., Williams, J., Shipton, L. and Demack, S. (2002) *Admission appeal panels: Research study in the operation of appeal panels, use of the code of practice and training for panel members*, Research Report RR344, London: Department for Education and Skills.

Council on Tribunals (2003) *School admission and exclusion appeal panels. Special report*, Cm 5788, London: The Stationery Office.

DCA (Department for Constitutional Affairs) (2004) *Transforming public services: Complaints, redress and tribunals*, Cm 6243, London: The Stationery Office.

DCSF (Department for Children, Schools and Families) (2008) *A new way of handling parents' complaints about school issues*, London: DCSF.

DCSF (2009) *School admission appeals code*, London: The Stationery Office.

DCSF (2010) *School admissions code*, London: The Stationery Office.

Dean, H. (2002) *Welfare rights and social policy*, Harlow: Prentice Hall.

DfE (Department for Education) (2010a) *Statistical first release. Admission appeals for maintained primary and secondary schools in England 2008/09*, SFR 15/2010, London: DfE.

DfE (2010b) *Children and young people with special educational needs and disabilities – Call for views*, Green Paper (e-consultation published 10 September 2010 at www.education.gov.uk/consultations/index.cfm ?action=conResults&consultationId=1736&external=no&menu=3).

DfE (2010c) *Permanent and fixed period exclusions from schools and exclusion appeals in England, 2008/09*, SFR 22/2010, London: DfE.

DfES (Department for Education and Skills) (2001) *Special educational needs code of practice*, London: DfES.

DfES (2002) *SEN toolkit*, London: DfES (www.teachernet.gov.uk/_ doc/4606/Toolkit%201%20Text.pdf for updated version).

DfES (2005) *Higher standards, better schools for all*, Cm 6677, London: The Stationery Office.

Evans, G.R. (2004) 'A higher education mediation service', *Education Law Journal*, vol 5, no 4, pp 218-23.

Evans, G.R. (2008) 'Mediation in higher education: the "improving dispute resolution" project', *Education Law Journal*, vol 9, no 2, pp 119-27.

Evans, J. (1998) *Getting it right: LEAs and the Special Educational Needs Tribunal*, Slough: National Foundation for Educational Research.

Fabre, C. (2000) *Social rights under the constitution. Government and the decent life*, Oxford: Clarendon Press.

Furedi, F. (2010) 'Introduction to the marketisation of higher education and the student as consumer', in M. Molesworth, R. Scullion and E. Nixon (eds) *The marketisation of higher education and the student as consumer*, London: Routledge, pp 1-7.

Genn, H. (2010a) 'Civil mediation: a measured approach?', *Journal of Social Welfare and Family Law*, vol 32, no 2, pp 195-205.

Genn, H. (2010b) *Judging civil justice*, Cambridge: Cambridge University Press.

Genn, H., Lever, B., Gray, L., Balmer, N. and National Centre for Social Research (2006) *Tribunals for diverse users*, DCA Research series 1/06, London: Department for Constitutional Affairs.

Gersch, I.S. and Gersch, A. (2003) *Resolving disagreement in special educational needs*, London: RoutledgeFalmer.

Hall, J. (1999) *Resolving disputes between parents, schools and LEAs: Some examples of best practice*, London: DfEE.

Harris, N. (1993) 'Local complaints procedures under the Education Reform Act 1988', *Journal of Social Welfare and Family Law*, vol 15, no 1, pp 19-39.

Harris, N. (1997) *Special educational needs and access to justice*, Bristol: Jordan Publishing Ltd.

Harris, N. (1999) 'The developing role and structure of the education appeal system', in M. Partington and M. Harris (eds) *Administrative justice in the 21st century*, Oxford: Hart, pp 296-325.

Harris, N. (2007) 'Resolution of student complaints in higher education institutions', *Legal Studies*, vol 27, no 4, pp 566-603.

Harris, N. and Eden, K., with Blair, A. (2000) *Challenges to school exclusion. Exclusion, appeals and the law*, London: RoutledgeFalmer.

Harris, N. and Smith E. (2008) *A survey of local authorities and parent partnership services in England*, Working Paper 6, ESRC Research: Resolving and Avoiding Disputes Concerning Special Educational Needs, Working Paper 6: Edinburgh: CREID (www.creid.ed.ac.uk/adr/pubs/adr_workingpaper6.pdf).

HEFCE (Higher Education Funding Council for England) (2010) *2010 student survey results for students in England*, Bristol: HEFCE (www.hefce.ac.uk/news/hefce/2010/nssresult.htm).

Henry, J. (2009) 'Hundreds of complaints from parents about schools – but less than 2% investigated', 21 February (www.telegragh.co.uk).

House of Commons Education and Skills Committee (2006) Third report of session 2005-06, *Special educational needs*, HC 478-I, London: The Stationery Office.

House of Lords Constitution Committee (2006) *First report session 2006-07. Tribunal, Courts and Enforcement Bill. Report with evidence*, London: The Stationery Office.

Ivens, C. (2008) *Survey of parents in England 2008*, Research Report DCSF-RW041, London: Department for Children, Schools and Families.

Jackson, J., Fleming, H., Koamvounias, P. and Varnham, S. (2010) 'Student complaint handling and disciplinary processes in the 21st century Australian university', *Education Law*, vol 11, no 2, pp 108-16.

Lamb, Sir B. (2009) *Lamb Inquiry: Special educational needs and parental confidence*, London: Department for Children, Schools and Families.

Leggatt, Sir A. (2001) *Tribunals for users: One system, one service*, London: The Stationery Office.

LGO (Local Government Ombudsman) (2004) *Special report: Schools admissions and appeals*, London: Commission for Local Administration in England.

LGO (2010) *Local Government Ombudsman. Annual report 200910* (sic), London: Commission for Local Administration in England.

Lister, R. (2007) 'Inclusive citizenship: realizing the potential', *Citizenship Studies*, vol 11, no 1, pp 49-61.

Marquand, D. (2004) *Decline of the public: The hollowing out of citizenship*, Cambridge: Polity Press.

Marshall, T.H. and Bottomore, T. (1992) *Citizenship and social class*, London: Pluto.

Mashaw, J.L. (1983) *Bureaucratic justice*, New Haven, CT: Yale University Press.

Ministry of Justice (2010) *Proposals for the reform of legal aid in England and Wales*, Cm 7967, London: The Stationery Office.

Mullen, T. (2010) 'A holistic approach to administrative justice?', in M. Adler (ed) *Administrative justice in context*, Oxford: Hart, pp 383-420.

NAO (National Audit Office) (Comptroller and Auditor-General) (2005) *Citizen's redress: What citizens can do if things go wrong with public services*, HC 21 Session 2004-2005, London: The Stationery Office.

National Consumer Council (1992) *When things go wrong at school: Redress procedures in the education service*, London: National Consumer Council.

Neuberger, Lord, of Abbotsbury (2010) 'Educating future mediators', Published speech given at the Fourth Civil Mediation Council National Conference, London, 11 May.

NUS (National Union of Students) (2009) *Review of institutional complaints and appeals procedures in England and Wales*, London: NUS.

Ofsted (Office for Standards in Education, Children's Services and Skills) (2007) *Parental complaints: Report on the consultation responses*, Ref 070166, London: Ofsted.

Ofsted (2010) *The special educational needs and disability review: A statement is not enough*, Ref 090221, London: Ofsted.

OIA (Office of the Independent Adjudicator) (2010a) *Annual report 2009* (www.oiahe.org.uk/downloads/OIA-annual-report-2009.pdf).

OIA (2010b) *The Pathway Report. Recommendations for the development of the OIA scheme*, Reading: OIA.

Penfold, C., Cleghorn, N., Tennant, R., Palmer I. and Read, J. (2009) *Parental confidence in the special educational needs assessment, statementing and tribunal system*, DCSF-RR117, London: Department for Children, Schools and Families.

PHSO (Parliamentary and Health Service Ombudsman) (2009) *Principles of good complaint handling*, London: PHSO.

QAA (Quality Assurance Agency) (2007a) *Code of practice for the assurance of academic quality and standards in higher education, Section 5, Academic appeals and student complaints on academic matters*, Gloucester: QAA.

QAA (2007b) *Procedure for identifying and handling causes for concern in English institutions offering higher education programmes or awards*, Gloucester: QAA.

Richardson, G. and Genn, H. (2007) 'Tribunals in transition: resolution or adjudication?', *Public Law*, pp 116-41.

Riddell, S. (2003) 'Procedural justice and special educational needs assessments in England and Scotland', *International Journal of Inclusive Education*, vol 7, no 3, pp 201-23.

Riddell, S., Harris, N., Smith, E. and Weedon, E. (2010) 'Dispute resolution in additional and special educational needs: local authority perspectives', *Journal of Education Policy*, vol 25, no 1, pp 55-71.

Rogers, R., Tod., J., Powell, S., Parsons, C., Godfrey, R., Graham-Matheson, L., Carlson, A., and Cornwall, J. (2006) *Evaluation of the special educational needs parent partnership services in England*, DfES Research Report, RR719, London: DFES.

Soar, K., Gersch, I.S. and Lawrence, J.A. (2006) 'Pupil involvement in special educational needs disagreement resolution: a parental perspective', *Support for Learning*, vol 21, no 3, pp 149-55.

Stafford, B. (2009) 'Service delivery and the user', in J. Millar (ed) *Understanding social security* (2nd edn), Bristol: The Policy Press, pp 255-73.

Stilitz, D. and Sheldon, C. (2007) 'Meeting education disputes', *Education Law Journal*, vol 8, no 3, pp 165-73.

Supperstone, M., Stilitz, D. and Sheldon, C. (2006) 'ADR and public law', *Public Law*, pp 299-319.

Tennant, R., Callanan, M., Snape, D., Palmer, I. and Read, J. (2008) *Special educational needs disagreement resolution services*, Research Report DCSF-RR054, London: Department for Children, Schools and Families.

Tilley, S. (2007) 'ADR professional: recognising gender differences in all issues mediation', *Family Law*, vol 37, pp 352-6.

Tribunals Service (2010) *Annual report and accounts 2009–10*, HC239, London: The Stationery Office.

Vidler, E. and Clarke, J. (2005) 'Creating consumer-citizens: New Labour and the remaking of public services', *Public Policy and Administration*, vol 20, no 2, pp 19-37.

Walsh, E. (2004) 'The future of family mediation', in J. Westcott (ed) *Family mediation. Past, present and future*, Bristol: Family Law, pp 101-20.

Wilkins, A. (2010) 'Citizens and/or consumers: mutations in the construction of concepts and practices of school choice', *Journal of Education Policy*, vol 25, no 2, pp 171-89.

Woods, P. (1988) 'A strategic view of parent participation', *Journal of Education Policy*, vol 3, no 4, pp 323-34.

Woolf, The Rt Hon Lord (1996), *Access to justice: Final report*, London: Lord Chancellor's Department.

THIRTEEN

A sin of omission: New Zealand's export education industry and foreign policy

Andrew Butcher and Terry McGrath

Introduction

Discussions of New Zealand's export education policies and the welfare of its international students are rarely found within literature concerning its international relations and foreign affairs. We suggest that this is a great omission. But it is not a surprising one. New Zealand's export education within trade policy is on quantifiable territory: data abounds on the economic impact of export education to the nation's economy. A less measurable but more long-term impact is on how New Zealand's place in the world is affected by its policies and practices toward international students. Such a view considers the nation's relationships with its international students for longer than just their period of study. This view also considers its export education policies in terms other than trade. It is our contention that New Zealand's foreign and export education policies are inextricably linked, even if that is not evident in the current formation of those policies. The education and wider life experiences international students have while in New Zealand will impact on their lives later on. They may become 'friends and allies' to the country and its interests in the world (McGrath et al, 2007). Or they may not.

International education and foreign policy in New Zealand

Most international students in New Zealand come from the Asian region and it is that region and those students that form much of the focus of this chapter. While students from China dominated in 2010, students from South East Asia, particularly Malaysia, Indonesia and Singapore, were among the first students in the country in 1951 and the largest group for many years afterwards. That is not the only reason we devote much of our discussion to Asia. As we show in this chapter, New Zealand's foreign policy interests have also recently veered towards Asia and, as the mandate of the not-for-profit Asia New Zealand Foundation (Asia:NZ), which was set up by the government in 1994, illustrates, the country's future is in Asia also.

The delineation between 'foreign' and 'domestic' policies is increasingly blurred and especially so with international education in New Zealand. Full fee-paying overseas students provide revenue to public educational institutions both at the compulsory education levels and at universities and polytechnics. They also provide funding to the private sector, but that is a matter that we will address momentarily. Issues around the age at which foreign students can study in New Zealand, the demands their presence places on teachers and other students, the management of their accommodation and general pastoral care, the length of their stay in New Zealand and the ability for them to advance from a student visa to a work visa are all issues that concern domestic policy agendas. However, many of these issues also have implications for foreign policy. When students have negative experiences these may attract the attention of both domestic and international media, which may turn into a diplomatic issue that requires government intervention and resolution. Such a turn of events is familiar to Australia (Wesley, 2009).

The significant impacts that export education in all its forms has on a national economy ensures the interest of trade and tourism agencies. However, the interests of the Ministry of Foreign Affairs and Trade are broader:

> The Ministry's primary role is to recognise and understand international trends, opportunities and risks that affect New Zealand, and offer the Government advice on how best to protect and advance New Zealand's interests and well-being. In this way it contributes to the Government's overall objective of transforming New Zealand into a dynamic, knowledge-based economy and society, underpinned by the values of fairness, opportunity and security for all. (MFAT, 2010)

Advancing 'New Zealand's interests and well-being' is not the exclusive prerogative of diplomats. As we see it, graduates may or may not advance those interests as well. However, the competing agency interests in New

Zealand's export education industry expose the fault lines of the industry as much as the inadequacies of the neoliberal project on which it was reformed and created in the 1980s. These fault lines, as detailed elsewhere in this chapter, were manifest in other ways also: the precipitous decline of students from the People's Republic of China (PRC), the collapse of two large private education providers and the over-leveraging by public institutions on revenue from international students. These fault lines exhibit the *particular* issues in relation to export education and foreign policy in New Zealand. As Lewis (2005, pp 6-7) remarks,

> [New Zealand] is an isolated, relatively wealthy, commodity exporting economy and a post-colonial trading nation peopled largely by immigrants, primarily from Britain and more recently from the Island Pacific, East Asia and South Africa. It has always been deeply immersed and implicated in globalising processes and associated imaginaries and faced with maintaining a cultural economy at a distance.

The extent of the neoliberal restructuring in New Zealand in the 1980s and 1990s has been the subject of rigorous scholarly and policy debate (Boston et al, 1996, 1999; Kelsey, 1997). By and large, however, the focus of these critiques has been on domestic policy.

New Zealand's foreign policy is relatively neglected in these analyses and yet it is a key aspect of the country's nation-building project. The hackneyed phrase 'punching above our weight' is frequently employed to illustrate New Zealand's role in the world, from its anti-nuclear stance to its internationally respected scientists and musicians to its role as the location for movie trilogy *The Lord of the Rings*. These examples and more are used as evidence that for a country of only 4.2 million population, New Zealand is a small but significant country in the world and should not be forgotten. This same aphorism is used in the context of its foreign policy, although it is a phrase that other countries freely adopt as well (Cook, 2010). The official phrases for New Zealand's foreign policy – at least with respect to Asia – are no less anodyne: better integrating ourselves into an integrated region; being a good neighbour; boosting New Zealand's growth by linking to the growth of Asian economies; and becoming more 'Asia literate' (MFAT, 2007). These motherhood-and-apple-pie ambitions reflect a committee of competing interests as much as a foreign policy that is struggling to find a place in a rapidly changing world and region where even New

Zealand's closest neighbour and ally Australia views it with disinterest and occasional disdain (Cook, 2010).

Firmly establishing New Zealand's place in the world and the correlate of its national identity exercises the minds of many of its international relations' scholars. So what interest then should it hold for scholars of social policy? We suggest because export education – as an industry, a significant export earner, a feature of globalisation and a growing revenue stream for public and privately funded educational institutions alike – cannot be left out of domestic policy concerns. As Boston (1999, p 217) notes, 'if New Zealand is to retain a relatively high-quality tertiary sector, together with equitable access and participation rates at least comparable to those of its major competitors, significant additional state investment in the tertiary sector will be essential'. This is especially prescient in 2010 as the New Zealand government has signalled that it will cap domestic student numbers (due to the cost of subsidising them) and will expect the tertiary sector to compensate the loss of revenue from export education.

But it is not only the tertiary sector that requires the revenue from international students. The primary and secondary school sectors also benefit from international students and in many cases have active international recruitment campaigns to attract them. During the peak of international students in New Zealand, in the late 1990s/early 2000s, new classrooms were built, new teachers hired and ambitious plans developed. All of these had to be shelved as student numbers precipitously declined.

The private sector is even more reliant on international student revenue and thus more vulnerable to fluctuating demand. In this same period, several private training establishments (PTEs) were set up seemingly overnight and with scant regulation. While some were competent and qualified, others were little more than factories whose interest in international students extended no further than the revenue they generated. Clearly, such an approach negatively impacted on quality and a slew of regulations from 2001 sought to address the negative practices and perceptions of the private sector. But even regulations could not save two of the largest providers, Carich and Modern Age, collapsing (due to a decline in students and revenue) and leaving many Asian students out of pocket, out of the classroom and out of sorts with their New Zealand experience. At the time, the Chinese government publicly called on the New Zealand government to improve education standards and safety at private schools attended by Chinese students. In so doing it added to growing negative perceptions of New Zealand's export education industry (*China Daily*, 2003).

The collapse of these two private training establishments was not unique or isolated. In November 2010 the weekend edition of the *New Zealand Herald*, New Zealand's largest metropolitan daily, ran a two-page spread on the failings of New Zealand's export education industry, especially at Private Training Establishments (Laxon, 2010). In an editorial a few days later, the same newspaper noted:

> Former staff of these 'schools' tell disturbing tales of fraud. They say students can be given answers to test questions to ensure a pass and sometimes the centres [PTEs] sell pass marks to students who have failed at other schools. They call the centres 'visa factories', providers of paper qualifications that help students gain permanent residency....The whole country and possibly its other exports stand to suffer in the long run if it becomes known as a place where education is corrupt and academic qualifications are unreliable. (Editorial, *New Zealand Herald*, 2010)

Recognising the economic benefit of its export education industry, the New Zealand government announced several proposed legislative changes to address the concerns raised by the media. (Although, as the same *Herald* editorial noted, 'the governments have been slow to act on persistent reports that question the standards and honesty of some of those providing export education in this country'.) These legislative changes are directed at both New Zealand's export education marketing agencies and the PTE sector. The *New Zealand Herald* reported that the government is investigating scrapping the current export education agency, Education New Zealand (ENZ) (of which more is said below) and creating a new crown entity. In its place would be an agency that would bring together the various parts of government departments and agencies under one body (Binning, 2010). Changes proposed to the PTE sector include giving the New Zealand Qualifications Authority (NZQA) stronger powers to monitor, investigate and enforce the compliance of PTEs and raising the threshold for PTE registration (Joyce, 2010). In announcing these proposed legislative changes, the Minister for Tertiary Education noted that:

> While the vast majority of providers are doing a good job, there have been incidents involving dishonest practices in some PTEs. It is important that steps are taken to ensure such practices are

not allowed to continue....The increased investment in the sector, and its growing economic value to New Zealand, increases the importance of a clear and effective regulatory regime.... *[F]urther development of the sector will bring real benefits in terms of economic growth plus additional income to allow our tertiary institutions to grow.* (Joyce, 2010, emphasis added)

But there is not only a compelling economic argument here. New Zealand's relationship with the Asian region and Asian peoples is thickening. The vast majority of international students to New Zealand come from Asia. New Zealand's population of Asian ethnicity at the 2006 Census of Population and Dwellings was 10 per cent and is projected to be 16 per cent by 2026 (Bedford and Ho, 2008), putting New Zealand's proportion of its Asian population alongside Canada and above Australia (Spoonley and Butcher, 2010). Increasingly migrants to New Zealand are coming from Asia (especially China and South Korea), with education for either themselves or their children as a primary motive.

Between 1986 and 2006, New Zealand's resident population that had been born in countries in Asia increased almost sevenfold, from 32,685 to 248,364, while the population that identified with Asian ethnicities (including New Zealand-born) increased by 550 per cent (Bedford and Ho, 2008). The total Chinese population in New Zealand increased by 456 per cent in the same period compared with increases of 562 per cent for the Indian population and 770 per cent for other Asian ethnic groups (Bedford and Ho, 2008).

An 'Asian' in New Zealand is perceived quite differently from how an 'Asian' is perceived in, for example, the UK. In its annual survey of New Zealanders' perceptions of Asia, Asia:NZ asks, 'when you think about Asia, which countries come to mind?'. The results from the 2009 survey were China (88 per cent) and Japan (70 per cent), followed some way behind by Thailand (32 per cent) and India (31 per cent) (Asia New Zealand Foundation, 2010). In New Zealand 'Indian' is often perceived and defined as distinct from 'Asian' (Bandyopadhyay, 2009, 2010).

Most of New Zealand's foreign policy priority countries are in Asia, as are two of the three largest economies in the world (China and Japan). The strategic regional and political shifts in Asia will invariably impact on New Zealand because of both its geographical and economic proximity to the region (cf White, 2009). We cannot artificially divide foreign, immigration, trade and defence policies; each impacts on the other.

New Zealand in the world

New Zealand's foreign relations with Asia came rather late in the scheme of things. Its foreign (as distinct from defence) policies followed rather than led its increasing economic engagement with the Asian region. This economic engagement came by compulsion rather than choice. With Britain figuratively turning its back on New Zealand's economy, the country had to look elsewhere for its trade partners. Australia was always an important partner but it was not enough to sustain, let alone grow, the country's economy.

Aligned with its growing economic interests in Asia, New Zealand saw potential for charging full-cost fees from international students from that region. Asian students had studied in the country since 1951, under the auspices of the Colombo Plan. This was a scheme designed ostensibly to educate scholars from developing countries in Asia so that they might return to their home countries and assist their development. The underlying reason for the Plan was to prevent communism sweeping through Asia Pacific to British-allied nations. While discussion about raising fees for international students had begun in the 1970s, the combination of neoliberal government policies in the late 1980s with Asia's growing economic importance to New Zealand marked a definitive shift from 'aid' to 'trade' in the country's international education policies.

International students in New Zealand: from aid to trade

The first tranche of overseas students to New Zealand can be put into three brief periods. The first period began in the late 1800s with students coming into the Auckland-based Anglican training seminary St John's College, with help from the church. The second period, involving New Zealand government-assisted students from the Pacific, began with trade-related courses in 1919. The third period began with the Colombo Plan Agreement signed in Sri Lanka (then known as Ceylon) in 1950. During these three periods many New Zealanders involved in tertiary education established and maintained lasting friendships and professional relationships with these overseas students. Many went on to become influential in their own countries in Asia (MFAT, 2001). These graduates became a conduit for ongoing goodwill between Asia and New Zealand.

Tarling (2004) has meticulously and comprehensively covered the minutiae of New Zealand's formulation of its international education policy and the details of that need not be rehearsed here. A quick scan of its landscape, however, reveals that it came as much out of pragmatic politics as it did out of shifting political ideologies. While the legislative shift from 'aid to trade' occurred in 1989, the ground had been moving long before then (Butcher, 2009; Tarling, 2004). In charging partial – and then full-cost – fees for international students in New Zealand, charges were seen as being beneficial to both the national economy and the educational system. It paralleled shifts elsewhere in the nation's social policies (Boston, 1999).

Changes to the Education Act in 1989 decisively marked an endpoint in the shift from 'aid' under the Colombo Plan to 'trade', the selling of New Zealand education to international students. However, there were increasing numbers of private (that is, non-Colombo Plan-funded) students in the nation from the 1960s onwards, although they are often considered within the Colombo Plan period of the nation's export education (Tarling, 2004).

These changes, both with respect to international student fees, and more broadly, were not without their critics. A key architect in these reforms, Sir Frank Holmes, noted that Trade Minister Mike Moore was 'surprised by the resistance he encountered' and that 'there was a good deal of vocal opposition'. While Holmes' report and similar reports on the education system generally were delivered in the mid-1980s, Tarling (2004) contends that the shift to exporting educational services had begun much earlier (1980–81), pre-dating the Labour government most associated with these social reforms with the substantive shift in 1984 with the election of that government (Tarling, 2004, pp 100, 130ff).

It is appropriate and justifiable that the changes to New Zealand's export education policies should be seen largely in domestic terms. But it presents only half the picture. While the foreign policy focus of this Labour government was dominated by its fallout with the US (over the refusal to admit nuclear-powered ships) and then France (over the French bombing of the Greenpeace ship the *Rainbow Warrior* in Auckland Harbour), there was nonetheless change in the wind.

The 1990s, under the National government, were a decade in which the nation's foreign policy credentials were greatly strengthened: New Zealand served on the United Nations (UN) Security Council from 1992–93 and, importantly for our purposes, moved its focus significantly towards Asia, a region which post-Cold War and the collapse of communist Europe was returning to the centre of the world economy. Action followed this focus: new embassies opened; language training was funded; and the Asia 2000 Foundation (now Asia New Zealand

Foundation, Asia:NZ) opened to promote and develop links between New Zealand and Asia (Capie, 2009, p 594). The move towards charging fees for foreign students from Asia was merely the precursor to this wider shift.

However, New Zealand's export education policies did not return to the umbrella of foreign affairs. Instead it moved from one ministry to another: from the government trade promotion body to the Ministry of Education, where it remains. However, as one of New Zealand's top five export earners, it remains an interest of trade agencies. The current promotion agency, Education New Zealand (ENZ), is self-described as:

> A not-for-profit charitable trust that is governed by the New Zealand export education industry, and is committed to an "NZ Inc" approach to the export of New Zealand's education services offshore. ENZ is recognised by the Government as the umbrella industry body for education exporters. (ENZ website, 27 August 2010, www.educationnz.org.nz)

Marketing New Zealand as an international education destination during the early 1990s resulted in increasing numbers of international students from a growing diversity of countries. Practice prior to the establishment of ENZ and its antecedents was less regulated, more ad hoc and highly competitive between institutions. The 'NZ Inc' approach of ENZ in recent years has sought to address some of these inadequacies, by presenting one uniform marketing campaign, building relationships and a register of appropriate agents, and engaging with the education sector more broadly.

After the policy shift in 1989 growth in international student numbers was gradual to begin with but then occurred at a rapid pace. In the late 1990s and early 2000s the growth rate rose to around 30 per cent per annum. This ultimately became unsustainable and decreased: many educational institutions struggled to keep pace with this growth of students and in addressing their particular needs. The needs were most marked among Chinese students from the PRC. These students dominated numbers, with over 50,000 recorded as studying in New Zealand in 2002. However, PRC student numbers halved in a short period and accounted for most of the drop in numbers in and around the early part of the 2000s. This drop was in part due to market forces and competition, appreciation of the dollar over the Yuan and the growing perception in the PRC of the lack of care and quality in New Zealand (Li, 2007). Consequently, attention in marketing New Zealand's education abroad diversified, largely so that it would not be overly reliant on the PRC. Hitherto, its reliance on that one market had been to the detriment of public and private providers alike who suffered when the numbers of students from the PRC market decreased. But as its focus went on diversifying markets, it came off providing appropriate and satisfactory levels of pastoral care. Indeed, the diversification of markets – and thus students – exacerbated rather than resolved concerns around pastoral care. Institutions that had developed skills for some student groups, such as Chinese groups, were ill-equipped to deal with students from new source countries, such as India and Saudi Arabia (see Figure 13.3 below).

Figures 13.1 and 13.2 illustrate first, the distribution of international fee-paying students in New Zealand by world region and second, international students in New Zealand by number in the period 2000–10. Together, these figures show both New Zealand's dependence on the Asian market for its international students and the fluctuations in that market from the early 2000s.

While students from the Asian and South East Asian regions are not at the same levels as they were at the peak of students in the early 2000s, they nonetheless remain dominant among international students in New

Figure 13.1: Distribution of international fee-paying students in New Zealand by world region, 2003–09

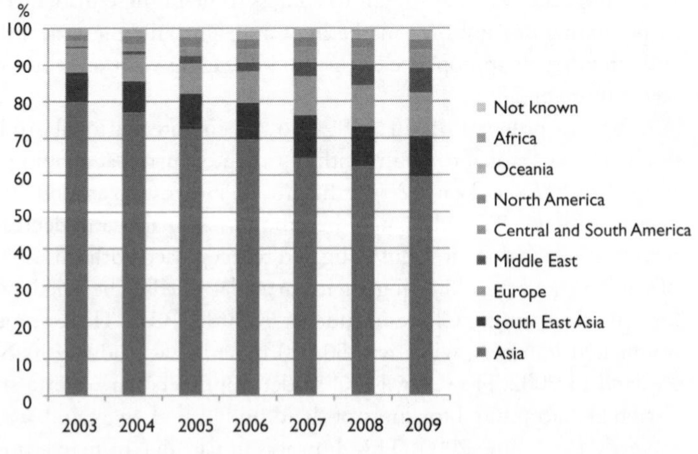

Note: World regions are based on classifications used for the New Zealand government's tertiary Single Data Return (SDR) system.

Source: Ministry of Education (2010b)

Figure 13.2: International student numbers in New Zealand, 2000–10

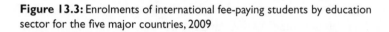

Source: Ministry of Education (2010b)

Figure 13.3: Enrolments of international fee-paying students by education sector for the five major countries, 2009

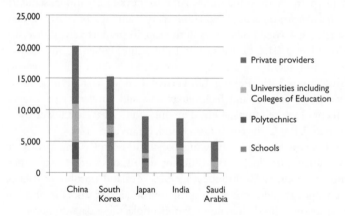

Source: Ministry of Education (2010b)

Zealand. The significant drop in students from the Asian region (see Figure 13.1) can be largely attributed to the decline in students from PRC (including Hong Kong Special Administrative Region [HK SAR]). However even at April 2010 they constituted 23.5 per cent of the total international student body in New Zealand. As shown in Figure 13.3 below, from 2009 to 2010, however, the largest numeric increases for international students came from India and Saudi Arabia (Ministry of Education, 2010b), indicating the increasing diversification of source countries and markets.

International trends and responses

New Zealand is not alone in deliberately recruiting and growing its international student population. According to UNESCO (2009) figures, the number of mobile university students (that is, those who leave their country/territory of origin and move to another with the objective of studying) has grown by almost 3.5-fold, from 0.8 million in 1975 to 2.8 million in 2007. Fifteen countries together account for 44 per cent of the world's mobile students, with the PRC the lead country by a significant margin. Six countries hosted 62 per cent of the world's mobile students in 2007 (US, UK, France, Australia, Germany and Japan), New Zealand is ranked 14th in the world and hosts 1.2 per cent of the world's mobile students (by comparison, Australia hosts 7.6 per cent).

Increasingly some Asian countries are also *receiving* international students, particularly as their universities achieve international status. In *The Times Higher Education* World University Rankings for 2010–11 there are seven Asia-based universities in the top 50 (respectively: University of Hong Kong, 21st, University of Tokyo, 26th, Pohang University of Science and Technology in South Korea, 28th, National University of Singapore, 34th, Peking University, China, 37th, Hong Kong University of Science and Technology, 41st and University of Science and Technology of China, 49th). The only New Zealand University in the top 200, the University of Auckland, is ranked at 145.

We have to be careful drawing conclusions and comparisons on international data due to the different definitions and statistics used country to country. With respect to New Zealand, enrolment data of foreign students does not also capture enrolment of students of other ethnicities (measured elsewhere). For example, these data do not show that at the country's largest university, the University of Auckland, one third of the student body are of Asian ethnicity, which reflects the large local-born and permanent resident Asian population in the Auckland region (Friesen, 2008).

Host community responses

Students' experiences extend well beyond the classroom and into the community and elsewhere. When Asian students first arrived in New

Zealand, host culture attitudes were generally supportive, but the large influx of Asian international students and the country's general under-preparedness for Asian migration resulted in increased barriers to engagement (see McGrath et al, 2005). Examples of negative social behaviour increased both towards and between international (Asian) students. Sometimes community attitudes were expressed as racism, which tended to have a greater impact on students than positive encounters (McGrath and Butcher, 2004b). Media portrayals added to host community views (Spoonley and Trlin, 2004). These portrayals identified Asian international students as being responsible for health problems and crime, and as visa abusers (Rotherham, 2003; Coddington, 2006; Spoonley and Butcher, 2010). High public exposure of negative incidents magnified influences on host community perceptions. Unlike during the Colombo Plan period, when Asian students were seen as a novelty, in the period of high growth in the 1990s and early 2000s, they were seen more as a nuisance.

A similar effect was reflected in origin countries where largely negative New Zealand headlines were subsequently reported in Asian media and where Asian students reported personal incidents on websites, blogs and in chat rooms (Li, 2007), and often in Chinese language media. Crime and safety issues began being reported back to countries of origin. Whatever the reality of the *actual* crime rate, the perception was consequential. Much of this may be seen as natural effects of the increased numbers of students. However, New Zealand's marketing promised a clean green, safe and purportedly 'crime-free' environment and on that it was not delivering.

The decade of growth for international education in New Zealand brought with it changes in the classroom and the lecture theatre. Frequently Asian students encountered large numbers of other Asian students. Therefore their socialisation occurred among co-nationals and other international students. In recent times Saudi students have encountered a similar effect. In national and targeted surveys, Asian students report that New Zealanders are superficially friendly but somewhat reticent to engage in quality relationships (Ward and Masgoret, 2004). The exceptions to this frequently relate to quality home-stay experiences and deep lasting friendships with some domestic students. Regrettably, some Asian students experience financial exploitation or poor treatment by service providers. The country's poor transport infrastructure (compared to their home countries) and the struggles to communicate well in English, along with experiencing cultural distance and being unable to make New Zealand friends, were the leading problems encountered by international students in New Zealand in these surveys (Ward and Masgoret, 2004; Deloitte, 2007). Asian students are less likely to maintain friendships with New Zealanders once they have returned home if they have not developed those friendships in the first instance (Butcher, 2009; McGrath et al, 2009, 2010).

Sector and official responses

Despite what can only be described as 'phenomenal' growth in numbers of Asian students to New Zealand, little or no attempt was made in official publications and responses to consider the effects of large numbers of Asian students entering education in New Zealand (Butcher, 2003a). In four large reports by the organisation set up to govern New Zealand's tertiary education sector, the Tertiary Education Advisory Commission (TEAC, 2000, 2001a, 2001b, 2001c), related to future directions in New Zealand tertiary education, international students received one fleeting reference, yet at the time they accounted for almost eight per cent of the student body and their numbers were rising.

As at June 2008, export education was New Zealand's fifth largest export industry, at NZ$2.3 billion per annum, after dairy, tourism, meat and mineral fuels respectively (Education NZ, 2010; see also Education NZ and Ministry of Education, 2008). New Zealand is a country of small businesses and the education sector is no exception. In shifting policy from 'aid' to 'trade' imbalances began to occur as the numbers and diversity of international students grew, as did the numbers and diversity of courses and education providers. As numbers began climbing in the late 1990s, commentators identified the need to exercise care in growing the sector (Groser, 2000; McGrath and Butcher, 2001).

Successive reports on the internationalisation of New Zealand's education (Back et al, 1998; McInnis et al, 2006) indicated limited progress in relation to building international relationships at interpersonal and organisational levels. These reports identified a need for government and educational institutions when developing and implementing policies to recognise the opportunities afforded by the presence of Asian students in the country as significant for long-term, sustainable engagement with the world and Asia in particular. The international student body in New Zealand and the country's international alumnus represent a unique resource for developing the country's international relationships, especially in the priority areas of its foreign relations. However, as these various documents illustrate, for many New Zealand universities at least, their interest in their alumni extend only as far as these alumni are prepared to financially contribute to their alma mater.

Some attention was given to engaging more fully with international alumni in the document, *The international education agenda for 2007–2012* (Ministry of Education, 2007). This document identified various aims for that agenda, including 'equipping New Zealand students to thrive in an interconnected world' and 'international students to be enriched by their education and living experiences in New Zealand'. But there has been scant other policy or programme developments to support these aims. There are, however, two exceptions. One is an immigration response to the international competition for skilled labour. This policy allows New Zealand-trained graduates to stay on in the country after completing their studies for an additional year, which is designed to allow time for them to secure a job that would fit with skilled migration policies. Another is the policy which allows PhD international students and their children of primary and secondary school age to study at domestic rates, plus their spouse being able to receive an open work permit, which has also been well received. However, these initiatives are not well supported by programmes and understanding related to securing appropriate employment for the graduate on completion (McGrath et al, 2010). These policies also have several unintended consequences. Graduate work permits do not take into account that few degrees ideally match a first job for a graduate. The scheme promoting PhDs presents significant and burdensome pastoral care challenges of the families of those PhD students, who are frequently neglected (McGrath et al, 2009; 2010).

New Zealand is not alone in trying to retain its foreign graduates. Other countries are also seeking to retain their foreign graduates through various policy and migration incentives (Suter and Jandi, 2006, p 15). Against this, however, China is encouraging its citizens to return to China (Ip, 2006; Zweig, 2006). This reflects a reversal in both practice and philosophy since the Colombo Plan era. Once host countries encouraged (indeed, mandated) foreign students to return to their countries of origin to assist with those countries' development (and to ward off communism). Now those same countries are developed or rapidly developing economies in their own right, while host countries are depending more on migration to fill gaps in their labour market.

Tim Groser, the Trade Minister and Associate Foreign Minister in the current government (at the time of writing), warned from his then role at the Asia 2000 Foundation against 'commoditisation' trade tendencies[1] as being inappropriate morally in educational contexts. He suggested that such practices would be viewed with abhorrence in Asia (Groser,

2000). This and other criticisms, alongside a string of institutional failures, provoked the then Labour government to intervene. The 'failure' by some education providers to deliver on what was promised (or at least marketed) put at risk the potential benefits that could accrue to New Zealand from the international education sector. One of New Zealand's largest and growing export industries was at risk. Government intervention took shape in regulation associated with the introduction of the *Code of practice for the pastoral care of international students* (Ministry of Education, 2003, 2010a) and an international student levy designed to provide funds to assist in promotion and communication, quality assurance, research, capability development and to fund the code office and its work. All education providers were required to meet course standards set by NZQA and to be signatories to the *Code* before they were permitted to enrol international students.

This intervention, alongside coordinated initiatives taken by the responsible associations within the sector and community institutions such as the police, city councils and community groups, have contributed much to arrest an erosion of confidence in the quality of care for international students in New Zealand. Successive research surveys have indicated the corrections enshrined in the *Code* has been successful and that international students have good levels of satisfaction with what is provided (Ward and Masgoret, 2004; Deloitte, 2007; McGrath et al, 2009).

Shifting responses and changing directions

The change of government in late 2008 appeared to continue the direction for international education as set by the previous Labour-led government. The promotion of export education would remain with ENZ and a 'NZ Inc' approach would be promoted (MFAT, 2009). The same messages are reinforced elsewhere: the appointment of a businessman to lead New Zealand's foreign affairs and trade ministry; the development 'NZ Inc' brand and offshore strategy; positioning New Zealand so it matches the Australian economy; building trade with Asia (particularly the PRC); growing the country's export education industry; putting a sinking lid on the funding of public sector departments and agencies (including public tertiary institutions); and reducing social science funding. These are all part of this current government's economic and social programme. Indeed, this government's preoccupation with Asia is exclusively through a trade lens, manifestly focused in securing further free trade agreements with various Asian countries.

New Zealand's Ministers of Education have indicated to the education sector that international education is to be a continuing and growing part of revenue generation for education institutions as a means of balancing the budget. In a joint press release of 28 July 2010, the two Ministers indicated that 'further development of the sector will bring real benefits in terms of economic growth plus additional income to allow our tertiary institutions to grow' (Tolley and Joyce, 2010). They went on to say that international students created diversity of cultures in the classroom that led to broader understanding of other cultures for domestic students. Joyce emphasised the importance of tertiary institutions developing the revenue streams through international education to at least the level of Australian universities. Extra revenue would enhance the experience of all students, he added. But whatever the rhetoric otherwise, there was no doubt that the government is expecting tertiary institutions to see international students primarily in revenue-generating terms – an echo of policies of 10 years ago.

The Ministry of Education, under the previous government, developed strategies for international education (Ministry of Education, 2007) that were evenly split between those that were educationally related for domestic and international students and those that were economic in regard to strengthening the financial positions of education providers as well as providing economic benefits to the community. Telling state-owned education providers to further utilise international students as a greater means to funding their operations is clearly an indication of the new government's intention to continue in that direction. Current export education policy has decisively moved away from intentional aid to intentional trade.

Discussion: friends and allies

Large numbers of Asian students studying in New Zealand provided an opportunity for growth in the country's relationships with Asian countries yet little attention has been given to this aspect. During the Colombo Plan era, there was a clear focus that students were brought to the country as part of its foreign policy interests. In moving to sell education internationally, the chance to affect bilateral and multilateral relationships at national, personal and community levels has not been given sufficient attention. The building of foundations for future relationships has occurred in ad hoc ways rather than being managed with clear public good objectives in view.

The significance of prior personal cross-cultural relationships and friendships to the effective development of other relationships such as trade and bilateral agreements is often not understood fully or at the opportune time when international students are still studying in New Zealand. Cannon (2000) argues that the value of the overseas experience lies primarily in what he calls a 'third place' – a distinct intercultural group in professional society, which gives advantage to employers, individuals and communities through its unique potential and relationships within global society. This 'third place' is where the graduate has made accommodations with family and friends, is comfortable in the lifestyle of the home community, has integrated their world view change and has adjusted to their situation within the work environment. Potentially this 'third place' can be one of significant influence, as graduates have adjusted back into their countries of origin, are equipped to work cross-culturally and have personal experience and understanding of both their own culture and New Zealand cultures.

New Zealand-educated international graduates live in 'third places' in their societies. They are invaluable resources, as they are instantly capable of being ambassadors for the country, commentators on New Zealand values, people and lifestyle, as well as witnesses to the net good obtained from education and experience while living in New Zealand. Their potential is enormous: from providing education about New Zealand in that community, to mutually enhancing relationships, to serving as a catalyst for further relationships of varying kinds.

Re-entry research clearly indicates the value of the New Zealand experience to the Asian graduate (McGrath, 1998; Butcher, 2003b; McGrath et al, 2007). It is also apparent that the experience could be improved on to enhance and build on positive relationships. Two key principles emerged from comments of New Zealand's Asian graduates: relationship or *guan xi* – the establishment of long-lasting and mutually trusted relationships; and relevance or *guan lian* – whatever we do needs to be relevant to those whom we seek to relate to, ideally of mutual relevance (McGrath et al, 2007, 2009).

Among many Colombo Plan graduates there is tremendous goodwill toward the country because of the positive experience many had had in New Zealand and the ongoing contacts they have with New Zealanders and other alumni. From national surveys we know that the experiences of recent students to New Zealand are more mixed (Ward and Masgoret, 2004; Ward et al, 2005; Deloitte, 2007). We also know that the pastoral care that students both expect and require (and some require more than others) is more often than not care by non-educational institutional groups, like churches or sports clubs (McGrath and Butcher, 2004a; Ward and Masgoret, 2004; Deloitte, 2007), despite the regulatory presence of the *Code of practice*. Australian Michael Wesley (2009, p 1) has referred to 'poisoned alumni' and the 'costs' of international education to his country, of which New Zealand needs to note the implications. Wesley (2009, p 1) comments:

> [S]tudents who return to their countries of origin with negative experiences could become a poisoned alumni, conveying critical attitudes in other countries about Australian society and poor impressions about Australia's reputation as an education provider. This could ultimately destroy a strong export product.

He goes on to note with respect to students from China and India in Australia that:

> The Australian government spends millions of dollars each year on public diplomacy, trying to foster a positive image of this country abroad. Any gains made by these programs can be reversed quickly by incidents such as attacks on foreign students ... the damage has the potential to contaminate some of Australia's most important diplomatic relationships. (Wesley, 2009, p 3)

The diplomatic fallout from foreign students being treated poorly in a host country is a severe issue. Equally severe, however, is disengaging with students – especially, in fact, those who have been *well*-treated – once they graduate. In New Zealand, there is no one database on foreign students who have graduated from a New Zealand university. Well-treated students will, naturally, be better disposed towards the country than poorly treated students, although both could end up in positions of influence and authority in their countries of origin or elsewhere in the world. For New Zealand, whose economic growth depends on economically engaging with Asia, this need is a pressing issue but not only in terms of trade. Bilateral relationships extend well beyond those who buy and sell. New Zealand, like Australia, risks 'poisoned alumni' damaging its international reputation. This could be remedied, in part at least, if the country's fifth biggest export earner, education, was also seen as an integral component of its foreign affairs.

Acknowledgements

We are grateful for the work of Brittany Chellew in preparing this chapter for publication and for the comments of Gaby Ramia and Chris Holden on an earlier draft. All errors or omissions otherwise remain our own.

Note

[1] In this context 'commodisation' trade tendency refers to New Zealand's economy being dependent on trade in agricultural commodities, which still provides the backbone of the economy. However, here Minister Groser is advocating that we need to understand that international education is a service industry involving real people who should not be treated as 'commodities'.

References

Asia New Zealand Foundation (2010) *Perceptions of Asia 2009* (www. asianz.org.nz/sites/asianz.org.nz/files/Perceptions_of_Asia_2009%20 (2).pdf).

Back, K., Davis D. and Olsen, A. (1998). *Internationalisation and tertiary education institutions in New Zealand,* Wellington: Ministry of Education.

Bandyopadhyay, S. (2009) 'A history of small numbers: Indians in New Zealand, c.1890s-1930s', *New Zealand Journal of History,* vol 43, no 2, pp 150-68.

Bandyopadhyay, S. (ed) (2010), *India in New Zealand: Local identities, global relations,* Dunedin: Otago University Press.

Bedford, R. and Ho, E. (2008) *Asians in New Zealand: Implications of a changing demography,* Wellington: Asia New Zealand Foundation.

Binning, E. (2010) 'Makeover for marketing of NZ to international students', *New Zealand Herald,* 15 November (www.nzherald.co.nz/ nz/news/article.cfm?c_id=1&objectid=10687656).

Boston, J. (1999) 'The funding of tertiary education: enduring issues and dilemmas', in J. Boston, P. Dalziel and S. St John (eds) *Redesigning the welfare state in New Zealand: Problems, policies, prospects,* Auckland: Oxford University Press.

Boston, J., Martin, J., Pallot, J. and Walsh, P. (1996) *Public management: The New Zealand model,* Auckland, Oxford University Press.

Boston, J., Dalziel, P. and St John, S. (eds) (1999) *Redesigning the welfare state in New Zealand: Problems, policies, prospects,* Auckland: Oxford University Press.

Butcher, A. (2003a) 'Whither international students? University reforms in New Zealand 1984-1999', *New Zealand Journal of Educational Studies*, vol 38, no 2, pp 151-64.

Butcher, A. (2003b) 'No place like home?: the experiences of South-East Asian international university students in New Zealand and their re-entry into their countries of origin', PhD thesis, Albany: Massey University.

Butcher, A. (2009) 'Friends, foreign and domestic: (re)converging New Zealand's export education and foreign policies', *Policy Quarterly*, vol 5, no 4, Wellington: Institute of Policy Studies, Victoria University of Wellington.

Cannon, R. (2000) 'The outcomes of an international education for Indonesian graduates: the third place?', *Higher Education Research and Development*, vol 19, no 3, pp 357-79.

Capie, D. (2009) 'New Zealand and the world: imperial, international and global relations', in G. Byrnes (ed) *The new Oxford history of New Zealand, Oxford:* Oxford University Press, pp 579-98.

China Daily (2003) www.chinadaily.co.cn/en/doc/2003-11/05/content_278761.htm

Coddington, D. (2006) 'Asian angst', *North and South*, December, pp 40-7.

Cook, M. (2010) *Standing together in single file: Australian views of New Zealand and Asia*, Wellington: Asia New Zealand Foundation (www.asianz.org.nz/files/AsiaNZ_Outlook_13_June.pdf).

Deloitte (2007) *The experiences of international students in New Zealand: Report on the results of the national survey*, Wellington: Ministry of Education (www.educationcounts.govt.nz/publications/international/22971).

Editorial, *New Zealand Herald* (2010) 'Rogue English schools risk NZ's reputation', *New Zealand Herald*, 16 November (www.nzherald.co.nz/nz/news/article.cfm?c_id=1&objectid=10687821).

Education New Zealand (2010) 'An important, lucrative industry comes of age', Press release, 25 January (www.educationnz.org.nz/documents/Export%20Education%20Coming%20of%20Age%20_for%20NZ%20Herald_.pdf).

Education New Zealand and Ministry of Education (2008) *The economic impact of export education*, Prepared by Infometrics, NRB and Skinnerstrategic, Wellington: Ministry of Education (www.educationcounts.govt.nz/__data/assets pdf_file/0007/35368/EconomicImpactReport08.pdf).

Friesen, W. (2008) *Diverse Auckland: The face of New Zealand in the 21st century?*, Asia Wellington: Asia New Zealand Foundation.

Groser,T. (2000) Keynote Address, 10th Graduation Address, International Pacific College, Palmerston North.

Ip, M. (2006) 'Returnees and transnationals: evolving identities of Chinese (PRC) immigrants in New Zealand', *Journal of Population Studies*, vol 3, pp 62-102.

Joyce, S. (2010) 'Greater accountability in international education', Press release from the Minister of Tertiary Education, 17 November.

Kelsey, J. (1997) *The New Zealand experiment. A world model for structural adjustment?*, 2nd edn, Auckland: Auckland University Press.

Laxon, A. (2010) 'Failure is not an option with pass-for-cash scams', *New Zealand Herald*, 13 November (www.nzherald.co.nz/nz/news/article. cfm?c_id=1&objectid=10687329).

Lewis, N. (2005) 'Code of practice for the pastoral care of international students: making a globalising industry in New Zealand', *Globalisation, Societies and Education*, vol 3, no 1, pp 5-47.

Li, M. (2007) 'The impact of the media on the New Zealand export education industry', Inaugural Australia – China International Business Research Conference, Beijing.

McGrath, T.M. (1998) 'Homecoming: reverse culture shock. An investigation of New Zealand trained graduates returning home to Singapore, Malaysia and Indonesia', Unpublished MPhil thesis, Massey University.

McGrath, T. and Butcher, A. (2001) *The governance of services for international students within the New Zealand tertiary education system*, Submission to the Tertiary Education Advisory Commission (http:// cunningham.acer.edu.au/dbtw-wpd/textbase/ndrie/ndrie534n.pdf).

McGrath, T. and Butcher, A. (2004a) *Campus community linkages in the pastoral care of international students, with specific reference to Palmerston North, Wellington and Christchurch*, Wellington: Ministry of Education.

McGrath, T. and Butcher, A. (2004b) 'International students in New Zealand: needs and responses', *International Education Journal*, vol 5, no 4, pp 540-51.

McGrath, T., Stock, P. and Butcher, A. (2007) *The impacts of returning Asian students on New Zealand–Asia relationships*, Wellington: Asia New Zealand Foundation (www.asianz.org.nz/sites/asianz.org.nz/files/ AsiaNZ percent20Outlook percent205.pdf).

McGrath, T., Butcher, A., Pickering, J. and Smith, H. (2005) *Engaging Asian communities in New Zealand*, Wellington: Asia New Zealand Foundation.

McGrath,T.,Anderson,V., Ching, C., Doi,A. and Stock, P. (2009) *Tracking study series of Asian business graduates: Report One*,Wellington:Asia New Zealand Foundation (www.asianz.org.nz/sites/asianz.dev.boost.co.nz/ files/Asia percent20NZ percent20Tracking percent20Study.pdf).

McGrath,T.,Anderson,V., Ching, C., Doi,A. and Stock, P. (2010) *Tracking study series of Asian business graduates: Report Two*,Wellington:Asia New Zealand Foundation.

McInnes, C., Peacock, R., Catherwood,V. (2006) *Internationalisation in New Zealand tertiary education organisations*, Wellington: Ministry of Education.

Ministry of Education, (2003) *The code of practice for the pastoral care of international students*,Wellington: Ministry of Education.

Ministry of Education (2007) *The international education agenda: A strategy for 2007-2012*,Wellington: Ministry of Education.

Ministry of Education (2010a) *The code of practice for the pastoral care of international students*,Wellington: Ministry of Education.

Ministry of Education (2010b) Export education levy key statistics for full-years 2003-2009 (www.educationcounts.govt. nz/statistics/international_education/export_education_levy_ statistics/29650/29680/29692).

MFAT (Ministry of Foreign Affairs and Trade) (2001) *The Colombo Plan at 50: A New Zealand perspective, 50th anniversary of the Colombo Plan, 1951–2001*,Wellington: MFAT.

MFAT (2007) *Our future with Asia*,Wellington: MFAT.

MFAT (2009) *Statement of intent 2009–2012*,Wellington: MFAT (www. mfat.govt.nz/downloads/media-and-publications/soi-mfat-2009-12. pdf).

MFAT (2010) 'About the Ministry' (http://mfat.govt.nz/About-the- Ministry/What-we-do/index.php).

Rotherham, F. (2003) 'Export education – blip or bust', *Unlimited Magazine*, 1 September (www.sharechat.co.nz/features/unlimited/ article).

Spoonley, P. and Butcher,A. (2010) 'Reporting superdiversity: the mass media and immigration in New Zealand', *Journal of Intercultural Studies*, vol 30, no 4, pp 355-72.

Spoonley, P. and Trlin A.D. (2004) *Immigration, immigrants and the media: Making sense of multicultural New Zealand*, Palmerston North: New Settlers Programme, Massey University.

Suter, B. and Jandi, M. (2006) *Comparative study on policies toward foreign graduates: Study on admission and retention policies towards foreign students in industrialised countries,* Vienna: International Centre for Migration Policy Development.

Tarling, N. (2004) *International students in New Zealand: The making of policy since 1950,* Auckland: New Zealand Asia Institute, University of Auckland.

TEAC (Tertiary Education Advisory Commission) (2000) *Shaping a shared vision,* Wellington: TEAC.

TEAC (2001a) *Shaping the system,* February, Wellington: TEAC.

TEAC (2001b) *Shaping the strategy,* July, Wellington: TEAC.

TEAC (2001c) *Shaping the funding framework,* November, Wellington: TEAC.

The Times Higher Education World University Rankings 2010-11 (www.timeshighereducation.co.uk/world-university-rankings/2010-2011/top-200.html).

Tolley, A. and Joyce, S. (2010) 'International student numbers increase', 28 July (www.beehive.govt.nz/release/international+student+numbers+increase).

UNESCO Institute of Statistics (2009) *Global education digest 2009: Comparing education statistics across the world,* Quebec: UNESCO Institute for Statistics.

Ward, C. and Masgoret, A. (2004) *The experiences of international students in New Zealand: Report on the results of the national survey,* Prepared for the Ministry of Education by the Centre for Applied Cross-cultural Research and School of Psychology, Victoria University of Wellington, Wellington.

Ward, C., Masgoret, A.-M., Ho, E., Holmes, P., Newton, J., Crabbe, D. and Cooper, J. (2005) *Interactions with international students,* Report for Education New Zealand, Wellington.

Wesley, M. (2009) *Australia's poisoned alumni: International education and the costs to Australia,* Sydney: Lowy Institute (www.lowyinstitute.org/Publication.asp?pid=1103).

White, H. (2009) *A focused force: Australia's defence priorities in the Asian century,* Lowy Institute Paper No 26. NSW: Longueville Media (http://lowyinstitute.org/Publication.asp?pid=1013).

Zweig, D. (2006) 'Learning to compete: China's efforts to encourage a reverse brain drain', *Competing for Global Talent,* Geneva: International Institute for Labour Studies, pp 187-213.

FOURTEEN

Student security in the global education market

Simon Marginson and Erlenawati Sawir

Introduction

According to the Organisation for Economic Co-operation and Development (OECD), in 2008, 3.3 million students were enrolled in tertiary education outside their country of citizenship for one year or more. From 2000 to 2008 the foreign student population grew at 11 per cent per year (OECD, 2010, p 315). Most of these students crossed national borders for educational purposes – such students are classified as 'international students' – although in some countries the data also included non-citizen permanent residents. More than four international students in ten enter English language countries (OECD, 2010, p 319).

The identity of the education provider nation determines the legal and policy regime that governs international student lives. These students do not enjoy the same rights, protections and entitlements as citizens. Their status as temporary migrants with student visas leaves them in a limbo they share with other mobile people such as short-term business and labour entrants, and refugees. The uncertain, vulnerable and de-powered existence of international students, their resulting problems, and what might be done to lift their dignity and position in the world, are the matters discussed here.

The chapter begins by outlining its assumptions about human security and rights. It provides a brief political economy of the global market in educational services. It then considers the legal and policy position of international (cross-border) foreign students, drawing on a recent Australian study, *International student security* (Marginson et al, 2010). The international student experience is mediated by non-citizen outsider status and the related facts of cultural difference, information asymmetry and communication problems. It differs from the experience of local students. The final section canvasses changes in national and global regulation.

Human rights and human security

In this chapter all people are normed as bearers of comprehensive human rights and entitlements to human security, universal rights that are not confined to national citizens or other selected groups. Charles Taylor argues in *Sources of the self* (1988) that it is 'utterly wrong and unfounded to draw the boundaries' of respect and concern for others 'any narrower than the whole human race' (pp 6-7). Some may question why international students should be viewed through the human rights lens, rather than, say, the lens of pastoral care, or consumer regulation. At bottom this is a normative question. It cannot be settled by investigation and evidence. Yet the whole matter turns on it. The founding assumption of this chapter is the United Nations' (UN) *Universal Declaration of Human Rights* (UN, 2010), which has been signed by most national governments, although implementation is radically incomplete. For globally mobile people, codified universal human rights are especially important. Outside their own countries they lack the entitlements of social citizenship. It is incumbent on those who believe international students should be viewed through another lens to explain why they should be seen as bearers of something less than comprehensive human rights.

The UN *Declaration* is the most widely acknowledged definition of human rights. It provides for the rights of self-determining people in a broad set of domains including personal safety and privacy; access to justice and equal recognition before the law; freedom of movement and expression; and 'economic, social and cultural rights', including access to social security and work, 'just and favourable' conditions of work and education and health. Article 28 of the *Declaration* states that: 'Everyone is entitled to a social and international order in which the rights and freedoms set forth in this Declaration can be fully realized'. These enabling clauses affect the definition of human security. If international students are the self-determining people of the *Declaration*, their human security rests on the exercise of stable human agency in the country of education. Only then can they access the full set of legal, industrial and civil rights: rights to welfare, healthcare, safe housing and other essential services; rights to education of adequate quality; rights to assistance in crisis; and rights to organise and advocate. This includes a capacity to differ from host country nationals within the terms of the law.

For mobile people, self-determining agency and rights depends in part on conditions provided by the host country, government and institutions. In addition, human security is affected in more than zones normally accessible to regulation such as housing, work and health services. Much of life takes place in the informal private domain. While not subject to direct regulation except at the extremes (such as family violence), the private domain interacts with the formal public domain and contributes to overall human security.

The global market in education

Cross-border student mobility has roots in globalisation, national government policies and market forces (Bashir, 2007; OECD, 2007; Verbik and Lasanowski, 2007). The drivers of the market are part commercial, part status-related and part political and cultural. In international education an 'exporting' nation includes institutions that offer educational services to citizens of other, 'importing', nations. Most such services are provided in the exporting nation itself. The institutions stay put and the students come to them. In addition institutions from some countries, including the US, Australia and the UK, provide educational services on the soil of importing countries, mostly in East and South East Asia ('transnational education'). This can take the form of actual campuses with buildings or distance-based learning. The service and institution are exported, the students stay put.[1]

In 2008 40.9 per cent of all mobile students were in the English language countries: US (18.7 per cent), UK (10.0 per cent), Australia (6.9 per cent), Canada (5.5 per cent) and New Zealand (1.8 per cent). Another 7.3 per cent were in Germany, 7.3 per cent in France, 4.3 per cent in Russia and 3.8 per cent in Japan. China (1.5 per cent) is an emerging provider. There are smaller intakes in Western Europe (OECD, 2010, p 314, Figure 1).

The largest education importers are China and India. Considerable numbers of students also come from Korea, Japan, Hong Kong China, Malaysia, Singapore, Pakistan, Bangladesh, Thailand and Indonesia. Another one quarter of the global total move between European countries, facilitated by subsidised mobility schemes and the part-integration of education systems in the Bologna reforms, whereby European education systems have become more closely aligned in their degree structures, facilitating mobility (Kehm et al, 2009). There is also growing movement within Asia. Figure 14.1 shows where international students go, and the weight of international student populations within the export nations.

Figure 14.1: Share of world tertiary education exports, and cross-border students as a proportion of all students, by export nation, 2008

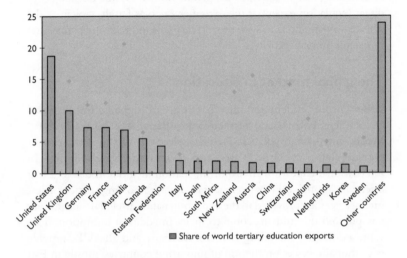

Note: In France, Germany, Italy, Korea and the Russian Federation the data are for non-citizen (foreign) students whether mobile or residential. In all other nations the data are for mobile ('international') students.

Source: OECD (2010, pp 314, 327)

For most students and their families, international education is a major financial commitment – an investment in upward social mobility designed to secure a better graduate career at home or transfer to a migration-friendly nation. 'The language spoken and used in instruction is an essential element in the choice of a foreign country in which to study' (OECD, 2010, p 315). English is the one global language of education and business (Crystal, 2003). This offers English-speaking nations a special opportunity for profit making.

International education has been estimated as a US$40 billion global industry. But it is a business as such only in some countries. All nations and universities compete for mobile students, up to a point. 'Tertiary education institutions ... have academic incentives to engage in international activities to build or maintain their reputation in the context of academic competition on an increasingly global scale' (OECD, 2007, p 303). International demand is a mark of national prestige, a means of magnifying global influence and a source of talent. Doctoral education is a one-world competition for mobile scholar-researchers. But not all international education takes the form of a commercial business. Doctoral education is scholarship-based, not tuition-based, and first degrees and Master's programmes vary. France, Germany and Japan provide free or subsidised places. The UK, Australia, New Zealand, Malaysian private colleges and Singapore use full price international education to generate surplus revenues. Full-fee international students in public universities study with subsidised locals and access common services. There are also for-profit providers such as the University of Phoenix.

The commercial sub-sector focuses mostly on business studies, technologies and mass professions like healthcare. Here international education is capitalism with no restrictions on growth. International students were 14.7 per cent of all tertiary students in the UK and 20.6 per cent in Australia, the highest level in the OECD region (OECD, 2010, p 327). In Australia education was the fourth largest export sector in 2009 (ABS, 2010), behind only coal, iron ore and gold. In the UK and Australia the introduction of the commercial approach triggered a decline in foreign aid to tertiary education (OECD, 2004), although the UK still provides a substantial scholarship programme.

The US is the most sought-after destination but international students constitute just 3.4 per cent of tertiary students. Despite their potential business advantages, non-profit US institutions do not run international education as a business. The main goals are foreign aid, integration of national elites into American culture and recruitment of research talent.

The status of foreign students

Despite trends to global integration and convergence (Held et al, 1999) and the growing awareness of global interdependence, we live in a nation-state world. There is no global state or other comprehensive global governance. We have a sketchy system of international law resting on multilateral consent; global agencies that operate partly inside and partly outside national governments; and a thickening global civil society so far beyond significant formal regulation. People are decisively regulated by national governments on the basis of where they reside and where they are citizens. National authority means sovereign control over bordered territory. This creates difficulties for globally mobile people such as international students, who are mostly citizens of one state while present within the jurisdiction of another. Dual citizenship is provided by some countries but rarely accessed by students and other temporary migrants like tourists, workers and business executives.

This regulatory terrain has three implications for international students, regardless of whether their education is subsidised or commercial. First, being outsiders, mobile students have ambiguous meanings for the country of education. Struggling to manage global people flows they never fully control, national governments flip between the benefits and the dangers (as they see it) of international students. These students are managed within two conflicting normative frameworks. On the one hand international education is a global market where the student is nominally valued, welcomed and sovereign and might become a future citizen. Education officials emphasise the revenues, research labour, international goodwill and cross-border cultural and economic integration. On the other hand international education triggers border anxiety and old-style bureaucratic force. Officials from immigration or homeland security, perhaps reflecting anti-migration sensitivities in the host country population, focus on the absorption of scarce national resources in education, health, welfare and housing, and the dangers to property, life and national character. International students overstay their student visas and attempt backdoor migration, it is said. Some are criminals or potential terrorists. In threat mode the nation-state focuses on its own welfare and security, asserts its own interests as a right and models the students as outsiders threatening *its* national security. It is difficult for that same nation-state to conceive of international students as (temporary) insiders with legitimate issues of *their* human security and rights.

Some of those who attacked New York and Washington in September 2001 had entered the US as students. After 9/11 the Bush government established the SEVIS surveillance system, which positioned international students as potentially dangerous aliens, infringed their liberties and imposed a regulatory burden on universities (Rosser et al, 2006). Meanwhile Australia cancelled the visas of many international students for often minor breaches of the rules governing student work, placing many in prison-like detention. The students had no recourse except protracted expensive appeals – often from within detention – against the visa cancellations. Yet a third of the cancellations were overturned (Marginson et al, 2010, pp 247-50). These failures of humanism point to the connections between borders, law and fear, and nations' customary use of pre-emptive violence to protect their arbitrarily defined territories. Imposed by force in the past, challenged by globalisation, borders must be continually remade (Vaughan-Williams, 2008, pp 326-8). Nations that have signed the *Universal Declaration of Human Rights* ignore it. The distinction between citizen and non-citizen is more potent. This highlights the weak point in multilateralism, where universal principles have to be regulated by sectional interests.

Second, students are affected by two national regimes and the political and legal relationship between them. The nation of education has the larger practical regulatory power. But the home country is not out of the picture. From time to time home governments take up individual and collective issues with the nation of education. In the last decade China has actively pursued student security within Australia and New Zealand. At one point it issued a website advisory against study in New Zealand, triggering a sharp decline in Chinese students there (Marginson et al, 2010, pp 8-9, 206-8, 217-19).

Third, notwithstanding the presence of two national jurisdictions in their lives, international students also experience an incomplete regulatory regime and less than full citizen agency. They fall into a gap between the two states. They cannot exercise the full rights and entitlements of citizens in either the home country or the country of temporary residence. They cannot fully access home country legal, welfare and political systems. The main point of formal contact is the embassy or consulate, itself a guest and unable to replicate all home government functions. Yet as aliens in the foreign country they have a different and inferior status to local citizens. What this means can vary. International students are affected by laws concerning aliens, and some nations with large numbers of international students also have specific laws, regulations and/or programmes for them. (The case of Australia is addressed below.) Status can also vary according to the nation of origin. For example, European Union (EU) countries grant other EU citizens favoured treatment – they pay lower tuition than non-EU foreigners. Australia offers quasi-citizen status to New Zealanders. Some nations discriminate against particular categories of foreigners. The Australian government imposes more stringent migration requirements on people from countries whose nationals are reckoned most likely to breach visa conditions, based on probabilistic data.

This 'Othering' of international students spreads beyond the formal jurisdiction. Often foreigners are seen as culturally exotic outsiders. There is no obligation to engage with the exotic, or include it in a common humanist regime; and it is a short trip from 'fascinating and mysterious' to 'dangerous'. The inferior status of mobile non-citizens renders them de-powered and vulnerable compared to national citizens. This might seem unexceptional in the case of short-term visitors such as tourists.

It is more problematic for people resident for several years, including students who complete degree programmes. They are classified as aliens yet must deal with the housing and employment markets. They are subject like local citizens to the authority of the police, the legal system and public bureaucracies. They pay the same taxes.

National governments that have signed the *Universal Declaration* nevertheless typically give priority to their own citizens. There are no international protocols enabling governments to determine whether, how much and how they differentiate resident foreign students from citizens. Which rights of the person, if any, should be extended to these students? Which services are universally accessed by citizens? And to what extent should government provide specific services in areas of international student need and vulnerability? How far can government go without prompting a backlash from local citizens that elect it? Should governments provide less to non-citizens? How much less? Given that many international students pay taxes, what financing arrangements are appropriate? Can firm benchmarks be applied, or are these matters shaped merely by pragmatic politics and shifting public reaction? Governments make varied responses.

The case of Australia

English-speaking nations for whom international education is primarily a commercial matter position international students as consumers with consumer protection rights. The modelling of global actors in economic terms is more familiar territory for nation-states than the regulation of global cultural flows, which spill freely beyond national control (Appadurai, 1996).[2] There is a long if chequered history of national and international regulation of trade. However, the commercial framing of international education is partial. Consumer protection addresses some areas of human rights and security but is absent from others.

Australia is formally committed to universal human rights (Australian Government, Attorney-General's Department, 2005, p 5). But this has no resonance in the regulation of international education. The students are imagined as aliens with no rights other than those donated by the host nation. International education is governed by the Education Services for Overseas Students (ESOS) Act. The Act includes *The national code of practice for registration of authorities and providers of education and training for overseas students* (DEEWR, 2007a). The second objective of the *National code* is to 'establish and safeguard Australia's international reputation as a provider of high quality education and training'. The third objective is to 'protect the interests of overseas students'. But there is no statement pertaining to universal humanism or comprehensive rights. The ESOS Act and *National code* are focused on the obligations of educational providers and concerned primarily with immigration law compliance and consumer protection (DEEWR, 2007a, Sections A.3.1, B.4). They do not mention personal safety, entitlements to learning or protection from discrimination.

The *National code* has five pages on the institution's responsibilities in relation to visa requirements concerning student progression, attendance and completion, including the obligation to monitor student compliance and report to the immigration authorities any changes of student circumstances and breaches of visa conditions (DEEWR, 2007a, Section 10.1). The notion of the student as consumer is not formalised in legislation governing the higher education of local students; it is used only for internationals.[3] 'The registered provider must enter into a written agreement with the student' that specifies the programme of study, monies payable, and 'information in relation to refunds of course money'. It is not mandatory to include educational or welfare provisions or standards (DEEWR, 2007a, Standard 3, Section 3.1). In this system, government devolves responsibility for the security of students to the provider, and the provider devolves much of the responsibility to the students themselves. There is no contract between students and government, and no references to political rights or channels of representation.

To facilitate Australia's reputation and protect consumers, the *National code* emphasises that marketing should provide information 'of a high standard, clear and unambiguous, so that intending students and their parents can make informed decisions about their preferred provider and course'. Consumers must have 'information about the course, fees, facilities, services and resources offered by the registered provider prior to enrolment', and data on the cost of living and housing options. Recruitment should be 'ethical'. This is little defined (DEEWR, 2007a, Section D, Preamble to Standards 1-4, 10-11; Standard 2, Section 2.1), but providers must not offer 'false or misleading information or advice' in areas like 'the employment outcomes associated with a course', 'automatic acceptance into another course' or 'possible migration outcomes' (DEEWR, 2007a, Standard 1, Section 1.2). Pre-departure information is not closely monitored. There is no prohibition of false claims in other respects. Students must be offered an internal mechanism for handling complaints and appeals. Providers must also guarantee a person or body external to the provider who can handle further complaints or appeals

(DEEWR, 2007a, Standard 8, Section 8.2). However, a genuinely independent external agent is not required.

Academic staffing must be 'adequate and have the capabilities as required by the quality assurance framework applying to the course'. This permits variable standards. The statement about learning resources and facilities is similar (DEEWR, 2007a, Standard 14, Sections 14.1-14.3). On welfare, providers should ensure 'access to support services and support staff to meet the needs of the students enrolled in their courses'. 'Needs' – defined by provider? by student? according to regulated standards? – are unspecified (DEEWR, 2007a, Preamble to Standard 6). The strongest statements are that 'the registered provider must have sufficient student support personnel to meet the needs of the students enrolled with the registered provider', and 'the registered provider must assist students to adjust to study and life in Australia', but again firm definitions of 'assist' and 'needs' are missing (DEEWR, 2007a, Standard 6, Sections 6.1, 6.6). For the most part the *National code* does not list mandatory services but instead lists services that students should be informed about, including 'student support services available to students in the transition to life and study in a new environment', 'legal services', 'emergency and health services', 'facilities and resources' and 'complaints and appeals processes' (DEEWR, 2007a, Standard 6, Section 6.1).

There are no common benchmarks in relation to service quality. It is assumed that students as consumers will regulate standards by making market choices, even though as the *National code* notes, 'overseas students usually cannot evaluate the quality of a course before purchase' (DEEWR, 2007a, Section A.6.1), and there is little students can do to pressure the provider to improve the product in institutions where the number of applications for study exceeds the number of places available. The consumer has leverage only when the provider breaches its contractual undertaking to provide the specified programme. There have been few claims in this area.

The *National code* is more prescriptive in relation to welfare at one point. The provider must offer free 'welfare-related support services to assist with issues that may arise during their study, including ... accommodation issues' (DEEWR, 2007a, Standard 6, Section 6.2), the only reference to post-enrolment housing services. Counselling is not mentioned. The *National code* also regulates 'emergency' services and critical incidents. It is it unclear how far beyond the campus the obligatory provision extends. Beyond ESOS there is no legal and policy basis for managing international student security in the general community, in relation to personal safety, accommodation, freedom from abuse and discrimination and access to transport, health and other services provided to citizens. Yet most breaches of student security occur off campus (for more detailed discussion, see Marginson et al, 2010).

In sum, the framework feints towards comprehensive security provision but assigns intrusive surveillance responsibilities to providers, minimises mandatory expenditure by them and is short of detail or silent in crucial areas. This limits potential student claims. Student agency is channelled into a consumer protection regime where the student is a market actor rather than democratic subject and constrained by information asymmetries acknowledged but only weakly addressed in the *National code*. This allows commercial considerations to take priority and enables the variable quality consistent with a price-based market. If institutions offer comprehensive student security they do so only as a market positioning strategy.

Nevertheless, it is not all a matter of rights reduction. While the notion of student as consumer is a regression from universal human rights, it does not eliminate agency altogether. Further, market-based rights are universal, cutting across differences of nation, culture, gender, age and social position. 'Consumer' is a global form of agency that offers international students from anywhere a common presence in national law, albeit as subordinates.

The international student experience in Australia

Data on international students' perceptions of their human security and rights were gathered in semi-structured interviews conducted in 2004-06 with 200 students from 35 nations enrolled at nine Australian public universities.[4] The student interviews lasted 30-60 minutes and included up to 63 questions in 12 domains common to the study. Interviews were voluntary and arranged through emails advertising the study or university international offices. A study of this kind does not constitute a representative sample of the 632,000 international students in all sectors (data for 2009 from AEI, 2010). However, 200 interviews is a large qualitative study and the group approximated the balances of the international student population in gender, field of study and national origin. PhD students, older students and students from Indonesia were over-represented (Marginson et al, 2010, pp 12-15). The findings are generally consistent with the prior research literature.

The research was funded by the Australian Research Council, and the Monash Institute for the Study of Global Movements at Monash University.

Findings from the interviews

The chapter now briefly summarises findings from the 200 international student interviews that go to questions of human agency, security and rights (see Marginson et al, 2010 for fuller results and discussion).

Most Australian universities assume students have full communicative competence from day 1, but one third of the interviewees had problems with academic English, including most of those from East Asia. Language-related difficulties are the most frequently reported item in research on international students in English-speaking countries. Many students in the study found their university's language-related support services to be very inadequate.

In relation to the immigration department, many students reported bad experiences including hostility from officials, time delays, administrative inefficiency and wrong advice. Respondents became more emotive in answering questions about immigration than about any other matter.

International students faced more difficulties with accommodation than local students who often lived with their parents. In Australia there is less on-campus student housing than in many Asian universities, and it is unsubsidised and beyond the reach of most students. In Sydney and Melbourne there is a severe shortage of rental housing. In the seller's market several interviewees stated that they had experienced discrimination. Often students lacked information about the housing market when they signed up for high-rent rooms in poor conditions. Whether by choice or necessity many had crowded into shared same-culture households of 10 or more at a time. Many such houses were unhygienic. Some were unsafe due to fire risk.

In relation to personal safety, nine in ten interviewees stated that they felt 'safe and secure' in Australia, and most said that Australia was safer than the home country (the exceptions were students from Japan and Singapore), but a small minority reported physical assaults. A larger number had been robbed, mostly house burglaries; and a still larger group, all non-white, had been subjected to hate crime in the form of verbal abuse in public places.

Most students experienced loneliness, especially in the first three to six months. For some, loneliness and/or isolation persisted throughout the period of study. Same-culture networks were often dominant in international students' lives. Many also found it relatively easy to make good friends with international students from other cultural backgrounds. There were barriers to making friends with local students. This was a strong finding of the study. Local students tended to self-segregate. They saw no need to move out of their comfort zone. In classrooms relations were at the 'hi-bye' level. This further encouraged international students to self-segregate. Cultural segregation compounded stereotyping by both groups, reinforcing separation. In a minority of cases differences of values, beliefs and activity appeared to be an obstacle. But the main barrier to intercultural relations between local and international students was that while most international students were open to personal change, local students had no motivation to change or to engage with other cultures. 'Who cares?', 'Why bother?', was the attitude.

In total 99 of the 200 students – just under 50 per cent of those interviewed – had experienced cultural hostility or prejudice in Australia. The rate was highest for students from Singapore and Malaysia, above average for those from China, and higher for women than for men. There were a small number of complaints about administrative or academic staff. But the great majority of problems occurred outside the campus, especially on the street or public transport; and also in shops, and in students' workplaces when dealing with local customers and sometimes when dealing with the boss. Several students reported unprovoked abusive incidents that were profoundly distressing. In these incidents they were made to feel outsiders, aliens, often with lasting effect. There was no process whereby they could claim respect and seek redress, reasserting their dignity, agency and their right to belong.

Differences between local and international students

The study carried out two further inquiries to more closely identify those aspects of student security and rights distinctive to international students.

The first compared the rights, entitlements and benefits available to international and local students respectively, in all domains of policy (Marginson et al, 2010, pp 17–20). The position of international students was inferior in 28 domains. Nearly all forms of public financial support, including welfare and housing, were inaccessible to them. In the two largest Australian States, they paid full fares on public transport, while local students paid concession rates. Public schooling was free for local families but most internationals paid full cost fees for their student children. International students received less financial support from universities although they paid higher tuition fees. Some postgraduate research scholarships were unavailable to them, and certain bank services. Both groups had access to health cover but internationals were not included in the public Medicare scheme and had to take out private insurance. This was more costly than the Medicare levy paid by locals via taxation. During semester international students could work for only 20 hours per week. Local students had unrestricted rights to work. International students from certain countries faced implied restrictions on political activity. Their visas included condition 8303: 'You must not become involved in any activities that are disruptive to, or in violence threaten harm to, the Australian community or a group within the Australian community'.

Second, in 2008 there were parallel interviews with 20 locals and 20 internationals from the same university. The 20 students were significantly more likely to have experienced difficulty with English in academic work, less likely to be aware of on-campus student services, more likely to have experienced loneliness and/or isolation and more likely to have experienced discrimination. Both groups agreed there were 'significant barriers in making friends across cultures' (Marginson et al, 2010, p 15).

In sum, four related factors distinguish international from local students and mediate the international student experience. First, international students are outsiders: temporary residents without citizen status, and always seen as such. Overall their lives are more marginal and more lonely. This outsider status is reinforced by communication problems, immigration department hostility, negative experiences in the housing market and instances of discrimination and abuse. It reinforces loneliness and isolation and difficulties in forming friendships with local students. Second, most international students experience an information gap, although the effects diminish over time. The interviews show that this problem plays out in many areas including housing, dealings with university administration, lack of local cultural knowledge in communication, and difficulties with local pedagogy. Third, most internationals are from countries where English is not in daily use and experience communication difficulties, although these also diminish over time. This affects not just academic progress but daily life and especially cross-cultural relations, inhibiting the potential for local friendships. Fourth, most international students experience cultural difference: the contrast between home country and education country practices. For example, this may include differences in politeness regimes, religion and the cultures of institutions and interpersonal relations. The differences diminish over time, and become easier to navigate, but rarely disappear altogether.

The four factors intersect. Recency of arrival, information gaps and outsider status emphasise perceived cultural difference. Communication problems, lack of knowledge and perceived cultural difference magnify outsiderness. Difference too readily becomes separation and stigma. 'Not only do international students need to adapt to a foreign education system and a foreign language and culture, like migrants, they also need to adjust to being part of a social minority … they encounter difficulties associated with being different' (Forbes-Mewett and Nyland, 2008, p 185). The *National code* addresses only one of the four issues, the information gap. The regulatory framework ignores cultural difference. It makes the implicit presumption that Anglo-Australian culture is neutral and normal. Yet the federal department's own student surveys show the international student experience is most fraught when cultural identity is at play (DEEWR, 2007b). This affects mostly non-white students and especially East and South East Asian students (Marginson et al, 2010, chs 9 and 12-15).

The differences between local and international students are less obvious in areas such as finance, work and health. Nevertheless, even where the statistical incidence of problems is similar for international and local students, the experience of those problems can be different, being articulated through lack of knowledge, cultural factors and outsider status. For example, students from both groups experience ultra exploitation and other problems at work. What makes the international student experience distinct – aside from less knowledge of labour markets – is immigration status. Despite the limit of 20 hours work a week during semester, internationals often work for longer to make ends meet. But students working outside their visa conditions are scarcely in a position to complain to public authorities about low rates of pay, demands for excessive hours or sexual harassment in the workplace.

Implications for regulation

International education is simultaneously local and institutional, national and global. Globalisation invokes the challenge of regulating activities such as education when they cross more than one national space. It is inefficient to sort all global matters through bilateral negotiation, and developments in international law place in question the traditional assumption that limits of national territory are also limits of governance (Vaughan-Williams, 2008, p 323). Nevertheless, global governance and regulation are underdeveloped. Decisions about the global movement of people between nations are made by national governments whose formal authority stops at the territorial border. The rights and lives of mobile individuals are regulated through the prism of national policy on aliens, rather than global citizenship.

The commercial character of international education in Australia, the UK, New Zealand and some other countries, where the needs and rights of students are understood in terms of bargains struck in the marketplace, creates further challenges. Part of the dynamism of international education derives from its commercial character but this generates limits, frustrations and abuses. Consumer bargains are unlikely to be configured so as to provide a common entitlement to human rights. What kind of international student security regime is consistent with both the healthy functioning of the global education market, and the human rights and security of the students?

This suggests three questions about regulation. First, should matters of the public good or public interest include the comprehensive human rights of non-citizen students even if that cuts across the profitability of educational trade? Second, if the answer is 'yes', should the scope of regulation be national alone or both national and global? Third, if global regulation of mobile students and others is desired, how should this be developed and managed?

Re-norming international education

International student security (Marginson et al, 2010) makes specific proposals for reforms by national government in each domain pertaining to human rights and security. It also argues for a re-norming of international education at national level. The elements of this re-norming are as follows:

- To ensure the common freedom and security of international students it is necessary to look beyond the economic market. Market forces prefer maximum price for minimum cost, human rights confined to rights of trade and consumer protection, and human security devolved to self-management by student and family. Markets must be regulated and where necessary, overridden.
- International students are not weak or people in 'deficit'. They are strong human agents, deciding for themselves, engaged in a process of complex self-formation through education and global mobility (Marginson, 2009). Their challenges and achievements mostly exceed those of native-speaking local students.
- If international students are worthy of equal respect with local students this does not mean their need for particularised services and support disappears. To exercise full human rights such services are essential, especially during the early months.

- If international students are self-determining people, managing their own identity and life trajectory, defining their own needs and values, they are bearers of the full range of acknowledged human rights. The principle of universal humanism suggests the same.
- Human rights apply in all domains of living, whether formally regulated or unregulated, whether in education institutions or in the general community. Human rights include protections such as safety, freedom of association and freedom from discrimination and abuse, as well as personal capacity in areas such as communications or housing.
- As far as possible, nations should extend to non-citizen international students the same rights and entitlements as apply to citizen students. (There may be exceptions in a small number of designated areas where national treatment is warranted, such as the right to vote in national elections.) The application of this norm of equivalence with local citizens would minimise the *outsider* element in the international student experience, the primary limitation on security and rights.

The strategic question at play is whether it is possible for nation-states to adopt a sufficiently global approach to the problem. Designating temporary residents as quasi-citizens would qualify national sovereignty and in some respects deals nations out of the game (although they would still control which students they admit). The same problem dogs multilateral discussions on climate change and world financial management. It is unlikely that operating on their own behalf without a change in the settings all nation-states would re-norm international education in more global terms. The core problem is how to develop the global public good in this area, in a world of nation-states.

A more global approach can evolve in two perhaps interdependent ways: the accumulation of bilateral negotiations, and the work of global agencies.

Bilateral negotiations

Home country governments have a potential role in the regulation of their international students abroad, as shown by China's interventions. This role can only be exercised in collaboration with the national government in the country of education. This suggests that student-sending (education-importing) countries might negotiate with the receiving (exporting) government a set of protocols covering the rights and entitlements of mobile students. These protocols could be developed with reference to the *Universal Declaration of Human Rights*, with provisions about student-specific domains such as education, housing, crisis support and intercultural relations.

If enough such agreements are reached on a bilateral basis, this begins to create sufficient momentum for the emergence of an informal global standard subject to widespread policy imitation. Thus a regime of international student security and rights could be constructed by an incremental process of voluntary agreement, whereby each nation makes its education system into a more globally responsible space.

Global agencies

In turn, this would create favourable conditions for the development of a universal global standard for multilateral consideration and/ or monitoring and regulation by a global agency, whether existing or purpose-built. Here international education could also lead the development of global approaches to other, more difficult areas of cross-border people movement – not just labour and business migration, but political refugees, and people displaced by global climate change. In principle the need for global agency involvement is obvious. The welfare and rights of mobile people should be seen primarily as a matter of *global public good*, not a matter of national private or public good, or global private good created in global markets. Everyone has a common interest in the freedom and security of cross-border movement.

The problem in providing global public goods is that there is no global state. Right now few people want a global government. If one was created tomorrow it would reflect one or another national political culture, not a global culture. While the expansion of synchronous communication is driving the growth of global civil society, this has limited capacity to shape global governance and in itself cannot provide for universal rights and protections. For global agencies to assume such obligations in relation to national citizens such as international students would be a radical innovation. Perhaps this is why global agencies are largely indifferent to the human rights and security of the students. For example, the International Labour Organization discusses migrant workers but does not include international students in that category, although nations often define such students as temporary migrants.

Cross-border agencies are more active in relation to stateless people and refugees from states. No national government has jurisdiction over such people. Nations readily accept the need for a supranational intervention. However, while international students are in a different position to refugees in some respects (they leave their homes voluntarily, and often have more favourable economic support and prospects), the two groups are positioned similarly in one crucial respect – as mobile people both groups have incomplete access to rights and protections in a nationally bordered world. The students can be regulated by the nation of citizenship and/or nation of education, but regulation by one or another government is incomplete. For both students and refugees the core problem is absence (whether full or partial) of nation-state coverage and its empowerment of the person.

Conclusion

Cross-border migration, whether permanent, or temporary for work or study, is challenging for those that undertake it. Mobile people move from familiar rules, conventions, supports and citizenship rights, to a country less familiar where they have less personal support and formal rights and the rules may be unknown. Global mobility demands adjustment by mobile people. On the face of it, global mobility also demands adjustments by the institutions and systems that mobile people encounter, especially when there are many such people. But institutions and systems in the country of education rarely adjust much to the 'strangers'. They would be more willing to adjust if international students were no longer defined as 'strangers'.

International students are investors in geographical and social mobility. They face many difficulties. Some have good personal, institutional and governmental backup. Others do not. Nevertheless, most will enter the top socioeconomic status quintile at home or somewhere in the world. International students are not proletarian subjects, but they are at the cutting edge of two problems of global governance, or rather its absence. One is the extent to which regulation should modify market forces. The other is the disjunction between mobile populations and national regulation.

Global mobility will increase. The number of international students is expanding. And in future there will be a marked increase in displaced people, including those affected by climate change. Ultimately cross-border people movement will have to be managed via a multilateral and/or global approach. No one nation can solve it. So why focus on international students? Refugees are more in need of immediate assistance, and there are more of them. The answer is that for many of the receiving nations international students are economically desired, because they create revenues and/or become skilled migrants. Nations have incentives to improve the conditions of international students, especially once better norms are established.

It is a familiar political logic. Human rights, such as the right to vote and gender equality, are first extended to middle-class populations and become progressively universalised to all. By getting the global protocols right on international students, the ultimate position of refugees can be advanced.

Ultimately it will be necessary to de-nationalise, globalise and humanise international student rights. The bedrock of a global student rights regime is not national strategic interest, but a global humanism in which every person is understood as a self-determining subject and worthy of equal respect.

Notes

[1] Transnational education is not discussed here, but see Ziguras and McBurnie (2006).

[2] Perhaps nations are always more comfortable with global mobility where global subjects are modelled in economic terms, whether as subjects of trade and commerce or as economically desired migrants. This is not because economic life is more intrinsically global than cultural flows. The opposite is the case. In many respects political economy is still nationally bordered (Held et al, 1999). Perhaps – paradoxically – politics more readily understands globalisation as an economic phenomenon and global actors in the context of economic bargains, because politics itself (which remains largely nation-centred) finds this easier to manage than global flows of images, information, ideas and knowledge.

[3] 'Overseas students differ from domestic students in that they are subject to migration controls and face different needs for consumer protection' (DEEWR, 2007a, Section 6.1).

[4] The institutions were the Universities of Ballarat, Melbourne, New South Wales and Sydney; and RMIT, Swinburne, Victoria, Deakin and Central Queensland (Rockhampton and Melbourne campuses). All interviews were conducted with permission of the universities concerned and the project received ethics clearance at Monash University where all of the researchers were then based.

References

ABS (Australian Bureau of Statistics) (2010) *International trade in goods and services, Australia*, December, ABS Catalogue no 5368.0, Canberra: ABS.

AEI (Australian Education International) (2010) *Statistical data on international education* (http://aei.gov.au/AEI/PublicationsAndResearch/Default. htm).

Appadurai, A. (1996) *Modernity at large: Cultural dimensions of globalization*, Minneapolis, MS: University of Minnesota Press.

Australian Government, Attorney-General's Department (2005) *Australia's national framework for human rights: National action plan*, Canberra: Commonwealth of Australia.

Bashir, S. (2007) *Trends in international trade in education: Implications and options for developing countries*, Education Working Paper Series, no 6, Washington, DC: The World Bank.

Crystal, D. (2003) *English as a global language* (2nd edn), Cambridge: Cambridge University Press.

DEEWR (Department of Education, Employment and Workplace Relations) (2007a) *National code of practice for registration authorities and providers of education and training to overseas students*, Australian Government (http://aei.gov.au/AEI/ESOS/NationalCodeOfPractice2007/ Default.htm).

DEEWR (2007b) *2006 international student survey: Higher education summary report*, Canberra: Australian Education International (AEI).

Forbes-Mewett, H. and Nyland, C. (2008) 'Cultural diversity, relocation, and the security of international students at an internationalised university', *Journal of Studies in International Education*, vol 12, no 2, pp 181-203.

Held, D., McLew, A., Goldblatt, D. and Perraton, J. (1999) *Global transformations: Politics, economics and culture*, Stanford, CA: Stanford University Press.

Kehm, B., Huisman, J. and Stensaker, B. (eds) (2009) *The European higher education area: Perspectives on a moving target*, Rotterdam: Sense Publishers, pp 297-321.

Marginson, S. (2009) 'Sojourning students and creative cosmopolitans', in M. Peters, S. Marginson and P. Murphy, *Creativity and the global knowledge economy*, New York: Peter Lang, pp 217-55.

Marginson, S., Nyland, C., Sawir, E. and Forbes-Mewett, H. (2010) *International student security*, Cambridge: Cambridge University Press.

OECD (Organisation for Economic Co-operation and Development) (2004) *Internationalisation and trade in higher education*, Paris: OECD.

OECD (2007) *Education at a glance, 2007*, Paris: OECD.

OECD (2010) *Education at a glance, 2010*, Paris: OECD.

Rosser, V., Hermsen, J., Mamiseishvili, K. and Wood, M. (2007) 'A national study examining the impact of SEVIS on international student and scholar advisers', *Higher Education*, vol 54, no 4, pp 525-42.

Taylor, C. (1988) *Sources of the self: The making of modern identity*, Cambridge, MA: Harvard University Press.

UN (United Nations) (2010) *The Universal Declaration of Human Rights* (www.un.org/en/documents/udhr/index.shtml).

Vaughan-Williams, N. (2008), 'Borders, territory, law', *International Political Sociology*, vol 4, no 2, pp 322-38.

Verbik, L. and Lasanowski, V. (2007) *International student mobility: Patterns and trends*, London: Observatory on Borderless Higher Education (OBHE).

Ziguras, C. and McBurnie, G. (2006), *Transnational education: Issues and trends in offshore higher education*, London, Routledge.

FIFTEEN

Exporting policy: the growth of multinational education policy businesses and new policy 'assemblages'

Stephen J. Ball

Introduction

In this chapter I address some particular aspects of global education policy, which are almost totally ignored in the current literatures on policy transfer and policy mobilities. That is, the role of policy as a profit opportunity for global edu-businesses, the 'selling of policy' and education services, and the participation of these businesses in national and international education policy communities (see Holden, 2009, on the export of public–private partnership [PPP]/private finance initiative [PFI] schemes in the health sector). I focus on some specific examples of these multinational education businesses (MNEBs),[1] and look at their business activities and some of the new policy 'assemblages' in which they are key players as part of what Larner (2002, p 663) calls 'a new specialist elite'. Thus, in a number of ways I explore the changing relationships between business, education policy and nation states, and the increasingly important role of corporate philanthropy in solving education policy problems, and touch on the concomitant changes in the form and modalities of the contemporary state. However, as I shall seek to illustrate, education policy analysis can no longer sensibly be limited to within the nation state, and policy analysis must also extend its purview to include transnational business practices.

The chapter begins with a discussion of policy transfer, and identifies some problems with the concept. The activities of MNEBs of different kinds are then discussed in four sections: *new policy assemblages* explores the developing relations between philanthropy and business to solve educational problems in low-income countries; *exporting and selling policy* looks at the policy work of a new breed of knowledge companies; *education as big business* focuses on consolidations and mergers and the emergence of transnational 'giants'; and *selling students* considers private higher education and the global market in educational institutions. In each case the analyses and discussions are indicative rather than exhaustive.

Policy transfer

The term *policy transfer* refers to a diverse rag bag of ideas that attempt to capture and model the ways in which policy knowledge circulates globally. It is an 'umbrella concept' (Stone, 1999) which is used in and which draws on diverse literatures. It refers to the 'import' of 'innovatory policy developed elsewhere' (Stone, 1999, p 52) by national policy-making elites; to the imposition of policy by multilateral agencies; and to processes of structural convergence. Policy transfer analysts ask a number of key questions about the mechanisms involved, including: 'who are the key actors involved' (Dolowitz and Marsh, 2000, p 8). However, 'policy businesses' fail to appear in either Dolowitz and Marsh's 'nine main categories' (2000, p 10) or Stone's (2004, p 556) list of eight, although Stone does include consultancy firms. Furthermore, in these contributions and many others, much more attention is paid to identifying the participants and the successes and failures of transfer than to analysing and explaining the processes involved (Dolowitz and Marsh, 2000, p 7) or to 'local' mediations and interpretations. In this chapter I want to emphasise the mobility of policies rather than their transfer. That is to say, I suggest that policies move through, and are adapted by, networks of social relations or assemblages (see below), involving diverse participants (see below), with a variety of interests, commitments, purposes and influence, which are held together by subscription to a common discourse, which circulates within and is legitimated by these network relations. In the case addressed here that common discourse is focused on 'enterprise' or entrepreneurship as the solution to social and economic problems of development. Transfer is thus in this case an emergent and multi-scaled process (Hannam et al, 2006).

Business is now directly engaged with education policy, in a number of different ways, and these are part of a broader set of complex processes effecting education policy which include changes in the form and modalities of the state, new modes of philanthropy and aid for educational development and the work of transnational advocacy networks (TANs) and individual policy entrepreneurs,[2] market processes of capital growth and expansion and the search by business for new opportunities for profit. The relationships involved here cross and erase traditional boundaries and form the basis for new kinds of *global assemblages* (Ong, 2005) within which education policies are produced and disseminated. To adapt Ong's meaning somewhat, these *assemblages* are 'sites' of mobilisation 'by diverse groups in motion' (2005, p 499) and 'new spaces of entangled possibilities' (p 499), or what Larner (2002, p 765) calls 'globalizing "micro-spaces"' within which new forms of policy expertise are performed.

New policy assemblages[3]

The Clinton Global Initiative (CGI) is one example of such a site of mobilisation. It brings together a set of international policy actors and groups operating at different levels and on different scales towards a single end. In particular it provides an infrastructure for and brokering of private sector participation in education services, and a policy network through which ideology, ideas and discourse flow. It constructs and animates a new *epistemic policy community*.

> Imagine a room filled with the most innovative, action-oriented, and socially responsible leaders in the world. The Clinton Global Initiative's Annual Meeting brings together heads of state, government and business leaders, scholars, and NGO [non-governmental organisation] directors. Participants analyze pressing global challenges, discuss the most effective solutions, and build lasting partnerships that enable them to create positive social change. (www.clintonglobalinitiative.org/ourmeetings/default. asp?Section=OurMeetings&PageTitle=Our%20Meetings)

In these new arenas and networks business is now an essential part of the policy process, re-defining policy problems and constructing and enacting new solutions. Pragmatically and ideologically the CGI (and other philanthropic and multilateral agencies) are committed to what the website calls 'strengthening market-based solutions':

> Traditional approaches to aid are not enough to address the great global challenges of our time. Market-based solutions show incredible promise to solve these daunting problems on a systemic and widespread level. These approaches, however, are still in a

nascent stage. Corporations are researching and developing better business practices that meet social and environmental bottom lines while producing profits. Non-profits are pioneering enterprise-based models that offer potential for long-term sustainability. Governments are contributing their resources to encourage and support market-based approaches. (www.clintonglobalinitiative. org/ourmeetings/2010/meeting_annual_actionareas.asp?Section =OurMeetings&PageTitle=Actions%20Areas)

In relation to the CGI the enterprise or business solution (and there are a number of different versions of this) is articulated from many disparate but connected points, via authoritative voices, backed by very large-scale funding (see Network 1). Two specific examples give some indication of the nature of the sorts of activities and relationships that are produced in and around the CGI – they are: Opportunity International and the Affordable Private School Symposium (APSS). These examples also give some indication of the joining up of method, money and ideology as so-called 'corporate social capitalism' (see Friscia, 2009).

> Opportunity International, a nonprofit microfinance organization founded in 1971 ... announced at the Clinton Global Initiative's Fifth Annual Meeting that it will expand its Banking on Education program to five additional countries over the next 24 months. Opportunity will commit USD 10 million to its education finance program, which provides loans for entrepreneurs to open schools in poor areas where it is difficult for children, particularly girls, to access public schools.... Opportunity currently invests in over 200 private schools in five countries, with loans ranging from USD 500 to USD 25,000 for terms of two to five years. The program reached over 8,000 children in 2007.... Opportunity aims to improve educational opportunities for up to 250,000 children by 2012.

> In addition to providing loans to entrepreneurs to start and expand schools, Opportunity offers interest-bearing tuition savings accounts and school fee loans for parents who cannot afford their children's education.

Figure 15.1: A new global policy assemblage

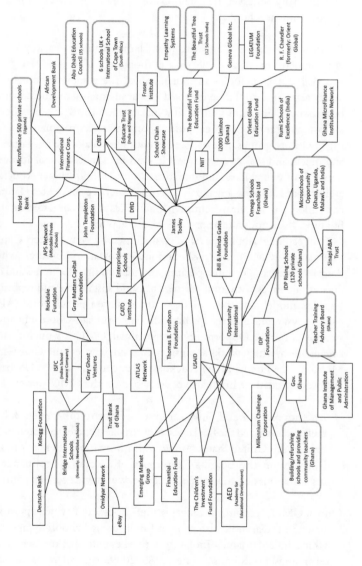

In a five-year study comparing 'schools for the poor' in India, China, Nigeria, Kenya and Ghana with government schools, Dr James Tooley, Professor of Education Policy at Newcastle University, observed that schools for the poor were superior to government schools.

In both this example and the next, James Tooley is a key policy entrepreneur, or what APSS calls a 'thought leader' (see Nambissan and Ball, 2010, on Tooley in India). Tooley is a paradigmatic network policy actor, he is mobile and hybrid – an academic, ideologue, advocate, businessman, philanthropist, policy maker. He moves, literally, indeed almost constantly, between policy communities, national settings, organisations, groups, interests and events. He speaks, writes, organises and meets, and seeks to persuade. He joins up a transnational advocacy network of policy ideas and initiatives around school choice, vouchers and private schooling. He is part of a new 'kinetic' policy elite (Hannam et al, 2006, p 6) and moves through 'fragile relays and contested locales', building 'fissiparous affiliations' (Rose, 1999, p 51).

The second example, the APSS, is organised by Gray Matters Capital Foundation (GMC), an off-shoot for Gray Matters Ventures, which describes itself as 'a private operating foundation that researches and co-creates initiatives with local partners to build sustainable and replicable business models for the benefit of underserved populations' (APSS website, www.graymatterscap.com/affordable-private-school-initiative/symposium). Like Opportunity International, GMC is a microfinance organisation, which works alongside 'sister enterprises', the Gray Ghost Microfinance Fund and the Rockdale Foundation. GMC is US-based and was founded by Bob Pattillo, described on the GMC website as:

> An entrepreneur and philanthropist.... Prior to this career, Bob built and managed the 8th largest industrial real estate development firm in the United States. Along with his own social enterprises Bob sits on the board of directors of several microfinance organizations and investment funds. (www.graymatterscap.com)

One of GMC's 'ventures' is EnterprisingSchools.com, which appears to be based in India, and it also runs an Enterprising Schools Symposium at which in 2010 James Tooley was the keynote speaker (see www.enterprisingschools.com/). The APSS 2009, as a micro-assemblage and networking event, is a fascinating and telling example of the new, complex and multifaceted relationships being established in these new sites of policy. In the list of participants there were 40 organisations, plus James Tooley. India is strongly represented but there were also participants from Africa, China and Latin America. These included philanthropies (for example, USAID, Opportunity International, Michael and Susan Dell Foundation), businesses (for example, SONG investment advisers, Indian School Finance Company, Educomp Solutions Ltd [now part-owned by Pearson], CfBT Education Trust, Faulu Kenya Ltd, Sunshine Fortune Education Investment & Consultancy Co Ltd [of which James Tooley is the Director]), microfinance banks (for example, SKS, K-Rep Bank Ltd) and the Ghana Ministry of Education and Kenya Independent Schools Association. In all of this the distinctions between businesses, social enterprises, not-for-profits and philanthropies is blurred. Relationships – initiatives, investments, partnerships, ownership, programmes, advocacy – are multifaceted, and people move between and speak on behalf of these different organisations in different roles. Like the CGI and in relation to it, the APSS is a setting for advocacy and making relationships and doing deals, for putting funders, sponsors and donors in contact with businesses and innovators and national governments to create new education programmes and initiatives. These projects, programmes and initiatives bring together philanthropies, charities and commercial banks, private equity companies, commercial education providers, social enterprises and governments, and are financing a new generation of multinational education businesses, some with diverse involvements in educational services and products, for example, New Globe schools (New Globe is developing a chain of private affordable schools in India and Kenya with funding and support from Deutsche Bank, the Kellogg Foundation and Gray Matters Ventures).

The CGI and these other networks and assemblages aim their activities primarily at low-income countries, and the private school initiatives indicated above are targeted at these countries and are concentrated in particular countries which are 'receptive' and which offer opportunities for profit – such as Nigeria, Ghana, Kenya and India. In 2007 School Ventures and the Economist Intelligence Unit launched the African Schools Investment Index (ASII) to compare 'the attractiveness of African markets as destination for private investment'. The private schools created are represented as supplementing existing state provision to achieve national and international policy goals. The entry of and role of edu-businesses in the education systems of these countries is clearly different from middle and higher-income countries. However, some of the players in these new markets are also already involved in or have aspirations to participate in high-income markets, and some of the policy 'importers' like India have their own indigenous edu-business sectors and export education services to other countries. The participants in these networks and initiatives range from lone, self-employed consultants, through local entrepreneurs, small and medium-size businesses to multinationals (as we shall see). Some are local providers (for example, store front schools) or run national or international chains of schools; others offer educational materials, services, software and consultancy and policy solutions; and others buy and sell educational institutions and businesses transnationally. There is as yet no workable taxonomy.

Exporting and 'selling' policy: a global market in policy ideas

There is increasing commercial interest in the processes of policy. Policy itself has become a profit opportunity in a number of ways. This involves a new generation of *knowledge companies* and consultants from whom governments are purchasing 'policy knowledge' (see Ball, 2009). In the UK, the Matrix Knowledge Group (which also operates in India) and A4e are examples of such 'knowledge' businesses.

> The Matrix Knowledge Group has a twenty-year international, national and local track record of supporting some of the biggest policy decisions by rapidly utilizing the best available evidence. Our team includes world-renowned consultants, researchers, experienced practitioners, and creative software developers who collaboratively create the organisational, knowledge and information infrastructures and evidence to deliver improvements in performance and value. (www.matrixknowledge.com/)

Matrix produces 'evidenced-based' policy knowledge using indicators of performance and value, and offers the possibilities of 'improvements' in delivery in these terms. Policy itself is rendered into a commodity in both senses. Policy solutions are for sale, and these solutions render policy into a set of measurable outcomes. When represented in this way service delivery becomes 'contractable' and can be 'contracted out' – there is a virtuous circle, for business, between the generation of policy knowledge, policy itself and new profit opportunities.

A4e, a broad-based UK public service company, which now also operates in France and Germany, offers to the state 'innovation' or 'reform knowledge', new solutions to intractable social problems. As their website asserts, they will 'Test new ways of delivering front line public services'.

> At A4e, we work with governments across the globe to 'square circles'. We tackle the difficult problems. We address market failure. We take pilot programmes and test new ways of delivering front line public services. And we deliver complex services at scale. Employing over 3100 people across 201 locations in eleven countries, we are the partner of choice for government organisations looking to deliver results. (www. mya4e.com/getdoc/45e90dbf-b4e7-4c2a-93f7-38ab844f347d/4-Governments.aspx)

There is now an extensive global flow of such policy knowledge in the field of education. Cambridge Education, a UK edu-business subsidiary of Mott Macdonald, and one of the five English school inspection contractors, is making inroads in the US and has worked in over 60 other countries. Among its 'products' it offers versions of the English school inspection model as a policy product to other countries; New York City and Beijing have both 'bought' this model.

> New York, the US's largest school district with 1.1m students has hired Cambridge Education to lead the introduction of a programme of 'school reviews' based on the English Inspections model (worth around $6.4m a year). CE is an Inspection contractor in England. CE is training New York reviewers so that they can assume full-control of the review system in coming years. As the tabloid *New York Sun* put it 'The British have arrived: They're Reviewing City Schools' (July 31st 2007).

Here experience, knowledge and expertise gained in the English education services market is repackaged, sold and exported often without much attention being given to the risks and problems associated with the policies or models involved (see Holden, 2009).

> The UK experience has served as the underlying model for much of the development internationally of SBM [School Based Management]. (www.cea.co.uk)

> Nord Anglia's reputation and expertise with British education gives it a rare opportunity to capitalise upon the demand in

overseas markets for improved quality in education provision. (Nord Anglia Company Annual Report, 2006, p 8)

Cambridge is also involved in various national settings in writing education policy, particularly for small states, as they explain on their website:

Our services are comprehensive: from assisting with education policy development and advising on education financing, through programme and project design and management, to social and institutional development. We have considerable *expertise* in capacity building, helping to form solid foundations for education development and reform. We provide technical assistance and training in all aspects of education – for example in developing curriculum and learning materials, and training teachers. (www. camb-ed.com/International/Internationalexpertise.aspx)

For example, the Asian Development Bank has paid Cambridge Education to 'support': 'the Maldives in drafting legislation for a new Education Act; in developing a sustainable financial framework for increased and equitable access to post-secondary education; and in enhancing capacity to develop learning and teaching materials for lower secondary grades' (www.camb-ed.com/International/internationalprojects/internationalcountries/MaldivesStrengtheningtheFrameworkofEducation/tabid/172/Default.aspx).

Here then education policy knowledge and experience are commodified and sold with the effect of moving policies, policy concepts and languages, between national settings, mostly from West to East and North to South. However, companies based in India, like NIIT, and Japan, like Benesse (with offices in Hong Kong, Korea and Taiwan), and others from Australia and New Zealand, are now expanding into this international trade in policies, policy ideas and educational services.

Education as big business

Edu-businesses are subject to the same market and business processes as other companies and there has been a series of significant acquisitions and mergers in this field. These take two forms. One, in which Pearson is the paradigm case, is the building of big education and information conglomerates. The other is the swallowing up of edu-businesses by generic professional and management services companies as in the

case of Cambridge and Mott Macdonald, and 3Es and Faber Maunsell/
AECOM, and further mergers and consolidations of these companies
in the case of Babcock and VT (see below). In these cases the education
services divisions in these companies sit alongside housing, transport,
defence and other specialist divisions.

The result is the emergence of multinational companies that are
vertically and horizontally integrated. Vertical integration takes two
forms: one form is business activities which address markets in curriculum,
pedagogy and assessment services (and support and administrative
services); the other form is markets in different education sectors,
from pre-school to higher education, and vocational and professional
education. Horizontal integration involves the development of generic
business approaches which involve professional and management
services of various kinds (for example, Mouchel Parkman and VT) and
information and business information services.

Here Pearson Education, the world's largest education company, will
serve as a particular example of the global reach and influence of these
MNEBs. Pearson owns the *Financial Times*, Penguin Books and several
other publishing houses, Edexcel (the University of London Examination
Board as was), and 50 per cent of the FTSE index and of *The Economist*.
Pearson's worldwide sales in 2009 were £5.1 billion (profit £710 million
after tax). Pearson has pursued an aggressive programme of acquisitions
and joint ventures. In May 2010 Pearson agreed to sell its stake in
financial data provider Interactive Data for US$3.4 billion 'to free up
funds for acquisitions in emerging markets' (Reuters).

Pearson generates 21 per cent of its income from US higher
education publishing, for example, MyLab digital learning, homework
and assessment programmes, CourseConnect online courses, and the
eCollege online management system. A further 21 per cent of income
comes from assessment and information work in the US including
running the Florida state testing programme, Powerschool and Chancery
student information systems, and 12 per cent comes from school
curriculum sales, for example, enVisionMATH, and Poptropica, a virtual
world for young children.

Pearson recently acquired America's Choice (an education and
information company), 'a leading provider of school improvement
services' (August 2010) for US$80 million cash. In July 2010 it established
a strategic partnership with Sistema Educacional Brasileiro (SEB) and
acquired SEB's school learning systems (for £326 million); this serves
450,000 students in public and private schools. Globally Pearson won
new contracts in Vietnam, Colombia (eCollege), South Africa and Malta,

Vietnam and UK (Pearson Learning Solutions) in 2009-10. The UK generates seven per cent of Pearson's income (it runs BTEC and the Edexcel examination board) and in May 2010 Pearson bought Melorio, a UK vocational training company that has 49 training centres, for £99 million (Melorio's profit after tax in 2010 was £520,000). In 2008 Melorio had purchased Zenos Learning for £20.6 million and Learning World Academies when it was floated on the stock exchange. Europe generates five per cent of income via, for example, Linx secondary science in Italy, and the development of a virtual business community in the Netherlands. Two per cent of income comes from Africa and the Middle East, including national contracts in Ethiopia for science learning materials, and a UNICEF contract to provide 13.5 million textbooks in Zimbabwe. A further four per cent comes from Asia, including a new joint venture with Educomp, and in 2009 Pearson paid US$30 million for a 50 per cent stake in Educomp's vocational training businesses, which have 12 million users in 23,000 schools in India, North America and Singapore, and invested in TutorVista that provides offshore online tutoring for US students. Latin America contributes two per cent of income, with new developments in Brazil, Mexico and Colombia. The Professional testing and publishing division produces six per cent of sales with new contracts in Saudi Arabia, Egypt, Bahrain and Colorado, US, for testing medical and business professionals. Alongside its business activities Pearson is also involved in educational philanthropy through the work of the Pearson Foundation.

Increasingly edu-businesses like Pearson, in their advertising and promotion, position themselves as offering 'solutions' to the national policy problems of raising standards and achieving educational improvements linked to both individual opportunity and national competitiveness. But such promotion also extends to active participation in policy influence relationships and policy networks as a means to agitate for policies which offer further opportunities for profit (see Burch, 2009, for examples of edu-business lobbying in the US in relation to the No Child Left Behind programme). Indeed, Pearson organises events that are aimed at attracting key policy actors:

Pearson International Education Conference Launched in Singapore

The Pearson Foundation hosted the first annual Pearson International Education Conference April 28-May 1, 2008, in Singapore. The summit, created in partnership with the Council of Chief State School Officers (CCSSO), convened delegates from around the world to share and consider key educational, assessment, and professional development practices that ensure student success in mathematics and science education.

Delegates from countries including Brazil, Canada, England, Italy, Japan, Korea, New Zealand, South Africa, Taiwan, the United Kingdom, and the United States met in small working teams to present and share best practices from their countries; learn from each other ways in which they can improve their own local efforts; and make recommendations that can be shared with an even broader group about methods, practice, and policy in math and science education. (Pearson website, www.pearsoned.com/)

All of this has a variety of consequences in terms of national education policy and policy influence and transnational standardisation, as well as signalling a further aspect of the wholesale commodification of education and educational processes. This also raises questions of national and foreign ownership that could have implications in terms of the ability of national governments to exert policy control over and regulate their education systems. Sweden is an interesting case in point. Sweden now has about 15 per cent of its school students educated in state-funded 'free schools', most of which are owned and run by private providers. The largest of these companies is John Bauer, which, aside from the Swedish schools, runs international schools in Spain, hotel and catering colleges in India and Norway, has other education ventures in China and Tanzania, and property development activities in Central America and Indo-China. In 2009, John Bauer was bought by Denmark's largest private equity company, Axcel (with a total revenue of approximately DKK 14 billion), which has its other main interests in housing, fashion and pet foods.[4] In 2010 another of the Swedish free school companies, Academedia, was bought by EQT, who outbid rivals Providence Equity Partners, a US private equity investor (who in 2009 bought Study Group, an Australian-based global private education provider for US\$570 million). Study Group has 38 campuses and 55,000 students in the UK, Australia, New Zealand and the US. Among other things Study Group runs International Study Centres in partnership with UK universities on their campuses, for example at Lincoln and Kingston.

Finally, in the UK in 2007 Babcock International (turnover in 2006, £836 million), a global engineering and support services company, formed a joint venture with Mouchel Parkman (a business process outsourcing company, with its own education services division, turnover in 2008, £656 million; see Ball, 2007) to create Mpb Education, a full-service education and building services company. Also in 2007 Mouchel bought Hyder Business Services, with its education division (heavily involved in continuing professional development [CPD], back-office work and outsourcing), from Terra Firma, a private equity company. In February 2010, the VT group, with its own education services division VTES, heavily involved in careers advice, consultancy and work-based learning (and 4S, a joint venture CPD company with Surrey Local Authority), launched a £330 million bid to buy Mouchel. Almost immediately Babcock announced a £1.29 billion offer for VT, but on the stipulation that it drop its bid for Mouchel. In March 2010 Babcock and VT agreed a £1.3 billion merger.

Two issues here are the relationship of ownership to policy and the alignments and misalignments between company and national interests, and the opacity of ownership, and change of ownership and the disconnects between brand and ownership. Here we see the growth of global brands which market standard services, products and policy solutions in diverse national settings and which in some cases wield considerable financial influence, especially in relation to small or weak nation states. As yet we have little sense of the significance of foreign ownership of national educational infrastructure or services or the limits that this may place on national policy options or the possibility that MNEBs will use their leverage to influence national policies in their interest or the possible impact of business failures.

Selling students

It is not only educational materials and services and policy ideas that are being sold by the edu-businesses. There is now a global market in educational institutions – schools, colleges and universities (and in effect their clients – students) are bought and sold (as in the cases of John Bauer and Academia above).

In 2008, 2.7 million higher education students were being educated overseas, a 50 per cent increase since 2000; the worth of this sector of higher education is currently US$400 billion; 25 per cent of these students are in the private sector that is expanding rapidly. There is a set of global higher education brands that are emerging and are increasingly dominant in the lucrative private higher education market. One such is Laureate Education, a US-based private higher education company which owns 51 universities around the world and which had an income of US$160 million in 2005. For example, included in their global portfolio of universities are two in Brazil: Universidade Anhembi Morumbi (UAM, Brazil) and Faculdade Unida da Pariba (UniPB, Brazil). UAM was founded in 1970 as a school of tourism. Several of UAM's undergraduate and graduate degree programs are ranked among the best in Brazil by *Melhores Universidades*, a special higher education edition of a leading Brazilian magazine. UniPB was founded in 2006 and serves more than 550 students, offering degrees in nutrition, nursing, environmental engineering and gastronomy.

This is a different sort of knowledge economy; the monetary value and profitability of education here are most self-evident and most direct. Again there are both opportunities and dangers involved for national governments. These institutional forms of higher education may provide quick and relatively cheap means to up-skill the local workforce in response to the supposed requirements of the knowledge economy, as well as satisfying the increased local demand for access to higher education, especially those which offer forms of certification with international currency, and thus potential entry into the global labour market. States like China have allowed the entry of foreign providers for exactly these reasons, and around 500 foreign campuses are up and running in China, but the government has now suspended further recognition of overseas providers. Other states, like Singapore, have encouraged 'elite' overseas providers to set up shop as a means of attracting overseas students from other parts of South East Asia and beyond, and in an effort to re-invent itself as a 'global classroom' and a regional hub for higher education. By 2003 there were 14 elite transnational campuses in Singapore including MIT, INSEAD (France), University of Chicago and NIIT (India). But these offshore enterprises may also be seen as part of a new educational colonialism. Business schools in particular have been key points for the articulation and flow of new, western, and particularly US, management ideas and metaphors. There are also difficult issues about quality and accountability involved. In many cases these private university chains employ poorly qualified teachers and have a limited involvement in research activities (McCowan, 2004). Indeed companies like Pearson can offer higher education companies software packages which provide curriculum materials, learning systems and online assessment and marking, together with administrative systems, which require only minimal design and teaching inputs.

One further example indicates a further dimension to the financial and network complexity embedded in these sorts of developments, and another kind of blurring between traditional public/private sector divisions. In 2000 the University of Nottingham opened a campus in Malaysia (UNiM). UNiM has 2,700 students from 50 countries and Nottingham's UK, Malaysia and Chinese campuses now enrol over 30,000 students. The majority shareholder of UNiM is the Boustead Group, an engineering services and geo-spatial technology company. Nottingham spent £5.3 million on the Malaysia campus, and it owns a 29.1 per cent share (*Times Higher Education*, 27 September 2007). It is not clear how Nottingham funded its investment in UNiM as it says the source of the University of Nottingham's investment is undisclosed. The other partner is YTL Corporation Berhad, which owns and manages utilities and 'infrastructural assets' and owns 19 per cent of UNiM. This is an example of what Kelsey (2006) terms 'an unsustainable hybrid form of a modern/neoliberal university' (p 1). UNiM awards University of Nottingham degrees. In effect, perhaps, Nottingham is licensing its trademark, but the Vice-Chancellor at the time, Sir Colin Campbell, was adamant that a 'Franchise arrangement is too great a risk to reputation' and that 'Exams, marking and quality assurance are consistent' (*Education Guardian*, 4 September 2007). The University describes its overseas strategy as 'exporting excellence' (Annual Report, 2005). The University of Nottingham won the Queens Award for Enterprise in 2006 and 2007.

This was not Boustead's only educational investment. An associate company of the Boustead group, Easycall International (China Education Ltd), owned Boustead College in China, a joint enterprise with Tianjin University of Commerce. And in 2004 Easycall purchased Spherion Education, a New Zealand company that runs 13 training institutes in Australia and New Zealand. Easycall has since been bought by the Raffles Education Corp, a Singapore-based company, which owns Oriental University City (China) and which has grown from its founding in 1990 to operate three universities and 26 colleges across 10 countries in the Asia-Pacific region.

Discussion

Policy transfer, policy colonisation and policy convergence are all being effected here, through the writing of policy, policy consultancy and recommendations, policy influence, the selling of materials, pedagogy and assessment products, and the growth and spread of multinational service providers with standardised methods and contents. At the same time educational processes, policies themselves and policy knowledge are all commodified. In these new processes of policy, states are changing, being changed and to some extent being residualised or, as Hannam et al (2006, p 2) put it, 'the nation itself is being transformed by [such] mobilities'. New policy networks and communities are being established through which discourses and knowledge flow and gain legitimacy and credibility, and 'these processes are located within a global architecture of political relations that not only involves national governments, but also intergovernmental organisations (IGOs), transnational corporations (TNCs) and NGOs. Policies are developed, enacted and evaluated in various global networks from where their authority is now partly derived' (Rizvi and Lingard, 2009, p 338). These are new assemblages with a diverse range of participants that exist in a new kind of policy space somewhere between multilateral agencies, national governments and international business, in and beyond the traditional sites and circulations of policy making.

Policy entrepreneurs, like James Tooley, move through and between these assemblages and networks, telling persuasive stories about policy (see Tooley, 2009), based on 'research' and experience, strategically naming problems and framing their solutions, using tropes and representational techniques that together produce a 'hegemonic imaginary' (Larner and Le Heron, 2002, p 762). Or, as Ward (2006, p 70) puts it, 'the "making-up" of policy is ... a profoundly geographical process, in and through which different places are constructed as facing similar problems in need of similar solutions'. Reports, articles, addresses, blogs, websites, Twitter, Facebook, PowerPoint presentations and 'micro-spaces of persuasion' like seminars, symposia and forums (Peet, 2002), work to circulate policy knowledge and 'stabilise' a particular set of rationalities, metadiscourses and logics (Larner and Le Heron, 2002, p 760). Policy makers, as 'policy travellers', attend and attend to these 'occasioned activities', 'learning' new policy possibilities as they go, and making those ideas 'actionable' through new 'weak ties' and financial 'commitments' (McCann, 2011). New policy relationships and spaces and media are constituted and used to re-embed mobile policies and their attendant discourses in national territories. As a result, national governments, especially those small and fragile states, may be experiencing a reduction in their capacity to steer their education systems. In addition, in his examination of the 'export' of PPP/PFI models, Holden (2009, p 313) makes the point that this goes on 'despite the fact that the public sector technical capacity needed to make the policy effective may be lacking in the target countries'.

Clearly, in some cases the private sector, privatisations and off-the-shelf policy solutions can serve national interests – like soaking up unmet demand for education, or modernising curriculum, learning and assessment, or meeting policy goals and commitments. Nonetheless, other things are also happening as indicated – processes of standardisation, westernisation and new forms of colonisation. Kelsey (2006, p 9) argues that 'University/business collaboration deepen the influence of corporate priorities and preferences and compress critical space'. Within all of this there are ongoing blurrings and emergent hybridities, as the boundaries between public and private, charity and profit, lending and donation collapse, and forms of *social capitalism* reconfigure policy problems as business opportunities. Our traditional categories and concepts no longer work here. And all of this is happening as the state itself changes, in part in response to the transfer and dissemination of models of good practice – like new public management, outsourcing, performance management and PPPs. These changes are part of the construction of new forms of state and new modes of political thinking which produce states which are ready for and open to various forms of privatisation, endogenous and exogenous, including various self-privatisations (see Ball, 2008). Through all of this, and despite the interpretation and modification of policy products at national and local levels (which I have not attended to here), there is clearly now something we can call 'global education policy' – a generic set of concepts, language and practices that is recognisable in various forms and is for sale!

In many ways this analysis and discussion raises more questions than it answers. There is much more research and analysis to be done. But I hope to have sketched a new terrain for global policy analysis, identified a useful extension to the current policy transfer literature, and pointed up some directions for the development of ways of understanding education policy mobilities.

Notes

[1] At this stage I am using the term 'MNEB' loosely and as a catch-all to identify a set of trends in global education policy making. Further work is needed to bring some greater precision and differentiation to this diverse and highly dynamic business sector, as I did previously with UK edu-businesses (Ball, 2007). The intention is that the examples given will provide some clarity. But in this chapter I am seeking to sketch out a new policy terrain and identify a set of policy mobilities, within which MNEBs are key players.

[2] See Nambissan and Ball (2010) for a discussion of the concept.

[3] I want to acknowledge ongoing work with Antonio Olmedo on the Clinton Global Initiative (CGI) that has contributed to this section and Figure 15.1.

[4] In the 2010 UK election campaign the Conservative Party manifesto

indicated that a Conservative government would introduce Swedish-style free schools.

References

Ball, S.J. (2007) *Education Plc: Understanding private sector participation in public sector education*, London: Routledge.

Ball, S.J. (2008) 'New philanthropy, new networks and new governance in education', *Political Studies*, vol 56, no 4, pp 747-65.

Ball, S.J. (2009) 'Privatising education, privatising education policy, privatising educational research: network governance and the "competition state"', *Journal of Education Policy*, vol 42, no 1, pp 83-99.

Burch, P.E. (2009) *Hidden markets: The new educational privatization*, New York: Routledge.

Dolowitz, D. and Marsh, D. (2000) 'Who learns what from whom: a review of the policy transfer literature', *Political Studies*, vol 44, no 1, pp 343-57.

Friscia, T. (2009) 'The 2009 Clinton Global Initiative: corporate social capitalism is the new basis of global competition', 2 October 2009 (www.amrresearch.com/content/view.aspx?compURI=tcm:7-48415).

Hannam, K., Sheller, M. et al (2006) 'Mobilities, immobilities and moorings', *Mobilities*, vol 1, no 1, pp 1-22.

Holden, C. (2009) 'Exporting public-private partnerships in healthcare: export strategy and policy transfer', *Policy Studies*, vol 33, no 3, pp 313-32.

Kelsey, J. (2006) 'Taking minds to market' (www.knowpol.uib.no/portal/files/ uplink/kelsey.pdf).

Larner, W. (2002) 'Globalization, governmentality and expertise: creating a call centre labour force', *Review of International Political Economy*, vol 9, no 4, pp 650-74.

Larner, W. and Le Heron, R. (2002) 'From economic globalisation to globalising economic processes: towards post-structural political economies', *Geoforum*, vol 33, no 4, pp 415-19.

McCann, E.J. (2011) 'Urban policy mobilities and global circuits of knowledge', *Annals of Association of American Geographers*, vol 101, no 1, pp 107-30.

McCowan, T. (2004) 'The growth of private higher education in Brazil: implications for equity and quality', *Journal of Education Policy*, vol 19, no 4, pp 453-72.

Nambissan, G.B. and Ball, S.J. (2010) 'Advocacy networks, choice and private schooling of the poor in India', *Global Networks*, vol 10, no 3, pp 324-43.

Ong, A. (2005) 'Mutations in citizenship', *Theory, Culture and Society*, vol 23, no 2-3, pp 499-531.

Peet, R. (2002) 'Ideology, discourse and the geography of hegemony', *Antipode*, vol 34, no 1, pp 54-84.

Rizvi, F. and Lingard, B. (2009) *Globalizing education policy*, London: Routledge.

Rose, N. (1999) *Powers of freedom: Reframing political thought*, Cambridge: Cambridge University Press.

Stone, D. (1999) 'Learning lessons and transferring policy across time, space and disciplines', *Politics*, vol 19, no 1, pp 51-9.

Stone, D. (2004) 'Transfer agents and global networks in the "transnationalization" of policy', *Journal of European Public Policy*, vol 11, no 3, pp 545-66.

Tooley, J. (2009) *The beautiful tree*, Washington, DC: Cato Institute.

Ward, K. (2006) '"Policies in motion", urban management and state restructuring: the trans-local expansion of Business Improvement Districts', *International Journal of Urban and Regional Research*, vol 30, pp 54-75.

Index

Note: page numbers followed by the letters *f* and *t* refer to information in figures and tables respectively.